Restoration Tragedies

EDITED WITH AN INTRODUCTION BY

JAMES SUTHERLAND

OXFORD UNIVERSITY PRESS

LONDON OXFORD NEW YORK

1977

Oxford University Press, Walton Street, Oxford OX2 6DP

OXFORD LONDON GLASGOW NEW YORK
TORONTO MELBOURNE WELLINGTON CAPE TOWN
IBADAN NAIROBI DAR ES SALAAM LUSAKA ADDIS ABABA
KUALA LUMPUR SINGAPORE JAKARTA HONG KONG TOKYO
DELHI BOMBAY CALCUTTA MADRAS KARACHI

ISBN 0 19 281176 2

First published as an Oxford University Press paperback
by Oxford University Press, London, 1977

British Library Cataloguing in Publication Data

Restoration tragedies.
Bibl.
ISBN 0-19-281176-2
1. Sutherland, James
822'.051 PR1266
English drama (tragedy)

Printed in Great Britain
at the University Press, Oxford
by Vivian Ridler
Printer to the University

Contents

Introduction

Restoration drama is so often equated with the work of Etherege, Wycherley, Congreve, and the other writers of comedy that we tend to forget how many of the plays presented at the two London theatres were tragedies. On the evidence of his famous diary Samuel Pepys had a decided preference for comedies, and his taste was probably shared by most playgoers of his own sex; his wife, on the other hand, if free to choose, would have been more likely to enjoy a good tragedy. It is true that when Pepys was keeping his diary in the 1660s few new tragedies were being written, and those he saw were mostly revivals from the Elizabethan and Jacobean theatre. Some of those old plays he enjoyed, notably *Macbeth*, which he saw many times; but others such as Webster's *The White Devil*, which he found to be 'a poor play', were not at all to his liking. The erratic and fluctuating judgements of Pepys on the many plays he saw are perhaps evidence of little more than his own unpredictable tastes; and how uncertain those can be is shown by his observation that he had always reckoned *Othello* 'a mighty good play', but after reading it one day as he was being rowed down the Thames to Deptford and comparing it with Sir Samuel Tuke's *The Adventures of Five Hours*, he realized that it was only 'a mean thing'.

At all events, the great supporters of tragedy (and of the heroic play) in the Restoration theatre were the ladies, and one clear indication of this is the polite addresses almost invariably made to them in prologues and epilogues. Appealed to as 'the softer sex', 'the shining circle', 'the fair ones who in judgement sit', they were invited to shed a pitying tear, and to make the sorrows of the tragic hero and heroine their own. It was the experience of Crowne's Sir Courtly Nice that 'comedies are always crammed with our odious sex', whereas 'at tragedies, the house is all lined with beauty'. Considering the nature of Restoration comedy and tragedy such preferences are not really surprising. Comedy almost invariably saw life from a masculine standpoint; and although Congreve can rise to a Millamant, or Etherege to a Harriet in *The Man of Mode*, women in Restoration comedy are usually not much more than the physical objects of male pursuit, the necessary concomitants of sexual satisfaction. Not so in tragedy. Here women came into their own—or, as the masculine Shadwell suggested, into more than their own: the female part of an audience, Shadwell grumbled, enjoyed romantic plays in which 'poor frail woman's made a deity', and in which the hero, so intrepid in battle, is the abject slave of his mistress—and 'if the dame once chides, the milksop hero swoons'. In tragedy, then, women were taken seriously, treated with respect and even reverence, given an importance and a dignity that they were rarely accorded in comedy; they were shown as capable of passionate love and heroic self-sacrifice. Above all, by dramatists like Otway, Banks, and Southerne, married love and marital fidelity were accepted as the norm. In comedy, marriage was the monotonous aftermath of love (*faute de mieux je me couche avec ma femme*); in tragedy it was normally a permanent relationship of mutual respect.

Tragedy, however, appealed in another way to both sexes in the Restoration audience: it was usually produced with elaborate and spectacular scenic effects and gorgeous costumes. The Restoration stage had made a considerable advance in scene-painting and theatrical 'machines'; and the public theatres were now offering the kind of visual spectacle that in the earlier part of the century had been seen only when plays or masques were performed at Court. On at least two occasions in the 1660s the affable Charles II lent his coronation robes for a performance in one of the public theatres; and in 1667 Pepys learnt from Henry Harris the actor that the King had promised £500 for a revival of Ben Jonson's *Catiline*, to be expended on dressing the play, 'there being, as they say, to be sixteen scarlet robes'. Royal promises that involved the payment of hard cash were not always kept, and the production of *Catiline* was indefinitely postponed; but when Pepys saw it at last over a year later he was duly impressed by the 'fine clothes, and a fine scene of the Senate', though he was clearly bored by the play itself.

Since the two theatres often played to half-empty houses, they were driven to competing for playgoers by gratifying them as spectators; and the chronic financial troubles of both theatres were partly due to the expense of mounting tragedies with new and striking scenic effects and with rich and exotic costumes. Here the heroic plays of the 1660s and early 1670s must have had a considerable influence. Since these were almost invariably concerned with kings and queens and imperial courts and set in remote parts of the world, they offered an obvious opportunity for spectacular effects. The opportunity was seized in the production of *The Indian Queen* (by Sir Robert Howard and Dryden), and John Evelyn, who was present at a performance on 3 February 1664, noted in his diary that the play was 'so beautified with rich scenes as the like had never been seen here . . . on a mercenary theatre'. *The Indian Queen* opens with 'an Indian boy and girl sleeping under two plantain trees', and draws to a close in 'the Temple of the Sun all of gold', with 'four priests in habits of white and red feathers attending by a bloody altar'. Addressing the audience in the epilogue, Montezuma commends

> the plot, the show,
> The poet's scenes, nay, more, the painter's too,

and goes on to remark,

> If all this fail, considering the cost,
> 'Tis a true voyage to the Indies lost.

When Dryden's successful sequel, *The Indian Emperor*, was produced a year later, the King's Company was able to use the same scenes and costumes, as Dryden frankly admitted in the prologue. Crowne's *The Destruction of Jerusalem* (1677) was produced 'at a vast expense in scenes and clothes': among the scenes are a palace and a garden, and as the dramatis personæ include several kings, a queen, a High Priest, a Roman general, and (in the second part) a Roman emperor, not to mention battling Parthians, Romans, and Pharisees, the vast expense in clothes is understandable.

Not all tragedies, it is true, were given such expensive production, but in general audiences had come to expect exotic visual effects; and songs, incidental music, and on occasion a masque or a ballet, contributed to the emotional appeal. And, finally, the heroes and heroines of Restoration tragedy were played by some outstanding actors and actresses, notably Charles Hart (the Antony of *All for Love*), Thomas Betterton (Lucius Junius Brutus in Lee's play, Jaffeir in *Venice Preserved*), and Elizabeth Barry (Teraminta in *Lucius Junius Brutus*, Belvidera in *Venice Preserved*).

Some or all of those considerations may account for the rapturous response of Mrs. Mary Evelyn (the wife of the diarist) after she had seen a performance of *The Conquest of Granada*, with Hart as Almanzor and Nell Gwyn as Almahide. For Mrs. Evelyn this was a play 'so full of ideas that the most refined romance I ever read is not to compare with it; love is made so pure, and valour so nice, that one would imagine it designed for an Utopia rather than our stage. I do not quarrel with the poet, but admire one born in the decline of morality should be able to feign such exact virtue; and as poetic fiction has been instructive in former ages, I wish this the same event in ours.' Behind these words, with their allusion to 'the decline of morality' and the implied disapproval of 'our stage', one can detect a distaste for the licentiousness of contemporary comedy, which was actively shared by John Evelyn, who usually stayed away from the theatre on account of its 'atheistical liberty, foul and undecent'. Tragedy, at any rate, continued to attract some sober-minded people to the theatre who would not have wished to be seen at *The Country Wife* or *The London Cuckolds*.

Although the heroic play was going out of fashion by the mid 1670s, its influence was felt on the structure of the tragic drama for many years to come. One marked feature that continued to dominate tragedy was the conflict in the mind of the hero or heroine, torn between the contending claims of love and honour, love and friendship, love and duty, with all the resulting dilemmas of choice between different lines of action, and the consequent suspense while the tragic character wrestled with his problem in a prolonged self-debate. In *All for Love* (which, as Dryden saw it, is almost a highly-developed version of the old Morality play) the conflict in the mind of Antony is powerfully dramatized through the pressure exerted on him by Cleopatra on the one side, and, on the other, by the virtuous Ventidius and the long-suffering and equally virtuous Octavia. In Dryden's tragic reading of this famous love story, Antony and Cleopatra were 'patterns of unlawful love; and their end accordingly was unfortunate'; they did not err 'by any necessity, or fatal ignorance', their actions were wholly voluntary. In Restoration comedy what Dryden calls unlawful love is treated very differently: it becomes almost the law of the comic world, and is usually admired and rewarded. But tragedy too can be much less overtly moral than Dryden is (or says he is) in *All for Love*. In Shakespeare's *Antony and Cleopatra*, which Dryden says he was 'imitating', the moral issue is almost never in the forefront. It is true that in the very first speech of the play Philotas, the critical bystander, sees Antony as 'the triple pillar of the world transformed into a strumpet's fool'; but Shakespeare, apart from the fact that he is also dramatizing several vital years of Roman history, seems more concerned in the scenes where Antony and Cleopatra are together to make us realize their irresistible attraction for each other, what fun they had in their shared experience, and the necessity, being what they are, of doing what they do,

> when such a mutual pair
> And such a twain can do't.

Incidentally, Dryden's sub-title, 'The World well Lost', is much more relevant to Shakespeare's *Antony and Cleopatra* than to the play Dryden wrote.

Emotional conflict and the divided mind are seen again in *The Unhappy Favourite* of John Banks, where Queen Elizabeth is torn between a secret love for one of her subjects and her royal duty to the State. No matter that the historical Queen Elizabeth was in her sixty-eighth year when Essex went to the block: such niceties meant little to Banks, or to most of his audience. Again, in Thomas Otway's *Venice Preserved*, Jaffeir is divided between love for his wife Belvidera (whose father he has sworn to kill), and, on the other side, his friendship with Pierre and his loyalty to the other conspirators. In Lee's *Lucius Junius Brutus* Titus has to make an agonizing choice between his love for Teraminta (a daughter of Tarquin), and his love for and duty to his father, who is engaged in driving the

Tarquins from Rome. Both Otway and Lee seek to generate the maximum amount of excitement from the alternating revulsions of feeling, but Lee, who is more usually accused of bombast and hyperbole, is on this occasion more controlled that Otway. At the end of *Venice Preserved*, when Pierre points to the wheel on which he is about to be broken and says to Jaffeir, 'Though thou'st betrayed me, do me some way justice', it is clear that he wants Jaffeir to stab him with his dagger, and so save him from a death unworthy of a man who has fought for the State. But Jaffeir can't see what is needed. Filled with remorse, and eager to express his passionate and undying friendship for Pierre, Jaffeir exclaims:

> No more of that. Thy wishes shall be satisfied.
> I have a wife and she shall bleed, my child too
> Yield up his little throat, and all t'appease you.

How this would help Pierre is not only not clear, but has never even been considered by Jaffeir—nor, one suspects, by Otway. The moment calls for a stupendous gesture, and this is it. For five acts Jaffeir has been spinning like a weathercock in conflicting gusts of passion, and living on a plane of hysterical extravagance. Taken in that context his last outburst is in character, if it is the nature of Jaffeir to react violently to every change in the theatrical situation. It would be charitable to suppose that in this tragedy Otway was less concerned with creating a heroic protagonist than with showing, by means of Jaffeir's impetuous and unsteady conduct, the unstable and irrational stuff of which conspirators (and Whig plotters) are made. That may well have been part of Otway's intention; but perhaps the main reason why Jaffeir is what he is (and isn't) is that Otway had inherited a dramatic tradition going back to Beaumont and Fletcher, which was less interested in retaining the credibility of character than with achieving those surprising turns of situation and feeling that aroused in an audience what Dryden called 'concernment'.

The five plays in this volume share in varying degrees another feature of Restoration tragedy. In the preface to his edition of Shakespeare, Johnson remarked that in modern European drama the universal agent, by which every action was 'quickened or retarded', was love:

> To bring a lover, a lady and a rival into the fable; to entangle them in contradictory obligations, perplex them with oppositions of interest, and harrass them with violence of desires inconsistent with each other; to make them meet in rapture and part in agony; to fill their mouths with hyperbolical joy and outrageous sorrow; to distress them as nothing human ever was distressed; to deliver them as nothing human ever was delivered, is the business of a modern dramatist. For this probability is violated, life is misrepresented, and language is depraved. But love is only one of many passions. . . .

The great exception to this monotonous concentration on love was Shakespeare, 'who knew that any other passion, as it was regular or exorbitant, was a cause of happiness or calamity'. Even when Shakespeare gave himself the opportunity to dwell on love in *Antony and Cleopatra*, the action of the play ranged far beyond the passionate relationship of his hero and heroine, and involved large events in world history. In so constructing his tragedy Shakespeare achieved a highly dramatic contrast between the loud world of action and public discord and the quiet inner world into which Antony could retreat with Cleopatra, content to 'let Rome in Tiber melt' while time stood still; but he also brought much more of life and a greater variety of human motives into his play. In *All for Love*, on the other hand, Dryden concentrates almost all the action on the fatal charm for Antony of his enchanting queen, and on the ensuing struggle with his divided self. Love with its 'contradictory obligations' again plays a large part in the action of *The Unhappy Favourite*, *Lucius Junius Brutus*, and *Venice Preserved*, and love of one kind or another accounts for most of what happens in *Oroonoko*.

But if love was undoubtedly the mainspring of most Restoration tragedy, and the dramatists would never have agreed with Johnson that 'it has no great influence upon the sum of life', they were not blind to other motives. In *Lucius Junius Brutus* and *Venice Preserved* political issues are seriously discussed, and are central to the action of both plays; and in *Oroonoko* Southerne has something to say about the slave trade and the treatment of slaves. Yet how much such issues interested the contemporary audience is open to question; and in the dedication of *Lucius Junius Brutus* Lee complained that his attempts to come to grips with a great tragic theme and to create a great patriot-hero had been wasted on 'a sparkish generation that have an antipathy to thought'. Dramatists had to take into account the conventional expectations and prejudices of their audiences; on the whole they gave the public what it wanted, and what it wanted was what it knew already. The best dramatists, however, could and did give that audience something finer than it wanted.

In preparing these plays for publication I have been able to benefit from the recent editions of *All for Love*, by David M. Vieth, *Lucius Junius Brutus*, by John Loftis, and *Venice Preserved*, by Malcolm Kelsall (all in the 'Regents Restoration Drama Series'). I have given some textual variants for all five plays, but only where they involved readings that seemed to affect the meaning. I have modernized spelling and, occasionally, punctuation, and have silently corrected misprints. I have silently restored blank verse where the seventeenth-century printer set it as prose, and occasionally restored to prose what he mistakenly tried to set as verse.

JAMES SUTHERLAND

Sutton Courtenay
1976

ALL FOR LOVE

John Dryden

1631–1700

From 1665 to 1675 Dryden wrote a succession of highly successful heroic plays, culminating in *Aureng-Zebe*, the most restrained and in some ways the best of them. Having got the heroic play out of his system, and no doubt realizing that the public appetite for the genre had been sated, he turned to tragedy proper and wrote his dramatic masterpiece, *All for Love*. The first recorded performance of the play was on 12 December 1677. As a writer for the stage he had always been aware that 'the drama's laws the drama's patrons give'; and reflecting some years later on certain passages in his heroic plays he admitted, 'I knew they were bad enough to please, even when I writ them'. But looking back on *All for Love* in his old age, he said something very different: 'I never writ anything for myself but *Antony and Cleopatra*.'

With this tragedy Dryden entered what, with reservations, may be called his neo-classical period. That he had long been aware of the virtues of a tauter dramatic form than he had so far used may be seen from the arguments he put into the mouth of Crites in *An Essay of Dramatic Poesy* (1668). Crites had there advocated 'one great and complete action', with the scene continued in the same place throughout the play; and in defending the Unity of Time he had claimed that it 'set the audience, as it were, at the post where the race is to be concluded; . . . saving them the tedious expectation of seeing the poet set out and ride the beginning of the course'. The action of *All for Love* takes place in the last days of Antony, when the great soldier-statesman is in his decline; and with the entrance of Ventidius early in the first act the pressure on Antony is felt at once. (Dryden understandably preferred 'the scene between Antony and Ventidius in the first act to anything which I have written in this kind'.) From that point on the tension rarely slackens, and the 'psychomachia' of Antony remains absorbing. Antony and Cleopatra are binary stars revolving around one another at the centre of their universe.

Like Shakespeare, Dryden made use of North's translation of Plutarch; but his claim to have written 'in imitation of Shakespeare's style' is puzzling. When we compare the two dramatists at work on the same situation and on the same source—for example, the journey of Cleopatra down the river Cydnus in Plutarch's 'Life of Antony'—the differences are more striking than the resemblances. In Shakespeare (II. ii) the description is given to Enobarbus; in *All for Love* (III. i), to Antony. Antony's speech is little more than an elegant variation of what Dryden found in North, but the eyewitness account that Shakespeare put into the mouth of Enobarbus is far more intensely realized. Enobarbus ends his memorable description with the whole city pouring out to see Cleopatra and leaving Antony alone in the market-place,

> Whistling to the air; which but for vacancy,
> Had gone to gaze on Cleopatra too
> And made a gap in nature.

The field of discourse in *All for Love* never reaches that imaginative level; but if we may doubt whether Dryden was capable of writing such a passage, we may also doubt whether, if he could, he would. Such wild and unfamiliar concepts as the air going to gaze on Cleopatra and leaving a gap in nature were not for the Restoration theatre. *All for Love* makes easier and more predictable demands on the responses of an audience. But it has nobility and grandeur, an action that moves in a succession of effective confrontations to its foreseen climax, a surprising variety of moods, emotions, and situations, and a rich and varied imagery that, in the thinner poetical atmosphere of the Restoration, is perhaps as near as Dryden could safely come to 'Shakespeare's style'.

Texts collated: *Q.* 1 (1678); *Q.* 2 (1692); *Q.* 3 (1696); *Works* (Collected Works, 1701). See also Selected Bibliography, pp. 439–41.

ALL FOR LOVE:
OR, THE
World well Lost.

A
TRAGEDY,

As it is Acted at the

THEATRE-ROYAL;

And Written in Imitation of *Shakespeare's* Stile.

By *John Dryden*, Servant to His Majesty.

Facile est verbum aliquod ardens (ut ita dicam) notare: idque restinctis animorum incendiis irridere. Cicero.

In the SAVOY:

Printed by *Tho. Newcomb*, for *Henry Herringman*, at the Blew Anchor in the Lower Walk of the *New-Exchange*. 1678.

To the Right Honourable,

Thomas, Earl of Danby, Viscount Latimer, and Baron Osborne of Kiveton in Yorkshire, Lord High Treasurer of England, One of His Majesty's most Honourable Privy-Council, and Knight of the Most Noble Order of the Garter, *&c.*

My LORD,

THE gratitude of poets is so troublesome a virtue to great men, that you are often in danger of your own benefits; for you are threatened with some epistle, and not suffered to do good in quiet, or to compound for their silence whom you have obliged. Yet, I confess, I neither am nor ought to be surprized at this indulgence; for your Lordship has the same right to favour poetry which the great and noble have ever had.

Carmen amat, quisquis carmine digna gerit.

There is somewhat of a tie in Nature betwixt those who are born for worthy actions, and those who can transmit them to posterity; and though ours be much the inferior part, it comes at least within the verge of alliance; nor are we unprofitable members of the commonwealth when we animate others to those virtues which we copy and describe from you.

'Tis indeed their interest who endeavour the subversion of governments, to discourage poets and historians; for the best which can happen to them is to be forgotten. But such who, under KINGS, are the fathers of their country, and by a just and prudent ordering of affairs preserve it, have the same reason to cherish the chroniclers of their actions as they have to lay up in safety the deeds and evidences of their estates; for such records are their undoubted titles to the love and reverence of after-ages. Your Lordship's administration has already taken up a considerable part of the English annals; and many of its most happy years are owing to it. His MAJESTY, the most knowing judge of men, and the best master, has acknowledged the ease and benefit he receives in the incomes of his treasury, which you found not only disordered, but exhausted. All things were in the confusion of a *Chaos*, without form or method, if not reduced beyond it, even to annihilation; so that you had not only to separate the jarring elements, but (if that

8 *Carmen . . . gerit.*] Whoever does things worthy of poetry, loves poetry (Claudian, xxiii. 6).

boldness of expression might be allowed me) to create them. Your enemies had so embroiled the management of your office, that they looked on your advancement as the instrument of your ruin. And as if the clogging of the revenue, and the confusion of accounts which you found in your entrance, were not sufficient, they added their own weight of malice to the public calamity by forestalling the credit which should cure it: your friends on the other side were only capable of pitying, but not of aiding you. No farther help or counsel was remaining to you but what was founded on yourself, and that indeed was your security; for your diligence, your constancy and your prudence wrought more surely within, when they were not disturbed by any outward motion. The highest virtue is best to be trusted with itself, for assistance only can be given by a genius superior to that which it assists. And 'tis the noblest kind of debt when we are only obliged to God and Nature. This then, My Lord, is your just commendation, that you have wrought out yourself a way to glory by those very means that were designed for your destruction: you have not only restored, but advanced the revenues of your Master without grievance to the subject; and as if that were little yet, the debts of the Exchequer, which lay heaviest both on the crown, and on private persons, have by your conduct been established in a certainty of satisfaction. An action so much the more great and honourable because the case was without the ordinary relief of laws; above the hopes of the afflicted, and beyond the narrowness of the Treasury to redress, had it been managed by a less able hand. 'Tis certainly the happiest and most unenvied part of all your fortune to do good to many, while you do injury to none: to receive at once the prayers of the subject, and the praises of the prince; and by the care of your conduct, to give him means of exerting the chiefest (if any be the chiefest) of his royal virtues, his distributive justice to the deserving, and his bounty and compassion to the wanting. The disposition of princes towards their people cannot better be discovered than in the choice of their ministers; who, like the animal spirits betwixt the soul and body, participate somewhat of both natures, and make the communication which is betwixt them. A king who is just and moderate in his nature, who rules according to the laws, whom God made happy by forming the temper of his soul to the constitution of his government, and who makes us happy by assuming over us no other sovereignty than that wherein our welfare and liberty consists; a prince, I say, of so excellent a character, and so suitable to the wishes of all good men, could not better have conveyed himself into his people's apprehensions than in your Lordship's person, who so lively express the same virtues, that you seem not so much a copy as an emanation of him. Moderation is

45 debts of the Exchequer] In January 1672 the King suspended for one year all payments on assignations in the Exchequer, and renewed the suspension a year later.

doubtless an establishment of greatness; but there is a steadiness of temper which is likewise requisite in a Minister of State: so equal a mixture of both virtues that he may stand like an isthmus betwixt the two encroaching seas of arbitrary power and lawless anarchy. The undertaking would be difficult to any but an extraordinary genius, to stand at the line, and to divide the limits; to pay what is due to the great representative of the Nation, and neither to enhance, nor to yield up, the undoubted prerogatives of the crown. These, My Lord, are the proper virtues of a noble Englishman, as indeed they are properly English virtues: no people in the world being capable of using them but we who have the happiness to be born under so equal, and so well-poised a government. A government which has all the advantages of liberty beyond a commonwealth, and all the marks of kingly sovereignty without the danger of a tyranny. Both my nature, as I am an Englishman, and my reason, as I am a man, have bred in me a loathing to that specious name of a republic: that mock-appearance of a liberty, where all who have not part in the government are slaves; and slaves they are of a viler note than such as are subjects to an absolute dominion. For no Christian monarchy is so absolute but 'tis circumscribed with laws. But when the executive power is in the law-makers, there is no farther check upon them; and the people must suffer without a remedy, because they are oppressed by their representatives. If I must serve, the number of my masters, who were born my equals, would but add to the ignominy of my bondage. The nature of our government, above all others, is exactly suited both to the situation of our country, and the temper of the natives: an island being more proper for commerce and for defence than for extending its dominions on the Continent; for what the valour of its inhabitants might gain, by reason of its remoteness, and the casualties of the seas, it could not so easily preserve, and therefore neither the arbitrary power of one in a monarchy, nor of many in a commonwealth, could make us greater than we are. 'Tis true that vaster and more frequent taxes might be gathered, when the consent of the people was not asked or needed, but this were only by conquering abroad to be poor at home; and the examples of our neighbours teach us that they are not always the happiest subjects whose kings extend their dominions farthest. Since therefore we cannot win by an offensive war, at least a land war, the model of our government seems naturally contrived for the defensive part; and the consent of a people is easily obtained to contribute to that power which must protect it. *Felices nimium bona si sua norint, Angligenæ!* And yet there are not wanting malcontents amongst us who, surfeiting themselves on too much happiness,

104–5 *Felices . . . Angligenæ!*] Happy Englishmen! blest beyond all bliss, did they but know their own happiness. (An adaptation of Virgil, *Georgics*, ii. 458–9. For Dryden's '*Angligenæ*' Virgil has '*agricolas*'.)

would persuade the people that they might be happier by a change. 'Twas indeed the policy of their old forefather, when himself was fallen from the station of glory, to seduce mankind into the same rebellion with him, by telling him he might yet be freer than he was; that is, more free than his nature would allow, or (if I may so say) than God could make him. We have already all the liberty which freeborn subjects can enjoy; and all beyond it is but licence. But if it be liberty of conscience which they pretend, the moderation of our Church is such that its practice extends not to the severity of persecution, and its discipline is withal so easy, that it allows more freedom to dissenters than any of the sects would allow to it. In the meantime, what right can be pretended by these men to attempt innovations in Church or State? Who made them the trustees, or (to speak a little nearer their own language) the keepers of the liberty of England? If their call be extraordinary, let them convince us by working miracles; for ordinary vocation they can have none to disturb the government under which they were born, and which protects them. He who has often changed his party, and always has made his interest the rule of it, gives little evidence of his sincerity for the public good: 'tis manifest he changes but for himself, and takes the people for tools to work his fortune. Yet the experience of all ages might let him know that they who trouble the waters first have seldom the benefit of the fishing; as they who began the late rebellion enjoyed not the fruit of their undertaking, but were crushed themselves by the usurpation of their own instrument. Neither is it enough for them to answer that they only intend a reformation of the government, but not the subversion of it. On such pretences all insurrections have been founded: 'tis striking at the root of power, which is obedience. Every remonstrance of private men has the seed of treason in it; and discourses which are couched in ambiguous terms are therefore the more dangerous, because they do all the mischief of open sedition, yet are safe from the punishment of the laws. These, My Lord, are considerations which I should not pass so lightly over, had I room to manage them as they deserve; for no man can be so inconsiderable in a nation as not to have a share in the welfare of it; and if he be a true Englishman, he must at the same time be fired with indignation, and revenge himself as he can on the disturbers of his country. And to whom could I more fitly apply myself, than to your Lordship, who have not only an inborn, but an hereditary loyalty? The memorable constancy and sufferings of your father, almost to the ruin of his estate for the royal cause, were an earnest of that which such a parent and such an institution would produce in the person of a son. But so unhappy an occasion of manifesting

119 *call*] vocation (with religious overtones) 122 He who has often changed his party] Shaftesbury is probably glanced at here. 129 instrument] Oliver Cromwell 143 your father] Sir Edward Osborne (1596–1647), a royalist commander in the Civil War

your own zeal in suffering for his present MAJESTY, the providence of God and the prudence of your administration will, I hope, prevent. That as your father's fortune waited on the unhappiness of his sovereign, so your own may participate of the better fate which attends his son. The relation which you have by alliance to the noble family of your lady serves to confirm to you both this happy augury. For what can deserve a greater place in the English chronicle than the loyalty and courage, the actions and death of the general of an army fighting for his prince and country? The honour and gallantry of the Earl of Lindsey is so illustrious a subject that 'tis fit to adorn an heroic poem; for he was the proto-martyr of the cause, and the type of his unfortunate royal master.

Yet, after all, My Lord, if I may speak my thoughts, you are happy rather to us than to yourself; for the multiplicity, the cares, and the vexations of your employment have betrayed you from yourself, and given you up into the possession of the public. You are robbed of your privacy and friends, and scarce any hour of your life you can call your own. Those who envy your fortune, if they wanted not good nature, might more justly pity it; and when they see you watched by a crowd of suitors, whose importunity 'tis impossible to avoid, would conclude with reason that you have lost much more in true content than you have gained by dignity, and that a private gentleman is better attended by a single servant than your Lordship with so clamorous a train. Pardon me, My Lord, if I speak like a philosopher on this subject; the fortune which makes a man uneasy cannot make him happy; and a wise man must think himself uneasy when few of his actions are in his choice.

This last consideration has brought me to another, and a very seasonable one for your relief; which is, that while I pity your want of leisure, I have impertinently detained you so long a time. I have put off my own business, which was my dedication, till 'tis so late that I am now ashamed to begin it. And therefore I will say nothing of the poem which I present to you, because I know not if you are like to have an hour which, with a good conscience, you may throw away in perusing it. And for the author, I have only to beg the continuance of your protection to him, who is,

MY LORD,

Your Lordship's, most Obliged,

most Humble, and most

Obedient Servant,

JOHN DRYDEN

154 Lindsey] Robert Bertie, first Earl of Lindsey (1582–1642), killed at the battle of Edgehill while in command of the royalist army. His son, the second earl, was Danby's father-in-law.

PREFACE

The death of Antony and Cleopatra is a subject which has been treated by the greatest wits of our nation, after Shakespeare; and by all so variously, that their example has given me the confidence to try myself in this bow of Ulysses amongst the crowd of suitors; and, withal, to take my own measures, in aiming at the mark. I doubt not but the same motive has prevailed with all of us in this attempt; I mean the excellency of the moral: for the chief persons represented were famous patterns of unlawful love, and their end accordingly was unfortunate. All reasonable men have long since concluded that the hero of the poem ought not to be a character of perfect virtue, for then he could not, without injustice, be made unhappy; nor yet altogether wicked, because he could not then be pitied. I have therefore steered the middle course; and have drawn the character of Antony as favourably as Plutarch, Appian, and Dion Cassius would give me leave: the like I have observed in Cleopatra. That which is wanting to work up the pity to a greater height was not afforded me by the story; for the crimes of love which they both committed were not occasioned by any necessity, or fatal ignorance, but were wholly voluntary, since our passions are, or ought to be, within our power. The fabric of the play is regular enough, as to the inferior parts of it; and the unities of time, place and action more exactly observed than, perhaps, the English theatre requires. Particularly, the action is so much one that it is the only of the kind without episode or underplot; every scene in the tragedy conducing to the main design, and every act concluding with a turn of it. The greatest error in the contrivance seems to be in the person of Octavia; for, though I might use the privilege of a poet to introduce her into Alexandria, yet I had not enough considered that the compassion she moved to herself and children was destructive to that which I reserved for Antony and Cleopatra, whose mutual love, being founded upon vice, must lessen the favour of the audience to them, when virtue and innocence were oppressed by it. And, though I justified Antony in some measure, by making Octavia's departure to proceed wholly from herself, yet the force of the first machine still remained; and the dividing of pity, like the cutting of a river into many channels, abated the strength of the natural stream. But this is an objection which none of my critics have urged against me; and therefore I might have let it pass, if I could have resolved to have been partial to myself.

2 the greatest wits of our nation] e.g. Samuel Daniel, John Fletcher, Thomas May, Sir Charles Sedley 11 pitied] cf. Aristotle, *Poetics*, xiii 31 machine] contrivance

The faults my enemies have found are rather cavils concerning little, and not essential decencies; which a master of the ceremonies may decide betwixt us. The French poets, I confess, are strict observers of these punctilios: they would not, for example, have suffered Cleopatra and Octavia to have met; or if they had met, there must only have passed betwixt them some cold civilities, but no eagerness of repartee, for fear of offending against the greatness of their characters, and the modesty of their sex. This objection I foresaw, and at the same time contemned; for I judged it both natural and probable that Octavia, proud of her new-gained conquest, would search out Cleopatra to triumph over her, and that Cleopatra, thus attacked, was not of a spirit to shun the encounter; and 'tis not unlikely that two exasperated rivals should use such satire as I have put into their mouths; for, after all, though the one were a Roman, and the other a queen, they were both women. 'Tis true, some actions, though natural, are not fit to be represented; and broad obscenities in words ought in good manners to be avoided: expressions therefore are a modest clothing of our thoughts, as breeches and petticoats are of our bodies. If I have kept myself within the bounds of modesty, all beyond it is but nicety and affectation; which is no more but modesty depraved into a vice: they betray themselves who are too quick of apprehension in such cases, and leave all reasonable men to imagine worse of them than of the poet.

Honest Montaigne goes yet farther: *Nous ne sommes que cérémonie; la cérémonie nous emporte, et laissons la substance des choses. Nous nous tenons aux branches, et abandonnons le tronc et le corps. Nous avons appris aux dames de rougir, oyans seulement nommer ce qu'elles ne craignent aucunement à faire: nous n'osons appeller à droit nos membres, et ne craignons pas de les employer à toute sorte de debauche. La cérémonie nous defend d'exprimer par paroles les choses licites et naturelles, et nous l'en croyons; la raison nous defend de n'en faire point d'illicites et mauvaises, et personne ne le'n croit.* My comfort is, that by this opinion my enemies are but sucking critics, who would fain be nibbling ere their teeth are come.

Yet in this nicety of manners does the excellency of French poetry consist: their heroes are the most civil people breathing; but their good breeding seldom extends to a word of sense. All their wit is in their ceremony; they want the genius which animates our stage; and therefore 'tis but necessary

57–64 *Nous . . . croit*] 'We are nought but ceremonie, ceremonie doth transport us, and wee leave the substance of things; we hold-fast by the boughs, and leave the trunke or body. Wee have taught Ladies to blush, onely by hearing that named, which they nothing fear to doe. Wee dare not call our members by their proper names, and feare not to employ them in all kind of dissolutenesse. Ceremonie forbids us by words to expresse lawfull and naturall things; and we beleeve it. Reason willeth us to doe no bad or unlawfull things, and no man giveth credit unto it' (Montaigne, *Essays*, 17; Florio's translation).

when they cannot please, that they should take care not to offend. But, as the civilest man in the company is commonly the dullest, so these authors, while they are afraid to make you laugh or cry, out of pure good manners make you sleep. They are so careful not to exasperate a critic that they never leave him any work; so busy with the broom, and make so clean a riddance, that there is little left either for censure or for praise: for no part of a poem is worth our discommending where the whole is insipid; as when we have once tasted of palled wine, we stay not to examine it glass by glass. But while they affect to shine in trifles, they are often careless in essentials. Thus their Hippolitus is so scrupulous in point of decency, that he will rather expose himself to death than accuse his stepmother to his father; and my critics, I am sure, will commend him for it; but we of grosser apprehensions are apt to think that this excess of generosity is not practicable but with fools and madmen. This was good manners with a vengeance; and the audience is like to be much concerned at the misfortunes of this admirable hero: but take Hippolitus out of his poetic fit, and I suppose he would think it a wiser part to set the saddle on the right horse, and choose rather to live with the reputation of a plain-spoken honest man than to die with the infamy of an incestuous villain. In the meantime we may take notice, that where the poet ought to have preserved the character as it was delivered to us by antiquity, when he should have given us the picture of a rough young man, of the Amazonian strain, a jolly huntsman, and both by his profession and his early rising a mortal enemy to love, he has chosen to give him the turn of gallantry, sent him to travel from Athens to Paris, taught him to make love, and transformed the Hippolitus of Euripides into Monsieur Hippolite. I should not have troubled myself thus far with French poets, but that I find our *chedreux* critics wholly form their judgements by them. But for my part, I desire to be tried by the laws of my own country; for it seems unjust to me that the French should prescribe here, till they have conquered. Our little sonneteers, who follow them, have too narrow souls to judge of poetry. Poets themselves are the most proper, though I conclude not the only critics. But till some genius, as universal as Aristotle, shall arise, one who can penetrate into all arts and sciences, without the practice of them, I shall think it reasonable that the judgement of an artificer in his own art should be preferable to the opinion of another man; at least where he is not bribed by interest, or prejudiced by malice. And this, I suppose, is manifest by plain induction; for, first, the crowd cannot be presumed to have more than a gross instinct of what pleases or displeases them: every man will grant me this; but then, by a particular kindness to

78 palled] stale 80 Hippolitus] Dryden is thinking of Racine's *Phèdre* 97 *chedreux*] a fashionable wig-maker of the period, whose name was given to the wigs he made. 100 sonneteers] song-writers.

himself, he draws his own stake first, and will be distinguished from the multitude, of which other men may think him one. But, if I come closer to those who are allowed for witty men, either by the advantage of their quality, or by common fame, and affirm that neither are they qualified to decide sovereignly concerning poetry, I shall yet have a strong party of my opinion; for most of them severally will exclude the rest, either from the number of witty men, or at least of able judges. But here again they are all indulgent to themselves; and everyone who believes himself a wit, that is, every man, will pretend at the same time to a right of judging. But to press it yet farther, there are many witty men, but few poets; neither have all poets a taste of tragedy. And this is the rock on which they are daily splitting. Poetry, which is a picture of Nature, must generally please; but 'tis not to be understood that all parts of it must please every man; therefore is not tragedy to be judged by a witty man, whose taste is only confined to comedy. Nor is every man who loves tragedy a sufficient judge of it: he must understand the excellencies of it too, or he will only prove a blind admirer, not a critic. From hence it comes that so many satires on poets, and censures of their writings, fly abroad. Men of pleasant conversation, (at least esteemed so) and endued with a trifling kind of fancy, perhaps helped out with some smattering of Latin, are ambitious to distinguish themselves from the herd of gentlemen, by their poetry;

Rarus enim ferme sensus communis in illa
Fortuna.

And is not this a wretched affectation, not to be contented with what fortune has done for them, and sit down quietly with their estates, but they must call their wits in question, and needlessly expose their nakedness to public view? Not considering that they are not to expect the same approbation from sober men which they have found from their flatterers after the third bottle? If a little glittering in discourse has passed them on us for witty men, where was the necessity of undeceiving the world? Would a man who has an ill title to an estate, but yet is in possession of it, would he bring it of his own accord to be tried at Westminster? We who write, if we want the talent, yet have the excuse that we do it for a poor subsistence; but what can be urged in their defence, who, not having the vocation of poverty to scribble, out of meer wantonness take pains to make themselves

119 witty men] What follows is directed particularly against the Earl of Rochester, who had attacked Dryden in his anonymous poem, *An Allusion to Horace*. 131–2 *Rarus . . . Fortuna*] for commonsense is usually rare in that station of life (Juvenal, *Satires*, viii. 73–4) 135 nakedness] a *double entendre*: Rochester and some of the other wits had done so literally on several occasions. 141 Westminster] Westminster Hall, at this time the seat of the lawcourts

ridiculous? Horace was certainly in the right, where he said that *no man is satisfied with his own condition.* A poet is not pleased, because he is not rich; and the rich are discontented, because the poets will not admit them of their number. Thus the case is hard with writers: if they succeed not, they must starve; and if they do, some malicious satire is prepared to level them for daring to please without their leave. But while they are so eager to destroy the fame of others, their ambition is manifest in their concernment: some poem of their own is to be produced, and the slaves are to be laid flat with their faces on the ground, that the monarch may appear in the greater majesty.

Dionysius and Nero had the same longings, but with all their power they could never bring their business well about. 'Tis true, they proclaimed themselves poets by sound of trumpet; and poets they were upon pain of death to any man who durst call them otherwise. The audience had a fine time on't, you may imagine; they sate in a bodily fear, and looked as demurely as they could; for 'twas a hanging matter to laugh unseasonably, and the tyrants were suspicious, as they had reason, that their subjects had 'em in the wind; so every man, in his own defence, set as good a face upon the business as he could. 'Twas known beforehand that the monarchs were to be crowned laureates; but when the show was over, and an honest man was suffered to depart quietly, he took out his laughter which he had stifled, with a firm resolution never more to see an Emperor's play, though he had been ten years a-making it. In the meantime the true poets were they who made the best markets, for they had wit enough to yield the prize with a good grace, and not contend with him who had thirty legions. They were sure to be rewarded if they confessed themselves bad writers, and that was somewhat better than to be martyrs for their reputation. Lucan's example was enough to teach them manners; and after he was put to death for overcoming Nero, the Emperor carried it without dispute for the best poet in his dominions. No man was ambitious of that grinning honour; for if he heard the malicious trumpeter proclaiming his name before his betters, he knew there was but one way with him. Mæcenas took another course, and we know he was more than a great man, for he was witty too: but finding himself far gone in poetry, which Seneca assures us was not his talent, he thought it his best way to be well with Virgil and with Horace, that at least he might be a poet at the second hand; and we

145–6 *no man . . . condition*] Horace, *Satires*, I. i. 1–3 155 Dionysius and Nero] Both had tried their hands at writing 162 in the wind] to windward; i.e. their subjects could scent what their writing was really like. 172 Lucan's example] Lucan imprudently entered a literary contest with Nero and was the victor. Provoked by the daily insults of the angry emperor, Lucan took part in a conspiracy against him and was condemned to death. 174–5 grinning honour] *1 Henry IV*, v. iii. 61

see how happily it has succeeded with him, for his own bad poetry is forgotten, and their panegyrics of him still remain. But they who should be our patrons are for no such expensive ways to fame: they have much of the poetry of Mæcenas, but little of his liberality. They are for persecuting Horace and Virgil, in the persons of their successors (for such is every man who has any part of their soul and fire, though in a less degree). Some of their little zanies yet go farther; for they are persecutors even of Horace himself, as far as they are able, by their ignorant and vile imitations of him; by making an unjust use of his authority, and turning his artillery against his friends. But how would he disdain to be copied by such hands! I dare answer for him, he would be more uneasy in their company than he was with Crispinus, their forefather, in the *Holy Way*; and would no more have allowed them a place amongst the critics than he would Demetrius the mimic, and Tigellius the buffoon;

> ——*Demetri*, *teque*, *Tigelli*,
> *Discipularum inter jubeo plorare cathedras.*

With what scorn would he look down on such miserable translators, who make doggerel of his Latin, mistake his meaning, misapply his censures, and often contradict their own? He is fixed as a landmark to set out the bounds of poetry,

> —— *Saxum*, *antiquum ingens* . . .
> *Limes agro positus*, *litem ut discerneret arvis.*

But other arms than theirs, and other sinews are required, to raise the weight of such an author; and when they would toss him against their enemies,

> *Genua labant*, *gelidus concrevit frigore sanguis.*
> *Tum lapis ipse viri*, *vacuum per inane volutus*,
> *Nec spatium evasit totum*, *nec pertulit ictum.*

For my part, I would wish no other revenge, either for myself or the rest of the poets, from this rhyming judge of the twelve-penny gallery, this

192 Crispinus] a mediocre poet ridiculed by Horace 192 the Holy Way] the *Via Sacra*, the oldest street in Rome 195–6 *Demetri* . . . *cathedras*] You, Demetrius, and you, Tigellius, I bid you lament amidst the easy chairs of your female disciples (Horace, *Satires*, I. x. 90–1: Dryden reads *Discipulorum*). 198 censures] judgements, opinions 201–2 *Saxum* . . . *arvis*] A stone, ancient and huge, a boundary mark lying in a field, that it may ward off disputes over the cultivated lands (Virgil, *Æneid*, xii. 897–8) 206–8 *Genua* . . . *ictum*] (His) knees totter, his blood is frozen cold. Then this hero's stone itself whirled through the empty void, neither passed over the whole distance nor brought the blow home (ibid. xii. 905–7). 210 twelve-penny gallery] the upper gallery, the cheapest part of a Restoration theatre

legitimate son of Sternhold, than that he would subscribe his name to his censure, or (not to tax him beyond his learning) set his mark; for, should he own himself publicly, and come from behind the lion's skin, they whom he condemns would be thankful to him, they whom he praises would choose to be condemned; and the magistrates whom he has elected would modestly withdraw from their employment, to avoid the scandal of his nomination. The sharpness of his satire, next to himself, falls most heavily on his friends, and they ought never to forgive him for commending them perpetually the wrong way, and sometimes by contraries. If he have a friend whose hastiness in writing is his greatest fault, Horace would have taught him to have minced the matter, and to have called it readiness of thought and a flowing fancy; for friendship will allow a man to christen an imperfection by the name of some neighbour virtue:

Vellem in amicitia sic erraremus; et isti
Errori nomen virtus posuisset honestum.

But he would never have allowed him to have called a slow man hasty, or a hasty writer a slow drudge, as Juvenal explains it:

—— *Canibus pigris, scabieque vetustae*
Laevibus, et siccæ lambentibus ora lucernæ
Nomen erit, Pardus, Tigris, Leo; si quid adhuc est
Quod fremit in terris violentius.

Yet Lucretius laughs at a foolish lover, even for excusing the imperfections of his mistress:

Nigra μελίχροος *est, immunda et fœtida* ἄκοσμος.
Balba loqui non quit, τραυλίζει; *muta pudens est, etc.*

But to drive it *ad Æthiopem cygnum* is not to be endured. I leave him to interpret this by the benefit of his French version on the other side,

211 Sternhold] Thomas Sternhold, who (with John Hopkins) produced a metrical version of the Psalms which was much ridiculed 224–5 *Vellem . . . honestum*] I could wish that we might err so in friendship, and that to such an error our ethics should have attached an honourable name (Horace, *Satires*, I. iii. 41–2) 227 drudge] In *An Allusion to Horace* (41 ff.) Rochester had referred to 'hasty Shadwell and slow Wycherley' 228–31 *Canibus . . . violentius*] 'Lazy hounds that are bald with chronic mange, and lick the edges of a dry lamp, will bear the name of "Pard", "Tiger", "Lion", or of any other animal in the world that roars more fiercely' (Juvenal, *Satires*, viii. 34–7; Loeb's translation). 234–5 *Nigra . . . etc.*] 'The black girl is a nut-brown maid, the dirty and rank is a sweet disorder, if she stutters and cannot speak—*elle zézaye*; the dumb is modest *etc.*' (Lucretius, *De Rerum Natura*, lv. 1160, 1164; Loeb's translation) 236 *ad Æthiopem cygnum*] Juvenal, *Satires*, viii. 32–3; *nanum cuiusdam Atlanta vocamus, / Æthiopem cygnum . . .*: we call someone's dwarf an 'Atlas', his blackamoor 'a swan'.

and without farther considering him than I have the rest of my illiterate censors, whom I have disdained to answer because they are not qualified for judges. It remains that I acquaint the reader that I have endeavoured in this play to follow the practice of the Ancients, who, as Mr. Rymer has judiciously observed, are and ought to be our masters. Horace likewise gives it for a rule in his Art of Poetry,

—— Vos exemplaria Græca
Nocturna versate manu, versate diurna.

Yet, though their models are regular, they are too little for English tragedy; which requires to be built in a larger compass. I could give an instance in the *Oedipus Tyrannus*, which was the masterpiece of Sophocles; but I reserve it for a more fit occasion, which I hope to have hereafter. In my style I have professed to imitate the divine Shakespeare; which that I might perform more freely, I have disencumbered myself from rhyme. Not that I condemn my former way, but that this is more proper to my present purpose. I hope I need not to explain myself, that I have not copied my author servilely: words and phrases must of necessity receive a change in succeeding ages, but 'tis almost a miracle that much of his language remains so pure; and that he who began dramatic poetry amongst us, untaught by any, and, as Ben Jonson tells us, without learning, should by the force of his own genius perform so much, that in a manner he has left no praise for any who come after him. The occasion is fair, and the subject would be pleasant to handle the difference of styles betwixt him and Fletcher, and wherein, and how far they are both to be imitated. But since I must not be over-confident of my own performance after him, it will be prudence in me to be silent. Yet I hope I may affirm, and without vanity, that by imitating him I have excelled myself throughout the play; and particularly, that I prefer the scene betwixt Antony and Ventidius in the first act, to anything which I have written in this kind.

241 Rymer] Dryden alludes to Thomas Rymer's *The Tragedies of the Last Age Considered*, which had appeared a few months earlier 244–5 *Vos . . . diurna*] As for you, reflect upon Greek models by night, reflect upon them by day (Horace, *Ars Poetica*, 268–9). 257 tells us] in his lines 'To the Memory of . . . William Shakespeare', prefixed to the First Folio, where he writes of Shakespeare's 'small Latin, and less Greek'

PROLOGUE

What flocks of critics hover here today,
As vultures wait on armies for their prey,
All gaping for the carcass of a play!
With croaking notes they bode some dire event,
And follow dying poets by the scent.
Ours gives himself for gone; y'have watched your time!
He fights this day unarmed, without his rhyme;
And brings a tale which often has been told,
As sad as Dido's, and almost as old.
His hero, whom you wits his bully call,
Bates of his mettle, and scarce rants at all:
He's somewhat lewd, but a well-meaning mind;
Weeps much, fights little, but is wondrous kind.
In short, a pattern and companion fit
For all the keeping tonies of the pit.
I could name more: a wife and mistress too,
Both (to be plain) too good for most of you;
The wife well-natured, and the mistress true.
Now, poets, if your fame has been his care,
Allow him all the candour you can spare.
A brave man scorns to quarrel once a day,
Like hectors, in at every petty fray.
Let those find fault whose wit's so very small,
They've need to show that they can think at all.
Errors like straws upon the surface flow;
He who would search for pearls must dive below.
Fops may have leave to level all they can,
As pygmies would be glad to lop a man.
Half-wits are fleas, so little and so light,
We scarce could know they live but that they bite.
But, as the rich, when tired with daily feasts,
For change become their next poor tenant's guests,

11 *bates of his mettle*] becomes dejected or depressed *scarce rants at all*] i.e. unlike the 'bully' heroes of his own heroic plays 15 *keeping tonies*] simpletons keeping mistresses 20 *candour*] kindness, favour 22 *hectors*] bullies 32 *next*] nearest

Drink hearty draughts of ale from plain brown bowls,
And snatch the homely rasher from the coals;
So you, retiring from much better cheer,
For once may venture to do penance here.
And since that plenteous autumn now is past,
Whose grapes and peaches have indulged your taste,
Take in good part from our poor poet's board,
Such rivelled fruits as winter can afford.

40 *rivelled*] dried, or stored up (*O.E.D.*, 1, 6) *winter*] The first recorded performance of the play was in December (see p. 1).

DRAMATIS PERSONAE

MARK ANTONY	*Mr. Hart*
VENTIDIUS, his general	*Mr. Mohun*
DOLABELLA, his friend	*Mr. Clark*
ALEXAS, the Queen's eunuch	*Mr. Goodman*
SERAPION, Priest of Isis	*Mr. Griffin*
ANOTHER PRIEST [Myris]	*Mr. Coysh*
SERVANTS TO ANTONY	
CLEOPATRA, Queen of Egypt	*Mrs. Boutell*
OCTAVIA, Antony's wife	*Mrs. Corey*
CHARMION } Cleopatra's maids	
IRAS } Cleopatra's maids	

ANTONY'S two little Daughters

Scene: Alexandria

ALL for LOVE;

OR,

The World well Lost

ACT I

The Temple of Isis

Enter Serapion, Myris, *Priests of Isis.*

Serap. Portents, and prodigies, are grown so frequent,
That they have lost their name. Our fruitful Nile
Flowed ere the wonted season, with a torrent
So unexpected, and so wondrous fierce,
That the wild deluge overtook the haste
Ev'n of the hinds that watched it. Men and beasts
Were borne above the tops of trees that grew
On th'utmost margin of the water-mark.
Then, with so swift an ebb the flood drove backward
It slipped from underneath the scaly herd:
Here monstrous phocae panted on the shore;
Forsaken dolphins there, with their broad tails,
Lay lashing the departing waves; hard by 'em,
Sea-horses flound'ring in the slimy mud
Tossed up their heads, and dashed the ooze about 'em.

Enter Alexas *behind them.*

Myr. Avert these omens, heaven!
Serap. Last night, between the hours of twelve and one,
In a lone aisle o'th' temple while I walked,
A whirlwind rose, that with a violent blast
Shook all the dome: the doors around me clapped,

11. phocae] seals   14 sea-horses] hippopotami   20 dome] building

The iron wicket, that defends the vault
Where the long race of Ptolomies is laid,
Burst open, and disclosed the mighty dead.
From out each monument, in order plac'd,
An armed ghost start up: the boy-king last
Reared his inglorious head. A peal of groans
Then followed, and a lamentable voice
Cried, 'Egypt is no more.' My blood ran back,
My shaking knees against each other knocked;
On the cold pavement down I fell entranced,
And so unfinished left the horrid scene.

Alex. [*Showing himself.*] And dreamed you this? or did invent the story
To frighten our Egyptian boys withal,
And train 'em up betimes in fear of priesthood?

Serap. My lord, I saw you not,
Nor meant my words should reach your ears; but what
I uttered was most true.

Alex. A foolish dream,
Bred from the fumes of indigested feasts,
And holy luxury.

Serap. I know my duty:
This goes no farther.

Alex. 'Tis not fit it should.
Nor would the times now bear it, were it true.
All southern, from yon hills, the Roman camp
Hangs o'er us black and threat'ning, like a storm
Just breaking on our heads.

Serap. Our faint Egyptians pray for Antony;
But in their servile hearts they own Octavius.

Myr. Why then does Antony dream out his hours,
And tempts not fortune for a noble day,
Which might redeem what Actium lost?

Alex. He thinks 'tis past recovery.

Serap. Yet the foe
Seems not to press the siege.

Alex. Oh, there's the wonder.
Maecenas and Agrippa, who can most

21 wicket] small gate or grill 25 start] started boy-king] Ptolomy XIV, Cleopatra's younger brother 49 Actium] the scene of the naval victory of Octavius over Antony and Cleopatra, 31 B.C. 52–3 who can most/with Cæsar] who can do most, has most influence

With Cæsar, are his foes. His wife Octavia,
Driven from his house, solicits her revenge;
And Dolabella, who was once his friend,
Upon some private grudge now seeks his ruin:
Yet still war seems on either side to sleep.

Serap. 'Tis strange that Antony, for some days past,
Has not beheld the face of Cleopatra;
But here in Isis' temple lives retired,
And makes his heart a prey to black despair.

Alex. 'Tis true; and we much fear he hopes by absence
To cure his mind of love.

Serap. If he be vanquished,
Or make his peace, Egypt is doomed to be
A Roman province; and our plenteous harvests
Must then redeem the scarceness of their soil.
While Antony stood firm, our Alexandria
Rivalled proud Rome (dominion's other seat),
And Fortune striding, like a vast Colossus,
Could fix an equal foot of empire here.

Alex. Had I my wish, these tyrants of all nature
Who lord it o'er mankind should perish, here,
Each by the other's sword; but, since our will
Is lamely followed by our power, we must
Depend on one, with him to rise or fall.

Serap. How stands the Queen affected?

Alex. Oh, she dotes,
She dotes, Serapion, on this vanquished man,
And winds herself about his mighty ruins;
Whom would she yet forsake, yet yield him up,
This hunted prey, to his pursuers' hands,
She might preserve us all; but 'tis in vain—
This changes my designs, this blasts my counsels,
And makes me use all means to keep him here,
Whom I could wish divided from her arms
Far as the earth's deep centre. Well, you know
The state of things; no more of your ill omens
And black prognostics; labour to confirm
The people's hearts.

53 Octavia] the sister of Octavius, married to Antony in 40 B.C. when he and Octavius divided up the Roman empire between themselves

Enter Ventidius, *talking aside with a* Gentleman of Antony's.

Serap. These Romans will o'erhear us.
But who's that stranger? By his warlike port,
His fierce demeanour and erected look,
He's of no vulgar note.
Alex. Oh, 'tis Ventidius,
Our Emp'ror's great lieutenant in the East,
Who first showed Rome that Parthia could be conquered.
When Antony returned from Syria last,
He left this man to guard the Roman frontiers.
Serap. You seem to know him well.
Alex. Too well. I saw him in Cilicia first,
When Cleopatra there met Antony:
A mortal foe he was to us, and Egypt.
But, let me witness to the worth I hate,
A braver Roman never drew a sword.
Firm to his prince, but as a friend, not slave.
He ne'er was of his pleasures, but presides
O'er all his cooler hours and morning counsels:
In short, the plainness, fierceness, rugged virtue
Of an old true-stamped Roman lives in him.
His coming bodes I know not what of ill
To our affairs. Withdraw, to mark him better;
And I'll acquaint you why I sought you here,
And what's our present work.

They withdraw to a corner of the stage; and Ventidius, *with the other, comes forwards to the front.*

Ventidius. Not see him, say you?
I say, I must, and will.
Gent. He has commanded,
On pain of death, none should approach his presence.
Ven. I bring him news will raise his drooping spirits,
Give him new life.
Gent. He sees not Cleopatra.
Ven. Would he had never seen her!
Gent. He eats not, drinks not, sleeps not, has no use
Of anything but thought; or, if he talks,
'Tis to himself, and then 'tis perfect raving:
Then he defies the world, and bids it pass;
Sometimes he gnaws his lip, and curses loud
The boy Octavius; then he draws his mouth

Into a scornful smile, and cries, 'Take all,
The world's not worth my care.'
Ven. Just, just his nature.
Virtue's his path; but sometimes 'tis too narrow
For his vast soul, and then he starts out wide,
And bounds into a vice that bears him far
From his first course, and plunges him in ills:
But, when his danger makes him find his fault,
Quick to observe, and full of sharp remorse,
He censures eagerly his own misdeeds,
Judging himself with malice to himself,
And not forgiving what as man he did
Because his other parts are more than man.
He must not thus be lost.

Alexas *and the* Priests *come forward.*

Alex. You have your full instructions, now advance;
Proclaim your orders loudly.
Serap. Romans, Egyptians, hear the Queen's command.
Thus Cleopatra bids, 'Let labour cease,
To pomp and triumphs give this happy day
That gave the world a lord: 'tis Antony's.'
Live, Antony; and Cleopatra live!
Be this the general voice sent up to heaven,
And every public place repeat this echo.
Ven. [*Aside.*] Fine pageantry!
Serap. Set out before your doors
The images of all your sleeping fathers,
With laurels crowned; with laurels wreath your posts,
And strew with flow'rs the pavement; let the priests
Do present sacrifice; pour out the wine,
And call the gods to join with you in gladness.
Ven. Curse on the tongue that bids this general joy!
Can they be friends of Antony, who revel
When Antony's in danger? Hide, for shame,
You Romans, your great grandsires' images,
For fear their souls should animate their marbles,
To blush at their degenerate progeny.
Alex. A love which knows no bounds to Antony
Would mark the day with honours; when all heaven
Laboured for him, when each propitious star

147 images] small statues

Stood wakeful in his orb, to watch that hour
And shed his better influence. Her own birthday
Our Queen neglected, like a vulgar fate
That passed obscurely by.
Ven. Would it had slept,
Divided far from his, till some remote
And future age had called it out, to ruin
Some other prince, not him!
Alex. Your emperor,
Though grown unkind, would be more gentle than
T'upbraid my queen for loving him too well.
Ven. Does the mute sacrifice upbraid the priest?
He knows him not his executioner.
Oh, she has decked his ruin with her love,
Led him in golden bands to gaudy slaughter,
And made perdition pleasing: she has left him
The blank of what he was;
I tell thee, eunuch, she has quite unmanned him:
Can any Roman see, and know him now,
Thus altered from the lord of half mankind,
Unbent, unsinewed, made a woman's toy,
Shrunk from the vast extent of all his honours,
And cramped within a corner of the world?
O, Antony!
Thou bravest soldier, and thou best of friends!
Bounteous as nature; next to nature's god!
Couldst thou but make new worlds, so wouldst thou give 'em
As bounty were thy being. Rough in battle,
As the first Romans when they went to war;
Yet, after victory, more pitiful,
Than all their praying virgins left at home!
Alex. Would you could add to those more shining virtues,
His truth to her who loves him.
Ven. Would I could not!
But wherefore waste I precious hours with thee?
Thou art her darling mischief, her chief engine,
Antony's other fate. Go, tell thy queen,
Ventidius is arrived to end her charms.
Let your Egyptian timbrels play alone,
Nor mix effeminate sounds with Roman trumpets.
You dare not fight for Antony; go pray,
And keep your coward's holiday in temples. [*Exeunt* Alexas, Serapion.

Enter a Gentleman of Mark Antony.

2. Gent. The emperor approaches, and commands,
On pain of death, that none presume to stay.
1. Gent. I dare not disobey him. [*Going out with the other.*
Ven. Well, I dare.
But, I'll observe him first unseen, and find
Which way his humour drives: the rest I'll venture. [*Withdraws.*

Enter Antony, *walking with a disturbed motion before he speaks.*

Ant. They tell me 'tis my birthday, and I'll keep it
With double pomp of sadness.
'Tis what the day deserves which gave me breath.
Why was I raised the meteor of the world,
Hung in the skies, and blazing as I travelled,
Till all my fires were spent; and then cast downward
To be trod out by Cæsar?
Ven. [*Aside.*] On my soul,
'Tis mournful, wondrous mournful!
Ant. Count thy gains.
Now, Antony, wouldst thou be born for this?
Glutton of fortune, thy devouring youth
Has starved thy wanting age.
Ven. [*Aside.*] How sorrow shakes him!
So, now the tempest tears him up by th' roots,
And on the ground extends the noble ruin.
Ant. [*Having thrown himself down.*]
Lie there, thou shadow of an emperor;
The place thou pressest on thy mother earth
Is all thy empire now. Now it contains thee;
Some few days hence, and then 'twill be too large,
When thou'rt contracted in thy narrow urn,
Shrunk to a few cold ashes. Then Octavia
(For Cleopatra will not live to see it),
Octavia then will have thee all her own,
And bear thee in her widowed hand to Cæsar;
Cæsar will weep, the crocodile will weep,
To see his rival of the universe
Lie still and peaceful there. I'll think no more on't.
Give me some music; look that it be sad:
I'll sooth my Melancholy, till I swell,

s.d. *Enter a Gentleman*] *Re-enter the Gentleman Q.* 1–3, *Works*

And burst myself with sighing— [*Soft music.*
'Tis somewhat to my humour. Stay, I fancy
I'm now turned wild, a commoner of nature;
Of all forsaken, and forsaking all,
Live in a shady forest's sylvan scene;
Stretched at my length beneath some blasted oak,
I lean my head upon the mossy bark,
And look just of a piece as I grew from it;
My uncombed locks, matted like mistletoe,
Hang o'er my hoary face; a murm'ring brook
Runs at my foot.
Ven. [*Aside.*] Methinks I fancy
Myself there too.
Ant. The herd come jumping by me,
And fearless, quench their thirst while I look on,
And take me for their fellow-citizen.
More of this image, more; it lulls my thoughts. [*Soft music again.*
Ven. I must disturb him; I can hold no longer. [*Stands before him.*
Ant. [*Starting up.*] Art thou Ventidius?
Ven. Are you Antony?
I'm liker what I was, than you to him
I left you last.
Ant. I'm angry.
Ven. So am I.
Ant. I would be private: leave me.
Ven. Sir, I love you,
And therefore will not leave you.
Ant. Will not leave me?
Where have you learnt that answer? Who am I?
Ven. My Emperor; the man I love next Heaven:
If I said more, I think 'twere scarce a sin;
Y'are all that's good, and good-like.
Ant. All that's wretched.
You will not leave me then?
Ven. 'Twas too presuming
To say I would not; but I dare not leave you:
And 'tis unkind in you to chide me hence
So soon, when I so far have come to see you.
Ant. Now thou hast seen me, art thou satisfied?
For, if a friend, thou hast beheld enough;
And, if a foe, too much.
Ven. [*Weeping.*] Look, Emperor, this is no common dew;

I have not wept this forty year, but now
My mother comes afresh into my eyes;
I cannot help her softness.

Ant. By heaven, he weeps, poor good old man, he weeps!
The big round drops course one another down
The furrows of his cheeks. Stop 'em, Ventidius,
Or I shall blush to death: they set my shame,
That caused 'em, full before me.

Ven. I'll do my best.

Ant. Sure there's contagion in the tears of friends:
See, I have caught it too. Believe me, 'tis not
For my own griefs, but thine—Nay, father!

Ven. Emperor!

Ant. Emperor! Why, that's the style of victory.
The conqu'ring soldier, red with unfelt wounds,
Salutes his general so; but never more
Shall that sound reach my ears.

Ven. I warrant you.

Ant. Actium, Actium! Oh!—

Ven. It sits too near you.

Ant. Here, here it lies; a lump of lead by day,
And, in my short distracted nightly slumbers,
The hag that rides my dreams—

Ven. Out with it; give it vent.

Ant. Urge not my shame.
I lost a battle.

Ven. So has Julius done.

Ant. Thou favour'st me, and speak'st not half thou think'st;
For Julius fought it out, and lost it fairly:
But Antony—

Ven. Nay, stop not.

Ant. Antony
(Well, thou wilt have it), like a coward, fled,
Fled while his soldiers fought; fled first, Ventidius.
Thou long'st to curse me, and I give thee leave.
I know thou cam'st prepared to rail.

Ven. I did.

Ant. I'll help thee—I have been a man, Ventidius—

Ven. Yes, and a brave one; but—

Ant. I know thy meaning.

280 Actium] See note on p. 24.

But I have lost my reason, have disgraced
The name of soldier with inglorious ease.
In the full vintage of my flowing honours,
Sat still and saw it pressed by other hands.
Fortune came smiling to my youth, and wooed it,
And purple greatness met my ripened years.
When first I came to empire, I was borne
On tides of people, crowding to my triumphs,
The wish of nations; and the willing world
Received me as its pledge of future peace.
I was so great, so happy, so beloved,
Fate could not ruin me; till I took pains
And worked against my fortune, chid her from me,
And turned her loose; yet still she came again.
My careless days and my luxurious nights
At length have wearied her, and now she's gone,
Gone, gone, divorced for ever. Help me, soldier,
To curse this madman, this industrious fool,
Who laboured to be wretched: prithee, curse me.

Ven. No.

Ant. Why?

Ven. You are too sensible already
Of what y'have done, too conscious of your failings,
And like a scorpion, whipped by others first
To fury, sting yourself in mad revenge.
I would bring balm, and pour it in your wounds,
Cure your distempered mind, and heal your fortunes.

Ant. I know thou wouldst.

Ven. I will.

Ant. Ha, ha, ha, ha!

Ven. You laugh.

Ant. I do, to see officious love
Give cordials to the dead.

Ven. You would be lost then?

Ant. I am.

Ven. I say, you are not. Try your fortune.

Ant. I have, to th'utmost. Dost thou think me desperate,
Without just cause? No, when I found all lost
Beyond repair, I hid me from the world,
And learnt to scorn it here; which now I do

298 pressed] i.e. as in a wine-press   321 officious] (1) obliging, (2) zealous

So heartily, I think it is not worth
The cost of keeping.
Ven. Cæsar thinks not so:
He'll thank you for the gift he could not take.
You would be killed like Tully, would you? Do,
Hold out your throat to Cæsar, and die tamely.
Ant. No, I can kill myself; and so resolve.
Ven. I can die with you too, when time shall serve;
But fortune calls upon us now to live,
To fight, to conquer.
Ant. Sure thou dream'st, Ventidius.
Ven. No; 'tis you dream; you sleep away your hours
In desperate sloth, miscalled philosophy.
Up, up, for honour's sake! twelve legions wait you,
And long to call you chief. By painful journeys
I led 'em, patient both of heat and hunger,
Down from the Parthian marches to the Nile.
'Twill do you good to see their sun-burnt faces,
Their scarred cheeks, and chopped hands; there's virtue in 'em:
They'll sell those mangled limbs at dearer rates
Than yon trim bands can buy.
Ant. Where left you them?
Ven. I said, in lower Syria.
Ant. Bring 'em hither;
There may be life in these.
Ven. They will not come.
Ant. Why didst thou mock my hopes with promised aids
To double my despair? They're mutinous.
Ven. Most firm and loyal.
Ant. Yet they will not march
To succour me. Oh, trifler!
Ven. They petition
You would make haste to head 'em.
Ant. I'm besieged.
Ven. There's but one way shut up: how came I hither?
Ant. I will not stir.
Ven. They would perhaps desire
A better reason.
Ant. I have never used

331 Tully] (Marcus Tullius) Cicero was condemned to death by the triumvirate (43 B.C.), and took to flight. When Antony's soldiers caught up with him, he put his head out of the litter in which he was travelling, and it was immediately cut off. 344 chopped] chapped

My soldiers to demand a reason of
My actions. Why did they refuse to march?
Ven. They said they would not fight for Cleopatra.
Ant. What was't they said?
Ven. They said they would not fight for Cleopatra.
Why should they fight, indeed, to make her conquer,
And make you more a slave? to gain you kingdoms,
Which, for a kiss, at your next midnight feast,
You'll sell to her? Then she new names her jewels,
And calls this diamond such or such a tax;
Each pendant in her ear shall be a province.
Ant. Ventidius, I allow your tongue free licence
On all my other faults; but, on your life,
No word of Cleopatra. She deserves
More worlds than I can lose.
Ven. Behold, you pow'rs,
To whom you have entrusted humankind;
See Europe, Afric, Asia put in balance,
And all weighed down by one light worthless woman!
I think the gods are Antonies, and give,
Like prodigals, this nether world away
To none but wasteful hands.
Ant. You grow presumptuous.
Ven. I take the privilege of plain love to speak.
Ant. Plain love! plain arrogance, plain insolence!
Thy men are cowards; thou, an envious traitor
Who, under seeming honesty, hast vented
The burden of thy rank o'erflowing gall.
Oh, that thou wert my equal, great in arms
As the first Cæsar was, that I might kill thee
Without a stain to honour!
Ven. You may kill me;
You have done more already, called me traitor.
Ant. Art thou not one?
Ven. For showing you yourself,
Which none else durst have done? But had I been
That name, which I disdain to speak again,
I needed not have sought your abject fortunes,
Come to partake your fate, to die with you;
What hindered me t'have led my conqu'ring eagles
To fill Octavius' bands? I could have been
A traitor then, a glorious happy traitor,

And not have been so called.
Ant. Forgive me, soldier:
I've been too passionate.
Ven. You thought me false;
Thought my old age betrayed you: kill me, sir;
Pray, kill me. Yet you need not; your unkindness
Has left your sword no work.
Ant. I did not think so;
I said it in my rage: prithee forgive me.
Why didst thou tempt my anger by discovery
Of what I would not hear?
Ven. No prince but you
Could merit that sincerity I used,
Nor durst another man have ventured it;
But you, ere love misled your wand'ring eyes,
Were sure the chief and best of human race,
Framed in the very pride and boast of nature,
So perfect, that the gods who formed you wondered
At their own skill, and cried, 'A lucky hit
Has mended our design.' Their envy hindered,
Else you had been immortal, and a pattern,
When heaven would work for ostentation' sake,
To copy out again.
Ant. But Cleopatra—

Go on; for I can bear it now.
Ven. No more.
Ant. Thou dar'st not trust my passion; but thou mayst:
Thou only lov'st; the rest have flattered me.
Ven. Heaven's blessing on your heart, for that kind word!
May I believe you love me? Speak again.
Ant. Indeed I do. Speak this, and this, and this. [*Hugging him.*
Thy praises were unjust; but I'll deserve 'em,
And yet mend all. Do with me what thou wilt;
Lead me to victory, thou know'st the way.
Ven. And—will you leave this—
Ant. Prithee, do not curse her,
And I will leave her; though, heaven knows, I love
Beyond life, conquest, empire, all but honour:
But I will leave her.
Ven. That's my royal master.
And—shall we fight?
Ant. I warrant thee, old soldier,

Thou shalt behold me once again in iron,
And at the head of our old troops that beat
The Parthians, cry aloud, 'Come follow me!'
Ven. Oh, now I hear my Emperor! In that word
Octavius fell. Gods, let me see that day,
And, if I have ten years behind, take all;
I'll thank you for th' exchange.
Ant. Oh Cleopatra!
Ven. Again?
Ant. I've done: in that last sigh, she went.
Cæsar shall know what 'tis to force a lover
From all he holds most dear.
Ven. Methinks you breathe
Another soul: your looks are more divine;
You speak a hero, and you move a god.
Ant. Oh, thou hast fired me; my soul's up in arms,
And mans each part about me. Once again
That noble eagerness of fight has seized me,
That eagerness with which I darted upward
To Cassius' camp: in vain the steepy hill,
Opposed my way, in vain a war of spears
Sung round my head, and planted all my shield;
I won the trenches while my foremost men
Lagged on the plain below.
Ven. Ye gods, ye gods,
For such another hour!
Ant. Come on, my soldier!
Our hearts and arms are still the same. I long
Once more to meet our foes, that thou and I,
Like Time and Death, marching before our troops,
May taste fate to 'em; mow 'em out a passage,
And, ent'ring where the foremost squadrons yield,
Begin the noble harvest of the field. [*Exeunt.*

---

444 Cassius' camp] at Philippi, where Cassius and Brutus were defeated by Antony and Octavius, 42 B.C. 453 May taste fate to 'em] i.e. may put them to the test of fate (*O.E.D.* 2)

ACT II

Cleopatra, Iras, *and* Alexas.

Cleo. What shall I do, or whither shall I turn?
Ventidius has o'ercome, and he will go.
Alex. He goes to fight for you.
Cleo. Then he would see me ere he went to fight.
Flatter me not: if once he goes, he's lost,
And all my hopes destroyed.
Alex. Does this weak passion
Become a mighty queen?
Cleo. I am no queen:
Is this to be a queen, to be besieged
By yon insulting Roman, and to wait
Each hour the victor's chain? These ills are small;
For Antony is lost, and I can mourn
For nothing else but him. Now come, Octavius,
I have no more to lose; prepare thy bands;
I'm fit to be a captive: Antony
Has taught my mind the fortune of a slave.
Iras. Call reason to assist you.
Cleo. I have none,
And none would have: my love's a noble madness
Which shows the cause deserved it. Moderate sorrow
Fits vulgar love, and for a vulgar man:
But I have loved with such transcendent passion,
I soared at first quite out of reason's view,
And now am lost above it.—No, I'm proud
'Tis thus: would Antony could see me now!
Think you he would not sigh? Though he must leave me,
Sure he would sigh, for he is noble-natured,
And bears a tender heart: I know him well.
Ah, no, I know him not; I knew him once,
But now 'tis past.
Iras. Let it be past with you:
Forget him, madam.
Cleo. Never, never, Iras!
He once was mine; and once, though now 'tis gone,
Leaves a faint image of possession still.

13 bands] bonds

Alex. Think him unconstant, cruel, and ungrateful.
Cleo. I cannot: if I could, those thoughts were vain;
Faithless, ungrateful, cruel though he be,
I still must love him.

Enter Charmion.

Now, what news, my Charmion?
Will he be kind? and will he not forsake me?
Am I to live, or die?—nay, *do* I live?
Or am I dead? for, when he gave his answer,
Fate took the word, and then I lived, or died.
Char. I found him, madam—
Cleo. A long speech preparing?
If thou bring'st comfort, haste, and give it me;
For never was more need.
Iras. I know he loves you.
Cleo. Had he been kind, her eyes had told me so,
Before her tongue could speak it: now she studies
To soften what he said. But give me death,
Just as he sent it, Charmion, undisguised,
And in the words he spoke.
Char. I found him, then,
Incompassed round, I think, with iron statues,
So mute, so motionless his soldiers stood,
While awfully he cast his eyes about,
And ev'ry leader's hopes or fears surveyed:
Methought he looked resolved, and yet not pleased.
When he beheld me struggling in the crowd,
He blushed, and bade make way.
Alex. There's comfort yet.
Char. Ventidius fixed his eyes upon my passage
Severely, as he meant to frown me back,
And sullenly gave place. I told my message,
Just as you gave it, broken and disordered;
I numbered in it all your sighs and tears,
And while I moved your pitiful request,
That you but only begged a last farewell,
He fetched an inward groan, and ev'ry time
I named you, sighed, as if his heart were breaking,
But shunned my eyes, and guiltily looked down;
He seemed not now that awful Antony
Who shook an armed assembly with his nod,

But making show as he would rub his eyes,
Disguised and blotted out a falling tear.
Cleo. Did he then weep? and was I worth a tear?
If what thou hast to say be not as pleasing,
Tell me no more, but let me die contented.
Char. He bid me say, he knew himself so well,
He could deny you nothing, if he saw you;
And therefore—
Cleo. Thou wouldst say, he would not see me?
Char. And therefore begged you not to use a power
Which he could ill resist; yet he should ever
Respect you as he ought.
Cleo. Is that a word
For Antony to use to Cleopatra?
Oh, that faint word, respect! how I disdain it!
Disdain myself, for loving after it!
He should have kept that word for cold Octavia.
Respect is for a wife: am I that thing,
That dull insipid lump, without desires,
And without power to give 'em?
Alex. You misjudge;
You see through love, and that deludes your sight,
As what is straight seems crooked through the water.
But I, who bear my reason undisturbed,
Can see this Antony, this dreaded man,
A fearful slave who fain would run away,
And shuns his master's eyes: if you pursue him,
My life on't, he still drags a chain along,
That needs must clog his flight.
Cleo. Could I believe thee!—
Alex. By ev'ry circumstance I know he loves.
True, he's hard pressed by int'rest and by honour;
Yet he but doubts, and parleys, and casts out
Many a long look for succour.
Cleo. He sends word
He fears to see my face.
Alex. And would you more?
He shows his weakness who declines the combat,
And you must urge your fortune. Could he speak
More plainly? To my ears, the message sounds:
'Come to my rescue, Cleopatra, come;
Come, free me from Ventidius; from my tyrant;

See me, and give me a pretence to leave him!'
I hear his trumpets. This way he must pass.
Please you, retire a while; I'll work him first,
That he may bend more easy.

Cleo. You shall rule me;
But all, I fear, in vain. [*Exit with* Charmion *and* Iras.

Alex. I fear so too,
Though I concealed my thoughts to make her bold;
But 'tis our utmost means, and fate befriend it. [*Withdraws.*

Enter lictors with fasces, one bearing the eagle. Then enter Antony *with* Ventidius, *followed by other commanders.*

Ant. Octavius is the minion of blind chance,
But holds from virtue nothing.

Ven. Has he courage?

Ant. But just enough to season him from coward.
Oh, 'tis the coldest youth upon a charge,
The most deliberate fighter! If he ventures
(As in Illyria once they say he did
To storm a town), 'tis when he cannot choose,
When all the world have fixed their eyes upon him;
And then he lives on that for seven years after,
But at a close revenge he never fails.

Ven. I heard you challenged him.

Ant. I did, Ventidius.
What think'st thou was his answer? 'Twas so tame:
He said he had more ways than one to die;
I had not.

Ven. Poor!

Ant. He has more ways than one;
But he would choose 'em all before that one.

Ven. He first would choose an ague or a fever.

Ant. No; it must be an ague, not a fever;
He has not warmth enough to die by that.

Ven. Or old age and a bed.

Ant. Ay, there's his choice.
He would live, like a lamp, to the last wink,
And crawl upon the utmost verge of life.
O Hercules! Why should a man like this,

s.d. *lictors*] officers whose function was to attend upon magistrates, and to carry the fasces (a bundle of rods bound up with an axe in the middle and its blade projecting) on public occasions
119 close] secret

Who dares not trust his fate for one great action,
Be all the care of heaven? Why should he lord it
O'er fourscore thousand men, of whom each one
Is braver than himself?

Ven. You conquered for him:
Philippi knows it; there you shared with him
That empire which your sword made all your own.

Ant. Fool that I was, upon my eagle's wings
I bore this wren, till I was tired with soaring,
And now he mounts above me.
Good heavens! Is this, is this the man who braves me?
Who bids my age make way—drives me before him
To the world's ridge, and sweeps me off like rubbish?

Ven. Sir, we lose time; the troops are mounted all.

Ant. Then give the word to march:
I long to leave this prison of a town,
To join thy legions, and, in open Field,
Once more to show my face. Lead, my deliverer.

Enter Alexas

Alex. Great Emperor,
In mighty arms renowned above mankind,
But, in soft pity to th' oppressed, a god,
This message sends the mournful Cleopatra
To her departing lord.

Ven. Smooth sycophant!

Alex. A thousand wishes, and ten thousand prayers,
Millions of blessings wait you to the wars;
Millions of sighs and tears she sends you too,
And would have sent
As many dear embraces to your arms,
As many parting kisses to your lips,
But those, she fears, have wearied you already.

Ven. [*Aside.*] False crocodile!

Alex. And yet she begs not now you would not leave her;
That were a wish too mighty for her hopes,
Too presuming for her low fortune, and your ebbing love,
That were a wish for her more prosperous days,
Her blooming beauty, and your growing kindness.

Ant. [*Aside.*] Well, I must man it out.—What would the Queen?

139 I bore this wren] At the battle of Philippi Octavius came near to defeat by the forces of Brutus, and was only rescued by the intervention of Antony.

Alex. First, to these noble warriors who attend
Your daring courage in the chase of fame
(Too daring, and too dangerous for her quiet),
She humbly recommends all she holds dear,
All her own cares and fears, the care of you.
Ven. Yes, witness Actium.
Ant. Let him speak, Ventidius.
Alex. You, when his matchless valour bears him forward,
With ardour too heroic, on his foes
Fall down, as she would do, before his feet;
Lie in his way, and stop the paths of death;
Tell him, this god is not invulnerable,
That absent Cleopatra bleeds in him;
And, that you may remember her petition,
She begs you wear these trifles, as a pawn
Which, at your wished return, she will redeem
[*Gives jewels to the commanders.*
With all the wealth of Egypt:
This, to the great Ventidius she presents,
Whom she can never count her enemy,
Because he loves her lord.
Ven. Tell her I'll none on't;
I'm not ashamed of honest poverty:
Not all the diamonds of the East can bribe
Ventidius from his faith. I hope to see
These, and the rest of all her sparkling store,
Where they shall more deservingly be placed.
Ant. And who must wear 'em then?
Ven. The wronged Octavia.
Ant. You might have spared that word.
Ven. And he that bribe.
Ant. But have I no remembrance?
Alex. Yes, a dear one:
Your slave, the Queen—
Ant. My mistress.
Alex. Then your mistress;
Your mistress would, she says, have sent her soul,
But that you had long since; she humbly begs
This ruby bracelet, set with bleeding hearts,
(The emblems of her own) may bind your arm.
[*Presenting a bracelet.*
Ven. Now, my best lord, in honour's name, I ask you,

For manhood's sake, and for your own dear safety,
Touch not these poisoned gifts,
Infected by the sender; touch 'em not;
Myriads of bluest plagues lie underneath 'em,
And more than aconite has dipped the silk.

Ant. Nay, now you grow too cynical, Ventidius.
A lady's favours may be worn with honour.
What, to refuse her bracelet! On my soul,
When I lie pensive in my tent alone,
'Twill pass the wakeful hours of winter nights,
To tell these pretty beads upon my arm,
To count for every one a soft embrace,
A melting kiss at such and such a time;
And now and then the fury of her love,
When—And what harm's in this?

Alex. None, none my lord,
But what's to her, that now 'tis past for ever.

Ant. [*Going to tie it.*] We soldiers are so awkward.—Help me tie it.

Alex. In faith, my lord, we courtiers too are awkward
In these affairs. So are all men indeed;
Even I, who am not one. But shall I speak?

Ant. Yes, freely.

Alex. Then, my lord, fair hands alone
Are fit to tie it; she who sent it can.

Ven. Hell, death! this eunuch pandar ruins you.
You will not see her?

[Alexas *whispers to an attendant, who goes out.*

Ant. But to take my leave.

Ven. Then I have washed an Ethiope. Y'are undone;
Y'are in the toils; y'are taken; y'are destroyed:
Her eyes do Cæsar's work.

Ant. You fear too soon.
I'm constant to myself: I know my strength.
And yet she shall not think me barbarous neither,
Born in the depths of Afric: I'm a Roman,
Bred to the rules of soft humanity.
A guest, and kindly used, should bid farewell.

Ven. You do not know
How weak you are to her, how much an infant;

205 bluest plagues] Blue was 'often made the colour of plagues and things hurtful' (*O.E.D.*, 8); compare 'blue devil'.

You are not proof against a smile, or glance;
A sigh will quite disarm you.
Ant. See, she comes!
Now you shall find your error. Gods, I thank you:
I formed the danger greater than it was,
And, now 'tis near, 'tis lessened.
Ven. Mark the end yet.

Enter Cleopatra, Charmion *and* Iras.

Ant. Well, madam, we are met.
Cleo. Is this a meeting?
Then, we must part?
Ant. We must.
Cleo. Who says we must?
Ant. Our own hard fates.
Cleo. We make those fates ourselves.
Ant. Yes, we have made 'em; we have loved each other
Into our mutual ruin.
Cleo. The gods have seen my joys with envious eyes;
I have no friends in heaven; and all the world
(As 'twere the business of mankind to part us),
Is armed against my love. Even you yourself
Join with the rest; you, you are armed against me.
Ant. I will be justified in all I do
To late posterity, and therefore hear me.
If I mix a lie
With any truth, reproach me freely with it;
Else, favour me with silence.
Cleo. You command me,
And I am dumb.
Ven. I like this well: he shows authority.
Ant. That I derive my ruin
From you alone—
Cleo. O heavens! I ruin you!
Ant. You promised me your silence, and you break it
Ere I have scarce begun.
Cleo. Well, I obey you.
Ant. When I beheld you first, it was in Egypt,
Ere Cæsar saw your eyes; you gave me love,
And were too young to know it. That I settled
Your father in his throne was for your sake;

I left the acknowledgement for time to ripen.
Cæsar stepped in, and with a greedy hand
Plucked the green fruit ere the first blush of red,
Yet cleaving to the bough. He was my lord,
And was, beside, too great for me to rival,
But, I deserved you first, though he enjoyed you.
When, after, I beheld you in Cilicia,
An enemy to Rome, I pardoned you.

Cleo. I cleared myself—

Ant. Again you break your promise.
I loved you still, and took your weak excuses,
Took you into my bosom, stained by Cæsar,
And not half mine: I went to Egypt with you
And hid me from the business of the world,
Shut out enquiring nations from my sight,
To give whole years to you.

Ven. Yes, to your shame be't spoken. [*Aside.*

Ant. How I loved,
Witness ye days and nights, and all your hours,
That danced away with down upon your feet,
As all your business were to count my passion.
One day passed by, and nothing saw but love;
Another came, and still 'twas only love:
The suns were wearied out with looking on,
And I untired with loving.
I saw you ev'ry day, and all the day;
And ev'ry day was still but as the first:
So eager was I still to see you more.

Ven. 'Tis all too true.

Ant. Fulvia, my wife, grew jealous,
As she indeed had reason; raised a war
In Italy, to call me back.

Ven. But yet
You went not.

Ant. While within your arms I lay,
The world fell mould'ring from my hands each hour,
And left me scarce a grasp (I thank your love for't).

Ven. Well pushed: that last was home.

Cleo. Yet may I speak?

Ant. If I have urged a falsehood, yes; else, not.
Your silence says I have not. Fulvia died;
(Pardon, you gods, with my unkindness died).

To set the world at peace, I took Octavia,
This Cæsar's sister; in her pride of youth
And flow'r of beauty did I wed that lady,
Whom blushing I must praise, because I left her.
You called; my love obeyed the fatal summons:
This raised the Roman arms; the cause was yours.
I would have fought by land, where I was stronger:
You hindered it; yet, when I fought at sea,
Forsook me fighting, and (oh, stain to honour!
Oh, lasting shame!) I knew not that I fled,
But fled to follow you.

Ven. What haste she made to hoist her purple sails!
And, to appear magnificent in flight,
Drew half our strength away.

Ant. All this you caused.
And would you multiply more ruins on me?
This honest man, my best, my only friend,
Has gathered up the shipwrack of my fortunes;
Twelve legions I have left, my last recruits,
And you have watched the news, and bring your eyes
To seize them too. If you have aught to answer,
Now speak, you have free leave.

Alex. [*Aside.*] She stands confounded:
Despair is in her eyes.

Ven. Now lay a sigh i'th way to stop his passage:
Prepare a tear, and bid it for his legions;
'Tis like they shall be sold.

Cleo. How shall I plead my cause, when you, my judge,
Already have condemned me? Shall I bring
The love you bore me for my advocate?
That now is turned against me, that destroys me;
For love once past is, at the best, forgotten,
But oft'ner sours to hate. 'Twill please my lord
To ruin me, and therefore I'll be guilty.
But, could I once have thought it would have pleased you,
That you would pry with narrow searching eyes
Into my faults, severe to my destruction,
And watching all advantages with care
That serve to make me wretched? Speak, my lord,
For I end here. Though I deserve this usage,
Was it like you to give it?

Ant. Oh, you wrong me

To think I sought this parting, or desired
To accuse you more than what will clear myself,
And justify this breach.

Cleo. Thus low I thank you.
And, since my innocence will not offend,
I shall not blush to own it.

Ven. After this
I think she'll blush at nothing.

Cleo. You seem grieved
(And therein you are kind) that Cæsar first
Enjoyed my love, though you deserved it better.
I grieve for that, my lord, much more than you;
For, had I first been yours, it would have saved
My second choice: I never had been his,
And ne'er had been but yours. But Cæsar first,
You say, possessed my love. Not so, my lord:
He first possessed my person; you my love;
Cæsar loved me; but I loved Antony.
If I endured him after, 'twas because
I judged it due to the first name of men;
And, half constrained, I gave, as to a tyrant,
What he would take by force.

Ven. O siren! siren!
Yet grant that all the love she boasts were true,
Has she not ruined you? I still urge that,
The fatal consequence.

Cleo. The consequence indeed,
For I dare challenge him, my greatest foe,
To say it was designed. 'Tis true I loved you,
And kept you far from an uneasy wife—
Such Fulvia was.
Yes, but he'll say you left Octavia for me.
And can you blame me to receive that love
Which quitted such desert for worthless me?
How often have I wished some other Cæsar,
Great as the first, and as the second young,
Would court my love to be refused for you!

Ven. Words, words; but Actium, sir, remember Actium.

Cleo. Even there I dare his malice. True, I counselled
To fight at sea, but I betrayed you not.
I fled, but not to the enemy. 'Twas fear.
Would I had been a man, not to have feared,

For none would then have envied me your friendship,
Who envy me your love.

Ant. We're both unhappy:
If nothing else, yet our ill fortune parts us.
Speak; would you have me perish by my stay?

Cleo. If as a friend you ask my judgement, go;
If as a lover, stay. If you must perish—
'Tis a hard word!—but stay.

Ven. See now th' effects of her so boasted love!
She strives to drag you down to ruin with her;
But, could she 'scape without you, oh, how soon
Would she let go her hold, and haste to shore,
And never look behind!

Cleo. Then judge my love by this. [*Giving* Antony *a writing.*
Could I have borne
A life or death, a happiness or woe
From yours divided, this had giv'n me means.

Ant. By Hercules, the writing of Octavius!
I know it well; 'tis that proscribing hand,
Young as it was, that led the way to mine,
And left me but the second place in murder.—
See, see, Ventidius! here he offers Egypt,
And joins all Syria to it as a present,
So, in requital, she forsake my fortunes,
And join her arms with his.

Cleo. And yet you leave me!
You leave me, Antony, and yet I love you.
Indeed I do: I have refused a kingdom—
That's a trifle;
For I could part with life, with anything,
But only you. Oh, let me die but with you!
Is that a hard request?

Ant. Next living with you,
'Tis all that heav'n can give.

Alex. [*Aside.*] He melts; we conquer.

Cleo. No, you shall go: your interest calls you hence;
Yes, your dear interest pulls too strong for these
Weak arms to hold you here.— [*Takes his hand.*

394 proscribing] publishing the names of persons condemned to death, banished, etc. This was done on a large scale by the second triumvirate of Octavius, Antony, and Lepidus, when they came to power in 43 B.C.

Go! leave me, soldier
(For you're no more a lover), leave me dying;
Push me all pale and panting from your bosom,
And, when your march begins, let one run after
Breathless almost for joy, and cry, 'She's dead!'
The soldiers shout; you then perhaps may sigh,
And muster all your Roman gravity;
Ventidius chides, and straight your brow clears up,
As I had never been.
Ant. Gods, 'tis too much;
Too much for man to bear!
Cleo. What is't for me, then,
A weak forsaken woman? and a lover?—
Here let me breathe my last. Envy me not
This minute in your arms: I'll die apace,
As fast as e'er I can, and end your trouble.
Ant. Die! Rather let me perish! Loosened nature
Leap from its hinges! Sink the props of heaven,
And fall the skies to crush the nether world!
My eyes, my soul; my all!— [*Embraces her.*
Ven. And what's this toy
In balance with your fortune, honour, fame?
Ant. What is't, Ventidius? It outweighs 'em all.
Why, we have more than conquered Cæsar now:
My Queen's not only innocent, but loves me.
This, this is she who drags me down to ruin!
'But, could she 'scape without me, with what haste
Would she let slip her hold, and make to shore,
And never look behind!'
Down on thy knees, blasphemer as thou art,
And ask forgiveness of wronged innocence.
Ven. I'll rather die than take it. Will you go?
Ant. Go! Whither? go from all that's excellent?
Faith, honour, virtue, all good things forbid
That I should go from her who sets my love
Above the price of kingdoms. Give, you gods,
Give to your boy, your Cæsar,
This rattle of a globe to play withal,
This gew-gaw world, and put him cheaply off:
I'll not be pleased with less than Cleopatra.
Cleo. She's wholly yours. My heart's so full of joy,
That I shall do some wild extravagance

Of love, in public; and the foolish world,
Which knows not tenderness, will think me mad.

Ven. O women! women! women! All the gods
Have not such pow'r of doing good to man,
As you of doing harm. [*Exit.*

Ant. Our men are armed.
Unbar the gate that looks to Cæsar's camp;
I would revenge the treachery he meant me,
And long security makes conquest easy.
I'm eager to return before I go;
For all the pleasures I have known beat thick
On my remembrance. How I long for night!
That both the sweets of mutual love may try,
And once triumph o'er Cæsar ere we die. [*Exeunt.*

ACT III

At one door, enter Cleopatra, Charmion, Iras, *and* Alexas, *a train of Egyptians; at the other*, Antony *and Romans. The entrance on both sides is prepared by music; the trumpets first sounding on Antony's part, then answered by timbrels, &c. on Cleopatra's.* Charmion *and* Iras *hold a laurel wreath betwixt them. A dance of Egyptians. After the ceremony*, Cleopatra *crowns* Antony.

Ant. I thought how those white arms would fold me in,
And strain me close, and melt me into love;
So pleased with that sweet image, I sprung forwards,
And added all my strength to every blow;

Cleo. Come to me, come, my soldier, to my arms!
You've been too long away from my embraces;
But, when I have you fast, and all my own,
With broken murmurs and with amorous sighs
I'll say you were unkind, and punish you,
And mark you red with many an eager kiss.

Ant. My brighter Venus!

Cleo. O my greater Mars!

456 security] freedom from apprehension

Ant. Thou join'st us well, my love!
Suppose me come from the Phlegræan plains,
Where gasping giants lay, cleft by my sword:
And mountain tops pared off each other blow,
To bury those I slew. Receive me, goddess!
Let Cæsar spread his subtle nets, like Vulcan;
In thy embraces I would be beheld
By heaven and earth at once,
And make their envy what they meant their sport.
Let those who took us blush; I would love on
With awful state, regardless of their frowns,
As their superior god.
There's no satiety of love in thee;
Enjoyed, thou still art new; perpetual Spring
Is in thy arms; the ripened fruit but falls,
And blossoms rise to fill its empty place,
And I grow rich by giving.

Enter Ventidius, *and stands apart.*

Alex. Oh, now the danger's past, your general comes.
He joins not in your joys, nor minds your triumphs;
But, with contracted brows, looks frowning on,
As envying your success.
Ant. Now, on my soul, he loves me, truly loves me;
He never flattered me in any vice,
But awes me with his virtue: even this minute
Methinks he has a right of chiding me.
Lead to the temple: I'll avoid his presence;
It checks too strong upon me. [*Exeunt the rest.*

As Antony *is going*, Ventidius *pulls him by the robe.*

Ven. Emperor!
Ant. [*Looking back.*] 'Tis the old argument; I prithee spare me.
Ven. But this one hearing, Emperor.
Ant. Let go
My robe; or, by my father Hercules—
Ven. By Hercules his father, that's yet greater,
I bring you somewhat you would wish to know.

13 Phlegræan plains] where the giants were said to have attacked the gods, and to have been defeated by Hercules 17 nets] Learning that his wife and Mars were lovers, Vulcan constructed a fine net and trapped them together in bed. 41 Hercules] Antony was thought to be descended from Hercules, the son of Jupiter and Alcmena.

Ant. Thou see'st we are observed; attend me here,
And I'll return. [*Exit.*
Ven. I'm waning in his favour, yet I love him;
I love this man who runs to meet his ruin,
And sure the gods, like me, are fond of him:
His virtues lie so mingled with his crimes,
As would confound their choice to punish one,
And not reward the other.

Enter Antony.

Ant. We can conquer,
You see, without your aid.
We have dislodged their troops;
They look on us at distance, and like curs
'Scaped from the lion's paws, they bay far off,
And lick their wounds, and faintly threaten war.
Five thousand Romans with their faces upward
Lie breathless on the plain.
Ven. 'Tis well: and he
Who lost 'em could have spared ten thousand more.
Yet if, by this advantage, you could gain
An easier peace, while Cæsar doubts the chance
Of arms!—
Ant. Oh, think not on't, Ventidius;
The boy pursues my ruin, he'll no peace:
His malice is considerate in advantage.
Oh, he's the coolest murderer, so staunch,
He kills, and keeps his temper.
Ven. Have you no friend
In all his army who has power to move him?
Mæcenas or Agrippa might do much.
Ant. They're both too deep in Cæsar's interests.
We'll work it out by dint of sword, or perish.
Ven. Fain I would find some other.
Ant. Thank thy love.
Some four or five such victories as this
Will save thy farther pains.
Ven. Expect no more; Cæsar is on his guard.
I know, sir, you have conquered against odds,
But still you draw supplies from one poor town,

64 His malice . . . advantage] i.e. he keeps his malice under control in his own interest

And of Egyptians: he has all the world,
And at his back nations come pouring in
To fill the gaps you make. Pray, think again.
Ant. Why dost thou drive me from myself, to search
For foreign aids? to hunt my memory,
And range all o'er a waste and barren place
To find a friend? The wretched have no friends.—
Yet I had one, the bravest youth of Rome,
Whom Cæsar loves beyond the love of women;
He could resolve his mind, as fire does wax,
From that hard rugged image, melt him down,
And mould him in what softer form he pleased.
Ven. Him would I see, that man of all the world:
Just such a one we want.
Ant. He loved me too;
I was his soul, he lived not but in me.
We were so closed within each other's breasts,
The rivets were not found that joined us first.
That does not reach us yet: we were so mixed
As meeting streams, both to our selves were lost;
We were one mass; we could not give or take,
But from the same; for he was I, I he.
Ven. [*Aside.*] He moves as I would wish him.
Ant. After this,
I need not tell his name: 'twas Dolabella.
Ven. He's now in Cæsar's camp.
Ant. No matter where,
Since he's no longer mine. He took unkindly
That I forbade him Cleopatra's sight
Because I feared he loved her. He confessed
He had a warmth which, for my sake, he stifled;
For 'twere impossible that two, so one,
Should not have loved the same. When he departed,
He took no leave; and that confirmed my thoughts.
Ven. It argues that he loved you more than her,
Else he had stayed; but he perceived you jealous,
And would not grieve his friend: I know he loves you.
Ant. I should have seen him then ere now.
Ven. Perhaps
He has thus long been lab'ring for your peace.

78 back] *Q.* 1–3; beck *Works*

Ant. Would he were here!
Ven. Would you believe he loved you?
I read your answer in your eyes; you would.
Not to conceal it longer, he has sent
A messenger from Cæsar's camp with letters.
Ant. Let him appear.
Ven. I'll bring him instantly.
[*Exit* Ventidius. *He re-enters immediately with* Dolabella.
Ant. 'Tis he himself, himself, by holy friendship! [*Runs to embrace him.*
Art thou returned at last, my better half?
Come, give me all myself. Let me not live,
If the young bridegroom, longing for his night,
Was ever half so fond.
Dola. I must be silent, for my soul is busy
About a nobler work: she's new come home,
Like a long-absent man, and wanders o'er
Each room, a stranger to her own, to look
If all be safe.
Ant. Thou hast what's left of me;
For I am now so sunk from what I was,
Thou find'st me at my lowest water-mark.
The rivers that ran in and raised my fortunes
Are all dried up, or take another course.
What I have left is from my native spring;
I've still a heart that swells, in scorn of fate,
And lifts me to my banks.
Dola. Still you are lord of all the world to me.
Ant. Why, then I yet am so; for thou art all.
If I had any joy when thou wert absent,
I grudged it to myself; methought I robbed
Thee of thy part. But oh, my Dolabella!
Thou hast beheld me other than I am.
Hast thou not seen my morning chambers filled
With sceptred slaves who waited to salute me?
With eastern monarchs who forgot the sun
To worship my uprising? Menial kings
Ran coursing up and down my palace-yard,
Stood silent in my presence, watched my eyes,
And, at my least command, all started out
Like racers to the goal.
Dola. Slaves to your fortune.

Ant. Fortune is Cæsar's now, and what am I?
Ven. What you have made yourself; I will not flatter.
Ant. Is this friendly done?
Dola. Yes, when his end is so, I must join with him;
Indeed I must, and yet you must not chide:
Why am I else your friend?
Ant. Take heed, young man,
How thou upbraid'st my love: the Queen has eyes,
And thou too hast a soul. Canst thou remember
When, swelled with hatred, thou beheld'st her first
As accessary to thy brother's death?
Dola. Spare my remembrance; 'twas a guilty day,
And still the blush hangs here.
Ant. To clear herself
For sending him no aid, she came from Egypt.
Her galley down the silver Cydnos rowed,
The tackling silk, the streamers waved with gold,
The gentle winds were lodged in purple sails:
Her nymphs, like Nereids, round her couch were placed,
Where she, another sea-born Venus, lay.
Dola. No more; I would not hear it.
Ant. Oh, you must!
She lay, and leant her cheek upon her hand,
And cast a look so languishingly sweet,
As if, secure of all beholders' hearts,
Neglecting she could take 'em. Boys like Cupids
Stood fanning with their painted wings the winds
That played about her face; but if she smiled,
A darting glory seemed to blaze abroad,
That men's desiring eyes were never wearied,
But hung upon the object. To soft flutes
The silver oars kept time; and while they played,
The hearing gave new pleasure to the sight,
And both to thought. 'Twas heaven, or somewhat more;
For she so charmed all hearts that gazing crowds
Stood panting on the shore, and wanted breath
To give their welcome voice.
Then, Dolabella, where was then thy soul?
Was not thy fury quite disarmed with wonder?
Didst thou not shrink behind me from those eyes,

162 Cydnos] a river in Cilicia, Asia Minor

And whisper in my ear, 'Oh tell her not
That I accused her of my brother's death'?
Dola. And should my weakness be a plea for yours?
Mine was an age when love might be excused,
When kindly warmth, and when my springing youth
Made it a debt to nature. Yours—
Ven. Speak boldly.
Yours, he would say, in your declining age,
When no more heat was left but what you forced,
When all the sap was needful for the trunk,
When it went down, then you constrained the course,
And robbed from nature to supply desire;
In you—I would not use so harsh a word,
But 'tis plain dotage.
Ant. Ha!
Dola. 'Twas urged too home.
But yet the loss was private that I made;
'Twas but myself I lost: I lost no legions;
I had no world to lose, no people's love.
Ant. This from a friend?
Dola. Yes, Antony, a true one;
A friend so tender that each word I speak
Stabs my own heart before it reach your ear.
Oh, judge me not less kind because I chide:
To Cæsar I excuse you.
Ant. O ye gods!
Have I then lived to be excused to Cæsar?
Dola. As to your equal.
Ant. Well, he's but my equal:
While I wear this, he never shall be more.
Dola. I bring conditions from him.
Ant. Are they noble?
Methinks thou shouldst not bring 'em else; yet he
Is full of deep dissembling, knows no honour,
Divided from his interest. Fate mistook him;
For nature meant him for an usurer:
He's fit indeed to buy, not conquer, kingdoms.
Ven. Then, granting this,
What pow'r was theirs who wrought so hard a temper
To honourable terms!

187 my brother's death] P. Cornelius Dolabella was besieged by Cassius in Laodicea, and, when he saw that further resistance was impossible, committed suicide. 209 this] i.e. his sword

Ant. It was my Dolabella, or some god.
Dola. Nor I, nor yet Mæcenas, nor Agrippa:
They were your enemies, and I a friend
Too weak alone; yet 'twas a Roman's deed.
Ant. 'Twas like a Roman done. Show me that man
Who has preserved my life, my love, my honour;
Let me but see his face.
Ven. That task is mine,
And heaven thou know'st, how pleasing. [*Exit* Ventidius.
Dola. You'll remember
To whom you stand obliged?
Ant. When I forget it,
Be thou unkind, and that's my greatest curse.
My Queen shall thank him too.
Dola. I fear she will not.
Ant. But she shall do't: the Queen, my Dolabella!
Hast thou not still some grudgings of thy fever?
Dola. I would not see her lost.
Ant. When I forsake her,
Leave me, my better stars; for she has truth
Beyond her beauty. Cæsar tempted her,
At no less price than kingdoms, to betray me,
But she resisted all; and yet thou chid'st me
For loving her too well. Could I do so?
Dola. Yes, there's my reason.

Re-enter Ventidius *with* Octavia, *leading* Antony's *two little daughters.*

Ant. Where?—Octavia there! [*Starting back.*
Ven. What, is she poison to you? a disease?
Look on her, view her well, and those she brings:
Are they all strangers to your eyes? has nature
No secret call, no whisper they are yours?
Dola. For shame, my lord, if not for love, receive 'em
With kinder eyes. If you confess a man,
Meet 'em, embrace 'em, bid 'em welcome to you.
Your arms should open, even without your knowledge,
To clasp 'em in; your feet should turn to wings,
To bear you to 'em; and your eyes dart out,
And aim a kiss ere you could reach the lips.

231 grudgings] symptoms 244 confess] acknowledge yourself

Ant. I stood amazed to think how they came hither.
Vent. I sent for 'em; I brought 'em in, unknown
To Cleopatra's guards.
Dola. Yet are you cold?
Octav. Thus long I have attended for my welcome,
Which, as a stranger, sure I might expect.
Who am I?
Ant. Cæsar's sister.
Octav. That's unkind!
Had I been nothing more than Cæsar's sister,
Know, I had still remained in Cæsar's camp;
But your Octavia, your much injured wife,
Though banished from your bed, driven from your house,
In spite of Cæsar's sister, still is yours.
'Tis true, I have a heart disdains your coldness,
And prompts me not to seek what you should offer;
But a wife's virtue still surmounts that pride:
I come to claim you as my own; to show
My duty first, to ask, nay, beg your kindness.
Your hand, my lord; 'tis mine, and I will have it. [*Taking his hand.*
Ven. Do, take it, thou deserv'st it.
Dola. On my soul,
And so she does. She's neither too submissive,
Nor yet too haughty; but so just a mean
Shows, as it ought, a wife and Roman too.
Ant. I fear, Octavia, you have begged my life.
Octav. Begged it, my lord?
Ant. Yes, begged it, my ambassadress;
Poorly and basely begged it of your brother.
Octav. Poorly and basely I could never beg;
Nor could my brother grant.
Ant. Shall I who to my kneeling slave could say,
'Rise up, and be a king', shall I fall down
And cry, 'Forgive me, Cæsar'? Shall I set
A man, my equal, in the place of Jove,
As he could give me being? No; that word
'Forgive' would choke me up,
And die upon my tongue.
Dola. You shall not need it.
Ant. I will not need it. Come, you've all betrayed me
(My friend too!) to receive some vile conditions.
My wife has bought me with her prayers and tears,

And now I must become her branded slave.
In every peevish mood she will upbraid
The life she gave: if I but look awry,
She cries, 'I'll tell my brother.'
Octav. My hard fortune
Subjects me still to your unkind mistakes.
But the conditions I have brought are such
You need not blush to take: I love your honour
Because 'tis mine; it never shall be said
Octavia's husband was her brother's slave.
Sir, you are free; free even from her you loathe;
For though my brother bargains for your love,
Makes me the price and cement of your peace,
I have a soul like yours: I cannot take
Your love as alms, nor beg what I deserve.
I'll tell my brother we are reconciled;
He shall draw back his troops, and you shall march
To rule the East: I may be dropped at Athens—
No matter where, I never will complain,
But only keep the barren name of wife,
And rid you of the trouble.
Ven. Was ever such a strife of sullen honour!
Both scorn to be obliged.
Dola. Oh, she has touched him in the tender'st part!
See how he reddens with despite and shame
To be outdone in generosity!
Ven. See how he winks! how he dries up a tear
That fain would fall!
Ant. Octavia, I have heard you, and must praise
The greatness of your soul,
But cannot yield to what you have proposed;
For I can ne'er be conquered but by love,
And you do all for duty. You would free me,
And would be dropped at Athens: was't not so?
Octav. It was, my lord.
Ant. Then I must be obliged
To one who loves me not, who to herself
May call me thankless and ungrateful man.
I'll not endure it, no.
Ven. I'm glad it pinches there.
Octav. Would you triumph o'er poor Octavia's virtue?
That pride was all I had to bear me up,

That you might think you owed me for your life,
And owed it to my duty, not my love.
I have been injured, and my haughty soul
Could brook but ill the man who slights my bed.

Ant. Therefore you love me not.

Octav. Therefore, my lord,
I should not love you.

Ant. Therefore you would leave me?

Octav. And therefore I should leave you—if I could.

Dola. Her soul's too great, after such injuries,
To say she loves; and yet she lets you see it.
Her modesty and silence plead her cause.

Ant. Oh, Dolabella, which way shall I turn?
I find a secret yielding in my soul;
But Cleopatra, who would die with me,
Must she be left? Pity pleads for Octavia,
But does it not plead more for Cleopatra?

Ven. Justice and pity both plead for Octavia;
For Cleopatra, neither.
One would be ruined with you, but she first
Had ruined you; the other, you have ruined,
And yet she would preserve you.
In everything their merits are unequal.

Ant. Oh, my distracted soul!

Octav. Sweet heaven, compose it!
Come, come, my lord, if I can pardon you,
Methinks you should accept it. Look on these:
Are they not yours? Or stand they thus neglected
As they are mine? Go to him, children, go;
Kneel to him, take him by the hand, speak to him,
For you may speak, and he may own you too,
Without a blush; and so he cannot all
His children. Go, I say, and pull him to me,
And pull him to yourselves from that bad woman.
You, Agrippina, hang upon his arms;
And you, Antonia, clasp about his waist:
If he will shake you off, if he will dash you
Against the pavement, you must bear it, children,
For you are mine, and I was born to suffer.

[*Here the children go to him, &c.*

Ven. Was ever sight so moving! Emperor!

Dola. Friend!

Octav. Husband!
Both Children. Father!
Ant. I am vanquished. Take me,
Octavia; take me, children; share me all. [*Embracing them.*
I've been a thriftless debtor to your loves,
And run out much, in riot, from your stock;
But all shall be amended.
Octav. O blessed hour!
Dola. O happy change!
Ven. My joy stops at my tongue;
But it has found two channels here for one,
And bubbles out above.
Ant. (*to Octavia.*) This is thy triumph. Lead me where thou wilt,
Even to thy brother's camp.
Octav. All there are yours.

Enter Alexas *hastily.*

Alex. The Queen, my mistress, sir, and yours—
Ant. 'Tis past.
Octavia, you shall stay this night. Tomorrow
Cæsar and we are one.
[*Exit, leading* Octavia; Dolabella *and the children follow.*
Ven. There's news for you. Run, my officious eunuch,
Be sure to be the first; haste forward;
Haste, my dear eunuch, haste. [*Exit.*
Alex. This downright fighting fool, this thick-skulled hero,
This blunt unthinking instrument of death,
With plain dull virtue, has outgone my wit.
Pleasure forsook my earliest infancy,
The luxury of others robbed my cradle,
And ravished thence the promise of a man.
Cast out from nature, disinherited
Of what her meanest children claim by kind,
Yet greatness kept me from contempt: that's gone.
Had Cleopatra followed my advice,
Then he had been betrayed who now forsakes.
She dies for love, but she has known its joys:
Gods, is this just, that I, who know no joys,
Must die because she loves?

Enter Cleopatra, Charmion, Iras, *and train.*

Oh, madam, I have seen what blasts my eyes!
Octavia's here!
Cleo. Peace with that raven's note!
I know it too, and now am in
The pangs of death.
Alex. You are no more a queen;
Egypt is lost.
Cleo. What tell'st thou me of Egypt?
My life, my soul is lost! Octavia has him!
O fatal name to Cleopatra's love!
My kisses, my embraces now are hers;
While I—But thou hast seen my rival; speak,
Does she deserve this blessing? Is she fair,
Bright as a goddess? and is all perfection
Confined to her? It is. Poor I was made
Of that coarse matter which, when she was finished,
The gods threw by for rubbish.
Alex. She's indeed a very miracle.
Cleo. Death to my hopes, a miracle!
Alex. [*Bowing.*] A miracle,
I mean of goodness; for in beauty, madam,
You make all wonders cease.
Cleo. I was too rash:
Take this in part of recompense. But oh, [*Giving a ring.*
I fear thou flatter'st me.
Char. She comes! she's here!
Iras. Fly, madam, Cæsar's sister!
Cleo. Were she the sister of the Thund'rer Jove,
And bore her brother's lightning in her eyes,
Thus would I face my rival. [*Meets* Octavia *with* Ventidius.
Octavia *bears up to her. Their trains come up on either side.*
Octav. I need not ask if you are Cleopatra;
Your haughty carriage—
Cleo. Shows I am a queen:
Nor need I ask you who you are.
Octav. A Roman:
A name that makes, and can unmake, a queen.
Cleo. Your lord, the man who serves me, is a Roman.
Octav. He was a Roman, till he lost that name

To be a slave in Egypt; but I come
To free him thence.
Cleo. Peace, peace, my lover's Juno.
When he grew weary of that household clog,
He chose my easier bonds.
Octav. I wonder not
Your bonds are easy; you have long been practised
In that lascivious art. He's not the first
For whom you spread your snares: let Cæsar witness.
Cleo. I loved not Cæsar; 'twas but gratitude
I paid his love. The worst your malice can
Is but to say the greatest of mankind
Has been my slave. The next, but far above him
In my esteem, is he whom law calls yours,
But whom his love made mine.
Oct. [*Coming up close to her.*] I would view nearer
That face which has so long usurped my right,
To find th'inevitable charms that catch
Mankind so sure, that ruined my dear lord.
Cleo. Oh, you do well to search; for had you known
But half these charms, you had not lost his heart.
Octav. Far be their knowledge from a Roman lady,
Far from a modest wife. Shame of our sex,
Dost thou not blush to own those black endearments
That make sin pleasing?
Cleo. You may blush, who want 'em.
If bounteous nature, if indulgent heaven
Have given me charms to please the bravest man,
Should I not thank 'em? Should I be ashamed,
And not be proud? I am, that he has loved me;
And when I love not him, heaven change this face
For one like that.
Octav. Thou lov'st him not so well.
Cleo. I love him better, and deserve him more.
Octav. You do not, cannot; you have been his ruin.
Who made him cheap at Rome but Cleopatra?
Who made him scorned abroad but Cleopatra?
At Actium, who betrayed him? Cleopatra.

424 clog] literally, 'a block or heavy piece of wood, or the like, attached to the leg or neck of a man or beast, to impede motion or prevent escape' (*O.E.D.*); often satirically applied to wives in Restoration drama 443 want 'em] don't have them

Who made his children orphans? and poor me
A wretched widow? Only Cleopatra.
Cleo. Yet she who loves him best is Cleopatra.
If you have suffered, I have suffered more.
You bear the specious title of a wife,
To gild your cause, and draw the pitying world
To favour it: the world contemns poor me;
For I have lost my honour, lost my fame,
And stained the glory of my royal house,
And all to bear the branded name of mistress.
There wants but life, and that too I would lose
For him I love.
Octav. Be't so then; take thy wish. [*Exit cum suis.*
Cleo. And 'tis my wish,
Now he is lost for whom alone I lived.
My sight grows dim, and every object dances,
And swims before me in the maze of death.
My spirits, while they were opposed, kept up;
They could not sink beneath a rival's scorn:
But now she's gone they faint.
Alex. Mine have had leisure
To recollect their strength, and furnish counsel
To ruin her, who else must ruin you.
Cleo. Vain promiser!
Lead me, my Charmion; nay, your hand too, Iras:
My grief has weight enough to sink you both.
Conduct me to some solitary chamber,
And draw the curtains round;
Then leave me to myself, to take alone
My fill of grief.
There I till death will his unkindness weep:
As harmless infants moan themselves asleep. [*Exeunt.*

ACT IV

Antony, Dolabella.

Dola. Why would you shift it from yourself on me?
Can you not tell her you must part?
Ant. I cannot.
I could pull out an eye and bid it go,
And t'other should not weep. Oh, Dolabella,
How many deaths are in this word *Depart*!
I dare not trust my tongue to tell her so:
One look of hers would thaw me into tears,
And I should melt till I were lost again.
Dola. Then let Ventidius;
He's rough by nature.
Ant. Oh, he'll speak too harshly;
He'll kill her with the news. Thou, only thou.
Dola. Nature has cast me in so soft a mould
That but to hear a story feigned, for pleasure,
Of some sad lover's death moistens my eyes,
And robs me of my manhood.—I should speak
So faintly, with such fear to grieve her heart,
She'd not believe it earnest.
Ant. Therefore, therefore,
Thou only, thou art fit: think thyself me,
And when thou speak'st (but let it first be long),
Take off the edge from every sharper sound,
And let our parting be as gently made
As other loves begin. Wilt thou do this?
Dola. What you have said so sinks into my soul
That, if I must speak, I shall speak just so.
Ant. I leave you then to your sad task. Farewell!
I sent her word to meet you. [*Goes to the door, and comes back.*
I forgot;
Let her be told I'll make her peace with mine:
Her crown and dignity shall be preserved,
If I have pow'r with Cæsar.—Oh, be sure
To think on that.
Dola. Fear not, I will remember.
[Antony *goes again to the door, and comes back.*

Ant. And tell her, too, how much I was constrained;
I did not this, but with extremest force.
Desire her not to hate my memory,
For I still cherish hers.—Insist on that.
Dola. Trust me, I'll not forget it.
Ant. Then that's all.
[*Goes out, and returns again.*
Wilt thou forgive my fondness this once more?
Tell her, though we shall never meet again,
If I should hear she took another love,
The news would break my heart.—Now I must go;
For every time I have returned, I feel
My soul more tender; and my next command
Would be to bid her stay, and ruin both. [*Exit.*
Dola. Men are but children of a larger growth,
Our appetites as apt to change as theirs,
And full as craving too, and full as vain;
And yet the soul, shut up in her dark room,
Viewing so clear abroad, at home sees nothing;
But, like a mole in earth, busy and blind,
Works all her folly up, and casts it outward
To the world's open view. Thus I discovered,
And blamed the love of ruined Antony,
Yet wish that I were he, to be so ruined.

Enter Ventidius *above.*

Ven. Alone? and talking to himself? concerned too?
Perhaps my guess is right; he loved her once,
And may pursue it still.
Dola. O friendship! friendship!
Ill canst thou answer this; and reason, worse.
Unfaithful in th' attempt; hopeless to win;
And, if I win, undone: mere madness all.
And yet th' occasion's fair. What injury
To him, to wear the robe which he throws by?
Ven. None, none at all. This happens as I wish,
To ruin her yet more with Antony.

Enter Cleopatra, *talking with* Alexas; Charmion, Iras *on the other side.*

Dola. She comes! What charms have sorrow on that face!
Sorrow seems pleased to dwell with so much sweetness;
Yet, now and then, a melancholy smile

Breaks loose, like lightning in a winter's night,
And shows a moment's day.
Ven. If she should love him too! Her eunuch there!
That porcpisce bodes ill weather. Draw, draw nearer,
Sweet devil, that I may hear.
Alex. Believe me, try
[*Dolabella goes over to Charmion and Iras; seems to talk with them.*
To make him jealous; jealousy is like
A polished glass held to the lips when life's in doubt:
If there be breath, 'twill catch the damp and show it.
Cleo. I grant you jealousy's a proof of love,
But 'tis a weak and unavailing med'cine;
It puts out the disease, and makes it show,
But has no pow'r to cure.
Alex. 'Tis your last remedy, and strongest too:
And then this Dolabella, who so fit
To practice on? He's handsome, valiant, young,
And looks as he were laid for nature's bait
To catch weak women's eyes.
He stands already more than half suspected
Of loving you; the least kind word or glance
You give this youth will kindle him with love:
Then, like a burning vessel set adrift,
You'll send him down amain before the wind,
To fire the heart of jealous Antony.
Cleo. Can I do this? Ah no; my love's so true,
That I can neither hide it where it is,
Nor show it where it is not. Nature meant me
A wife, a silly harmless household dove,
Fond without art, and kind without deceit;
But Fortune, that has made a mistress of me,
Has thrust me out to the wide world, unfurnished
Of falsehood to be happy.
Alex. Force yourself.
Th' event will be, your lover will return
Doubly desirous to possess the good
Which once he feared to lose.
Cleo. I must attempt it;
But oh, with what regret! [*Exit Alexas. She comes up to Dolabella.*
Ven. So, now the scene draws near; they're in my reach.

68 porcpisce] porpoise

Cleo. [*To Dolabella.*] Discoursing with my women! Might not I
Share in your entertainment?
Char. You have been
The subject of it, madam.
Cleo. How! and how?
Iras. Such praises of your beauty!
Cleo. Mere poetry.
Your Roman wits, your Gallus and Tibullus,
Have taught you this from Cytheris and Delia.
Dola. Those Roman wits have never been in Egypt;
Cytheris and Delia else had been unsung.
I, who have seen—had I been born a poet,
Should choose a nobler name.
Cleo. You flatter me.
But 'tis your nation's vice: all of your country
Are flatterers, and all false. Your friend's like you.
I'm sure he sent you not to speak these words.
Dola. No, madam; yet he sent me—
Cleo. Well, he sent you—
Dola. Of a less pleasing errand.
Cleo. How less pleasing?
Less to yourself, or me?
Dola. Madam, to both;
For you must mourn, and I must grieve to cause it.
Cleo. You, Charmion, and your fellow, stand at distance.
[*Aside.*] Hold up, my spirits.—Well, now your mournful matter;
For I'm prepared, perhaps can guess it too.
Dola. I wish you would, for 'tis a thankless office
To tell ill news; and I, of all your sex,
Most fear displeasing you.
Cleo. Of all your sex,
I soonest could forgive you, if you should.
Ven. Most delicate advances! Woman! Woman!
Dear damned, inconstant sex!
Cleo. In the first place,
I am to be forsaken; is't not so?
Dola. I wish I could not answer to that question.
Cleo. Then pass it o'er because it troubles you:
I should have been more grieved another time.

105 Gallus] Gaius Cornelius Gallus, d. 26 B.C., famous for his love elegies on Cytheris, no longer extant. Tibullus, d. 19 B.C., similarly celebrated his Delia.

Next, I'm to lose my kingdom.—Farewell, Egypt!
Yet, is there any more?
Dola. Madam, I fear
Your too deep sense of grief has turned your reason.
Cleo. No, no, I'm not run mad; I can bear fortune:
And love may be expelled by other love,
As poisons are by poisons.
Dola. You o'erjoy me, madam,
To find your griefs so moderately borne:
You've heard the worst; all are not false, like him.
Cleo. No; heaven forbid they should.
Dola. Some men are constant.
Cleo. And constancy deserves reward, that's certain.
Dola. Deserves it not; but give it leave to hope.
Ven. I'll swear thou hast my leave. I have enough;
But how to manage this! Well, I'll consider. [*Exit.*
Dola. I came prepared,
To tell you heavy news; news which I thought
Would fright the blood from your pale cheeks to hear.
But you have met it with a cheerfulness
That makes my task more easy; and my tongue,
Which on another's message was employed,
Would gladly speak its own.
Cleo. Hold, Dolabella!
First tell me, were you chosen by my lord?
Or sought you this employment?
Dola. He picked me out; and, as his bosom-friend,
He charged me with his words.
Cleo. The message then
I know was tender, and each accent smooth,
To mollify that rugged word *Depart.*
Dola. Oh, you mistake! He chose the harshest words,
With fiery eyes, and with contracted brows,
He coined his face in the severest stamp,
And fury shook his fabric like an earthquake;
He heaved for vent, and burst like bellowing Etna
In sounds scarce human: 'Hence, away for ever!
Let her begone, the blot of my renown,
And bane of all my hopes:
Let her be driven as far as men can think
From man's commerce! She'll poison to the centre.
[*All the time of this speech,* Cleopatra *seems more and more concerned, till she sinks quite down.*

Cleo. Oh, I can bear no more!
Dola. Help, help! O wretch! O cursed, cursed wretch!
What have I done?
Char. Help, chafe her temples, Iras.
Iras. Bend, bend her forward quickly.
Char. Heaven be praised,
She comes again.
Cleo. Oh, let him not approach me.
Why have you brought me back to this loathed being,
Th' abode of falsehood, violated vows,
And injured love? For pity, let me go;
For if there be a place of long repose,
I'm sure I want it. My disdainful lord
Can never break that quiet, nor awake
The sleeping soul with holloing in my tomb
Such words as fright her hence. Unkind, unkind!
Dola. [*Kneeling*.] Believe me, 'tis against myself I speak:
That sure deserves belief. I injured him:
My friend ne'er spoke those words. Oh, had you seen
How often he came back, and every time
With something more obliging and more kind
To add to what he said; what dear farewells;
How almost vanquished by his love he parted,
And leaned to what unwillingly he left!—
I, traitor as I was, for love of you
(But what can you not do, who made me false!),
I forged that lie; for whose forgiveness kneels
This self-accused, self-punished criminal.
Cleo. With how much ease believe we what we wish!
Rise, Dolabella; if you have been guilty,
I have contributed, and too much love
Has made me guilty too.
Th' advance of kindness which I made was feigned,
To call back fleeting love by jealousy,
But 'twould not last. Oh, rather let me lose
Than so ignobly trifle with his heart.
Dola. I find your breast fenced round from human reach,
Transparent as a rock of solid crystal,
Seen through, but never pierced. My friend, my friend!
What endless treasure hast thou thrown away,
And scattered, like an infant, in the ocean,
Vain sums of wealth which none can gather thence!

Cleo. Could you not beg
An hour's admittance to his private ear?
Like one who wanders through long barren wilds,
And yet foreknows no hospitable inn
Is near to succour hunger, eats his fill,
Before his painful march:
So would I feed a while my famished eyes
Before we part; for I have far to go,
If death be far, and never must return.

Ventidius *with* Octavia, *behind*.

Ven. From hence you may discover—Oh, sweet, sweet!
Would you indeed? the pretty hand in earnest?
Dola. [*Takes her hand*.] I will, for this reward.—Draw it not back,
'Tis all I e'er will beg.
Ven. They turn upon us.
Octav. What quick eyes has guilt!
Ven. Seem not to have observed 'em, and go on.

They enter.

Dola. Saw you the Emperor, Ventidius?
Ven. No.
I sought him; but I heard that he was private,
None with him, but Hipparchus his freedman.
Dola. Know you his business?
Ven. Giving him instructions,
And letters, to his brother Cæsar.
Dola. Well,
He must be found. [*Exeunt* Dolabella *and* Cleopatra.
Octav. Most glorious impudence!
Ven. She looked, methought,
As she would say, 'Take your old man, Octavia;
Thank you, I'm better here.' Well, but what use
Make we of this discovery?
Octav. Let it die.
Ven. I pity Dolabella; but she's dangerous:
Her eyes have pow'r beyond Thessalian charms
To draw the moon from heaven. For eloquence,
The sea-green Sirens taught her voice their flatt'ry;

232 Thessalian charms] The inhabitants of Thessaly were noted for their addiction to magic and sorcery.

And while she speaks, night steals upon the day,
Unmarked of those that hear. Then she's so charming,
Age buds at sight of her, and swells to youth;
The holy priests gaze on her when she smiles,
And with heaved hands, forgetting gravity,
They bless her wanton eyes. Even I who hate her,
With a malignant joy behold such beauty,
And while I curse, desire it. Antony
Must needs have some remains of passion still,
Which may ferment into a worse relapse
If now not fully cured. I know, this minute,
With Cæsar he's endeavouring her peace.

Octav. You have prevailed.—But for a farther purpose [*Walks off.*
I'll prove how he will relish this discovery.
What, make a strumpet's peace! it swells my heart:
It must not, sha' not be.

Ven. His guards appear.
Let me begin, and you shall second me.

Enter Antony.

Ant. Octavia, I was looking you, my love:
What, are your letters ready? I have given
My last instructions.

Octav. Mine, my Lord, are written.

Ant. Ventidius! [*Drawing him aside.*

Ven. My lord?

Ant. A word in private.
When saw you Dolabella?

Ven. Now, my lord,
He parted hence, and Cleopatra with him.

Ant. Speak softly. 'Twas by my command he went,
To bear my last farewell.

Ven. [*Aloud.*] It looked indeed
Like your farewell.

Ant. More softly.—My farewell?
What secret meaning have you in those words
Of my farewell? He did it by my order.

Ven. [*Aloud.*] Then he obeyed your order. I suppose
You bid him do it with all gentleness,
All kindness, and all—love.

248 prove] try, test

Ant. How she mourned,
The poor forsaken creature!
Ven. She took it as she ought; she bore your parting
As she did Cæsar's, as she would another's,
Were a new love to come.
Ant. [*Aloud.*] Thou dost belie her;
Most basely and maliciously belie her.
Ven. I thought not to displease you; I have done.
Octav. [*Coming up.*] You seem disturbed, my lord.
Ant. A very trifle.
Retire, my love.
Ven. It was indeed a trifle.
He sent—.
Ant. [*Angrily.*] No more! Look how thou disobey'st me;
Thy life shall answer it.
Octav. Then 'tis no trifle.
Ven. [*To Octavia.*] 'Tis less; a very nothing: you too saw it,
As well as I, and therefore 'tis no secret.
Ant. She saw it!
Ven. Yes: she saw young Dolabella—
Ant. Young Dolabella!
Ven. Young, I think him young,
And handsome too; and so do others think him,
But what of that? He went by your command,
Indeed 'tis probable, with some kind message,
For she received it graciously. She smiled;
And then he grew familiar with her hand,
Squeezed it, and worried it with ravenous kisses;
She blushed, and sighed, and smiled, and blushed again.
At last she took occasion to talk softly,
And brought her cheek up close, and leaned on his;
At which, he whispered kisses back on hers,
And then she cried aloud that 'constancy
Should be rewarded.'
Octav. This I saw and heard.
Ant. What woman was it, whom you heard and saw
So playful with my friend! Not Cleopatra?
Ven. Even she, my lord!
Ant. My Cleopatra?
Ven. Your Cleopatra;
Dolabella's Cleopatra;
Every man's Cleopatra.

Ant. Thou liest.
Ven. I do not lie, my lord.
Is this so strange? Should mistresses be left,
And not provide against a time of change?
You know she's not much used to lonely nights.
Ant. I'll think no more on't.
I know 'tis false, and see the plot betwixt you.
You needed not have gone this way, Octavia.
What harms it you that Cleopatra's just?
She's mine no more. I see, and I forgive:
Urge it no farther, love.
Octav. Are you concerned
That she's found false?
Ant. I should be, were it so;
For, though 'tis past, I would not that the world
Should tax my former choice, That I loved one
Of so light note. But I forgive you both.
Ven. What has my age deserved, that you should think
I would abuse your ears with perjury?
If heaven be true, she's false.
Ant. Though heaven and earth
Should witness it, I'll not believe her tainted.
Ven. I'll bring you then a witness
From Hell to prove her so.—Nay, go not back; [*Seeing* Alexas *just entering, and starting back.*
For stay you must and shall.
Alex. What means my lord?
Ven. To make you do what most you hate: speak truth.
You are of Cleopatra's private counsel,
Of her bed-counsel, her lascivious hours;
Are conscious of each nightly change she makes,
And watch her, as Chaldeans do the moon;
Can tell what signs she passes through, what day.
Alex. My noble lord.
Ven. My most illustrious pander,
No fine set speech, no cadence, no turned periods,
But a plain homespun truth is what I ask.
I did, myself, o'erhear your Queen make love
To Dolabella. Speak; for I will know,
By your confession, what more passed betwixt 'em;
How near the business draws to your employment,
And when the happy hour.

Ant. Speak truth, Alexas. Whether it offend
Or please Ventidius, care not: justify
Thy injured Queen from malice; dare his worst.
Octav. [*Aside.*] See, how he gives him courage! how he fears
To find her false! and shuts his eyes to truth,
Willing to be misled!
Alex. As far as love may plead for woman's frailty,
Urged by desert and greatness of the lover,
So far, divine Octavia! may my Queen
Stand even excused to you for loving him
Who is your lord; so far, from brave Ventidius,
May her past actions hope a fair report.
Ant. 'Tis well, and truly spoken. Mark, Ventidius.
Alex. To you, most noble Emperor, her strong passion
Stands not excused, but wholly justified.
Her beauty's charms alone, without her crown,
From Ind and Meroë drew the distant vows
Of sighing kings; and at her feet were laid
The sceptres of the earth, exposed on heaps,
To choose where she would reign.
She thought a Roman only could deserve her;
And, of all Romans, only Antony.
And, to be less than wife to you, disdained
Their lawful passion.
Ant. 'Tis but truth.
Alex. And yet, though love, and your unmatched desert,
Have drawn her from the due regard of honour,
At last heaven opened her unwilling eyes
To see the wrongs she offered fair Octavia,
Whose holy bed she lawlessly usurped.
The sad effects of this improsperous war,
Confirmed those pious thoughts.
Ven. [*Aside.*] Oh, wheel you there?
Observe him now; the man begins to mend,
And talk substantial reason. Fear not, eunuch,
The Emperor has given thee leave to speak.
Alex. Else had I never dared t' offend his ears
With what the last necessity has urged
On my forsaken mistress; yet I must not
Presume to say her heart is wholly altered.

348 Meroë] ancient Egyptian city on the Nile, in what is now the Sudan

Ant. No, dare not for thy life, I charge thee dare not
Pronounce that fatal word!
Octav. [*Aside.*] Must I bear this? Good heaven, afford me patience!
Ven. On, sweet eunuch; my dear half-man, proceed.
Alex. Yet Dolabella
Has loved her long: he, next my godlike lord,
Deserves her best; and should she meet his passion,
Rejected as she is by him she loved—
Ant. Hence, from my sight; for I can bear no more!
Let Furies drag thee quick to Hell; let all
The longer damned have rest; each torturing hand
Do thou employ, till Cleopatra comes,
Then join thou too, and help to torture her! [*Exit* Alexas, *thrust out by* Antony.
Octav. 'Tis not well;
Indeed, my lord, 'tis much unkind to me
To show this passion, this extreme concernment
For an abandoned, faithless prostitute.
Ant. Octavia, leave me: I am much disordered.
Leave me, I say.
Octav. My lord?
Ant. I bid you leave me.
Ven. Obey him, madam: best withdraw a while,
And see how this will work.
Octav. Wherein have I offended you, my lord,
That I am bid to leave you? Am I false,
Or infamous? Am I a Cleopatra?
Were I she,
Base as she is, you would not bid me leave you,
But hang upon my neck, take slight excuses,
And fawn upon my falsehood.
Ant. 'Tis too much,
Too much, Octavia; I am pressed with sorrows
Too heavy to be borne, and you add more:
I would retire, and recollect what's left
Of man within, to aid me.
Octav. You would mourn
In private for your love, who has betrayed you.
You did but half return to me: your kindness
Lingered behind with her. I hear, my lord,
You make conditions for her,
And would include her treaty. Wondrous proofs
Of love to me!

Ant. Are you my friend, Ventidius?
Or are you turned a Dolabella too,
And let this Fury loose?
Ven. Oh, be advised,
Sweet madam, and retire.
Octav. Yes, I will go; but never to return.
You shall no more be haunted with this Fury.
My Lord, my lord, love will not always last,
When urged with long unkindness and disdain.
Take her again whom you prefer to me;
She stays but to be called. Poor cozened man!
Let a feigned parting give her back your heart,
Which a feigned love first got. For injured me,
Though my just sense of wrongs forbid my stay,
My duty shall be yours.
To the dear pledges of our former love
My tenderness and care shall be transferred,
And they shall cheer, by turns, my widowed nights:
So, take my last farewell, for I despair
To have you whole, and scorn to take you half. [*Exit.*
Ven. I combat heaven, which blasts my best designs:
My last attempt must be to win her back,
But oh! I fear in vain. [*Exit.*
Ant. Why was I framed with this plain, honest heart,
Which knows not to disguise its griefs and weakness,
But bears its workings outward to the world?
I should have kept the mighty anguish in,
And forced a smile at Cleopatra's falsehood:
Octavia had believed it, and had stayed.
But I am made a shallow-forded stream,
Seen to the bottom: all my clearness scorned,
And all my faults exposed!—See, where he comes

Enter Dolabella.

Who has profaned the sacred name of friend,
And worn it into vileness!
With how secure a brow, and specious form
He gilds the secret villain! Sure that face
Was meant for honesty; but heaven mis-matched it,
And furnished treason out with nature's pomp,
To make its work more easy.
Dola. Oh, my friend!

Ant. Well, Dolabella, you performed my message?
Dola. I did, unwillingly.
Ant. Unwillingly?
Was it so hard for you to bear our parting?
You should have wished it.
Dola. Why?
Ant. Because you love me.
And she received my message with as true,
With as unfeigned a sorrow as you brought it?
Dola. She loves you, even to madness.
Ant. Oh, I know it.
You, Dolabella, do not better know
How much she loves me. And should I
Forsake this beauty, this all-perfect creature?
Dola. I could not, were she mine.
Ant. And yet you first
Persuaded me: how come you altered since?
Dola. I said at first I was not fit to go;
I could not hear her sighs, and see her tears,
But pity must prevail. And so, perhaps,
It may again with you, for I have promised
That she should take her last farewell; and see!
She comes to claim my word.

Enter Cleopatra.

Ant. False Dolabella!
Dola. What's false, my lord?
Ant. Why, Dolabella's false,
And Cleopatra's false; both false and faithless.
Draw near, you well-joined wickedness, you serpents,
Whom I have in my kindly bosom warmed
Till I am stung to death.
Dola. My lord, have I
Deserved to be thus used?
Cleo. Can heaven prepare
A newer torment? Can it find a curse
Beyond our separation?
Ant. Yes, if fate
Be just, much greater: heaven should be ingenious
In punishing such crimes. The rolling stone
And gnawing vulture were slight pains, invented
When Jove was young, and no examples known

Of mighty ills; but you have ripened sin
To such a monstrous growth, 'twill pose the gods
To find an equal torture. Two, two such—
Oh, there's no farther name! two such—to me,
To me who locked my soul within your breasts,
Had no desires, no joys, no life but you.
When half the globe was mine, I gave it you
In dowry with my heart; I had no use,
No fruit of all, but you: a friend and mistress
Was what the world could give. Oh, Cleopatra!
Oh, Dolabella! how could you betray
This tender heart, which with an infant-fondness
Lay lulled betwixt your bosoms, and there slept
Secure of injured faith?

Dola. If she has wronged you,
Heaven, Hell, and you revenge it.

Ant. If she wronged me!
Thou wouldst evade thy part of guilt; but swear
Thou lov'st not her.

Dola. Not so as I love you.

Ant. Not so? Swear, swear, I say, thou dost not love her.

Dola. No more than friendship will allow.

Ant. No more?
Friendship allows thee nothing: thou art perjured.—
And yet thou didst not swear thou lov'dst her not,
But not so much, no more. Oh trifling hypocrite,
Who dar'st not own to her thou dost not love,
Nor own to me thou dost! Ventidius heard it;
Octavia saw it.

Cleo. They are enemies.

Ant. Alexas is not so: he, he confessed it;
He who, next hell, best knew it, he avowed it.
[*To Dolabella.*] Why do I seek a proof beyond yourself?
You whom I sent to bear my last farewell,
Returned to plead her stay.

Dola. What shall I answer?
If to have loved be guilt, then I have sinned;
But if to have repented of that love
Can wash away my crime, I have repented.
Yet, if I have offended past forgiveness,
Let not her suffer: she is innocent.

476 pose] puzzle 488 Secure of] with no apprehension of

Cleo. Ah, what will not a woman do who loves!
What means will she refuse to keep that heart
Where all her joys are placed? 'Twas I encouraged,
'Twas I blew up the fire that scorched his soul,
To make you jealous, and by that regain you.
But all in vain; I could not counterfeit:
In spite of all the dams, my love broke o'er,
And drowned my heart again. Fate took th' occasion;
And thus one minute's feigning has destroyed
My whole life's truth.
Ant. Thin cobweb arts of falsehood,
Seen and broke through at first.
Dola. Forgive your mistress.
Cleo. Forgive your friend.
Ant. You have convinced yourselves,
You plead each other's cause. What witness have you
That you but meant to raise my jealousy?
Cleo. Ourselves, and heaven.
Ant. Guilt witnesses for guilt. Hence, love and friendship!
You have no longer place in human breasts;
These two have driven you out. Avoid my sight;
I would not kill the man whom I have loved,
And cannot hurt the woman; but avoid me.
I do not know how long I can be tame;
For, if I stay one minute more to think
How I am wronged, my justice and revenge
Will cry so loud within me that my pity
Will not be heard for either.
Dola. Heaven has but
Our sorrow for our sins, and then delights
To pardon erring man. Sweet mercy seems
Its darling attribute, which limits justice;
As if there were degrees in infinite;
And infinite would rather want perfection
Than punish to extent.
Ant. I can forgive
A foe, but not a mistress, and a friend:
Treason is there in its most horrid shape

521 convinced yourselves] proved yourselves guilty (convicted: *O.E.D.*, 4) 528 I have loved] I lov'd *Q.* 1–3, *Works* 540 to extent] Dryden's metaphor is probably a legal one (cf. 'which limits justice'). 'Extent' was a 'seizure of lands etc. in execution of a writ' (*O.E.D.*, 2b).

Where trust is greatest, and the soul resigned
Is stabbed by its own guards. I'll hear no more;
Hence from my sight, for ever!
Cleo. How? for ever!
I cannot go one moment from your sight,
And must I go for ever?
My joys, my only joys, are centred here:
What place have I to go to? My own kingdom?
That I have lost for you. Or to the Romans?
They hate me for your sake. Or must I wander
The wide world o'er, a helpless, banished woman,
Banished for love of you—banished from you?
Ay, there's the banishment! Oh hear me, hear me
With strictest justice, for I beg no favour;
And if I have offended you, then kill me,
But do not banish me.
Ant. I must not hear you.
I have a fool within me takes your part;
But honour stops my ears.
Cleo. For pity hear me!
Would you cast off a slave who followed you,
Who crouched beneath your spurn?—He has no pity!
See, if he gives one tear to my departure;
One look, one kind farewell. Oh, iron heart!
Let all the gods look down and judge betwixt us
If he did ever love!
Ant. No more.—Alexas!
Dola. A perjured villain!
Ant. [*To Cleopatra.*] Your Alexas; yours.
Cleo. Oh, 'twas his plot, his ruinous design
T'ingage you in my love by jealousy.
Hear him; confront him with me; let him speak.
Ant. I have, I have.
Cleo. And if he clear me not—
Ant. Your creature! one who hangs upon your smiles,
Watches your eye to say or to unsay
Whate'er you please! I am not to be moved.
Cleo. Then must we part? Farewell, my cruel lord!
Th' appearance is against me; and I go,
Unjustified, for ever from your sight.
How I have loved, you know; how yet I love,
My only comfort is, I know myself.

I love you more, even now you are unkind,
Than when you loved me most; so well, so truly,
I'll never strive against it, but die pleased
To think you once were mine.

Ant. Good heaven, they weep at parting!
Must I weep too? That calls 'em innocent.
I must not weep; and yet I must, to think
That I must not forgive.—
Live, but live wretched, 'tis but just you should,
Who made me so. Live from each other's sight;
Let me not hear you meet. Set all the earth
And all the seas betwixt your sundered loves;
View nothing common but the sun and skies.
Now, all take several ways;
And each your own sad fate with mine deplore;
That you were false, and I could trust no more.

[*Exeunt severally.*

ACT V

Cleopatra, Charmion, Iras.

Char. Be juster, heaven: such virtue punished thus
Will make us think that chance rules all above,
And shuffles with a random hand the lots
Which man is forced to draw.

Cleo. I could tear out these eyes that gained his heart
And had not pow'r to keep it. Oh the curse
Of doting on, even when I find it dotage!
Bear witness, gods, you heard him bid me go;
You whom he mocked with imprecating vows
Of promised faith.—I'll die, I will not bear it!
You may hold me— [*She pulls out her dagger, and they hold her.*
But I can keep my breath; I can die inward,
And choke this love.

Enter Alexas.

Iras. Help, O Alexas, help!
The Queen grows desperate, her soul struggles in her,

With all the agonies of love and rage,
And strives to force its passage.

Cleo. Let me go.
Art thou there, traitor!—Oh,
Oh, for a little breath to vent my rage!
Give, give me way, and let me loose upon him.

Alex. Yes, I deserve it, for my ill-timed truth.
Was it for me to prop
The ruins of a falling majesty?
To place myself beneath the mighty flaw,
Thus to be crushed and pounded into atoms
By its o'erwhelming weight? 'Tis too presuming
For subjects to preserve that wilful pow'r
Which courts its own destruction.

Cleo. I would reason
More calmly with you. Did not you o'er-rule,
And force my plain, direct, and open love
Into these crooked paths of jealousy?
Now, what's th' event? Octavia is removed,
But Cleopatra's banished. Thou, thou villain!
Has pushed my boat to open sea, to prove,
At my sad cost, if thou canst steer it back.
It cannot be; I'm lost too far; I'm ruined.
Hence, thou impostor, traitor, monster, devil!—
I can no more: thou, and my griefs, have sunk
Me down so low that I want voice to curse thee.

Alex. Suppose some shipwracked seaman near the shore,
Dropping and faint with climbing up the cliff,
If, from above, some charitable hand
Pull him to safety, hazarding himself
To draw the other's weight—would he look back
And curse him for his pains? The case is yours:
But one step more, and you have gained the height.

Cleo. Sunk, never more to rise.

Alex. Octavia's gone, and Dolabella banished.
Believe me, madam, Antony is yours.
His heart was never lost, but started off
To jealousy, love's last retreat and covert,
Where it lies hid in shades, watchful in silence,
And list'ning for the sound that calls it back.
Some other, any man ('tis so advanced),

32 Thou, thou villain!] Thou, thou, villain, *Q.* 1 45 But] only

May perfect this unfinished work, which I
(Unhappy only to myself) have left
So easy to his hand.

Cleo. Look well thou do't; else—

Alex. Else, what your silence threatens.—Antony
Is mounted up the Pharos, from whose turret
He stands surveying our Egyptian galleys,
Engaged with Cæsar's fleet. Now death, or conquest!
If the first happen, fate acquits my promise:
If we o'ercome, the conqueror is yours.

A distant shout within.

Char. Have comfort, madam: did you mark that shout?

Second shout nearer.

Iras. Hark! they redouble it.

Alex. 'Tis from the port.
The loudness shows it near: good news, kind heavens!

Cleo. Osiris make it so!

Enter Serapion.

Serap. Where, where's the Queen?

Alex. How frightfully the holy coward stares!
As if not yet recovered of th' assault,
When all his gods, and what's more dear to him,
His offerings were at stake.

Serap. O horror, horror!
Egypt has been; our latest hour is come:
The Queen of Nations from her ancient seat,
Is sunk for ever in the dark abyss;
Time has unrolled her glories to the last,
And now closed up the volume.

Cleo. Be more plain:
Say, whence thou com'st—though fate is in thy face,
Which from thy haggard eyes looks wildly out,
And threatens ere thou speak'st.

Serap. I came from Pharos;
From viewing (spare me and imagine it)
Our land's last hope, your navy.—

Cleo. Vanquished?

Serap. No.
They fought not.

67 How frightfully] with what fear 78 Pharos] the lighthouse at Alexandria

Cleo. Then they fled.
Serap. Nor that. I saw,
With Antony, your well-appointed fleet
Row out; and thrice he waved his hand on high,
And thrice with cheerful cries they shouted back.
'Twas then false Fortune, like a fawning strumpet,
About to leave the bankrupt prodigal,
With a dissembled smile would kiss at parting,
And flatter to the last: the well-timed oars
Now dipped from every bank, now smoothly run
To meet the foe; and soon indeed they met,
But not as foes. In few, we saw their caps
On either side thrown up; th' Egyptian galleys
(Received like friends) passed through, and fell behind
The Roman rear; and now they all come forward,
And ride within the port.
Cleo. Enough, Serapion:
I've heard my doom.—This needed not, you gods:
When I lost Antony, your work was done;
'Tis but superfluous malice. Where's my lord?
How bears he this last blow?
Serap. His fury cannot be expressed by words.
Thrice he attempted headlong to have fall'n
Full on his foes, and aimed at Cæsar's galley;
Withheld, he raves on you, cries, he's betrayed.
Should he now find you—
Alex. Shun him; seek your safety
Till you can clear your innocence.
Cleo. I'll stay.
Alex. You must not. Haste you to your Monument,
While I make speed to Cæsar.
Cleo. Cæsar! No,
I have no business with him.
Alex. I can work him
To spare your life, and let this madman perish.
Cleo. Base fawning wretch! wouldst thou betray him too?
Hence from my sight! I will not hear a traitor;
'Twas thy design brought all this ruin on us.—
Serapion, thou art honest; counsel me:
But haste, each moment's precious.

89 bank] tier (of oars) 91 In few] in brief 106 Monument] mausoleum

Serap. Retire; you must not yet see Antony.
He who began this mischief,
'Tis just he tempt the danger: let him clear you.
And since he offered you his servile tongue
To gain a poor precarious life from Cæsar,
Let him expose that fawning eloquence,
And speak to Antony.
Alex. O heavens! I dare not,
I meet my certain death.
Cleo. Slave, thou deserv'st it.
Not that I fear my lord, will I avoid him;
I know him noble: when he banished me
And thought me false, he scorned to take my life;
But I'll be justified, and then die with him.
Alex. Oh pity me, and let me follow you.
Cleo. To death, if thou stir hence. Speak, if thou canst,
Now for thy life, which basely thou wouldst save;
While mine I prize at—this! Come, good Serapion.
[*Exeunt* Cleopatra, Serapion, Charmion, Iras.
Alex. Oh that I less could fear to lose this being,
Which, like a snowball in my coward hand,
The more 'tis grasped, the faster melts away.
Poor reason! what a wretched aid art thou!
For still, in spite of thee,
These two long lovers, soul and body, dread
Their final separation. Let me think:
What can I say to save myself from death?
No matter what becomes of Cleopatra.
Ant. [*Within.*] Which way? where?
Ven. [*Within.*] This leads to th' Monument.
Alex. Ah me! I hear him; yet I'm unprepared:
My gift of lying's gone;
And this court-devil, which I so oft have raised,
Forsakes me at my need. I dare not stay,
Yet cannot far go hence. [*Exit.*

Enter Antony *and* Ventidius.

Ant. O happy Cæsar! Thou hast men to lead:
Think not 'tis thou hast conquered Antony,
But Rome has conquered Egypt. I'm betrayed.
Ven. Curse on this treach'rous train!
Their soil and heaven infect 'em all with baseness,

And their young souls come tainted to the world
With the first breath they draw.
Ant. Th' original villain sure no god created;
He was a bastard of the sun by Nile,
Aped into Man, with all his mother's mud
Crusted about his Soul.
Ven. The Nation is
One universal traitor; and their queen
The very spirit and extract of 'em all.
Ant. Is there yet left
A possibility of aid from valour?
Is there one god unsworn to my destruction?
The least unmortgaged hope? for, if there be,
Methinks I cannot fall beneath the fate
Of such a boy as Cæsar.
The world's one half is yet in Antony;
And from each limb of it that's hewed away
The soul comes back to me.
Ven. There yet remain
Three legions in the town: the last assault
Lopped off the rest. If death be your design
(As I must wish it now), these are sufficient.
To make a heap about us of dead foes,
An honest pile for burial.
Ant. They're enough.
We'll not divide our stars, but side by side
Fight emulous, and with malicious eyes
Survey each other's acts: so every death
Thou giv'st, I'll take on me as a just debt,
And pay thee back a soul.
Ven. Now you shall see I love you. Not a word
Of chiding more. By my few hours of life,
I am so pleased with this brave Roman fate
That I would not be Cæsar, to outlive you.
When we put off this flesh and mount together,
I shall be shown to all th' ethereal crowd:
'Lo, this is he who died with Antony!'
Ant. Who knows but we may pierce through all their troops,
And reach my veterans yet? 'Tis worth the tempting
T' o'er-leap this gulf of fate,
And leave our wond'ring destinies behind.

186 tempting] attempting 188 wond'ring] *Q.* 1; wand'ring *Q.* 2–3, *Works*

Enter Alexas, *trembling.*

Ven. See, see, that villain;
See Cleopatra stamped upon that face,
With all her cunning, all her arts of falsehood!
How she looks out through those dissembling eyes!
How he has set his count'nance for deceit,
And promises a lie before he speaks!
Let me dispatch him first. [*Drawing.*
Alex. Oh, spare me, spare me!
Ant. Hold, he's not worth your killing. On thy life
(Which thou mayst keep, because I scorn to take it),
No syllable to justify thy queen;
Save thy base tongue its office.
Alex. Sir, she's gone,
Where she shall never be molested more
By love, or you.
Ant. Fled to her Dolabella!
Die, traitor! I revoke my promise, die! [*Going to kill him.*
Alex. Oh hold! she is not fled.
Ant. She is: my eyes
Are open to her falsehood; my whole life
Has been a golden dream of love and friendship.
But now I wake, I'm like a merchant roused
From soft repose to see his vessel sinking,
And all his wealth cast o'er. Ingrateful woman!
Who followed me but as the swallow summer,
Hatching her young ones in my kindly beams,
Singing her flatt'ries to my morning wake;
But, now my winter comes, she spreads her wings,
And seeks the spring of Cæsar.
Alex. Think not so:
Her fortunes have in all things mixed with yours.
Had she betrayed her naval force to Rome,
How easily might she have gone to Cæsar,
Secure by such a bribe!
Ven. She sent it first,
To be more welcome after.
Ant. 'Tis too plain;
Else would she have appeared to clear herself.
Alex. Too fatally she has. She could not bear
To be accused by you, but shut herself

Within her Monument; looked down and sighed,
While from her unchanged face the silent tears
Dropped, as they had not leave but stole their parting.
Some undistinguished words she inly murmured;
At last, she raised her eyes, and with such looks
As dying Lucrece cast—

Ant. My heart forebodes—

Ven. All for the best: go on.

Alex. She snatched her poniard,
And, ere we could prevent the fatal blow,
Plunged it within her breast, then turned to me:
'Go, bear my lord', said she, 'my last farewell,
And ask him if he yet suspect my faith.'
More she was saying, but death rushed betwixt.
She half pronounced your name with her last breath,
And buried half within her.

Ven. Heaven be praised.

Ant. Then art thou innocent, my poor dear love?
And art thou dead?
O those two words! their sound should be divided:
Hadst thou been false, and died; or hadst thou lived,
And hadst been true—but innocence and death!
This shows not well above. Then what am I,
The murderer of this truth, this innocence!
Thoughts cannot form themselves in words so horrid
As can express my guilt!

Ven. Is't come to this? The gods have been too gracious—
And thus you thank 'em for't.

Ant. [*To Alexas.*] Why stay'st thou here?
Is it for thee to spy upon my soul,
And see its inward mourning? Get thee hence;
Thou art not worthy to behold what now
Becomes a Roman emperor to perform.

Alex. [*Aside.*] He loves her still:
His grief betrays it. Good! The joy to find
She's yet alive completes the reconcilement.
I've saved myself and her. But, oh! the Romans!
Fate comes too fast upon my wit,
Hunts me too hard, and meets me at each double. [*Exit.*

Ven. Would she had died a little sooner, though,

256 double] the doubling back of a hunted animal (e.g. a hare)

Before Octavia went: you might have treated.
Now 'twill look tame, and would not be received.
Come, rouse yourself, and let's die warm together.

Ant. I will not fight: there's no more work for war.
The business of my angry hours is done.

Ven. Cæsar is at your gates.

Ant. Why, let him enter;
He's welcome now.

Ven. What lethargy has crept into your soul?

Ant. 'Tis but a scorn of life, and just desire
To free myself from bondage.

Ven. Do it bravely.

Ant. I will; but not by fighting. Oh, Ventidius!
What should I fight for now? My queen is dead.
I was but great for her; my pow'r, my empire
Were but my merchandise to buy her love,
And conquered kings, my factors. Now she's dead,
Let Cæsar take the world—
An empty circle since the jewel's gone
Which made it worth my strife: my being's nauseous,
For all the bribes of life are gone away.

Ven. Would you be taken?

Ant. Yes, I would be taken,
But as a Roman ought—dead, my Ventidius;
For I'll convey my soul from Cæsar's reach,
And lay down life myself. 'Tis time the world
Should have a lord, and know whom to obey.
We two have kept its homage in suspense,
And bent the globe on whose each side we trod,
Till it was dinted inwards. Let him walk
Alone upon 't; I'm weary of my part.
My torch is out, and the world stands before me
Like a black desert at th' approach of night:
I'll lay me down, and stray no farther on.

Ven. I could be grieved,
But that I'll not outlive you. Choose your death;
For I have seen him in such various shapes,
I care not which I take. I'm only troubled
The life I bear is worn to such a rag,
'Tis scarce worth giving. I could wish, indeed,

258 treated] negotiated, discussed a settlement 271 factors] mercantile agents

We threw it from us with a better grace;
That like two lions taken in the toils,
We might at least thrust out our paws, and wound
The hunters that inclose us.

Ant. I have thought on't.
Ventidius, you must live.

Ven. I must not, sir.

Ant. Wilt thou not live, to speak some good of me?
To stand by my fair fame, and guard th' approaches
From the ill tongues of men?

Ven. Who shall guard mine,
For living after you?

Ant. Say, I command it.

Ven. If we die well, our deaths will speak themselves,
And need no living witness.

Ant. Thou hast loved me,
And fain I would reward thee. I must die:
Kill me, and take the merit of my death
To make thee friends with Cæsar.

Ven. Thank your kindness.
You said I loved you, and, in recompense,
You bid me turn a traitor. Did I think
You would have used me thus? that I should die
With a hard thought of you?

Ant. Forgive me, Roman.
Since I have heard of Cleopatra's death,
My reason bears no rule upon my tongue,
But lets my thoughts break all at random out:
I've thought better; do not deny me twice.

Ven. By heaven, I will not.
Let it not be t' outlive you.

Ant. Kill me first,
And then die thou; for 'tis but just thou serve
Thy friend before thyself.

Ven. Give me your hand.
We soon shall meet again. Now, farewell, Emperor! [*Embrace.*
Methinks that word's too cold to be my last:
Since Death sweeps all distinctions, farewell, friend!
That's all.—
I will not make a business of a trifle.
And yet I cannot look on you, and kill you;
Pray turn your face.

Ant. I do: strike home, be sure.
Ven. Home, as my sword will reach. [*Kills himself.*
Ant. Oh, thou mistak'st!
That wound was none of thine. Give it me back:
Thou robb'st me of my death.
Ven. I do, indeed;
But think 'tis the first time I e'er deceived you,
If that may plead my pardon. And you, gods,
Forgive me, if you will; for I die perjured
Rather than kill my friend. [*Dies.*
Ant. Farewell! Ever my leader, even in death!
My Queen and thou have got the start of me,
And I'm the lag of honour.—Gone so soon?
Is Death no more? He used him carelessly,
With a familiar kindness: ere he knocked,
Ran to the door, and took him in his arms,
As who should say, 'Y'are welcome at all hours,
A friend need give no warning.' Books had spoiled him;
For all the learn'd are cowards by profession.
'Tis not worth
My farther thought; for death, for aught I know,
Is but to think no more. Here's to be satisfied. [*Falls on his sword.*
I've missed my heart. O unperforming hand!
Thou never couldst have erred in a worse time.
My fortune jades me to the last; and death,
Like a great man, takes state, and makes me wait
For my admittance.— [*Trampling within.*
Some perhaps from Cæsar:
If he should find me living, and suspect
That I played booty with my life! I'll mend
My work ere they can reach me. [*Rises upon his knees.*

Enter Cleopatra, Charmion, Iras.

Cleo. Where is my lord? where is he?
Char. There he lies,
And dead Ventidius by him.
Cleo. My fears were prophets; I am come too late.
O that accursed Alexas! [*Runs to him.*
Ant. Art thou living?

336 the lag] the hindmost 349 takes state] stands upon ceremony (*O.E.D.*, 19b)
353 played booty] played badly with the intention of losing the game (i.e. did not mean to kill himself)

Or am I dead before I knew? and thou
The first kind ghost that meets me?
Cleo. Help me seat him.
Send quickly, send for help! [*They place him in a chair.*
Ant. I am answered.
We live both. Sit thee down, my Cleopatra:
I'll make the most I can of life, to stay
A moment more with thee.
Cleo. How is it with you?
Ant. 'Tis as with a man
Removing in a hurry; all packed up,
But one dear jewel that his haste forgot,
And he for that returns upon the spur:
So I come back, for thee.
Cleo. Too long, you heavens, you have been cruel to me;
Now show your mended faith, and give me back
His fleeting life.
Ant. It will not be, my love.
I keep my soul by force.
Say but thou art not false.
Cleo. 'Tis now too late
To say I'm true: I'll prove it, and die with you.
Unknown to me, Alexas feigned my death;
Which, when I knew, I hasted to prevent
This fatal consequence. My fleet betrayed
Both you and me.
Ant. And Dolabella?—
Cleo. Scarce
Esteemed before he loved; but hated now.
Ant. Enough: my life's not long enough for more.
Thou say'st thou wilt come after: I believe thee,
For I can now believe whate'er thou say'st,
That we may part more kindly.
Cleo. I will come.
Doubt not, my life, I'll come, and quickly too:
Cæsar shall triumph o'er no part of thee.
Ant. But grieve not, while thou stay'st
My last disastrous times:
Think we have had a clear and glorious day,
And heaven did kindly to delay the storm
Just till our close of evening. Ten years' love,

373 I keep my soul by force] i.e. I stay alive by sheer force of will

And not a moment lost, but all improved
To th' utmost joys! What ages have we lived!
And now to die each other's; and so dying,
While hand in hand we walk in groves below,
Whole troops of lovers' ghosts shall flock about us,
And all the train be ours.

Cleo. Your words are like the notes of dying swans,
Too sweet to last. Were there so many hours
For your unkindness, and not one for love?

Ant. No, not a minute.—This one kiss—more worth
Than all I leave to Cæsar. [*Dies.*

Cleo. Oh, tell me so again,
And take ten thousand kisses for that word.
My lord, my lord! speak, if you yet have being;
Sigh to me if you cannot speak, or cast
One look: do anything that shows you live.

Iras. He's gone too far to hear you;
And this you see, a lump of senseless clay,
The leavings of a soul.

Char. Remember, madam,
He charged you not to grieve.

Cleo. And I'll obey him.
I have not loved a Roman not to know
What should become his wife; his wife, my Charmion;
For 'tis to that high title I aspire,
And now I'll not die less. Let dull Octavia
Survive, to mourn him dead: my nobler fate
Shall knit our spousals with a tie too strong
For Roman laws to break.

Iras. Will you then die?

Cleo. Why shouldst thou make that question?

Iras. Cæsar is merciful.

Cleo. Let him be so
To those that want his mercy: my poor lord
Made no such cov'nant with him to spare me
When he was dead. Yield me to Cæsar's pride?
What, to be led in triumph through the streets,
A spectacle to base plebeian eyes;
While some dejected friend of Antony's,
Close in a corner, shakes his head, and mutters
A secret curse on her who ruined him?
I'll none of that.

Char. Whatever you resolve,
I'll follow even to death.
Iras. I only feared
For you, but more should fear to live without you.
Cleo. Why, now 'tis as it should be. Quick, my friends,
Dispatch; ere this, the town's in Cæsar's hands.
My lord looks down concerned, and fears my stay,
Lest I should be surprised;
Keep him not waiting for his love too long.
You, Charmion, bring my crown and richest jewels;
With 'em, the wreath of victory I made
(Vain augury!) for him who now lies dead.
You, Iras, bring the cure of all our ills.
Iras. The aspics, madam?
Cleo. Must I bid you twice?
[*Exeunt* Charmion *and* Iras.
'Tis sweet to die when they would force life on me,
To rush into the dark abode of Death,
And seize him first; if he be like my love,
He is not frightful, sure.
We're now alone, in secrecy and silence,
And is not this like lovers? I may kiss
These pale, cold lips; Octavia does not see me,
And, oh! 'tis better far to have him thus
Than see him in her arms.—O welcome, welcome.

Enter Charmion, Iras.

Char. What must be done?
Cleo. Short ceremony, friends;
But yet it must be decent. First, this laurel
Shall crown my hero's head: he fell not basely,
Nor left his shield behind him. Only thou
Couldst triumph o'er thyself; and thou alone
Wert worthy so to triumph.
Char. To what end
These ensigns of your pomp and royalty?
Cleo. Dull that thou art! Why, 'tis to meet my love,
As when I saw him first, on Cydnos' bank,
All sparkling like a goddess. So adorned,
I'll find him once again; my second spousals
Shall match my first in glory. Haste, haste, both,
And dress the bride of Antony!

Char. 'Tis done.
Cleo. Now seat me by my lord. I claim this place;
For I must conquer Cæsar too, like him,
And win my share o'th' world.—Hail, you dear relics
Of my immortal love!
Oh, let no impious hand remove you hence,
But rest for ever here! Let Egypt give
His death that peace which it denied his life.
Reach me the casket.
Iras. Underneath the fruit
The aspic lies.
Cleo. [*Putting aside the leaves.*] Welcome, thou kind deceiver!
Thou best of thieves, who, with an easy key,
Dost open life, and, unperceived by us,
Even steal us from ourselves—discharging so
Death's dreadful office better than himself,
Touching our limbs so gently into slumber
That death stands by, deceived by his own image,
And thinks himself but Sleep.
Serap. [*Within.*] The Queen, where is she?
The town is yielded, Cæsar's at the gates.
Cleo. He comes too late t'invade the rites of death.
Haste, bare my arm, and rouse the serpent's fury. [*Holds out her arm, and draws it back.*
Coward flesh!—
Wouldst thou conspire with Cæsar to betray me,
As thou wert none of mine? I'll force thee to 't,
And not be sent by him,
But bring myself, my soul to Antony.
[*Turns aside, and then shows her arm bloody.*
Take hence; the work is done.
Serap. [*Within.*] Break ope the door,
And guard the traitor well.
Char. The next is ours.
Iras. Now, Charmion, to be worthy
Of our great queen and mistress. [*They apply the aspics.*
Cleo. Already, Death, I feel thee in my veins;
I go with such a will to find my lord
That we shall quickly meet.
A heavy numbness creeps through every limb,
And now 'tis at my head; my eyelids fall,
And my dear love is vanished in a mist.
Where shall I find him, where? Oh, turn me to him,

And lay me on his breast!—Cæsar, thy worst;
Now part us, if thou canst. [*Dies.* Iras *sinks down at her feet, and dies;*
Charmion *stands behind her chair, as dressing her head.*

Enter Serapion, *Two Priests,* Alexas *bound, Egyptians.*

Two Priests. Behold, Serapion,
What havoc death has made!
Serap. 'Twas what I feared.—
Charmion, is this well done?
Char. Yes, 'tis well done, and like a queen, the last
Of her great race: I follow her. [*Sinks down; dies.*
Alex. 'Tis true,
She has done well: much better thus to die
Than live to make a holiday in Rome.
Serap. See, see how the lovers sit in state together,
As they were giving laws to half mankind.
Th' impression of a smile left in her face
Shows she died pleased with him for whom she lived,
And went to charm him in another world.
Cæsar's just ent'ring: grief has now no leisure.
Secure that villain as our pledge of safety
To grace th' imperial triumph. Sleep, blessed pair,
Secure from human chance, long ages out,
While all the storms of fate fly o'er your tomb;
And Fame to late posterity shall tell,
No lovers lived so great, or died so well.

FINIS

EPILOGUE

Poets, like disputants when reasons fail,
Have one sure refuge left—and that's to rail.
'Fop, coxcomb, fool!' are thundered through the pit,
And this is all their equipage of wit.
We wonder how the devil this diff'rence grows
Betwixt our fools in verse, and yours in prose:
For, 'faith, the quarrel rightly understood,
'Tis Civil War *with their own flesh and blood.*
The threadbare author hates the gaudy coat,
And swears at the gilt coach, but swears afoot:
For 'tis observed of every scribbling man,
He grows a fop as fast as e'er he can,
Prunes up, and asks his oracle, the glass,
If pink or purple best become his face.
For our poor wretch, he neither rails nor prays,
Nor likes your wit just as you like his plays;
He has not yet so much of Mr. Bayes.
He does his best; and, if he cannot please,
Would quietly sue out his writ of ease.
Yet, if he might his own Grand Jury call,
By the fair sex he begs to stand or fall.
Let Cæsar's pow'r the men's ambition move,
But grace you him who lost the world for love!
Yet if some antiquated lady say,
The last age is not copied in his play,
Heaven help the man who for that face must drudge,
Which only has the wrinkles of a judge.
Let not the young and beauteous join with those;
For should you raise such numerous hosts of foes,
Young wits and sparks he to his aid must call:
'Tis more than one man's work to please you all.

17 *Mr. Bayes*] the character in Buckingham's *The Rehearsal*, intended as a caricature of Dryden 19 writ of ease] a certificate of discharge from employment 25 *The last age*] the age of Shakespeare, Ben Jonson, etc.

LUCIUS JUNIUS BRUTUS

Nathaniel Lee

1649–1692

This tragedy, in some ways Lee's finest work, was produced at Drury Lane early in December 1680. He had already succeeded several times on the stage, notably with *The Rival Queens* (1677), and he could fairly expect the same good fortune with *Lucius Junius Brutus*. Like his earlier plays, this new tragedy showed some traces of an ungoverned imagination, and he continued (as he had put it in the dedication of *Theodosius*) to 'leap hedges and ditches sometimes, and run at all'; yet there is now a new effort at control, and his political theme, together with his sense of the grandeur of old Rome, led him to speak out 'without cracking the voice, or straining the lungs', and to think as well as to feel. But the success he deserved was denied him. After his play had been running for a few days complaints must have reached the Lord Chamberlain, for on 11 December an order was issued forbidding further acting of the play on the grounds that it contained 'very scandalous expressions and reflections upon the government'.

It is hard to tell whether Lee knew what he was doing, or whether he was so politically naïve that it never occurred to him that some passages in his tragedy were political dynamite in 1680. At all events, at a time when the King was at loggerheads with his parliament, and the Whigs were pressing their Exclusion Bill and seemed even to be threatening the survival of the monarchy, Lee chose to bring forward an anti-monarchical tragedy based on the overthrow of Tarquin and the establishment of a republic in Rome. When Brutus accuses Tarquin of arbitrary rule (II. i. 180ff.), or, still more, in his great speech (V. ii. 34ff.), when he looks forward to a Rome 'where no man shall offend because he's great', where there are no innovations in religion, 'no desperate factions gaping for rebellion', no preferment of strangers or knaves 'for luxury, for wit, or glorious vice', he might be talking about the England of Charles II; and 1680 was a dangerous time for such talk. In his dedication of the play Lee makes no direct mention of its suppression, but he is clearly referring to it when he admits, 'I was troubled for my dumb play, like a father for his dead child'. So far as is known, it was never again acted on the London stage, but in 1703 Charles Gildon made it the basis of a new tragedy, *The Patriot*, incorporating many passages from Lee.

Most of the material for *Lucius Junius Brutus* came from two sources, (*a*) Livy, and (*b*) Madeleine de Scudéry's romance *Clélie*, which contains a romanticized version of the life of Brutus, and in which Lee also found the love story of Titus and Teraminta. In his edition of the play Professor John Loftis has suggested very plausibly that Lee may have expected most of his audience to be familiar with Mlle de Scudéry's popular romance, and that this 'enabled him to assume a knowledge of events in Brutus's life not explained in the play: the reason, for example, why Brutus had assumed the disguise of stupidity (to protect himself from Tarquin, who had killed his brother and father and confiscated his property)'.

Texts collated: *Q.* 1 (1681); *Works* (Collected Works, 1713). See Selected Bibliography, pp. 439–41.

LUCIUS JUNIUS BRUTUS;

FATHER of his COUNTRY.

A

TRAGEDY.

Acted at the Duke's Theater, by their Royal Highnesses Servants.

Written by *Nat. Lee.*

——*cæloque invectus aperto*
Flectit equos, curruque volans dat lora Secunda, Virg. lib. 4.

LONDON,

Printed for *Richard Tonson*, and *Jacob Tonson*, at *Grays-Inn* Gate, and at the Judges-Head in *Chancery-Lane* near *Fleet-street*, 1681.

To the Right Honourable

CHARLES,

Earl of DORSET and MIDDLESEX,

One of the Gentlemen of His

MAJESTY'S

BEDCHAMBER, etc.

My Lord,

With an assurance I hope becoming the justice of my cause, I lay this tragedy at your Lordship's feet, not as a common persecution but as an offering suitable to your virtue, and worthy of the greatness of your name. There are some subjects that require but half the strength of a great poet, but when Greece or old Rome come in play, the nature, wit and vigour of foremost Shakespeare, the judgement and force of Jonson, with all his borrowed mastery from the Ancients, will scarce suffice for so terrible a grapple. The poet must elevate his fancy with the mightiest imagination, he must run back so many hundred years, take a just prospect of the spirit of those times without the least thought of ours; for if his eye should swerve so low, his Muse will grow giddy with the vastness of the distance, fall at once, and for ever lose the majesty of the first design. He that will pretend to be a critic of such a work must not have a grain of Cecilius, he must be Longin throughout or nothing, where even the nicest, best remarks must pass but for alloy to the imperial fury of this old Roman gold. There must be no dross through the whole mass, the furnace must be justly heated, and the bullion stamped with an unerring hand. In such a writing there must be greatness of thought without bombast, remoteness without monstrousness, virtue armed with severity, not in iron bodies, solid wit without modern affectation, smoothness without gloss, speaking out without cracking the voice or straining the lungs. In short, my Lord, he that will write as he ought on so noble an occasion must write like you. But I fear there are few that know how to copy after so great an original as your Lordship, because

Title. Dorset] Charles Sackville, sixth Earl of Dorset and Earl of Middlesex (1638–1706), poet and patron of poets 14 Cecilius] Cecilius Statius, a native of Gaul (d. 68 B.C.), who wrote numerous comedies, but was called by Cicero 'malum Latinatis auctorem' 15 Longin] Longinus

there is scarce one genius extant of your own size that can follow you *passibus æquis*, that has the felicity and mastery of the old poets, or can half match the thoughtfulness of your soul. How far short I am cast of such inimitable excellence, I must with shame, my Lord, confess I am but too too sensible. Nature, 'tis believed (if I am not flattered and do not flatter myself) has not been niggardly to me in the portion of a genius, though I have been so far from improving it that I am half afraid I have lost of the principal. It behoves me then for the future to look about me to see whether I am a Lag in the race, to look up to your Lordship and strain upon the track of so fair a glory. I must acknowledge, however I have behaved myself in drawing, nothing ever presented itself to my fancy with that solid pleasure as Brutus did in sacrificing his sons. Before I read Machivel's notes upon the place, I concluded it the greatest action that was ever seen throughout all ages on the greatest occasion. For my own endeavour, I thought I never painted any man so to the life before.

Vis et Tarquinios reges, animamque superbam
Ultoris Bruti fascesque videre receptos?
Infelix utcunque ferent ea facta minores!

No doubt that divine poet imagined it might be too great for any people but his own; perhaps I have found it so, but Jonson's Catiline met no better fate as his motto from Horace tells us.

— *His non plebecula gaudet etc.*

Nay, Shakespeare's Brutus with much ado beat himself into the heads of a blockish age, so knotty were the oaks he had to deal with. For my own opinion, in spite of all the obstacles my modesty could raise, I could not help inserting a vaunt in the title-page, *Cœloque, etc.*

And having gained the list that he designed,
Bold as the billows driving with the wind,
He loosed the Muse that winged his free-born mind.

On this I armed and resolved not to be stirred with the little exceptions of a sparkish generation that have an antipathy to thought. But, alas, how

25–6 *Passibus æquis*] with equal steps 36 Machivel's notes] in his *Discorsi* on Livy 40–2 *Vis . . . minores!*] Will you see too the Tarquin kings, and the proud soul of the avenging Brutus, and the *fasces* regained? Unhappy man, however posterity may tolerate those deeds! (*Aeneid*, vi. 817–18, 822.) 46 *His . . . gaudet*] In these things the rabble takes no delight (Horace, *Epistles*, II. i. 186–8; Horace wrote: *His nam plebecula*). 53 free-born mind] in those three lines Lee appears to be offering a free paraphrase of the motto (from *Aeneid*, I. 155–6) on his title page. (list: what he wished for—*O.E.D.*, sb.[4] 3. But perhaps Lee wrote 'lift': i.e. the sky, upper regions.)

frail are our best resolves in our own concerns! I showed no passion outward, but whether through an over-conceit of the work, or because perhaps there was indeed some merit, the fire burnt inward, and I was troubled for my dumb play, like a father for his dead child. 'Tis enough that I have eased my heart by this dedication to your Lordship. I comfort myself, too, whatever our partial youth allege, your Lordship will find something in it worth your observation; which with my future diligence, resolution to study, devotion to vertue, and your Lordship's service, may render me not altogether unworthy the protection of your Lordship.

My Lord,

Your Lordship's most humble

and devoted Servant,

NAT. LEE.

PROLOGUE TO BRUTUS,

written by Mr. Duke.

Long has the tribe of poets on the stage
Groaned under persecuting critics' rage,
But with the sound of railing and of rhyme,
Like bees united by the tinkling chime,
The little stinging insects swarm the more
And buzz is greater than it was before.
But oh! you leading voters of the pit,
That infect others with your too much wit,
That well-affected members do seduce,
And with your malice poison half the house,
Know your ill managed arbitrary sway,
Shall be no more endured but ends this day.
Rulers of abler conduct we will choose,
And more indulgent to a trembling Muse;
Women for ends of government more fit,
Women shall rule the boxes and the pit,
Give laws to love and influence to wit.
Find me one man of sense in all your roll,
Whom some one woman has not made a fool.
Even business that intolerable load
Under which man does groan and yet is proud,
Much better they can manage would they please,
'Tis not their want of wit, but love of ease.
For, spite of art, more wit in them appears,
Though we boast ours, and they dissemble theirs.
Wit once was ours, and shot up for a while,
Set shallow in a hot and barren soil;
But when transplanted to a richer ground
Has in their Eden its perfection found.

Title. Mr. Duke] Richard Duke (1659?–1711), minor poet 4 *tinkling chime*] it was an old custom when bees swarmed to try to concentrate them by beating on a brass or copper pan 27 *Set*] planted

And 'tis but just they should our wit invade,
Whilst we set up their painting, patching trade;
As for our courage, to our shame 'tis known,
As they can raise it, they can pull it down.
At their own weapons they our bullies awe,
Faith, let them make an antisalic law,
Prescribe to all mankind, as well as plays,
And wear the breeches, as they wear the bays.

31 *patching*] the custom of wearing patches on the face had spread from the women to the beaux 35 *make an antisalic law*] i.e. reverse the Salic law, which excluded female succession to a throne 37 *bays*] the wreath or garland of bay laurel traditionally worn by celebrated poets. If the reference is to dramatists, the only obvious candidate is Mrs. Aphra Behn, who by 1680 had had eleven of her plays produced. Towards the end of the century several other women were writing for the stage.

DRAMATIS PERSONAE

LUCIUS JUNIUS BRUTUS	*Mr. Betterton*
TITUS 〈sons of Brutus〉	*Mr. Smith*
TIBERIUS 〈sons of Brutus〉	*Mr. Williams*
COLLATINUS 〈nephew of Tarquin〉	*Mr. Wiltshire*
VALERIUS	*Mr. Gillow*
HORATIUS	*Mr. Norris*
AQUILIUS	
VITELLIUS	
JUNIUS	
FECIALIAN PRIESTS	*Mr. Percival*, *Mr. Freeman*
VINDITIUS	*Mr. Nokes*
FABRITIUS	*Mr. Jeron*
CITIZENS, etc.	

WOMEN

SEMPRONIA	*Lady Slingsby*
LUCRECE 〈wife of Collatinus〉	*Mrs. Betterton*
TERAMINTA	*Mrs. Barry*

Scene: Rome

〈Characters not listed. *Men*: FLAMINIAS, LARTIUS, LUCRETIUS (Lucrece's father), MUTIUS, HERMINIUS, TREBONIUS, SERVILLIUS, MINUTIUS, POMPONIUS. *Women*: AQUILIA, VITELLIA.〉

Lucius Junius Brutus;

Father of his Country

ACT I SCENE I

Enter Titus, Teraminta.

Tit. O Teraminta, why this face of tears?
Since first I saw thee, till this happy day,
Thus hast thou passed thy melancholy hours,
Even in the Court retired; stretched on a bed
In some dark room, with all the curtains drawn;
Or in some garden o'er a flow'ry bank
Melting thy sorrows in the murmuring stream;
Or in some pathless wilderness a-musing,
Plucking the mossy bark of some old tree,
Or poring, like a sybil, on the leaves:
What, now the priest should join us! Oh, the gods!
What can you proffer me in vast exchange
For this ensuing night? Not all the days
Of crowning kings, of conquering generals,
Not all the expectation of hereafter,
With what bright fame can give in th'other world
Should purchase thee this night one minute from me.
Ter. Oh, Titus! if since first I saw the light,
Since I began to think on my misfortunes,
And take a prospect of my certain woes,
If my sad soul has entertained a hope
Of pleasure here, or harboured any joy,
But what the presence of my Titus gave me;
Add, add, you cruel gods, to what I bear,
And break my heart before him.

Tit. Break first th'eternal chain; for when thou'rt gone
The world to me is chaos. Yes, Teraminta,
So close the everlasting Sisters wove us,
Whene'er we part, the strings of both must crack:
Once more I do entreat thee give the grave
Thy sadness; let me press thee in my arms,
My fairest bride, my only lightness here,
Tune of my heart, and charmer of my eyes.
Nay, thou shalt learn the ecstasy from me,
I'll make thee smile with my extravagant passion,
Drive thy pale fears away; and e'er the morn
I swear, O Teraminta, O my love,
Cold as thou art, I'll warm thee into blushes.
Ter. Oh, Titus! may I, ought I to believe you?
Remember, sir, I am the blood of Tarquin;
The basest too.
Tit. Thou art the blood of heaven,
The kindest influence of the teeming stars;
No seed of Tarquin; no, 'tis forged t'abuse thee:
A god thy father was, a goddess was his wife;
The wood-nymphs found thee on a bed of roses,
Lapped in the sweets and beauties of the Spring,
Diana fostered thee with nectar dews,
Thus tender, blooming, chaste, she gave thee me
To build a temple sacred to her name,
Which I will do, and wed thee there again.
Ter. Swear then, my Titus, swear you'll ne'er upbraid me,
Swear that your love shall last like mine for ever;
No turn of state or empire, no misfortune,
Shall e'er estrange you from me. Swear, I say;
That, if you should prove false, I may at least
Have something still to answer to my fate;
Swear, swear, my lord, that you will never hate me,
But to your death still cherish in your bosom
The poor, the fond, the wretched Teraminta.
Tit. Till death! nay, after death if possible.
Dissolve me still with questions of this nature,
While I return my answer all in oaths:

26 th'eternal chain] the great chain of being, the divine principle of order and harmony. Cf. Drayton, *Pastorals*, Eclogue vii. 168–9: '. . . the everlasting chain/Which together all things tied.' 28 Sisters] the three Fates 41 basest] Teraminta was illegitimate (cf. 'Tarquin's bastard', I. 208). 61 Dissolve] melt, soften

More than thou canst demand I swear to do.
This night, this night shall tell thee how I love thee:
When words are at a loss, and the mute soul
Pours out herself in sighs and gasping joys,
Life grasps, the pangs of bliss, and murmuring pleasures,
Thou shalt confess all language then is vile,
And yet believe me most without my vowing.

Enter Brutus *with a* Flamen.

But see, my father with a Flamen here!
The Court comes on; let's slip the busy crowd,
And steal into the eternal knot of love. [*Exeunt.*

Brut. Did Sextus, say'st thou, lie at Collatia,
At Collatine's house last night?
Fla. My lord, he did,
Where he, with Collatine and many others,
Had been some nights before.
Brut. Ha! if before,
Why did he come again?
Fla. Because, as rumour spreads,
He fell most passionately in love with her.
Brut. What then?
Fla. Why, is't not strange?
Brut. Is she not handsome?
Fla. Oh, very handsome.
Brut. Then 'tis not strange at all.
What, for a king's son to love another man's wife!
Why, sir, I've known the king has done the same.
Faith, I myself, who am not used to caper,
Have sometimes had th'unlawful itch upon me:
Nay, prithee priest, come thou and help the number.
Ha! my old boy; the company is not scandalous:
Let's go to Hell together. Confess the truth:
Did'st thou ne'er steal from the gods an hour or so
To mumble a new prayer—
With a young fleshy whore in a bawdy corner? ha!
Fla. My lord, your servant. [*Aside.*] Is this the fool? the madman?

67 grasps] embraces (noun) Life grasps, the] *Q. 1*; Life grasps the . . . *works*
70 Flamen] priest 73 Sextus] Tarquin's son, who raped Lucrece. 78 her] i.e. Collatinus' wife, Lucrece 82 the king] perhaps an allusion to Charles II

Let him be what he will, he spoke the truth:
If other fools be thus, they're dangerous fellows. [*Exit.*

Brut. [*Solus.*] Occasion seems in view; something there is
In Tarquin's last abode at Collatine's:
Late entertained, and early gone this morning?
The matron ruffled, wet, and dropping tears,
As if she had lost her wealth in some black storm!
As in the body, on some great surprise,
The heart still calls from the discoloured face,
From every part the life and spirits down,
So Lucrece comes to Rome, and summons all her blood.
Lucrece is fair; but chaste as the fanned snow
Twice bolted o'er by the bleak northern blasts:
So lies this starry cold and frozen beauty,
Still watched and guarded by her waking virtue,
A pattern, though I fear inimitable,
For all succeeding wives. O Brutus! Brutus!
When will the tedious gods permit thy soul
To walk abroad in her own majesty,
And throw this vizor of thy madness from thee?
Oh, what but infinite spirit, propped by fate,
For empire's weight to turn on, could endure
As thou hast done, the labours of an age,
All follies, scoffs, reproaches, pities, scorns,
Indignities almost to blows sustained,
For twenty pressing years, and by a Roman?
To act deformity in thousand shapes,
To please the greater monster of the two,
That cries, 'Bring forth the beast, and let him tumble':
With all variety of aping madness,
To bray, and bear more than the ass's burden;
Sometimes to hoot and scream, like midnight owls,
Then screw my limbs like a distorted satyr,
The world's grimace, th'eternal laughing-stock,
Of town and Court, the block, the jest of Rome;
Yet all the while not to my dearest friend,
To my own children, nor my bosom wife,
Disclose the weighty secret of my soul.
O Rome, O mother, be thou th'impartial judge
If this be virtue, which yet wants a name,

94 Occasion . . . view] An opportunity seems to be at hand 104 bolted] sifted 126 block] blockhead

Which never any age could parallel,
And worthy of the foremost of thy sons.

Enter Horatius, Mutius.

Mut. Horatius, heard'st thou where Sextus was last night?
Hor. Yes, at Collatia: 'tis the buzz of Rome;
'Tis more than guessed that there has been foul play,
Else, why should Lucrece come in this sad manner
To old Lucretius' house, and summon thither
Her father, husband, each distinct relation?

Enter Fabritius, *with courtiers.*

Mut. Scatter it through the city, raise the people,
And find Valerius out. Away, Horatius. [*Exeunt severally.*

Fabr. Prithee, let's talk no more on't. Look, here's Lord Brutus. Come, come, we'll divert ourselves; for 'tis but just that we who sit at the helm should now and then unruffle our state affairs with the impertinence of a fool. Prithee, Brutus, what's a clock?

Brut. Clotho, Lachesis, Atropos; the Fates are three: let them but strike, and I'll lead you a dance, my masters.

Fab. But hark you, Brutus, dost thou hear the news of Lucrece?

Brut. Yes, yes; and I heard of the wager that was laid among you, among you whoring lords at the Siege of Ardea. Ha, boy! about your handsome wives:

Fab. Well; and how, and how?

Brut. How you bounced from the board, took horse, and rode like madmen, to find the gentle Lucrece at Collatia. But how found her? Why, working with her maids at midnight. Was not this monstrous, and quite out of the fashion? Fine stuff indeed, for a lady of honour, when her husband was out of the way, to sit weaving, and pinking, and pricking of arras? Now, by this light, my lord, your wife made better use of her pincushion.

Fab. My wife, my lord? by Mars, my wife!

Brut. Why should she not, when all the royal nurses do the same? What? What, my Lord, did you not find 'em at it, when you came from Collatia to Rome? Lartius, your wife, and yours, Flaminius, with Tullia's boys, turning the crystals up, dashing the windows, and the Fates defying? Now, by the gods, I think 'twas civil in you, discreetly done, sirs, not to interrupt 'em. But for your wife, Fabritius, I'll be sworn for her, she would not keep 'em company.

139 distinct] individual 150 Ardea] a town in Latium 157 pinking] ornamenting cloth, leather, etc., by cutting or punching eyelet-holes 162 Tullia's boys] the sons of Tullia, Tarquin's wife 163 crystals] (wine) glasses

Fab. No, marry, would she not; she hates debauches. How have I heard her rail at Terentia, and tell her next her heart upon the qualms, that drinking wine so late and tippling spirits would be the death of her?

Brut. Hark you, gentlemen, if you would but be secret now, I could unfold such a business; my life on't, a very plot upon the Court.

Fab. Out with it; we swear secrecy.

Brut. Why, thus then. Tomorrow Tullia goes to the camp; and I being Master of the Household, have command to sweep the Court of all its furniture, and send it packing to the wars: panders, sycophants, upstart rogues; fine knaves and surly rascals; flatterers, easy, supple, cringing, passing, smiling villains: all, all to the wars.

Fab. By Mars, I do not like this plot.

Brut. Why, is it not a plot, a plot upon yourselves, your persons, families, and your relations; even to your wives, mothers, sisters, all your kindred? For whores too are included, setters too, and whore-procurers; bag and baggage; all, all to the wars. All hence, all rubbish, lumber out; and not a bawd be left behind to put you in hope of hatching whores hereafter.

Fab. Hark, Lartius, he'll run from fooling to direct madness, and beat our brains out. The Devil take the hindmost: your servant, sweet Brutus; noble, honourable Brutus.

[*Exeunt* ⟨Fabritius *and courtiers.*⟩

Enter Titus.

Tit. 'Tis done, 'tis done, auspicious heaven has joined us,
And I this night shall hold her in my arms.
Oh, sir!
Brut. Oh, sir! that exclamation was too high:
Such raptures ill become the troubled times;
No more of 'em. And by the way, my Titus,
Renounce your Teraminta.
Tit. Ha, my lord!
Brut. How now, my boy?
Tit. Your counsel comes too late, sir.
Brut. Your reply, sir,
Comes too ill-mannered, pert and saucy, sir.
Tit. Sir, I am married.
Brut. What, without my knowledge?
Tit. My lord, I ask your pardon; but that Hymen—

175 furniture] i.e. human furniture, occupants 177 passing] surpassing 181 setters] pimps. (In cock-fighting the 'setter' placed the cocks together.)

Brut. Thou liest: that honourable god would scorn it.
Some bawdy flamen shuffled you together;
Priapus locked you, while the bacchanals
Sung your detested epithalamium.
Which of thy blood were the cursed witnesses?
Who would be there at such polluted rites
But goats, baboons, some chatt'ring old silenus,
Or satyrs grinning at your slimy joys?

Tit. Oh, all the gods! my lord, your son is married
To Tarquin's—

Brut. Bastard.

Tit. No, his daughter.

Brut. No matter:
To any of his blood; if it be his,
There is such natural contagion in it,
Such a congenial devil in his spirit,
Name, lineage, stock, that but to own a part
Of his relation is to profess thyself
Sworn slave of Hell, and bondman to the Furies.
Thou art not married.

Tit. Oh, is this possible?
This change that I behold? no part of him
The same; nor eyes, nor mien, nor voice, nor gesture!

Brut. Oh, that the gods would give my arm the vigour
To shake this soft, effeminate, lazy soul
Forth from thy bosom. No, degenerate boy,
Brutus is not the same; the gods have waked him
From dead stupidity to be a scourge,
A living torment to thy disobedience.
Look on my face, view my eyes flame, and tell me
If aught thou seest but glory and revenge,
A blood-shot anger, and a burst of fury,
When I but think of Tarquin. Damn the monster;
Fetch him, you judges of th'eternal deep,
Arraign him, chain him, plunge him in double fires:
If after this thou seest a tenderness,
A woman's tear come o'er my resolution,
Think, Titus; think, my son, 'tis nature's fault,
Not Roman Brutus, but a father now.

Tit. Oh, let me fall low as the earth permits me,

201 Priapus] the god of procreation locked] interlocked 205 silenus] satyr

And thank the gods for this most happy change,
That you are now, although to my confusion,
That awful, god-like, and commanding Brutus
Which I so oft have wished you, which sometimes
I thought imperfectly you were, or might be,
When I have taken unawares your soul
At a broad glance, and forced her to retire.
Ah, my dear lord, you need not add new threats,
New marks of anger to complete my ruin,
Your Titus has enough to break his heart
When he remembers that you durst not trust him:
Yes, yes, my lord, I have a thousand frailties;
The mould you cast me in, the breath, the blood,
And spirit which you gave me are unlike
The god-like author; yet you gave 'em, sir:
And sure, if you had pleased to honour me,
T'immortalize my name to after ages
By imparting your high cares, I should have found
At least so much hereditary virtue
As not to have divulged them.

Brut. Rise, my son;
Be satisfied thou art the first that know'st me:
A thousand accidents and fated causes
Rush against every bulwark I can raise,
And half unhinge my soul. For now's the time,
To shake the building of the tyrant down.
As from night's womb the glorious day breaks forth,
And seems to kindle from the setting stars:
So from the blackness of young Tarquin's crime
And furnace of his lust, the virtuous soul
Of Junius Brutus catches bright occasion.
I see the pillars of his kingdom totter;
The rape of Lucrece is the midnight lantern
That lights my genius down to the foundation.
Leave me to work, my Titus, oh, my son;
For from this spark a lightning shall arise
That must e'er night purge all the Roman air:
And then the thunder of his ruin follows.
No more; but haste thee to Lucretius:
I hear the multitude, and must among them.
Away, my son.

Tit. Bound, and obedient ever. [*Exit.*

Enter Vinditius *with plebeians.*

1. *Cit.* Jupiter defend us! I think the firmament is all on a light fire. Now, neighbour, as you were saying, as to the cause of lightning and thunder, and for the nature of prodigies—

Vin. What! a tailor, and talk of lightning and thunder? Why, thou walking shred, thou moving bottom, thou upright needle, thou shaving edging skirt, thou flip-flap of a man, thou vaulting flea, thou nit, thou nothing, dost thou talk of prodigies when I am by? *O tempora*, *O mores!* But, neighbours, as I was saying, what think you of Valerius?

All. Valerius, Valerius!

Vin. I know you are piping hot for sedition; you all gape for rebellion; but what's the near? For look you, sirs, we the people in the body politic are but the guts of government; therefore we may rumble and grumble, and croak our hearts out, if we have never a head. Why, how shall we be nourished? Therefore, I say, let us get us a head, a head my masters.

Brut. Protect me, Jove, and guard me from the phantom!
Can this so horrid apparition be;
Or is it but the making of my fancy?
Vin. Ha, Brutus! what, where is this apparition?
1. *Cit.* This is the tribune of the Celeres
A notable head-piece, and the King's jester.
Brut. By Jove, a prodigy!
Vin. Nay, like enough; the gods are very angry:
I know they are, they told me so themselves;
For look you, neighbours, I for my own part
Have seen today fourscore and nineteen prodigies and a half.
Brut. But this is a whole one. Oh, most horrible!
Look, Vinditius, yonder, o'er that part
O' the Capitol, just, just there man, yonder, look.
Vin. Ha, my lord!
Brut. I always took thee for a quick-sighted fellow:
What, art thou blind? Why, yonder, all o'fire,
It vomits lightning; 'tis a monstrous dragon.
Vin. Oh, I see it: O Jupiter and Juno! By the gods I see it.
Oh neighbours, look, look, look, on his filthy nostrils!
'T has eyes like flaming saucers, and a belly
Like a burning cauldron, with such a swingeing tail!
And oh, a thing, a thing that's all o'fire!

279 bottom] a clew on which to wind thread; also a skein or ball of thread (*O.E.D.*, 15)
285 what's the near?] what nearer are you to your purpose? (*O.E.D.* 'near', adv.[1] 5b)
293 tribune of the Celeres] captain of the royal bodyguard
294 head-piece] intellect
310 swingeing] huge

Brut. Ha! now it fronts us with a head that's marked
With Tarquin's name; and see, 'tis thunder-struck!
Look yonder how it whizzes through the air!
The gods have struck it down; 'tis gone, 'tis vanished.
Oh, neighbours, what, what should this portent mean?
Vin. Mean! Why, it's plain; did we not see the mark
Upon the beast? Tarquin's the dragon, neighbours,
Tarquin's the dragon, and the gods shall swinge him.
All. A dragon! a Tarquin!
1. *Cit*. For my part, I saw nothing.
Vin. How, rogue? Why, this is prodigy on prodigy!
Down with him, knock him down; what not see the dragon?
1. *Cit*. Mercy! I did, I did; a huge monstrous dragon.
Brut. So; not a word of this, my masters, not for your lives:
Meet me anon at the Forum; but not a word.
Vinditius, tell 'em the Tribune of the Celeres
Intends this night to give them an oration.
[*Exeunt* Vinditius *and rabble*.

Enter Lucrece, Valerius, Lucretius, Mutius, Herminius, Horatius, Titus, Tiberius, Collatinus.

Brut. Ha! in the open air? so near, you gods?
So ripe your judgements? Nay, then let 'em break
And burst the hearts of those that have deserved them.
Lucrece. O Collatine! art thou come?
Alas, my husband! O my love! my lord!
Coll. O Lucrece! see, I have obeyed thy summons:
I have thee in my arms; but speak, my fair,
Say, is all well?
Lucrece. Away, and do not touch me:
Stand near, but touch me not. My father too!
Lucretius, art thou here?
Luc. Thou seest I am.
Haste, and relate thy lamentable story.
Lucrece. If there be gods, oh, will they not revenge me?
Draw near, my lord; for sure you have a share
In these strange woes. Ah, sir, what have you done?
Why did you bring that monster of mankind
The other night, to curse Collatia's walls?
Why did you blast me with that horrid visage,
And blot my honour with the blood of Tarquin?

319 swinge] chastise

Coll. Oh, all the gods!
Lucrece. Alas, they are far off;
Or sure they would have helped the wretched Lucrece.
Hear then, and tell it to the wond'ring world:
Last night the lustful bloody Sextus came
Late and benighted to Collatia,
Intending, as he said, for Rome next morning;
But in the dead of night, just when soft sleep
Had sealed my eyes, and quite becalmed my soul,
Methought a horrid voice thus thundered in my ear,
'Lucrece, thou'rt mine, arise and meet my arms.'
When straight I waked, and found young Tarquin by me;
His robe unbuttoned, red and sparkling eyes,
The flushing blood that mounted in his face,
The trembling eagerness that quite devoured him,
With only one grim slave that held a taper,
At that dead stillness of the murd'ring night
Sufficiently declared his horrid purpose.
Coll. Oh, Lucrece, oh!
Lucrece. How is it possible to speak the passion
The fright, the throes, and labour of my soul?
Ah, Collatine! half dead I turned away
To hide my shame, my anger, and my blushes,
While he at first with a dissembled mildness
Attempted on my honour—
But hastily repulsed, and with disdain,
He drew his sword, and locking his left hand
Fast in my hair, he held it to my breast,
Protesting by the gods, the fiends and furies,
If I refused him he would give me death,
And swear he found me with that swarthy slave
Whom he would leave there murdered by my side.
Brut. Villain! Damned villain!
Lucrece. Ah Collatine! Oh father! Junius Brutus!
All that are kin to this dishonoured blood,
How will you view me now? Ah, how forgive me?
Yet think not, Collatine, with my last tears,
With these last sighs, these dying groans, I beg you,
I do conjure my love, my lord, my husband,
Oh, think me not consenting once in thought,
Though he in act possessed his furious pleasure:
For, oh, the name, the name of an adult'ress!—

But here I faint; oh, help me:
Imagine me, my lord, but what I was,
And what I shortly shall be—cold and dead.
Coll. Oh, you avenging gods! Lucrece, my love,
I swear I do not think thy soul consenting,
And therefore I forgive thee.
Lucrece. Ah, my lord!
Were I to live, how should I answer this?
All that I ask you now is to revenge me;
Revenge me, father, husband, oh revenge me.
Revenge me, Brutus; you his sons, revenge me;
Herminius, Mutius, thou Horatius too,
And thou Valerius—all, revenge me all:
Revenge the honour of the ravished Lucrece.
All. We will revenge thee.
Lucrece. I thank you all; I thank you, noble Romans:
And that my life, though well I know you wish it,
May not hereafter ever give example
To any that, like me, shall be dishonoured,
To live beneath so loathed an infamy,
Thus I for ever lose it, thus set free
My soul, my life, and honour all together: ⟨*Stabs herself.*⟩
Revenge me; oh, revenge, revenge, revenge! [*Dies.*
Lucretius. Struck to the heart, already motionless.
Coll. Oh, give me way t'embalm her with my tears;
For who has that propriety of sorrow?
Who dares to claim an equal share with me?
Brut. That, sir, dare I; and every Roman here.
What now? At your laments? Your puling sighs?
And woman's drops? Shall these quit scores for blood?
For chastity, for Rome, and violated honour?
Now, by the gods, my soul disdains your tears:
There's not a common harlot in the shambles
But for a drachma shall out-weep you all.
Advance the body nearer. See, my lords,
Behold, you dazzled Romans, from the wound
Of this dead beauty, thus I draw the dagger,
All stained and reeking with her sacred blood.
Thus to my lips I put the hallowed blade,
To yours Lucretius, Collatinus yours,

411 propriety] ownership 418 shambles] brothel

To yours Herminius, Mutius, and Horatius,
And yours, Valerius: kiss the poniard round.
Now join your hands with mine, and swear, swear all,
By this chaste blood, chaste ere the royal villain
Mixed his foul spirits with the spotless mass,
Swear, and let all the gods be witnesses,
That you with me will drive proud Tarquin out,
His wife, th'imperial fury, and her sons,
With all the race; drive 'em with sword and fire
To the world's limits, profligate accurst:
Swear from this time never to suffer them,
Nor any other king to reign in Rome.

All. We swear.

Brut. Well have you sworn; and oh, methinks I see
The hovering spirit of the ravished matron
Look down; she bows her airy head to bless you,
And crown th'auspicious sacrament with smiles.
Thus with her body high exposed to view,
March to the Forum with this pomp of death.
Oh, Lucrece! Oh!
When to the clouds thy pile of fame is raised
While Rome is free thy memory shall be praised:
Senate and people, wives and virgins all,
Shall once a year before thy statue fall;
Cursing the Tarquins, they thy fate shall mourn:
But, when the thoughts of liberty return,
Shall bless the happy hour when thou wert born. [*Exeunt.*

ACT II SCENE I

The Forum

Enter Tiberius, Fabritius, Lartius, Flaminius.

Tib. Fabritius, Lartius, and Flaminius,
As you are Romans, and obliged by Tarquin,
I dare confide in you; I say again,
Though I could not refuse the oath he gave us,
I disapprove my father's undertaking:

I'm loyal to the last, and so will stand.
I am in haste, and must to Tullia.

Fab. Leave me, my lord, to deal with the multitude.

Tib. Remember this in short. A king is one
To whom you may complain when you are wronged;
The throne lies open in your way for justice:
You may be angry, and may be forgiven.
There's room for favour, and for benefit,
Where friends and enemies may come together,
Have present hearing, present composition,
Without recourse to the litigious laws;
Laws that are cruel, deaf, inexorable,
That cast the vile and noble altogether,
Where, if you should exceed the bounds of order,
There is no pardon. Oh, 'tis dangerous,
To have all actions judged by rigorous law.
What, to depend on innocence alone,
Among so many accidents and errors
That wait on human life? Consider it;
Stand fast, be loyal: I must to the Queen. [*Exit*.

Fab. A pretty speech, by Mercury! Look you, Lartius, when the words lie like a low wrestler, round, close and short, squat, pat and pithy.

Lar. But what should we do here, Fabritius? The multitude will tear us in pieces.

Fab. 'Tis true, Lartius, the multitude is a mad thing; a strange blunder-headed monster, and very unruly. But eloquence is such a thing, a fine, moving, florid, pathetical speech! But see, the Hydra comes: let me alone; fear not, I say, fear not.

Enter Vinditius, *with plebeians.*

Vin. Come, neighbours, rank yourselves, plant yourselves, set yourselves in order; the gods are very angry, I'll say that for 'em. Pough, pough, I begin to sweat already; and they'll find us work enough today, I'll tell you that. And to say truth, I never liked Tarquin, before I saw the mark in his forehead: for look you, sirs, I am a true commonwealth's man, and do not naturally love kings, though they be good; for why should any one man have more power than the people? Is he bigger, or wiser than the people? Has he more guts, or more brains than the people? What can he do for the people that the people can't do for themselves? Can he make

32 Hydra] the fabulous many-headed monster was often equated with 'the many-headed multitude' 37–8 mark in his forehead] i.e. the mark made by Tarquin's crown. (Horns, the mark of a cuckold, do not seem relevant here.)

corn grow in a famine? can he give us rain in drought? or make our pots boil, though the Devil piss in the fire?

1. *Cit.* For my part, I hate all courtiers; and I think I have reason for't.

Vin. Thou reason! Well, tailor, and what's thy reason?

1. *Cit.* Why, sir, there was a crew of 'em t'other night got drunk, broke my windows, and handled my wife.

Vin. How, neighbours? Nay, now the fellow has reason, look you: his wife handled! Why, this is a matter of moment.

1. *Cit.* Nay, I know there were some of the princes, for I heard Sextus his name.

Vin. Ay, ay, the King's sons, my life for't; some of the King's sons. Well, these roaring lords never do any good among us citizens: they are ever breaking the peace, running in our debts, and swingeing our wives.

Fab. How long at length, thou many-headed monster,
You bulls and bears, you roaring beasts and bandogs,
Porters and cobblers, tinkers, tailors, all
You rascally sons of whores in a civil government,
How long, I say, dare you abuse our patience?
Does not the thought of rods and axes fright you?
Does not our presence, ha! these eyes, these faces
Strike you with trembling? Ha!

Vin. Why, what have we here? A very spitfire, the crack-fart of the Court. Hold, let me see him nearer. Yes, neighbours, this is one of 'em, one of your roaring squires that poke us in the night, beat the watch, and deflower our wives. I know him, neighbours, for all his bouncing and his swearing; this is a Court-pimp, a bawd, one of Tarquin's bawds.

Fab. Peace, thou obstreperous rascal; I am a man of honour. One of the equestrian order; my name Fabritius.

Vin. Fabritius! Your servant, Fabritius. Down with him. Neighbours, an upstart rogue; this is he that was the Queen's coachman, and drove the chariot over her father's body. Down with him, down with 'em all; bawds, pimps, panders.

Fab. O mercy, mercy, mercy!

Vin. Hold, neighbours, hold: as we are great, let us be just. You, sirrah; you of the equestrian order, knight? Now, by Jove, he has the look of a pimp; I find we can't save him. Rise, Sir Knight; and tell me before the

43–4 make our pots boil, etc.] cf. L'Estrange, *The Visions of Quevedo, made English* (1667): 'Money will make the pot boil, though the Devil piss in the fire'. 55 swingeing] copulating with 57 bandogs] large dogs kept tied up. 61 rods and axes] the *fasces* carried by the lictors before Roman magistrates 72 the Queen's coachman] When Tullia's father, Servius Tullius, King of Rome, was assassinated in 534 B.C., she had her chariot driven over his mangled body as it lay in the street.

majesty of the people, what have you to say that you should not have your neck broke down the Tarpeian rock, your body burnt, and your ashes thrown in the Tiber?

Fab. Oh! oh! oh!

Vin. A courtier! a sheep biter. Leave off your blubbering, and confess.

Fab. Oh! I will confess, I will confess.

Vin. Answer me then. Was not you once the Queen's coachman?

Fab. I was, I was.

Vin. Did you not drive her chariot over the body of her father, the dead King Tull[i]us?

Fab. I did, I did: though it went against my conscience.

Vin. So much the worse. Have you not since abused the good people by seducing the citizens' wives to Court for the King's sons? Have you not by your bawd's tricks been the occasion of their making assault on the bodies of many a virtuous-disposed gentlewoman?

Fab. I have, I have.

Vin. Have you not wickedly held the door while the daughters of the wise citizens have had their vessels broken up?

Fab. Oh, I confess, many a time and often.

Vin. For all which services to your princes, and so highly deserving of the commonwealth, you have received the honour of knighthood?

Fab. Mercy, mercy: I confess it all.

Vin. Hitherto I have helped you to spell; now pray put together for yourself, and confess the whole matter in three words.

Fab. I was at first the son of a carman, came to the honour of being Tullia's coachman, have been a pimp, and remain a knight at the mercy of the people.

Vin. Well, I am moved, my bowels are stirred: take 'em away, and let 'em only be hanged. Away with 'em, away with 'em!

Fab. Oh mercy! help, help!

Vin. Hang 'em, rogues, pimps; hang 'em, I say. Why, look you, neighbours, this is law, right, and justice: this is the people's law; and I think that's better than the arbitrary power of kings. Why, here was trial, condemnation, and execution, without more ado. Hark, hark; what have we here? Look, look, the Tribune of the Celeres! Bring forth the pulpit, the pulpit.

80 Tarpeian rock] the precipitous rock in Rome, about eighty feet high, from which condemned criminals were thrown to their deaths 83 a sheep biter] a sneaking fellow 101 spell] speak, talk

Trumpets sound a dead march.

Enter Brutus, Valerius, Herminius, Mutius, Horatius,
Lucretius, Collatinus, Tiberius, Titus,
with the body of Lucrece.

Val. I charge you fathers, nobles, Romans, friends,
Magistrates, all you people, hear Valerius.
This day, O Romans, is a day of wonders,
The villainies of Tarquin are complete:
To lay whose vices open to your view,
To give you reasons for his banishment,
With the expulsion of his wicked race,
The gods have chosen Lucius Junius Brutus,
The stupid, senseless, and illiterate Brutus,
Their orator in this prodigious cause:
Let him ascend, and silence be proclaimed.
Vin. A Brutus, a Brutus, a Brutus! Silence there;
Silence, I say, silence on pain of death.
Brut. Patricians, people, friends, and Romans all,
Had not th'inspiring gods by wonder brought me
From clouded sense to this full day of reason,
Whence, with a prophet's prospect, I behold
The state of Rome, and danger of the world;
Yet in a cause like this, methinks the weak,
Enervate, stupid Brutus might suffice:
O the eternal gods! bring but the statues
Of Romulus and Numa, plant 'em here
On either hand of this cold Roman wife,
Only to stand and point that public wound;
O Romans, oh, what use would be of tongues!
What orator need speak while they were by?
Would not the majesty of those dumb forms
Inspire your souls, and arm you for the cause?
Would you not curse the author of the murder,
And drive him from the earth with sword and fire?
But where, methinks I hear the people shout,
I hear the cry of Rome, where is the monster?
Bring Tarquin forth, bring the destroyer out,
By whose cursed offspring, lustful bloody Sextus,
This perfect mould of Roman chastity,
This star of spotless and immortal fame,

This pattern for all wives, the Roman Lucrece,
Was foully brought to a disastrous end.
Vin. Oh, neighbours, oh! I buried seven wives without crying,
Nay, I never wept before in all my life.
Brut. O the immortal gods, and thou great stayer
Of falling Rome, if to his own relations
(For Collatinus is a Tarquin too),
If wrongs so great to them, to his own blood,
What then to us, the nobles and the commons?
Not to remember you of his past crimes,
The black ambition of his furious Queen,
Who drove her chariot through the Cyprian street
On such a damned design, as might have turned
The steeds of day, and shocked the starting gods,
Blessed as they are, with an uneasy moment:
Add yet to this, oh! add the horrid slaughter
Of all the princes of the Roman senate,
Invading fundamental right and justice,
Breaking the ancient customs, statutes, laws,
With positive power, and arbitrary lust;
And those affairs which were before dispatched
In public by the fathers, now are forced
To his own palace, there to be determined
As he, and his portentous council please.
But then for you—
Vin. Ay, for the people, come;
And then, my myrmidons, to pot with him.
Brut. I say, if thus the nobles have been wronged,
What tongue can speak the grievance of the people?
Vin. Alas, poor people!
Brut. You that were once a free-born people, famed
In his forefathers' days for wars abroad,
The conquerors of the world. Oh Rome! Oh glory!
What are you now? what has the tyrant made you?
The slaves, the beasts, the asses of the earth;
The soldiers of the gods mechanic labourers,
Drawers of water, taskers, timber-fellers;
Yoked you like bulls, his very jades for luggage,

155 great stayer] i.e. Jupiter Stator (Lat. *stator*: one who rallies, or prevents flight), here thought of as the supporter or stayer of 'falling Rome' 162 drove her chariot] cf. II. i. 72. 170 positive] absolute 186 taskers] piece-workers 187 luggage] i.e. lugging, hauling (heavy goods)

Drove you with scourges down to dig in quarries,
To cleanse his sinks, the scavengers o'th'Court;
While his lewd sons, though not on work so hard,
Employed your daughters and your wives at home.

Vin. Yes, marry, did they.

Brut. O all the gods! what, are you Romans? ha!
If this be true, why have you been so backward?
Oh sluggish souls! Oh fall of former glory!
That would not rouse unless a woman waked you!
Behold she comes, and calls you to revenge her;
Her spirit hovers in the air, and cries
'To arms, to arms; drive, drive the Tarquins out!'
Behold this dagger, taken from her wound,
She bids you fix this trophy on your standard,
This poniard which she stabbed into her heart,
And bear her body in your battle's front:
Or will you stay till Tarquin does return,
To see your wives and children dragged about,
Your houses burnt, the temples all profaned,
The city filled with rapes, adulteries,
The Tiber choked with bodies, all the shores
And neighb'ring rocks besmeared with Roman blood?

Vin. Away, away! let's burn his palace first.

Brut. Hold, hold, my friends. As I have been th'inspirer
Of this most just revenge, so I entreat you,
Oh, worthy Romans, take me with you still:
Drive Tullia out, and all of Tarquin's race;
Expel 'em without damage to their persons,
Though not without reproach. Vinditius, you
I trust in this. So prosper us the gods,
Prosper our cause, prosper the commonwealth,
Guard and defend the liberty of Rome.

Vin. Liberty, liberty, liberty!

All. Liberty! &c.

[*Exeunt*, Vinditius *and others.*

Val. O Brutus, as a god, we all survey thee;
Let then the gratitude we should express
Be lost in admiration. Well we know
Virtue like thine, so fierce, so like the gods
That more than thou presents we could not bear,

189 sinks] cess-pits 213 take me with you] understand what I am saying

Looks with disdain on ceremonious honours;
Therefore accept in short the thanks of Rome.
First with our bodies thus we worship thee,
Thou guardian genius of the commonwealth,
Thou father and redeemer of thy country;
Next we, as friends, with equal arms embrace thee,
That Brutus may remember, though his virtue
Soar to the gods, he is a Roman still.

Brut. And when I am not so, or once in thought
Conspire the bondage of my countrymen,
Strike me, you gods; tear me, O Romans, piecemeal,
And let your Brutus be more loathed than Tarquin.
But now to those affairs that want a view.
Imagine then the fame of what is done
Has reached to Ardea, whence the trembling King,
By guilt and nature quick and apprehensive,
With a bent brow comes post for his revenge
To make examples of the mutineers:
Let him come on. Lucretius, to your care
The charge and custody of Rome is given;
While we, with all the force that can be raised,
Waiving the Tarquins on the common road,
Resolve to join the army at the camp.
What thinks Valerius of the consequence?

Val. As of a lucky hit. There is a number
Of malcontents that wish for such a time:
I think that only speed is necessary
To crown the whole event.

Brut. Go then yourself,
With these assistants, and make instant head
Well as you can, numbers will not be wanting,
To Mars's field: I have but some few orders
To leave with Titus that must be dispersed,
And Brutus shall attend you.

Val. The gods direct you.

[*Exeunt with the body of* Lucrece.

Manent Brutus, Titus.

Brut. Titus, my son?

Tit. My ever honoured lord.

229 genius] attendant spirit
240 Ardea] at this time under siege by Tarquin
247 Waiving] declining combat with, avoiding. Waving *Q.* 1; Waiting *Works*

Brut. I think, my Titus,
Nay, by the gods, I dare protest it to thee,
I love thee more than any of my children.
Tit. How, sir, oh how, my lord, have I deserved it?
Brut. Therefore I love thee more, because, my son,
Thou hast deserved it; for, to speak sincerely,
There's such a sweetness still in all thy manners,
An air so open, and a brow so clear,
A temper so removed from villainy,
With such a manly plainness in thy dealing,
That not to love thee, O my son, my Titus,
Were to be envious of so great a virtue.
Tit. Oh, all the gods, where will this kindness end?
Why do you thus, O my too gracious lord,
Dissolve at once the being that you gave me,
Unless you mean to screw me to performance
Beyond the reach of man?
Ah why, my lord, do you oblige me more
Than my humanity can e'er return?
Brut. Yes, Titus, thou conceiv'st thy father right,
I find our genii know each other well;
And minds, my son, of our uncommon make
When once the mark's in view, never shoot wide,
But in a line come level to the white,
And hit the very heart of our design:
Then, to the shocking purpose. Once again
I say, I swear, I love thee, O my son;
I like thy frame, the fingers of the gods
I see have left their mastery upon thee,
They have been tapering up thy Roman form,
And the majestic prints at large appear:
Yet something they have left for me to finish,
Which thus I press thee to, thus in my arms
I fashion thee, I mould thee to my heart.
What? dost thou kneel? nay, stand up now a Roman,
Shake from thy lids that dew that hangs upon 'em,
And answer to th'austerity of my virtue.
Tit. If I must die, you gods, I am prepared:
Let then my fate suffice; but do not rack me
With something more.

283 white] i.e. target

Brut. Titus, as I remember,
You told me you were married.
Tit. My lord, I did.
Brut. To Teraminta, Tarquin's natural daughter.
Tit. Most true, my lord, to that poor virtuous maid,
Your Titus, sir, your most unhappy son,
Is joined for ever.
Brut. No, Titus, not for ever.
Not but I know the virgin beautiful;
For I did oft converse her, when I seemed
Not to converse at all. Yet more, my son,
I think her chastely good, most sweetly framed,
Without the smallest tincture of her father;
Yet, Titus,—Ha! what, man? what, all in tears?
Art thou so soft, that only saying 'yet'
Has dashed thee thus? Nay, then I'll plunge thee down,
Down to the bottom of this foolish stream
Whose brink thus makes thee tremble. No, my son,
If thou art mine, thou art not Teraminta's;
Or, if thou art, I swear thou must not be,
Thou shalt not be hereafter.
Tit. O the gods!
Forgive me, blood and duty, all respects
Due to a father's name. Not Teraminta's!
Brut. No, by the gods I swear, not Teraminta's.
No, Titus, by th'eternal fates, that hang
I hope auspicious o'er the head of Rome,
I'll grapple with thee on this spot of earth
About this theme till one of us fall dead:
I'll struggle with thee for this point of honour,
And tug with Teraminta for thy heart
As I have done for Rome: Yes, ere we part,
Fixed as you are by wedlock joined and fast,
I'll set you far asunder: nay, on this,
This spotted blade, bathed in the blood of Lucrece,
I'll make thee swear on this thy wedding night
Thou wilt not touch thy wife.
Tit. Conscience, heart and bowels,
Am I a man? have I my flesh about me?
Brut. I know thou hast too much of flesh about thee;
'Tis that, my son, that and thy blood I fear

336 blood] sensual appetite

More than thy spirit, which is truly Roman:
But let the heated channels of thy veins
Boil o'er, I still am obstinate in this:
Thou shalt renounce thy father or thy love.
Either resolve to part with Teraminta,
To send her forth, with Tullia, to her father,
Or shake hands with me, part, and be accursed;
Make me believe thy mother played me false,
And, in my absence, stamped thee with a Tarquin.

Tit. Hold, sir, I do conjure you by the gods,
Wrong not my mother, though you doom me dead;
Curse me not till you hear what I resolve,
Give me a little time to rouse my spirits,
To muster all the tyrant-man about me,
All that is fierce, austere, and greatly cruel
To Titus and his Teraminta's ruin.

Brut. Remember me; look on thy father's suff'rings,
What he has borne for twenty rolling years:
If thou hast nature, worth, or honour in thee,
The contemplation of my cruel labours
Will stir thee up to this new act of glory.
Thou want'st the image of thy father's wrongs:
Oh, take it then, reflected with the warmth
Of all the tenderness that I can give thee:
Perhaps it stood in a wrong light before;
I'll try all ways to place it to advantage.
Learn by my rigorous Roman resolution
To stiffen thy unharassed infant virtue:
I do allow thee fond, young, soft, and gentle,
Trained by the charms of one that is most lovely;
Yet, Titus, this must all be lost, when honour,
When Rome, the world, and the gods come to claim us.
Think then thou hear'st 'em cry, 'Obey thy Father';
If thou art false, or perjured, there he stands
Accountable to us; but swear t'obey;
Implicitly believe him, that, if aught
Be sworn amiss, thou may'st have naught to answer.

Tit. What is it, sir, that you would have me swear,
That I may 'scape your curse, and gain your blessing?

Brut. That thou this night will part with Teraminta.
For once again I swear, if here she stays,

364 unharassed] untroubled, not yet put to the test. (Qy. unharnessed?)

What for the hatred of the multitude.
And my resolves to drive out Tarquin's race,
Her person is not safe.
Tit. Here, take me, sir;
Take me before I cool: I swear this night
That I will part with (oh!) my Teraminta.
Brut. Swear too, and by the soul of ravished Lucrece,
Though on thy bridal night, thou wilt not touch her.
Tit. I swear, even by the soul of her you named,
The ravished Lucrece—O th'immortal gods!
I will not touch her.
Brut. So; I trust thy virtue:
And, by the gods, I thank thee for the conquest.
Once more, with all the blessings I can give thee,
I take thee to my arms; thus on my breast,
The hard and rugged pillow of thy honour,
I wean thee from thy love. Farewell; be fast
To what thou'st sworn, and I am thine for ever. [*Exit.*
Tit. [*Solus*]. To what thou'st sworn! Oh, heaven and earth, what's that?
What have I sworn? to part with Teraminta?
To part with something dearer to my heart
Than my life's drops? What! not this night enjoy her?
Renounce my vows, the rights, the dues of marriage,
Which now I gave her, and the priest was witness,
Blessed with a flood that streamed from both our eyes,
And sealed with sighs, and smiles, and deathless kisses;
Yet after this to swear thou wilt not touch her!
Oh, all the gods, I did forswear myself
In swearing that, and will forswear again:
Not touch her! O thou perjured braggart! where,
Where are thy vaunts, thy protestations now?

Enter Teraminta.

She comes to strike thy staggering duty down:
'Tis fall'n, 'tis gone; Oh, Teraminta, come,
Come to my arms thou only joy of Titus,
Hush to my cares, thou mass of hoarded sweets,
Selected hour of all life's happy moments;
What shall I say to thee?
Ter. Say anything;

378 What for] in consequence of (more usually, 'what with')

For while you speak, methinks a sudden calm,
In spite of all the horror that surrounds me,
Falls upon every frighted faculty
And puts my soul in tune. O Titus, oh!
Methinks my spirit shivers in her house,
Shrugging, as if she longed to be at rest;
With this foresight, to die thus in your arms
Were to prevent a world of following ills.

Tit. What ills, my love? what power has fortune now
But we can brave? 'Tis true, my Teraminta,
The body of the world is out of frame,
The vast distorted limbs are on the rack
And all the cable sinews stretched to bursting,
The blood ferments, and the majestic spirit,
Like Hercules in the envenomed shirt,
Lies in a fever on the horrid pile:
My father, like an Æsculapius
Sent by the gods, comes boldly to the cure.
But how, my love? By violent remedies;
And says that Rome, ere yet she can be well,
Must purge and cast, purge all th'infected humours
Through the whole mass; and vastly, vastly bleed.

Ter. Ah, Titus! I myself but now beheld
Th'expulsion of the Queen, driven from her palace
By the enraged and madding multitude;
And hardly 'scaped myself to find you here.

Tit. Why, yet, my Teraminta, we may smile.
Come then to bed, ere yet the night descends
With her black wings to brood o'er all the world.
Why, what care we? let us enjoy those pleasures
The gods have given; locked in each other's arms
We'll lie for ever thus, and laugh at fate.

Ter. No, no, my lord; there's more than you have named,
There's something at your heart that I must find;
I claim it with the privilege of a wife:
Keep close your joys; but for your griefs, my Titus,
I must not, will not lose my share in them.

418 Shrugging] shivering 420 prevent] evade (*O.E.D.*, 9) 427–8 Hercules . . . pile] In mortal agony caused by a poisoned shirt sent to him by his wife, Hercules erected a funeral pile, and had himself burnt to death. 432 And says that . . .] i.e. And my father says that . . .

Ah, the good gods, what is it stirs you thus?
Speak, speak, my lord, or Teraminta dies.
Oh heavens, he weeps! nay, then upon my knees
I thus conjure you speak, or give me death.

Tit. Rise, Teraminta. Oh, if I should speak
What I have rashly sworn against my love,
I fear that I should give thee death indeed.

Ter. Against your love! No, that's impossible;
I know your god-like truth: nay, should you swear,
Swear to me now that you forswore your love,
I would not credit it. No, no, my lord,
I see, I know, I read it in your eyes,
You love the wretched Teraminta still:
The very manner of your hiding it,
The tears you shed, your backwardness to speak
What you affirm you swore against your love
Tell me, my lord, you love me more than ever.

Tit. By all the gods, I do: Oh, Teraminta,
My heart's discerner, whither wilt thou drive me?
I'll tell thee, then. My father wrought me up,
I know not how, to swear I know not what,
That I would send thee hence with Tullia,
Swear not to touch thee, though my wife; yet, oh,
Hadst thou been by thyself, and but beheld him,
Thou wouldst have thought, such was his majesty,
That the gods lightened from his awful eyes,
And thundered from his tongue.

Ter. No more, my lord:
I do conjure you by all those powers
Which we invoked together at the altar;
And beg you by the love I know you bear me,
To let this passion trouble you no farther;
No, my dear lord, my honoured god-like husband,
I am your wife, and one that seeks your honour:
By heaven, I would have sworn you thus myself.
What, on the shock of empire, on the turn
Of state, and universal change of things,
To lie at home and languish for a woman!
No, Titus, he that makes himself thus vile,
Let him not dare pretend to aught that's princely;
But be, as all the warlike world shall judge him,
The droll of th'people and the scorn of kings.

Enter Horatius.

Hor. My lord, your father gives you thus in charge,
Remember what you swore: the guard is ready;
And I am ordered to conduct your bride,
While you attend your father.
Tit. Oh, Teraminta!
Then we must part.
Ter. We must, we must, my lord:
Therefore be swift, and snatch yourself away,
Or I shall die with ling'ring.
Tit. Oh, a kiss,
Balmy as cordials that recover souls,
Chaste as maids' sighs, and keen as longing mothers.
Preserve thyself; look well to that, my love;
Think on our covenant: when either dies,
The other is no more.
Ter. I do remember;
But have no language left.
Tit. Yet we shall meet,
In spite of sighs we shall, at least in heaven.
Oh, Teraminta, once more to my heart,
Once to my lips, and ever to my soul.
Thus the soft mother, though her babe is dead,
Will have the darling on her bosom laid,
Will talk, and rave, and with the nurses strive,
And fond it still, as if it were alive;
Knows it must go, yet struggles with the crowd,
And shrieks to see 'em wrap it in the shroud.

ACT III SCENE I

Enter Collatinus, Tiberius, Vitellius, Aquilius.

Coll. Th' expulsion of the Tarquins now must stand;
Their camp to be surprised, while Tarquin here
Was scolded from our walls! I blush to think
That such a master in the art of war
Should so forget himself.
Vit. Triumphant Brutus,

510 fond] fondle

Like Jove when followed by a train of gods,
To mingle with the fates and doom the world,
Ascends the brazen steps o'th' Capitol,
With all the humming senate at his heels;
Even in that Capitol which the King built
With the expense of all the royal treasure:
Ingrateful Brutus there in pomp appears,
And sits the purple judge of Tarquin's downfall.
Aquil. But why, my lord, why are not you there too?
Were you not chosen consul by whole Rome?
Why are you not saluted too like him?
Where are your lictors? where your rods and axes?
Or are you but the ape, the mimic god
Of this new thunderer, who appropriates
Those bolts of power which ought to be divided?
Tib. Now, by the gods, I hate his upstart pride,
His rebel thoughts of the imperial race,
His abject soul that stoops to court the vulgar,
His scorn of princes, and his lust to th' people.
Oh, Collatine, have you not eyes to find him?
Why are you raised but to set off his honours?
A taper by the sun, whose sickly beams
Are swallowed in the blaze of his full glory:
He, like a meteor, wades th'abyss of light,
While your faint lustre adds but to the beard
That awes the world. When late through Rome he passed
Fixed on his courser, marked you how he bowed
On this, on that side, to the gazing heads
That paved the streets and all embossed the windows,
That gaped with eagerness to speak, but could not,
So fast their spirits flowed to admiration,
And that to joy; which thus at last broke forth:
'Brutus, god Brutus, Father of thy Country!
Hail genius, hail! Deliverer of lost Rome!
Shield of the commonwealth, and sword of justice!
Hail, scourge of tyrants, lash for lawless kings!
All hail,' they cried, while the long peal of praises
Tormented with a thousand echoing cries,
Ran like the volley of the gods along.
Coll. No more on't; I grow sick with the remembrance.

7 doom] judge 29 meteor] comet

Tib. But when you followed, how did their bellying bodies
That ventured from the casements more than half,
To look at Brutus, nay, that stuck like snails
Upon the walls, and from the houses' tops
Hung down like clust'ring bees upon each other;
How did they all draw back at sight of you
To laze, and loll, and yawn, and rest from rapture!
Are you a man? have you the blood of kings,
And suffer this?
Coll. Ha! is he not his father?
Tib. I grant he is.
Consider this, and rouse yourself at home:
Commend my fire, and rail at your own slackness.
Yet more; remember but your last disgrace,
When you proposed, with reverence to the gods,
A king of sacrifices should be chosen,
And from the consuls. Did he not oppose you,
Fearing, as well he might, your sure election,
Saying it smelt too much of royalty,
And that it might rub up the memory
Of those that loved the tyrant? Nay, yet more;
That if the people chose you for the place,
The name of king would light upon a Tarquin,
Of one that's doubly royal, being descended
From two great princes that were kings of Rome?
Coll. But, after all this, whither wouldst thou drive?
Tib. I would to justice; for the restoration
Of our most lawful prince. Yes, Collatine,
I look upon my father as a traitor;
I find that neither you, nor brave Aquilius,
Nor young Vitellius dare confide in me:
But that you may, and firmly, to the hazard
Of all the world holds precious, once again
I say, I look on Brutus as a traitor,
No more my father, by th'immortal gods.
And to redeem the time, to fix the King
On his imperial throne, some means proposed
That favour of a governed policy,
Where there is strength and life to hope a fortune,

60 A king of sacrifices] 'priest of high rank who performed certain rites formerly devolving on the king' (Loftis)

Not to throw all upon one desperate chance,
I'll on as far as he that laughs at dying.
Coll. Come to my arms: O thou so truly brave
Thou may'st redeem the errors of thy race!
Aquilius and Vitellius, oh embrace him,
And ask his pardon that so long we feared
To trust so rich a virtue. But behold,

Enter Brutus *and* Valerius.

Brutus appears. Young man, be satisfied,
I sound thy politic father to the bottom;
Plotting the assumption of Valerius,
He means to cast me from the consulship:
But now I heard how he cajoled the people
With his known industry, and my remissness,
That still in all our votes, proscriptions, edicts
Against the King, he found I acted faintly,
Still closing every sentence, 'He's a Tarquin.'
Brut. No, my Valerius, till thou art my mate,
Joint master in this great authority,
However calm the face of things appear,
Rome is not safe. By the majestic gods,
I swear, while Collatine sits at the helm,
A universal wrack is to be feared:
I have intelligence of his transactions,
He mingles with the young hot blood of Rome,
Gnaws himself inward, grudges my applause,
Promotes cabals with highest quality,
Such headlong youth as, spurning laws and manners,
Shared in the late debaucheries of Sextus,
And therefore wish the tyrant here again.
As the inverted seasons shock wise men,
And the most fixed philosophy must start
At sultry winters, and at frosty summers,
So at this most unnatural stillness here,
This more than midnight silence through all Rome,
This deadness of discourse, and dreadful calm
Upon so great a change, I more admire
Than if a hundred politic heads were met,
And nodded mutiny to one another;

86 brave] *Q.* 1: brave, *Works* 95 But] only 119 admire] wonder at

More fear, than if a thousand lying libels
Were spread abroad, nay, dropped among the senate.
Val. I have myself employed a busy slave,
His name Vinditius, given him wealth and freedom,
To watch the motions of Vitellius,
And those of the Aquilian family:
Vitellius has already entertained him,
And something thence important may be gathered,
For these of all the youth of quality
Are most inclined to Tarquin and his race
By blood and humour.
Brut. Oh, Valerius!
That boy, observ'st thou? Oh, I fear, my friend,
He is a weed, but rooted in my heart,
And grafted to my stock; if he prove rank,
By Mars, no more but thus, away with him!
I'll tear him from me, though the blood should follow.
—Tiberius.
Tib. My lord?
Brut. Sirrah, no more of that Vitellius;
I warned you too of young Aquilius:
Are my words wind that thus you let 'em pass?
Hast thou forgot thy father?
Tib. No, my lord.
Brut. Thou liest. But though thou 'scape a father's rod,
The consul's axe may reach thee: think on that.
I know thy vanity, and blind ambition;
Thou dost associate with my enemies.
When I refused the consul Collatine
To be the King of Sacrifices, straight,
As if thou hadst been sworn his bosom fool,
He named thee for the office. And since that,
Since I refused thy madness that preferment,
Because I would have none of Brutus' blood
Pretend to be a king, thou hang'st thy head,
Contriv'st to give thy father new displeasure,
As if imperial toil were not enough
To break my heart without thy disobedience.
But by the majesty of Rome I swear,
If after double warning thou despise me,

128 entertained] received, had conversation with
135 rank] corrupt, rebellious
153 Pretend to] have pretensions to, lay claim to

By all the gods, I'll cast thee from my blood,
Doom thee to forks and whips as a barbarian,
And leave thee to the lashes of the lictor.
Tarquinius Collatinus, you are summoned
To meet the senate on the instant time.

Coll. Lead on: my duty is to follow Brutus.

[*Exeunt* Brutus, Valerius, ⟨Collatinus⟩.

Tib. Now, by those gods with which he menaced me,
I here put off all nature; since he turns me
Thus desperate to the world, I do renounce him:
And when we meet again he is my foe.
All blood, all reverence, fondness be forgot:
Like a grown savage on the common wild,
That runs at all, and cares not who begot him,
I'll meet my lion sire, and roar defiance,
As if he ne'er had nursed me in his den.

Enter Vinditius, *with the people, and two* Fecialian Priests *crowned with laurels, two spears in their hands, one bloody and half burnt.*

Vin. Make way there, hey, news from the tyrant! Here come envoys, heralds, ambassadors; whether in the gods' name or in the Devil's I know not, but here they come, your Fecialian priests. Well, good people, I like not these priests; why, what the devil have they to do with state affairs? What side soever they are for, they'll have heaven for their part, I'll warrant you: they'll lug the gods in whether they will or no.

1. *Pri.* Hear, Jupiter, and thou, O Juno, hear;
Hear, O Quirinus; hear us, all you gods
Celestial, terrestrial, and infernal.

2. *Pri.* Be thou, O Rome, our judge: hear, all you people.

Vin. Fine canting rogues! I told you how they'd be hooking the gods in at first dash: why, the gods are their tools and tackle; they work with heaven and hell; and let me tell you, as things go, your priests have a hopeful trade on't.

1. *Pri.* I come ambassador to thee, O Rome,
Sacred and just, the legate of the King.

2. *Pri.* If we demand, or purpose to require,
A stone from Rome that's contrary to justice,

160 forks] forked stake, whipping-post (Latin, *furca*) *s.d.* Fecialian Priests] These were chiefly employed in declaring war and making peace. 181 Quirinus] a surname of Mars, but also of Romulus, who is probably meant here

May we be ever banished from our country,
And never hope to taste this vital air.

Tib. Vinditius, lead the multitude away:
Aquilius, with Vitellius and myself,
Will straight conduct 'em to the Capitol.

Vin. I go, my lord; but have a care of 'em: sly rogues I warrant 'em. Mark that first priest; do you see how he leers? A lying elder; the true cast of a holy juggler. Come, my masters, I would think well of a priest, but that he has a commission to dissemble: a patent hypocrite that takes pay to forge lies by law, and lives by the sins of the people.

[*Exeunt with people.*

Aquil. My life upon't, you may speak out, and freely;
Tiberius is the heart of our design.

1. *Pri.* The gods be praised. Thus then: the King commends
Your generous resolves, longs to be with you,
And those you have engaged, divides his heart
Amongst you; which more clearly will be seen
When you have read these packets. As we go,
I'll spread the bosom of the King before you. [*Exeunt.*

SCENE II

The Senate.

Brut. Patricians, that long stood, and 'scaped the tyrant,
The venerable moulds of your forefathers,
That represent the wisdom of the dead;
And you the conscript chosen for the people,
Engines of power, severest counsellors,
Courts that examine treasons to the head,
All hail. The consul begs th' auspicious gods,
And binds Quirinus by his tutelar vow,
That plenty, peace, and lasting liberty
May be your portion, and the lot of Rome.
Laws, rules, and bounds, prescribed for raging kings,
Like banks and bulwarks for the mother seas,
Though 'tis impossible they should prevent

198 elder] old man (but perhaps with an allusion to elders of the church among Presbyterians)
201 forge lies] *Works*; forge; lies *Q*. 1

A thousand daily wracks and nightly ruins,
Yet help to break those rolling inundations
Which else would overflow and drown the world.
Tarquin, to feed whose fathomless ambition
And ocean luxury, the noblest veins
Of all true Romans were like rivers emptied,
Is cut from Rome, and now he flows full on;
Yet, fathers, ought we much to fear his ebb,
And strictly watch the dams that we have raised.
Why should I go about? The Roman people
All, with one voice, accuse my fellow consul.

Coll. The people may; I hope the nobles will not.
The people! Brutus does indulge the people.

Brut. Consul, in what is right, I will indulge 'em;
And much I think 'tis better so to do,
Than see 'em run in tumults through the streets,
Forming cabals, plotting against the senate,
Shutting their shops and flying from the town,
As if the gods had sent the plague among 'em.
I know too well, you and your royal tribe
Scorn the good people, scorn the late election,
Because we chose these fathers for the people
To fill the place of those whom Tarquin murdered:
And, though you laugh at this, you and your train,
The irreligious harebrained youth of Rome,
The ignorant, the slothful, and the base,
Yet wise men know, 'tis very rarely seen,
That a free people should desire the hurt
Of common liberty. No, Collatine,
For those desires arise from their oppression,
Or from suspicion they are falling to it;
But put the case that those their fears were false,
Ways may be found to rectify their errors;
For grant the people ignorant of themselves,
Yet they are capable of being told,
And will conceive a truth from worthy men.
From you they will not, nor from your adherents,
Rome's infamous and execrable youth,
Foes to religion and the commonwealth,
To virtue, learning, and all sober arts

23 go about] use circumlocution

That bring renown and profit to mankind;
Such as had rather bleed beneath a tyrant
To become dreadful to the populace,
To spread their lusts and dissoluteness round,
Though at the daily hazard of their lives,
Than live at peace in a free government,
Where every man is master of his own,
Sole lord at home, and monarch of his house,
Where rancour and ambition are extinguished,
Where universal peace extends her wings,
As if the Golden Age returned, where all
The people do agree, and live secure,
The nobles and the princes loved and reverenced,
The world in triumph, and the gods adored.

Col. The consul, conscript fathers, says the people,
For divers reasons, grudge the dignity
Which I possessed by general approbation,
I hear their murmurs, and would know of Brutus
What they would have me do, what's their desire.

Brut. Take hence the royal name, resign thy office;
Go as a friend, and of thy own accord,
Lest thou be forced to what may seem thy will.
The city renders thee what is thy own
With vast increase, so thou resolve to go;
For till the name, the race and family
Of Tarquin be removed, Rome is not free.

Col. Brutus, I yield my office to Valerius,
Hoping, when Rome has tried my faith by exile,
She will recall me. So the gods preserve you. [*Exit.*

Brut. Welcome Publicola, true son of Rome;
On such a pilot in the roughest storm
She may securely sleep and rest her cares.

Enter Tiberius, Aquilius, Vitellius, *and the priests.*

1. *Pri.* Hear Jupiter, Quirinus, all you gods,
Thou father, judge commissioned for the message,
Pater Patratus for the embassy,
And sacred oaths which I must swear for truth,
Dost thou commission me to seal the peace,

83 Publicola] a name given to (Publius) Valerius on account of his popularity 88 *Pater Patratus*] the chief Fecialian priest deputed to negotiate war or peace

If peace they choose; or hurl this bloody spear
Half burnt in fire, if they enforce a war?

2. *Pri.* Speak to the senate and the Alban people
The words of Tarquin: this is your commission.

1. *Pri.* The King, to show he has more moderation
Than those that drove him from his lawful empire,
Demands but restitution of his own,
His royal household-stuff, imperial treasure,
His gold, his jewels, and his proper state
To be transported where he now resides.
I swear that this is all the King requires;
Behold his signet set upon the wax.
'Tis sealed and written in these sacred tables.
To this I swear; and as my oath is just,
Sincere and punctual, without all deceit,
May Jupiter and all the gods reward me:
But if I act, or otherwise imagine,
Think, or design, than what I here have sworn,
All you the Alban people being safe,
Safe in your country, temples, sepulchres,
Safe in your laws, and proper household gods;
Let me alone be struck, fall, perish, die,
As now this stone falls from my hand to earth.

Brut. The things you ask being very controversial,
Require some time. Should we deny the tyrant
What was his own, 'twould seem a strange injustice,
Though he had never reigned in Rome; yet, fathers,
If we consent to yield to his demand,
We give him then full power to make a war.
'Tis known to you, the Fecialian priests,
No act of senate after sunset stands;
Therefore your offers being of great moment,
We shall defer your business till the morn:
With whose first dawn we summon all the fathers,
To give th' affair dispatch. So Jove protect,
Guard, and defend the commonwealth of Rome.

[*Exeunt. Manent* Tiberius, Aquilius, Vitellius, *priests.*

Tib. Now to the garden, where I'll bring my brother.
Fear not, my lord; we have the means to work him;
It cannot fail.

93 Alban people] the Romans 99 his proper state] his own possessions 103 tables] tablets 105 punctual] explicit, precise 117 Though] i.e. Even if

1. *Pri.* And you, Vitellius, haste
With good Aquilius, spread the news through Rome,
To all of royal spirit; most to those
Young noble men that used to range with Sextus!
Persuade a restitution of the King,
Give 'em the hint to let him in by night,
And join their forces with th'imperial troops,
For 'tis a shove, a push of fate, must bear it.
For you, the hearts and souls of enterprise,
I need not urge a reason after this:
What good can come of such a government
Where though two consuls, wise and able persons
As are throughout the world, sit at the helm,
A very trifle cannot be resolved;
A trick, a start, a shadow of a business,
That would receive dispatch in half a minute,
Were the authority but rightly placed,
In Rome's most lawful king? But now no more;
The Fecialian garden is the place
Where more of our sworn function will be ready
To help the royal plot. Disperse, and prosper.

SCENE III

The Fecialian garden.

Titus *solus.*

Tit. She's gone; and I shall never see her more:
Gone to the camp, to the harsh trade of war,
Driven from thy bed, just warm within thy breast,
Torn from her harbour by thy father's hand,
Perhaps to starve upon the barren plain,
Thy virgin wife, the very blush of maids,
The softest bosom sweet, and not enjoyed.
O the immortal gods! and as she went,
Howe'er she seemed to bear our parting well,
Methought she mixed her melting with disdain,
A cast of anger through her shining tears:

11 cast] look, expression

So to abuse her hopes, and blast her wishes,
By making her my bride, but not a woman!

Enter Tiberius, Aquilius, Vitellius *and priests, with* Teraminta.

Tib. See where he stands, drowned in his melancholy.
1. *Pri.* Madam, you know the pleasure of the Queen;
And what the royal Tullia did command
I've sworn to execute.
Ter. I am instructed.
Since then my life's at stake, you need not doubt
But I will act with all the force I can:
Let me entreat you leave me here alone
Some minutes, and I'll call you to the conquest.
[*Exeunt* Tiberius, Aquilius, Vitellius, *priests.*
Tit. Choose then the gloomiest place through all the grove,
Throw thy abandoned body on the ground,
With thy bare breast lie wedded to the dew;
Then, as thou drink'st the tears that trickle from thee,
So stretched resolve to lie till death shall seize thee;
Thy sorrowful head hung o'er some tumbling stream,
To rock thy griefs with melancholy sounds,
With broken murmurs and redoubled groans,
To help the gurgling of the waters' fall,
Ter. Oh, Titus, oh, what scene of death is this!
Tit. Or if thy passion will not be kept in,
As in that glass of nature thou shalt view
Thy swoll'n drowned eyes with the inverted banks,
The tops of willows and their blossoms turned,
With all the under sky ten fathom down,
Wish that the shadow of the swimming globe
Were so indeed, that thou might'st leap at fate,
And hurl thy fortune headlong at the stars:
Nay, do not bear it, turn thy wat'ry face
To yond misguided orb, and ask the gods
For what bold sin they doom the wretched Titus
To such a loss as that of Teraminta?
O Teraminta! I will groan thy name
Till the tired echo faint with repetition,
Till all the breathless grove and quiet myrtles
Shake with my sighs, as if a tempest bowed 'em.
Nothing but 'Teraminta: O Teraminta!'

Ter. Nothing but 'Titus: Titus and Teraminta!'
Thus let me rob the fountains and the groves,
Thus gird me to thee with the fastest knot
Of arms and spirits that would clasp thee through;
Cold as thou art, and wet with night's fall'n dews,
Yet dearer so, thus richly dressed with sorrows,
Than if the gods had hung thee round with kingdoms.
Oh, Titus, oh!
Tit. I find thee Teraminta,
Waked from a fearful dream, and hold thee fast:
'Tis real, and I give thee back thy joys,
Thy boundless love with pleasures running o'er;
Nay, as thou art, thus with thy trappings, come,
Leap to my heart, and ride upon the pants,
Triumphing thus, and now defy our stars.
But, oh, why do we lose this precious moment!
The bliss may yet be barred if we delay,
As 'twas before. Come to thy husband's bed;
I will not think this true till there I hold thee,
Locked in my arms. Leave this contagious air;
There will be time for talk how thou cam'st hither
When we have been beforehand with the gods:
Till then—
Ter. Oh, Titus, you must hear me first.
I bring a message from the furious Queen;
I promised, nay, she swore me not to touch you,
Till I had charmed you to the part of Tarquin.
Tit. Ha, Teraminta! not to touch thy husband,
Unless he prove a villain?
Ter. Titus, no;
I'm sworn to tell you that you are a traitor,
If you refuse to fight the royal cause.
Tit. Hold, Teraminta.
Ter. No, my lord; 'tis plain,
And I am sworn to lay my reasons home.
Rouse then, awake, recall your sleeping virtue;
Side with the King, and arm against your father,
Take part with those that loyally have sworn
To let him in by night. Vitellius,
Aquilius, and your brother wait without;

60 trappings] the dress in which Teraminta had been married to Titus

Therefore I charge you haste, subscribe your name,
And send your vowed obedience to the King.
'Tis Teraminta that entreats you thus,
Charms, and conjures you. Tell the royal heralds
You'll head their enterprise; and then, my lord,
My love, my noble husband, I'll obey you,
And follow to your bed.

Tit. Never, I swear.
Oh, Teraminta, thou hast broke my heart:
By all the gods, from thee this was too much.
Farewell, and take this with thee. For thy sake,
I will not fight against the King, nor for him:
I'll fly my father, brother, friends for ever,
Forsake the haunts of men; converse no more
With aught that's human; dwell with endless darkness;
For, since the sight of thee is now unwelcome,
What has the world besides that I can bear?

Ter. Come back, my lord. By those immortal pow'rs
You now invoked, I'll fix you in this virtue.
Your Teraminta did but try how strong
Your honour stood; and now she finds it lasting,
Will die to root you in this solid glory.
Yes, Titus, though the Queen has sworn to end me,
Though both the Fecialians have commission
To stab me in your presence, if not wrought
To serve the King, yet by the gods I charge you
Keep to the point your constancy has gained.
Tarquin, although my father, is a tyrant,
A bloody black usurper; so I beg you
Even in my death to view him.

Tit. Oh you gods!

Ter. Yet guilty as he is, if you behold him
Hereafter with his wounds upon the earth,
Titus, for my sake, for poor Teraminta,
Who rather died than you should lose your honour,
Do not you strike him, do not dip your sword
In Tarquin's blood, because he was my father.

Tit. No, Teraminta, no: by all the gods,
I will defend him, even against my father.
See, see, my love; behold the flight I take:
What all the charms of thy expected bed
Could not once move my soul to think of acting,

Thy tears and menaced death, by which thou striv'st
To fix me to the principles of glory,
Have wrought me off. Yes, yes, you cruel gods,
Let the eternal bolts that bind this frame
Start from their order: since you push me thus
Even to the margin of this wide despair,
Behold I plunge at once in this dishonour,
Where there is neither shore, nor hope of haven,
No floating mark through all the dismal vast;
'Tis rockless too, no cliff to clamber up
To gaze about and pause upon the ruin.

Ter. Is then your purposed honour come to this?
What now, my Lord?

Tit. Thy death, thy death, my love:
I'll think on that, and laugh at all the gods.
Glory, blood, nature, ties of reverence,
The dues of birth, respect of parents, all,
All are as this, the air I drive before me.
What ho! Vitellius, and Aquilius, come,
And you the Fecialian heralds, haste;
I'm ready for the leap, I'll take it with you
Though deep as to the fiends.

Ter. Thus hear me, Titus.

Tit. Off from my knees, away!
What, on this theme, thy death? Nay, stabbed before me!

Enter priests, with Tiberius, Aquilius, Vitellius.

Speak not; I will not know thee on this subject,
But push thee from my heart, with all persuasions
That now are lost upon me. O, Tiberius,
Aquilius, and Vitellius, welcome, welcome;
I'll join you in the conjuration. Come:
I am as free as he that dares be foremost.

Ter. My lord, my husband.

Tit. Take this woman from me.
Nay, look you, sirs, I am not yet so gone,
So headlong neither in this damned design
To quench this horrid thirst with Brutus' blood:
No, by th' eternal gods, I bar you that;
My father shall not bleed.

Tib. You could not think

136 purposed] resolute   152 conjuration] conspiracy

Your brother sure so monstrous in his kind
As not to make our father's life his care.
Tit. Thus then, my lords, I list myself among you,
And with my style in short subscribe myself
The servant to the King. My words are these:
'Titus to the King—
Sir, you need only know my brother's mind
To judge of me, who am resolved to serve you.'
1. *Pri.* 'Tis full enough.
Tit. Then leave me to the hire
[*Exeunt* Tiberius, Aquilius, Vitellius, *and priests.*
Of this hard labour, to the dear-bought prize,
Whose life I purchased with my loss of honour.
Come to my breasts, thou tempest-beaten flower,
Brimful of rain, and stick upon my heart.
O short lived rose! yet I some hours will wear thee:
Yes, by the gods, I'll smell thee till I languish,
Rifle thy sweets, and run thee o'er and o'er,
Fall like the night upon thy folding beauties,
And clasp thee dead: then, like the morning sun,
With a new heat kiss thee to life again,
And make the pleasure equal to the pain.

ACT IV SCENE I

Tiberius, Vitellius.

Tib. Hark, are we not pursued?
Vit. No; 'tis the tread
Of our own friends that follow in the dark.
Tib. What's now the time?
Vit. Just dead of night,
And 'tis the blackest that e'er masked a murder.
Tib. It likes me better; for I love the scowl,
The grimmest low of fate on such a deed;
I would have all the charnel houses yawn,
The dusty urns, and monumental bones

163 style] sharp-pointed instrument used for incising letters on a wax tablet

Removed, to make our massacre a tomb.
Hark! who was that that holloa'd 'Fire'?
Vit. A slave,
That snores i'th' hall, he bellows in his sleep,
And cries, 'The Capitol's o' fire!'
Tib. I would it were,
And Tarquin at the gates: 'twould be a blaze,
A beacon fit to light a king of blood,
That vows at once the slaughter of the world.
Down with their temples, set 'em on a flame!
What should they do with houses for the gods,
Fat fools, the lazy magistrates of Rome,
Wise citizens, the politic heads o'th' people,
That preach rebellion to the multitude?
Why, let 'em off, and roll into their graves:

Enter Aquilius, Trebonius, Minutius, Pomponius *with prisoners.*

I long to be at work. See, good Aquilius,
Trebonius too, Servilius and Minutius;
Pomponius, hail! Nay, now you may unmask,
Browbeat the fates, and say they are your slaves.
Aquil. What are those bodies for?
Tib. A sacrifice.
These were two very busy commonwealth's men,
That, ere the King was banished by the senate,
First set the plot on foot in public meetings,
That would be holding forth 'twas possible
That kings themselves might err, and were but men.
The people were not beasts for sacrifice;
Then jogged his brother, this crammed statesman here,
The bolder rogue, whom even with open mouth
I heard once belch sedition from a stall.
Go, bear him to the priests; he is a victim
That comes as wished for them, the cooks of heaven,
And they will carve this brawn of fat rebellion,
As if he were a dish the gods might feed on.

Vin. [*From a window.*] Oh, the gods! Oh, the gods! what will they do with him? Oh, these priests, rogues, cut-throats! A dish for the gods, but the devil's cooks to dress him.

Tib. Thus then. The Fecialians have set down
A platform, copied from the King's design:

The Pandane or the Romulide, the Roman,
Carmental and Janiculan ports of Rome,
The Cirque, the Capitol, and Sublician Bridge
Must all be seized by us that are within;
'Twill not be hard in the surprise of night
By us, the consuls' children and their nephews,
To kill the drowsy guards, and keep the holds,
At least so long till Tarquin force his entrance
With all the royalists that come to join us:
Therefore, to make his broader squadrons way,
Tarquinian is designed to be the entry
Of his most pompous and resolved revenge.

Aquil. The first decreed in this great execution
Is here set down your father and Valerius.

Tib. That's as the King shall please; but for Valerius,
I'll take myself the honour of his head
And wear it on my spear. The senate all
Without exception shall be sacrificed:
And those that are the mutinous heads o'th' people
Whom I have marked to be the soldiers' spoil,
For plunder must be given, and who so fit
As those notorious limbs, your commonwealth's men?
Their daughters to be ravished; and their sons
Quartered like brutes upon the common shambles.

Vit. Now for the letters, which the Fecialians
Require us all to sign and send to Tarquin,
Who will not else be apt to trust his heralds
Without credentials under every hand,
The business being indeed of vast import,
On which the hazard of his life and empire,
As well as all our fortunes, does depend.

Tib. It were a break to the whole enterprise
To make a scruple in our great affair;
I will sign first: and for my brother Titus,
Whom his new wife detains, I have his hand
And seal to show, as fast and firm as any.

Vin. [*From the window.*] Oh, villainy! villainy! What would they do with me, if they should catch me peeping? Knock out my brains at least; another

45–7 The Pandane . . . Bridge] Lee found those various places named in his source, Madeleine de Scudéry's, *Clélie* (Stroup-Cooke). The 'cirque' is presumably the *Circus Maximus*. 51 the holds] the strong points of defence mentioned above

dish for the priests, who would make fine sauce of 'em for the haunch of a fat citizen!

Tib. All hands have here subscribed, and that your hearts
Prove resolute to what your hands have given,
Behold the messengers of heaven to bind you,
Charms of religion, sacred conjurations,
With sounds of execration, words of horror,
Not to disclose or make least signs or show,
Of what you have both heard, and seen, and sworn,
But bear yourselves as if it ne'er had been.
Swear by the gods celestial and infernal,
By Pluto, Mother Earth, and by the Furies,
Not to reveal, though racks were set before you,
A syllable of what is past and done.
Hark, how the offered brutes begin to roar!
Oh, that the hearts of all the traitor senate,
And heads of that foul hydra multitude,
Were frying with their fat upon this pile,
That we might make an off'ring worth an empire,
And sacrifice rebellion to the King.

The scene draws, showing the sacrifice: one burning, and another crucified; the priests coming forward with goblets in their hands, filled with human blood.

1. *Pri.* Kneel, all you heroes of this black design,
Each take his goblet filled with blood and wine;
Swear by the Thunderer, swear by Jove,
Swear by the hundred gods above;
Swear by Dis, by Proserpine,
Swear by the Berecynthian Queen.

2. *Pri.* To keep it close till Tarquin comes,
With trumpets' sound and beat of drums:
But then to thunder forth the deed,
That Rome may blush, and traitors bleed.
Swear all.

All. We swear.

1. *Pri.* Now drink the blood,
To make the conjuration good.

Tib. Methinks I feel the slaves' exalted blood
Warm at my heart: oh, that it were the spirits

108 Berecynthian Queen] Cybele, the mother of the gods

Of Rome's best life, drawn from her grizzled fathers!
That were a draught indeed to quench ambition,
And give new fierceness to the King's revenge.

Vin. [*From the window.*] Oh, the gods! What, burn a man alive! O cannibals, hellhounds! Eat one man, and drink another! Well, I'll to Valerius; Brutus will not believe me, because his sons and nephews are in the business. What, drink a man's blood! Roast him, and eat him alive! A whole man roasted! Would not an ox serve the turn? Priests to do this! Oh, you immortal gods! For my part, if this be your worship, I renounce you. No; if a man can't go to heaven unless your priests eat him and drink him, and roast him alive, I'll be for the broad way, and the Devil shall have me at a venture. [*Exit.*

Enter Titus.

Tit. What ho, Tiberius! give me back my hand.
What have you done? Horrors and midnight murders!
The gods, the gods awake you to repentance,
As they have me. Would'st thou believe me brother?
Since I delivered thee that fatal scroll,
That writing to the King, my heart rebelled
Against itself; my thoughts were up in arms
All in a roar, like seamen in a storm,
My reason and my faculties were wracked,
The mast, the rudder, and the tackling gone;
My body, like the hull of some lost vessel,
Beaten and tumbled with my rolling fears;
Therefore I charge thee give me back my writing.

Tib. What means my brother?

Tit. Oh, Tiberius, oh!
Dark as it seems, I tell thee that the gods
Look through a day of lightning on our city:
The heaven's on fire; and from the flaming vault
Portentous blood pours like a torrent down.
There are a hundred gods in Rome tonight,
And every larger spirit is abroad,
Monuments emptied, every urn is shaken
To fright the state, and put the world in arms:
Just now I saw three Romans stand amazed
Before a flaming sword, then dropped down dead,
Myself untouched: while through the blazing air

127 broad way] cf. Matthew 7: 13

A fleeting head, like a full riding moon,
Glanced by, and cried, 'Titus, I am Egeria;
Repent, repent, or certain death attends thee;
Treason and tyranny shall not prevail;
Kingdom shall be no more; Egeria says it:
And that vast turn imperial fate designed
I saw, O Titus, on th' eternal loom;
'Tis ripe, 'tis perfect, and is doomed to stand.'

1. *Pri.* Fumes, fumes; the phantoms of an ill digestion;
The gods are as good quiet gods as may be,
They're fast asleep, and mean not to disturb us,
Unless your frenzy wake 'em.

Tit. Peace, fury, peace.
May the gods doom me to the pains of hell
If I enjoyed the beauties that I saved:
The horror of my treason shocked my joys,
Enervated my purpose, while I lay
Colder than marble by her virgin side,
As if I had drunk the blood of elephants,
Drowsy mandragora, or the juice of hemlock.

1. *Pri.* I like him not; I think we had best dispatch him.

Tit. Nothing but images of horror round me,
Rome all in blood, the ravished vestals raving,
The sacred fire put out; robbed mothers' shrieks,
Deaf'ning the gods with clamours for their babes
That sprawled aloft upon the soldiers' spears;
The beard of age plucked off by barbarous hands,
While from his piteous wounds and horrid gashes
The labouring life flowed faster than the blood.

Enter Valerius, Vinditius, *with guards, who seize all but the priests, who slip away.* Vinditius *follows them.*

Val. Horror upon me! what will this night bring forth?
Yes, you immortal gods, strike, strike the consul;
Since these are here, the crime will look less horrid
In me, than in his sons. Titus, Tiberius!
Oh, from this time let me be blind and dumb,
But haste there. Mutius, fly; call hither Brutus,

155 Egeria] a nymph who (according to Ovid) became the wife of Numa, second King of Rome, and gave him wise counsel in his law-making 171 the blood of elephants] This was believed to cause impotence (Stroup-Cooke). 172 mandragora] a narcotic drug from the root of the mandrake

Bid him for ever leave the down of rest,
And sleep no more. If Rome were all on fire,
And Tarquin in the streets bestriding slaughter,
He would less wonder than at Titus here.

Tit. Stop there, oh, stop that messenger of fate;
Here, bind, Valerius, bind this villain's hands,
Tear off my robes, put me upon the forks,
And lash me like a slave till I shall howl
My soul away; or hang me on a cross,
Rack me a year within some horrid dungeon,
So deep, so near the hells that I must suffer,
That I may groan my torments to the damned.
I do submit, this traitor, this cursed villain,
To all the stings of most ingenious horror,
So thou dispatch me ere my father comes.
But hark! I hear the tread of fatal Brutus!
By all the gods, and by the lowest Furies,
I cannot bear his face. Away with me!
Or like a whirlwind I will tear my way
I care not whither. [*Exit with* Tiberius.

Val. Take 'em hence together.

Enter Vinditius *with the priests.*

Vin. Here, here, my lord, I have unkennelled two:
Those there are rascals made of flesh and blood,
Those are but men, but these are the gods' rogues.

Val. Go, good Vinditius, haste and stop the people,
Get 'em together to the Capitol:
Where all the senate with the consuls early,
Will see strict justice done upon the traitors.
For thee, the senate shall decree rewards
Great as thy service.

Vin. I humbly thank your lordship.
[*Aside.*] Why, what! They'll make me a senator at least,
And then a consul; oh, th' immortal gods!—

My lord, I go—[*Aside.*] to have the rods and axes carried before me, and a long purple gown trailing behind my honourable heels. Well, I am made for ever! [*Exit.*

Enter Brutus *attended.*

Brut. Oh, my Valerius, are these horrors true?

194 forks] cf. III. i. 160 n.

Hast thou, O gods, this night embowelled me?
Ransacked thy Brutus' veins, thy fellow consul,
And found two villains lurking in my blood?

Val. The blackest treason that e'er darkness brooded.
And who, to hatch these horrors for the world,
Who to seduce the noble youth of Rome,
To draw 'em to so damned a conjuration,
To bind 'em too by new invented oaths,
Religious forms, and devilish sacrifices,
A sacrament of blood, for which Rome suffered
In two the worthiest of her martyred sons—
Who to do this but messengers from heaven?
These holy men that swore so solemnly
Before the senate, called the gods to curse 'em
If they intended aught against the state,
Or harboured treason more than what they uttered?

Brut. Now all the fiends and furies thank 'em for it.
You sons of murder that get drunk with blood,
Then stab at princes, poison commonwealths,
Destroy whole hecatombs of innocent souls,
Pile 'em like bulls and sheep upon your altars,
As you would smoke the gods from out their dwelling:
You shame of earth, and scandal of the heavens,
You deeper fiends than any of the Furies,
That scorn to whisper envy, hate, sedition,
But with a blast of privilege proclaim it;
Priests that are instruments designed to damn us,
Fit speaking trumpets for the mouth of Hell.
Hence with 'em, guards; secure 'em in the prison
Of Ancus Martius. Read the packets o'er,
I'll bear it as I'm able; read 'em out.

Val. 'The sum of the conspiracy to the King:
It shall begin with both the consuls' deaths,
And then the senate; every man must bleed,
But those that have engaged to serve the King.
Be ready therefore, sir, to send your troops
By twelve tomorrow night, and come yourself
In person, if you'll reascend the throne:
All that have sworn to serve Your Majesty
Subscribe themselves by name your faithful subjects:

223 embowelled] disembowelled 229 conjuration] cf. III. iii. 152 252 Ancus Martius] fourth King of Rome, grandson of Numa

Tiberius, Aquilius, Vitellius,
Trebonius, Servilius, Minutius,
Pomponius, and your Fecialian priests.'
Brut. Ha! my Valerius, is not Titus there?
Val. He's here, my lord; a paper by itself.
'Titus to the King:
Sir, you need only know my brother's mind
To judge of me, who am resolved to serve you.'
What do you think, my lord?
Brut. Think, my Valerius?
By my heart, I know not:
I'm at a loss of thought, and must acknowledge
The councils of the gods are fathomless;
Nay, 'tis the hardest task perhaps of life
To be assured of what is vice or virtue:
Whether when we raise up temples to the gods
We do not then blaspheme 'em. Oh, behold me,
Behold the game that laughing Fortune plays;
Fate, or the will of heaven, call't what you please,
That mars the best designs that prudence lays,
That brings events about perhaps to mock
At human reach, and sport with expectation.
Consider this, and wonder not at Brutus
If his philosophy seems at a stand,
If thou behold'st him shed unmanly tears
To see his blood, his children, his own bowels
Conspire the death of him that gave 'em being.
Val. What heart but yours could bear it without breaking?
Brut. No, my Valerius, I were a beast indeed
Not to be moved with such prodigious suffering;
Yet after all I justify the gods,
And will conclude there's reason supernatural
That guides us through the world with vast discretion,
Although we have not souls to comprehend it,
Which makes by wondrous methods the same causes
Produce effects though of a different nature.
Since then, for man's instruction, and the glory
Of the immortal gods, it is decreed
There must be patterns drawn of fiercest virtue,
Brutus submits to the eternal doom.

287 bowels] offspring

Val. May I believe there can be such perfection,
Such a resolve in man?
Brut. First, as I am their father,
I pardon both of 'em this black design;
But, as I am Rome's consul, I abhor 'em,
And cast 'em from my soul with detestation:
The nearer to my blood, the deeper grained
The colour of their fault, and they shall bleed.
Yes, my Valerius, both my sons shall die.

Enter Teraminta.

Nay, I will stand unbowelled by the altar,
See something dearer to me than my entrails
Displayed before the gods and Roman people,
The sacrifice of justice and revenge.
Ter. What sacrifice, what victims, sir, are these
Which you intend? O, you eternal powers,
How shall I vent my sorrows! Oh, my lord,
Yet ere you seal the death you have designed,
The death of all that's lovely in the world,
Hear what the witness of his soul can say,
The only evidence that can, or dare
Appear for your unhappy guiltless son.
The gods command you, virtue, truth, and justice,
Which you with so much rigour have adored,
Beg you would hear the wretched Teraminta.
Brut. Cease thy laments: though of the blood of Tarquin,
Yet more, the wife of my forgotten son,
Thou shalt be heard.
Ter. Have you forgot him then?
Have you forgot yourself? The image of you,
The very picture of your excellence,
The portraiture of all your manly virtues,
Your visage stamped upon him; just those eyes,
The moving greatness of 'em, all the mercy,
The shedding goodness; not so quite severe,
Yet still most like: and can you then forget him?
Brut. Will you proceed?
Ter. My lord, I will. Know then,
After your son, your son that loves you more

310 unbowelled] having no 'bowels', pitiless. (It is possible, however, that Titus is saying he will be bereft of his 'bowels', i.e. his offspring: cf. l. 287 above.)

Than I love him—after our common Titus,
The wealth o'th' world unless you rob 'em of it,
Had long endured th' assaults of the rebellious,
And still kept fixed to what you had enjoined him;
I, as fate ordered it, was sent from Tullia,
With my death menaced, even before his eyes,
Doomed to be stabbed before him by the priests,
Unless he yielded not t'oppose the King.
Consider, sir; oh make it your own case;
Just wedded, just on the expected joys,
Warm for my bed, and rushing to my arms,
So loving too, alas, as we did love—
Granted in haste, in heat, in flame of passion
He knew not what himself, and so subscribed.
But now, sir, now, my lord, behold a wonder,
Behold a miracle to move your soul!
Though in my arms, just in the grasps of pleasure,
His noble heart, struck with the thoughts of Brutus,
Of what he promised you, till then forgot,
Leapt in his breast and dashed him from enjoyment;
He shrieked, 'Y' immortal gods, what have I done!
No, Teraminta, let us rather perish,
Divide for ever with whole seas betwixt us,
Rather than sin against so good a father.'
Though he before had barred your life and fortune,
Yet would not trust the traitors with the safety
Of him he called the image of the gods.

Val. O saint-like virtue of a Roman wife!
O eloquence divine! now all the arts
Of women's tongues, the rhetoric of the gods
Inspire thy soft and tender soul to move him.

Ter. On this he roused; swore by the powers divine,
He would fetch back the paper that he gave,
Or leave his life amongst 'em; kept his word,
And came to challenge it, but, oh! too late;
For, in the midst of all his piety,
His strong persuasions to a swift repentance,
His vows to lay their horrid treasons open,
His execration of the barbarous priests,
How he abhorred that bloody sacrament

361 barred] excluded from the general destruction contemplated

As much as you, and cursed the conjuration;
Vinditius came that had before alarmed
The wise Valerius, who with all the guards
Found Titus here, believed him like the rest,
And seized him too, as guilty of the treason.
Val. But, by the gods, my soul does now acquit him.
Blessed be thy tongue, blessed the auspicious gods
That sent thee, O true pattern of perfection!
To plead his bleeding cause. There needs no more,
I see his father's moved. Behold a joy,
A wat'ry comfort rising in his eyes,
That says, ''Tis more than half a heaven to hear thee.'
Brut. Haste, O Valerius, haste and send for Titus.
Ter. For Titus! Oh, that is a word too distant;
Say, for your son, for your beloved son,
The darling of the world, the joy of heaven,
The hope of earth, your eyes not dearer to you,
Your soul's best wish, and comfort of your age.

Enter Titus, *with* Valerius.

Tit. Ah, sir! Oh whither shall I run to hide me?
Where shall I lower fall? how shall I lie
More grovelling in your view, and howl for mercy?
Yet 'tis some comfort to my wild despair,
Some joy in death that I may kiss your feet,
And swear upon 'em by these streaming tears,
Black as I am with all my guilt upon me,
I never harboured aught against your person:
Ev'n in the height of my full-fraught distraction,
Your life my lord, was sacred; ever dear,
And ever precious, to unhappy Titus.
Brut. Rise, Titus: rise, my son.
Tit. Alas, I dare not;
I have not strength to see the majesty
Which I have braved: if thus far I aspire,
If on your knees I hang and vent my groans,
It is too much, too much for thousand lives.
Brut. I pity thee, my son, and I forgive thee:
And, that thou mayst believe my mercy true,
I take thee in my arms.
Tit. Oh, all the gods!

Brut. Now rise; I charge thee, on my blessing, rise.
Ter. Ah! See, sir, see, against his will, behold,
He does obey, though he would choose to kneel
An age before you; see how he stands and trembles!
Now, by my hopes of mercy, he's so lost,
His heart's so full, brimful of tenderness,
The sense of what you've done has struck him speechless:
Nor can he thank you now but with his tears.
Brut. My dear Valerius, let me now entreat thee
Withdraw a while with gentle Teraminta,
And leave us to ourselves.
Ter. Ah, sir, I fear you now;
Nor can I leave you with the humble Titus,
Unless you promise me you will not chide,
Nor fall again to anger. Do not, sir,
Do not upbraid his soft and melting temper
With what is past. Behold he sighs again!
Now by the gods that hitherto have blest us,
My heart forebodes a storm, I know not why:
But say, my lord; give me your god-like word
You'll not be cruel, and I'll not trust my heart,
Howe'er it leaps, and fills me with new horror.
Brut. I promise thee.
Ter. Why, then I thank you, sir;
Ev'n from my soul I thank you, for this goodness:
The great, good, gracious gods reward and bless you.
Ah Titus, ah my soul's eternal treasure,
I fear I leave thee with a hard usurer;
But I perforce must trust thee. Oh, farewell. [*Exit with* Valerius.
Brut. Well, Titus, speak; how is it with thee now?
I would attend awhile this mighty motion,
Wait till the tempest were quite overblown,
That I might take thee in the calm of nature,
With all thy gentler virtues brooding on thee,
So hushed a stillness, as if all the gods
Looked down, and listened to what we were saying.
Speak then, and tell me, O my best belov'd,
My son, my Titus, is all well again?
Tit. So well, that saying how must make it nothing;
So well, that I could wish to die this moment,
For so my heart with powerful throbs persuades me:
That were indeed to make you reparation,

That were, my lord, to thank you home, to die,
And that for Titus too would be most happy.
Brut. How's that, my son? would death for thee be happy?
Tit. Most certain, sir; for in my grave I 'scape
All those affronts which I in life must look for,
All those reproaches which the eyes and fingers
And tongues of Rome will daily cast upon me;
From whom, to a soul so sensible as mine,
Each single scorn would be far worse than dying:
Besides, I 'scape the stings of my own conscience,
Which will for ever rack me with remembrance,
Haunt me by day, and torture me by night,
Casting my blotted honour in the way
Where'er my melancholy thoughts shall guide me.
Brut. But is not death a very dreadful thing?
Tit. Not to a mind resolved. No, sir, to me
It seems as natural as to be born:
Groans and convulsions and discoloured faces,
Friends weeping round us, blacks and obsequies,
Make it a dreadful thing; the pomp of death
Is far more terrible than death itself.
Yes, sir; I call the powers of heaven to witness,
Titus dares die, if so you have decreed;
Nay, he shall die with joy, to honour Brutus,
To make your justice famous through the world,
And fix the liberty of Rome for ever:
Not but I must confess my weakness too;
Yet it is great thus to resolve against it,
To have the frailty of a mortal man,
But the security of th' immortal gods.
Brut. O Titus, oh, thou absolute young man!
Thou flatt'ring mirror of thy father's image,
Where I behold myself at such advantage!
Thou perfect glory of the Junian race!
Let me endear thee once more to my bosom,
Groan an eternal farewell to thy soul;
Instead of tears weep blood, if possible,
Blood, the heart blood of Brutus, on his child,
For thou must die, my Titus, die, my son,
I swear the gods have doomed thee to the grave;

454 home] thoroughly, to the heart

The violated genius of thy country
Rears his sad head, and passes sentence on thee.
This morning sun, that lights my sorrows on
To the tribunal of this horrid vengeance,
Shall never see thee more.

Tit. Alas, my lord!
Why are you moved thus? why am I worth your sorrow?
Why should the god-like Brutus shake to doom me?
Why all these trappings for a traitor's hearse?
The gods will have it so.

Brut. They will, my Titus:
Nor heaven, nor earth can have it otherwise.
Nay, Titus, mark; the deeper that I search,
My harrassed soul returns the more confirmed:
Methinks I see the very hand of Jove
Moving the dreadful wheels of this affair
That whirl thee, like a machine, to thy fate.
It seems as if the gods had preordained it
To fix the reeling spirits of the people,
And settle the loose liberty of Rome.
'Tis fixed. Oh, therefore let not fancy fond thee:
So fixed thy death, that 'tis not in the power
Of gods or men to save thee from the axe.

Tit. The axe! O heaven! then must I fall so basely?
What, shall I perish by the common hangman?

Brut. If thou deny me this, thou givest me nothing.
Yes, Titus, since the gods have so decreed
That I must lose thee, I will take th' advantage
Of thy important fate, cement Rome's flaws,
And heal her wounded freedom with thy blood.
I will ascend myself the sad tribunal,
And sit upon my sons; on thee, my Titus;
Behold thee suffer all the shame of death,
The lictor's lashes, bleed before people;
Then, with thy hopes and all thy youth upon thee,
See thy head taken by the common axe,
Without a groan, without one pitying tear,
If that the gods can hold me to my purpose,
To make my justice quite transcend example.

Tit. Scourged like a bondman! ha! a beaten slave!

500 doom] sentence, pass judgement 512 fond] delude

But I deserve it all; yet here I fail:
The image of this suff'ring quite unmans me,
Nor can I longer stop the gushing tears.
O sir! O Brutus! must I call you father,
Yet have no token of your tenderness?
No sign of mercy? What, not bate me that!
Can you resolve—O all th' extremity
Of cruel rigour!—to behold me too?
To sit unmoved, and see me whipped to death?
Where are your bowels now? Is this a father?
Ah, sir, why should you make my heart suspect
That all your late compassion was dissembled?
How can I think that you did ever love me?
Brut. Think that I love thee by my present passion,
By these unmanly tears, these earthquakes here,
These sighs that twitch the very strings of life:
Think that no other cause on earth could move me
To tremble thus, to sob, or shed a tear,
Nor shake my solid virtue from her point
But Titus' death: oh, do not call it shameful,
That thus shall fix the glory of the world.
I own thy suff'rings ought t' unman me thus,
To make me throw my body on the ground,
To bellow like a beast, to gnaw the earth,
To tear my hair, to curse the cruel Fates
That force a father thus to drag his bowels.
Tit. O rise, thou violated majesty,
Rise from the earth; or I shall beg those Fates
Which you would curse, to bolt me to the centre.
I now submit to all your threatened vengeance:
Come forth, you executioners of justice,
Nay, all you lictors, slaves, and common hangmen,
Come, strip me bare, unrobe me in his sight,
And lash me till I bleed; whip me like Furies;
And when you've scourged me till I foam and fall,
For want of spirits grovelling in the dust,
Then take my head, and give it his revenge:
By all the gods I greedily resign it.
Brut. No more, farewell, eternally farewell:
If there be gods, they will reserve a room,

557 drag] perhaps in the sense of using a grapnel or hook

A throne for thee in heaven. One last embrace.
What is it makes thy eyes thus swim again?
Tit. I had forgot. Be good to Teraminta
When I am ashes.
Brut. Leave her to my care.
See her thou must not; for thou canst not bear it.
Oh for one more, this pull, this tug of heartstrings:
Farewell for ever!
Tit. O Brutus! O my father!
Brut. Canst thou not say farewell?
Tit. Farewell for ever.
Brut. For ever then. But oh, my tears run o'er:
Groans choke my words, and I can speak no more. [*Exeunt.*

ACT V SCENE I

Enter Valerius, Horatius, Herminius, Mutius.

Hor. His sons condemned?
Val. Doomed to the rods and axes.
Hor. What, both of 'em?
Val. Both, sir, both, both his sons.
Hor. What, Titus too?
Val. Yes, sir, his darling Titus.
Nay, though he knows him innocent as I am,
'Tis all one, sir; his sentence stands like fate.
Hor. Yet I'll entreat him.
Mut. So will I.
Her. And I.
Val. Entreat him! yes, you may, my lords, and move him,
As I have done. Why, he's no more a man;
He is not cast in the same common mould,
His spirit moves not with our springs and wards.
He looks and talks, as if that Jove had sent him
To be the judge of all the under world;
Tells me, this palace of the universe,
With that vast moat, the ocean, running round us,

11 springs and wards] mechanisms 13 under world] i.e. the Earth

Th' eternal stars so fiercely rolling o'er us,
With all that circulation of heaven's orbs,
Were so established from before all ages
To be the dowry of majestic Rome;
Then looks as if he had a patent for it
To take account of all this great expense,
And see the layings out of the round world.
Her. What shall be done then? for it grieves my soul
To think of Titus' loss.
Val. There is no help
But thus to shake your head, and cross your arms,
And wonder what the gods and he intend.
Her. There's scarce one man of this conspiracy
But is some way related, if not nearly,
To Junius Brutus. Some of the Aquilians
Are nephews to him; and Vitellius' sister,
The grave Sempronia, is the consul's wife.
Val. Therefore I have engaged that groaning matron
To plead the cause of her unhappy sons.

Enter Titus, *with lictors*.

But see, O gods, behold the gallant Titus,
The mirror of all sons, the white of virtue,
Filled up with blots, and writ all o'er with blood,
Bowing with shame his body to the ground;
Whipped out of breath by these inhuman slaves!
Oh, Titus! is this possible? this shame?
Tit. Oh, my Valerius, call it not my shame:
By all the gods, it is to Titus' honour,
My constant suff'rings are my only glory:
What have I left besides? But ask, Valerius,
Ask these good men that have performed their duty,
If all the while they whipped me like a slave,
If when the blood from every part ran down,
I gave one groan, or shed a woman's tear:
I think, I swear, I think, O my Valerius,
That I have borne it well, and like a Roman.
But oh! far better shall I bear my death,
Which, as it brings less pain, has less dishonour.

22 layings out] expenditure

Enter Teraminta *wounded.*

Ter. Where is he? where, where is this god-like son
Of an inhuman, barbarous bloody, father?
Oh, bear me to him.
Tit. Ha! my Teraminta!
Is't possible? the very top of beauty,
This perfect face drawn by the gods at council,
Which they were long a-making, as they had reason,
For they shall never hit the like again,
Defiled and mangled thus! What barbarous wretch
Has thus blasphemed this bright original?
Ter. For me it matters not, nor my abuses;
But, oh, for thee, why have they used thee thus?
Whipped, Titus, whipped! and could the gods look on?
The glory of the world thus basely used?
Lashed, whipped, and beaten by these upright dogs?
Whose souls, with all the virtue of the senate,
Will be but foils to any fault of thine,
Who hast a beauty even in thy offending.
And did thy father doom thee thus? Oh Titus,
Forgive thy dying part, if she believes
A wretch so barbarous never could produce thee:
Some god, some god, my Titus, watched his absence,
Slipped to thy mother's bed and gave thee to the world.
Tit. Oh, this last wound, this stab to all my courage!
Hadst thou been well, I could have borne more lashes:
And is it thus my father does protect thee?
Ter. Ah Titus! what, thy murd'rer my protector!
No, let me fall again among the people,
Let me be hooted like a common strumpet,
Tossed, as I was, and dragged about the streets,
The bastard of a Tarquin, foiled in dirt,
The cry of all those bloodhounds that did hunt me
Thus to the goal of death, this happy end
Of all my miseries, here to pant my last,
To wash thy gashes with my farewell tears,
To murmur, sob, and lean my aching head
Upon thy breast, thus like a cradle babe
To suck thy wounds and bubble out my soul.

81 foil'd] fouled, defiled (*O.E.D.*, 6); possibly a misprint for 'soiled'.

Enter Sempronia, Aquilia, Vitellia, *mourners, &c.*

Semp. Come ladies, haste, and let us to the senate;
If the gods give us leave, we'll be to day
Part of the council. Oh, my son, my Titus!
See here the bloody justice of a father,
See how the vengeance rains from his own bowels!
Is he not mad? If he refuse to hear us,
We'll bind his hands, as one bereft of reason.
Haste then. Oh Titus, I would stay to moan thee,
But that I fear his orders are gone out
For something worse, for death, to take the heads
Of all the kindred of these wretched women.
Ter. Come then: I think I have some spirits left,
To join thee, O most pious, best of mothers,
To melt this rocky heart. Give me your hand;
Thus let us march before this wretched host,
And offer to that god of blood our vows:
If there be aught that's human left about him,
Perhaps my wounds and horrible abuses,
Helped with the tears and groans of this sad troop,
May batter down the best of his resolves.
Tit. Hark, Teraminta.
Ter. No, my lord, away. [*Exeunt.*
Tit. Oh, my Valerius! was there ever day
Through all the legends of recorded time
So sad as this? But see, my father comes!

Enter Brutus, Tiberius, *lictors.*

Tiberius too has undergone the lash.
Give him the patience, gods, of martyred Titus,
And he will bless those hands that have chastised him.
Tib. Enjoy the bloody conquest of thy pride,
Thou more tyrannical than any Tarquin,
Thou fiercer sire of these unhappy sons,
Than impious Saturn or the gorged Thyestes.
This cormorant sees and owns us for his children,
Yet preys upon his entrails, tears his bowels
With thirst of blood, and hunger fetched from Hell,
Which famished Tantalus would start to think on;
But end, barbarian! end the horrid vengeance
Which thou so impiously hast begun,

Perfect thy justice, as thou, tyrant, call'st it,
Sit like a Fury on thy black tribunal,
Grasp with thy monstrous hands these gory heads,
And let thy flatt'ring orators adore thee
For triumphs which shall make thee smile at horror.

Brut. Lead to the senate.

Tib. Go then to the senate,
There make thy boast how thou hast doomed thy children
To forks and whips; for which, the gods reward thee.
Away: my spirit scorns more conference with thee.
The axe will be as laughter; but the whips
That drew these stains, for this I beg the gods
With my last breath, for every drop that falls
From these vile wounds, to thunder curses on thee. [*Exit.*

Brut. Valerius, haste; the senate does attend us. [*Exit.*

Tit. Valerius, ere you go, let me conjure thee,
By all the earth holds great or honourable,
As thou art truly Roman, stamped a man,
Grant to thy dying Titus one request.

Val. I'll grant thee anything, but do not talk
Of dying yet; for much I dare confide
In that sad company that's gone before:
I know they'll move him to preserve his Titus;
For, though you marked him not, as hence he parted
I could perceive with joy a silent shower
Run down his silver beard. Therefore have hope.

Tit. Hope, say'st thou! O the gods! what hope of life?
To live, to live! and after this dishonour!
No, my Valerius, do not make me rave;
But if thou hast a soul that's sensible
Let me conjure thee, when we reach the senate,
To thrust me through the heart.

Val. Not for the world.

Tit. Do't; or I swear thou hast no friendship for me.
First, thou wilt save me from the hated axe,
The hangman's hand; for by the gods I tell thee
Thou mayst as well stop the eternal sun,
And drive him back, as turn my father's purpose:
Next, and what most my soul entreats thee for,
I shall perhaps in death procure his pity;
For to die thus, beneath his killing frown,
Is damning me before my execution.

Val. 'Tis granted. By the gods, I swear to end thee;
For when I weigh with my more serious thought
Thy father's conduct in this dreadful justice,
I find it is impossible to save thee.
Come then, I'll lead thee, O thou glorious victim,
Thus to the altar of untimely death,
Thus in thy trim, with all thy bloom of youth,
These virtues on thee, whose eternal spring
Shall blossom on thy monumental marble
With never fading glory.
Tit. Let me clasp thee,
Boil out my thanks thus with my farewell spirits.
And now away, the taper's almost out,
Never, Valerius, to be kindled more!
Or, if it be, my friend, it shall continue,
Burn through all winds against the puff of fortune,
To dazzle still, and shine like the fixed stars,
With beams of glory that shall last for ever. [*Exeunt.*

SCENE II

Senate.

Brut. Health to the senate! To the fathers hail!
Jupiter Horscius and Diespiter
Hospital and Feretrian, Jove the Stayer,
With all the hundred gods and goddesses,
Guard and defend the liberty of Rome.
It has been found a famous truth in story,
Left by the ancient sages to their sons,
That on the change of empires or of kingdoms,
Some sudden execution, fierce and great,
Such as may draw the world to admiration,
Is necessary to be put in act
Against the enemies of the present state.
Had Hector, when the Greeks and Trojans met
Upon the truce, and mingled with each other,
Brought to the banquet of those demigods

173 These] *Works*; This *Q*. 1. [Qy. This virtue's on thee, (?)] 2–3 Jupiter . . . Stayer] various titles given to Jupiter

The fatal head of that illustrious whore;
Troy might have stood till now; but that was wanting.
Jove having from eternity set down
Rome to be head of all the under world,
Raised with this thought, and big with prophecy
Of what vast good may grow by such examples,
Brutus stands forth to do a dreadful justice;
I come, O conscript fathers, to a deed
Wholly portentous, new, and wonderful,
Such as, perhaps, has never yet been found
In all memorials of former ages,
Nor ever will again. My sons are traitors,
Their tongues and hands are witnesses confessed;
Therefore I have already passed their sentence,
And wait with you to see their execution.

Hor. Consul, the senate does not ask their deaths;
They are content with what's already done,
And all entreat you to remit the axe.

Brut. I thank you, fathers, but refuse the offer.
By the assaulted majesty of Rome,
I swear there is no way to quit the grace,
To right the commonwealth, and thank the gods,
But by the sacrificing of my bowels:
Take then, you sad revengers of the public,
These traitors hence; strike off their heads, and then
My sons'. No more: their doom is passed. Away.
Thus shall we stop the mouth of loud sedition,
Thus show the difference betwixt the sway
Of partial tyrants, and of a freeborn people,
Where no man shall offend because he's great,
Where none need doubt his wife's or daughter's honour,
Where all enjoy their own without suspicion,
Where there's no innovation of religion,
No change of laws, nor breach of privilege,
No desperate factions gaping for rebellion,
No hopes of pardon for assassinates,
No rash advancements of the base or stranger,
For luxury, for wit, or glorious vice;
But on the contrary, a balanced trade,
Patriots encouraged, manufactors cherished,

36 quit] requite 38 bowels] cf. V. i. 38

Vagabonds, walkers, drones, and swarming braves,
The froth of states, scummed from the commonwealth;
Idleness banished, all excess repressed,
And riots checked by sumptuary laws.
Oh, conscript fathers, 'tis on these foundations
That Rome shall build her empire to the stars,
Send her commanders with her armies forth,
To tame the world, and give the nations law,
Consuls, proconsuls, who to the Capitol
Shall ride upon the necks of conquered kings;
And when they die, mount from the gorgeous pile
In flames of spice, and mingle with the gods.

Hor. Excellent Brutus! all the senate thanks thee,
And says that thou thyself art half a god.

Enter Sempronia, Teraminta, *with the rest of the mourners*; Titus, Valerius, Junius.

Sem. Gone, gone to death! already sentenced! Doomed
To lose the light of this dear world for ever?
What, my Tiberius too! Ah, barbarous! Brutus!
Send, haste, revoke the order of their fate.
By all the pledges of our marriage bed,
If thou, inhuman judge, hast left me one
To put thee yet in mind thou art a father;
Speak to him, oh, you mothers of sad Rome,
Sisters and daughters, ere the execution
Of all your blood; haste, haste, and run about him,
Groan, sob, howl out the terrors of your souls,
Nay, fly upon him like robbed savages,
And tear him for your young.

Brut. Away, and leave me.

Sem. Or if you think it better for your purpose,
Because he has the pow'r of life and death,
Entreat him thus: throw all your heartless breasts
Low at his feet, and like a god adore him;
Nay, make a rampier round him with your bodies
And block him up. I see he would be going;
Yet that's a sign that our complaints have moved him.
Continued falls of ever streaming tears,
Such, and so many, and the chastest too,

56 walkers] vagrants; but compare also 'night-walker' = (1) bully, thief, and (2) prostitute
87 rampier] rampart

Of all the pious matrons throughout Rome
Perhaps may melt this adamantine temper.
Not yet! Nay, hang your bodies then upon him,
Some on his arms, and some upon his knees,
And lay this innocent about his neck,
This little smiling image of his father:
See how he bends, and stretches to his bosom!
Oh, all you pitying pow'rs, the darling weeps!
His pretty eyes, ruddy and wet with tears,
Like two burst cherries rolling in a storm,
Plead for our griefs more than a thousand tongues.

Jun. Yes, yes, my father will be good to us,
And spare my brothers; oh, I know he will.
Why, do you think he ever was in earnest?
What, to cut off their heads? I warrant you
He will not; no, he only meant to fright 'em,
As he will me, when I have done a fault:
Why, mother, he has whipped 'em for't already,
And do you think he has the heart to kill 'em?
No, no, he would not cut their little fingers
For all the world; or if he should, I'm sure
The gods would pay him for't.

Brut. What ho! without there!
Slaves, villains, ha! are not my orders heard?

Hor. Oh Brutus, see, they are too well performed!
See here the bodies of the Roman youth
All headless by your doom, and there Tiberius.

Ter. See, sir, behold, is not this horrid slaughter,
This cutting off one limb from your own body,
Is't not enough? Oh, will it not suffice
To stop the mouth of the most bloody law?
Oh, it were highest sin to make a doubt,
To ask you now to save the innocent Titus,
The common wish, and general petition
Of all the Roman senate, matrons, wives,
Widows, and babes; nay, even the madding people
Cry out at last that treason is revenged,
And ask no more. Oh, therefore spare him, sir.

Brut. I must not hear you. Hark, Valerius—

Ter. By all these wounds upon my virgin breast,
Which I have suffered by your cruelty,
Although you promised Titus to defend me—

Sem. Yet hold thy bloody hand, tyrannic Brutus,
And I'll forgive thee for that headless horror:
Grant me my Titus, oh, in death I ask thee.
Thou hast already broke Sempronia's heart;
Yet I will pardon that, so Titus live.
Ah, cruel judge! thou pitiless avenger!
What art thou whisp'ring? Speak the horror out,
For in thy glaring eyes I read a murder.

Brut. I charge thee, by thy oath, Valerius,
As thou art here deputed by the gods,
And not a subject for a woman's folly,
Take him away, and drag him to the axe.

Val. It shall be thus then; not the hangman's hand.
[*Runs him through. The women shriek.*

Tit. Oh bravely struck! thou hast hit me to the earth
So nobly, that I shall rebound to heaven,
Where I will thank thee for this gallant wound. [Sempronia *swoons.*

Brut. Take hence this woman; haste, and bear her home.
Why, my Valerius, didst thou rob my justice?

Tit. I wrought him to it, sir, that thus in death
I might have leave to pay my last obedience,
And beg your blessing for the other world.

Ter. Oh, do not take it, Titus; whate'er comes
From such a monstrous nature must be blasting.
Ah, thou inhuman tyrant! but, alas,
I loiter here, when Titus stays for me:
Look here, my love; thou shalt not be before me. [*Stabs herself.*
Thus, to thy arms then. Oh, make haste, my Titus,
I'm got already in the grove of death;
The heaven is all benighted, not one star
To light us through the dark and pathless maze.
I have lost thy spirit; oh, I grope about
But cannot find thee: now I sink in shadows. [*Dies.*

Tit. I come, thou matchless virtue. Oh, my heart!
Farewell, my love; we'll meet in heaven again.
My lord, I hope your justice is atoned;
I hope the glorious liberty of Rome,
Thus watered by the blood of both your sons,
Will get imperial growth and flourish long.

Brut. Thou hast so nobly borne thyself in dying,
That not to bless thee were to curse myself;
Therefore I give thee thus my last embrace,

Print this last kiss upon thy trembling lips:
And, ere thou goest, I beg thee to report me
To the great shades of Romulus and Numa,
Just with that majesty and rugged virtue
Which they inspired, and which the world has seen.
So, for I see thou'rt gone, farewell for ever.
Eternal Jove, the king of gods and men,
Reward and crown thee in the other world.

Tit. What happiness has life to equal this?
By all the gods I would not live again;
For what can Jove or all the gods give more:
To fall thus crowned with virtue's fullest charms,
And die thus blessed, in such a father's arms? [*Dies.*

Val. He's gone; the gallant spirit's fled for ever.
How fares this noble vessel that is robbed
Of all its wealth, spoiled of its top-mast glory,
And now lies floating in this world of ruin?

Brut. Peace, consul, peace; let us not soil the pomp
Of this majestic fate with woman's brawls.
Kneel, fathers, friends, kneel all you Roman people,
Hushed as dead calms, while I conceive a pray'r
That shall be worthy Rome, and worthy Jove.

Val. Inspire him, gods; and thou, O Rome, attend.

Brut. Let heaven and earth for ever keep their bound,
The stars unshaken go their constant round;
In harmless labour be our steel employed,
And endless peace through all the world enjoyed;
Let every bark the waves in safety plough,
No angry tempest curl the ocean's brow;
No darted flames from heaven make mortals fear,
Nor thunder fright the weeping passenger;
Let not poor swains for storms at harvest mourn,
But smile to see their hoards of bladed corn;
No dreadful comets threaten from the skies,
No venom fall, nor pois'nous vapours rise.
Thou, Jove, who dost the fates of empires doom,
Guard and defend the liberty of Rome.

FINIS

189 top-mast] *Q.* 1; topmost *Works*

EPILOGUE

Spoken by Mrs. Barry

No cringing, sirs; the poet's champion I
Have sworn to stand, and ev'ry judge defy;
But why each bullying critic should I name
A judge, whose only business is to damn.
While you your arbitrary fist advance
At wit, and dust it like a boor of France,
Who without show of reason or pretence
Condemn a man to die for speaking sense?
Howe'er we termed you once the wise, the strong,
Know we have borne your impotence too long.
You that above your sires presume to soar,
And are but copies daubed in miniature;
You that have nothing right in heart nor tongue
But only to be resolute in wrong.
Who sense affect with such an awkward air,
As if a Frenchman should become severe;
Or an Italian make his wife a jest,
Like Spaniards pleasant, or like Dutchmen dressed;
That rank the noblest poets with the vile
And look yourselves in a plebeian style.
But with an oath—
False as your wit and judgement now I swear
By the known maidenheads of each Theatre—
Nay, by my own—the poets shall not stand,
Like shrovetide cocks, the palt of every hand.
Let not the purblind critic's sentence pass,
That shoots the poet through an optic glass,
No peals of ill-placed praise from galleries come,
Nor punk below to clap or hiss presume;

6 *dust it*] strike violently 25 *shrovetide cocks*] cocks 'tied up and pelted with sticks on Shrove Tuesday' (*O.E.D.*) *palt*] pelt (here, the thing pelted, the target)

Let her not cackle at the fops that flout her,
Nor cluck the squires that use to pip about her;
No full-blown blockhead bloated like an ox
Traverse the pit with 'Damme! what a pox!'
Know then, for ev'ry misdemeanour here
I'll be more stabbing, sharp, and more severe,
Then the fell she that on her keeper comes
Who in his drink last night laid waste her rooms,
Thundered her china, damned her quality,
Her glasses broke, and tore her point venie;
That dragged her by the hair, and broke her head,
A chamber lion, but a lamb in bed.
Like her I'll tease you for your midnight storming,
For your all talking, and your no-performing.
You that with monstrous judgement force the stage,
You fribbling, fumbling keepers of the age.

31 *pip*] peep, chirp 36 *fell she*] enraged woman 39 *point venie*] i.e. *point de Venise*, a fashionable lace of the period. 45 *fribbling*] acting foolishly, footling

THE UNHAPPY FAVOURITE

John Banks

c. 1650–*c.* 1700

Although *The Unhappy Favourite* was published in 1682 it was almost certainly first performed in 1681. John Banks (about whose life singularly little is known) began by writing two heroic plays, but he went on to specialize in what came to be known as 'she-tragedies', based on the lives of Queen Elizabeth, Ann Boleyn, Mary, Queen of Scots, and Lady Jane Gray. His choice of themes from fairly recent English history brought his plays a little closer to the life his audience knew than did those based on oriental courts or on ancient Greece or Rome, but on two occasions their real or supposed relevance to contemporary events exposed him to political censorship: his tragedies on Mary, Queen of Scots and Lady Jane Gray were both banned.

For the plot of *The Unhappy Favourite* he went to *The Secret History of the Most Renowned Queen Elizabeth and the Earl of Essex* (1681—and earlier?). In this piece of romantic fiction the Queen is secretly in love with Essex and very nearly declares her passion for him; and here too Banks found the story of the ring given by the Queen to Essex, and his treacherous betrayal by the Countess of Nottingham. Most of the historical mistakes in *The Unhappy Favourite* are due to Banks following his source.

The reputation of Banks in his own day and later is instructive. He was condemned by the critics and sneered at by the polite; but ordinary play-goers whose minds were not 'prepossessed by mechanical criticism' continued for several generations to weep at his tragedies. In the *Tatler* for 12 May 1709, Steele characterized *The Unhappy Favourite* as a play 'in which there is not one good line', and yet 'the incidents in this drama are laid together so happily that the spectator makes the play for himself, by the force which the circumstance has upon his imagination'. Steele's view that Banks succeeded in spite of being a wretched writer may have been in Colley Cibber's mind when, in his *Apology* (1740), he too observed that the plays of Banks were written 'in a most barren, barbarous style', but went on to remark on 'the happy disposition of his fables', in which 'the chief characters are thrown into such natural circumstances of distress that their misery, or affliction, wants very little assistance from the ornaments of style, or words to speak them'. What Cibber is saying here is that Banks could write good parts for actors; and as Cibber was an actor himself he ought to have known. Banks has admittedly a hit-or-miss style, and he peppers his dialogue mercilessly with classical allusions remembered from his schooldays; his technique is sometimes crude, his soliloquies are inordinately prolonged, and his blank verse can be baffling. But he holds fast to his action, and, above all, he works consistently in accordance with the principles that Matthew Arnold was to lay down for the poet: 'Choose a fitting action, penetrate yourself with the feeling of its situations; this done, everything else will follow.' With all his technical crudities Banks was a natural dramatist.

Texts collated: *Q.* 1 (1682); *Q.* 2 (1685); *Q.* 3 (1693); *Q.* 4 (1699). See Select Bibliography, pp. 439–41.

THE

Unhappy Favourite:

OR THE

Earl of ESSEX.

A

TRAGEDY

Acted at the

Theatre Royal

By their Majesty's Servants.

Written by *John Bankes.*

——qui nimios optabat Honores,
Et nimias poscebat Opes, numerosa parabat
Excelsæ turris tabulata, unde altior esset
Casus & impulsæ præceps immane Ruinæ. Juven. Sat. 10.

L O N D O N,
Printed for *Richard Bentley* and *Mary Magnes* in *Russel-street* near the *Piazza* in *Covent-Garden,* 1682.

To the Most High, and Most Illustrious

PRINCESS

The LADY

ANN,

Daughter to His

Royal Highness

MADAM,

I humbly lay before your Highness' feet an Unhappy Favourite, but 'tis in your power to make him no longer so. Not his Queen's repentance, nor her tears could rescue him from the malice of his enemies, nor from the violence of a most unfortunate death; but your Highness with this unspeakable favour, and so divine a condescension in protecting this once pitied hero, will make him live eternally; and those who could scarce behold him on the stage without weeping, when they shall see him thus exalted, will all turn envious of his fortune, which they can never think deplorable while he is graced by your Highness. For my own part, I tremble to express my thanks in so mean language, but much more when I would pay my tribute of just praises to your Highness; 'tis not to be attempted by any pen, Heaven has done it to a miracle in your own person, where are written so many admirable characters, such illustrious beauties on a body so divinely framed, that there is none so dull and ignorant that cannot read 'em plainly. And when you vouchsafe to cast your eyes on those beneath you, they speak their own excellencies with greater art and eloquence, and attract more admiration than ever Virgil did in his divinest flight of fancy, than Ovid in speaking of his princess, or Appelles in drawing of his Venus. Nor are your virtues, or your royal blood less admirable, sprung from the inestimable fountain of so many illustrious Plantagenets, that I stand amazed at the mightiness of the subject which I have chosen; besides the awful genius of your Highness bids me beware how I come too near, lest I profane so many

Title. Ann] Anne, second daughter of James, Duke of York (later James II), who became Queen Anne in 1702. When Banks dedicated this play to her she was seventeen years old
9 Appelles] a celebrated Greek painter who lived in the age of Alexander the Great

incomparable perfections in so sacred a shrine as your Highness' person, where you ought to be adored, and not seen: for, like the ancient Jews in their religious worship, 'tis a favour for me to remain on the outward steps, and not approach nigh the veil where the crowd never come. This, most illustrious Princess, ought to check my hand, lest in attempting your Highness' character my apprehension of the excellence of the subject, and the danger of miscarrying, should make my fancy sink beneath so glorious a burden. Therefore I will forbear troubling your Highness any further with the rashness of my zeal; nor dare I be dictated any longer by it, but will conclude, in hopes that, when hereafter I may chance to record the memory of a princess, whose beauty, fortune and merits are greater than Homer ever feigned, or Tasso copied, I may have leave to draw her pattern from your Highness, and when that is done, the rest of my life shall be employed in prayers for your eternal happiness, which be pleased to interpret as the duty of,

MADAM,

Your Highness's Most Obedient,
Most humble, and
Most Devoted Servant,

JOHN BANKS

DRAMATIS PERSONAE

The Earl of Essex	*Mr. Clarke*
Earl of Southampton	*Mr. Gryffin*
Burleigh	*Major Mohun*
Sir Walter Rawleigh	*Mr. Disney*
Lieutenant of the Tower	
Queen Elizabeth	*Mrs. Quyn*
Countess of Rutland, secretly married to the Earl of Essex	*Mrs. Cook*
Countess of Nottingham	*Mrs. Corbett*

Women
Gentlemen, Guards and Attendants

Scene: Whitehall and the Tower

BURLEIGH] Banks has confused Robert Cecil (1563?–1612) with his father, William Cecil, Lord Burleigh. Robert Cecil inherited his father's skill in statesmanship, but not, as a younger son, his title. In the reign of James I he was created successively Baron Cecil, Viscount Cranborne, and finally Earl of Salisbury.

RUTLAND] The wife of Essex was never Countess of Rutland, see p. 205n.

PROLOGUE

Spoken by Major Mohun, the first four days

The merchant, joyful with the hopes of gain,
Ventures his life and fortunes on the main;
But the poor poet oft'ner does expose
More than his life, his credit, for applause.
The play's his vessel, and his venture, wit:
Hopes are his Indies, *rocks and seas, the* Pit.
Yet our good-natured author bids me swear
He'll court you still, the more his fate draws near;
And cannot choose but blame their feeble rage
That crow at you, upon their dunghill stage;
A certain sign they merit to be cursed,
When, to excuse their faults, they cry 'whore' first.
So oft, in their dull prologues, 'tis expressed
That Critic now's become no more a jest,
Methinks self-int'rest in 'em more should rule;
There's none so impudent to ask a dole,
And then to call his benefactor fool?
They merit to be damned as well as poor,
For who that's in a storm, and hears it roar,
But then would pray, that never prayed before?
Yet seas are calm sometimes; and you, like those,
Are necessary friends, but cursed foes:
But if amongst you all he has no friend,
He humbly begs that you would be so kind,
Lay malice by, and use him as you find.

6 *the* Pit] the part of the theatre where the critics habitually sat. Many of them were playwrights, and so on the free list (cf. 'ask a dole', l. 16).

PROLOGUE

Spoken to the King and Queen at their coming to the House, and written on purpose

By Mr. Dryden

When first the Ark was landed on the shore,
And Heaven had vowed to curse the ground no more,
When tops of hills the longing Patriarch saw,
And the new scene of earth began to draw;
The dove was sent to view the waves' decrease,
And first brought back to man the pledge of peace:
'Tis needless to apply when those appear
Who bring the olive, and who plant it here.
We have before our eyes the royal dove,
Still innocence is harbinger to love,
The Ark is opened to dismiss the train,
And people with a better race the plain.
Tell me, you Powers, why should vain man pursue,
With endless toil, each object that is new,
And for the seeming substance leave the true?
Why should he quit for hopes his certain good,
And loathe the manna of his daily food?
Must England still the scene of changes be,
Tossed and tempestuous like our ambient sea?
Must still our weather and our wills agree?
Without our blood our liberties we have;
Who that is free would fight to be a slave?
Or what can wars to after times assure,
Of which our present age is not secure?
All that our monarch would for us ordain,
Is but t'enjoy the blessings of his reign.
Our land's an Eden, and the main's our fence,
While we preserve our state of innocence;

6 *peace*] The whole of Dryden's prologue reflects the political crisis that followed upon the disclosure, or fabrication, of the Popish Plot by Titus Oates in 1678. 21 *Without our blood*] i.e. without having to shed our blood

That lost, then beasts their brutal force employ,
And first their lord, and then themselves destroy:
What civil broils have cost we knew too well,
Oh, let it be enough that once we fell,
And every heart conspire with every tongue,
Still to have such a King, and this King long.

32 *once we fell*] i.e. when Charles I was executed in 1649

THE

Unhappy Favourite,

OR THE

EARL of ESSEX

ACT I SCENE I

Enter Countess of Nottingham, Burleigh *at several doors. The Countess reading a letter.*

C. Nott. Help me to rail, prodigious-minded Burleigh,
Prince of bold English councils, teach me how
This hateful breast of mine may dart forth words,
Keen as thy wit, malicious as thy person;
Then I'll caress thee, stroke thee into shape.
This rocky dismal form of thine that holds
The most seraphic mind that ever was,
I'll heal and mould thee with a soft embrace;
Thy mountain back shall yield beneath these arms,
And thy pale withered cheeks that never glow
Shall then be decked with roses of my own—
Invent some new strange curse that's far above
Weak woman's rage to blast the man I love.
Burl. What means the fairest of the Court, say what
More cruel darts are forming in those eyes
To make adoring Cecil more unhappy?
If such a wretched and declared hard fate
Attends the man you love, what then, bright star,
Has your malignant beauty yet in store
For him that is the object of your scorn?
Tell me that most unhappy happy man;

3 hateful] full of hate 6 rocky] lumpish. Cecil was almost a dwarf, and he suffered from curvature of the spine (cf. 'Thy mountain back', l. 9).

Declare who is this most ungrateful lover,
And to obey my lovely Nottingham
I will prefer this dear cabal and her
To all the other councils in the world;
Nay, though the Queen and her two nations called,
And sinking England stood this hour in need
For this supporting head, they all should sue,
Or perish all for one kind look from you.

C. Nott. There spoke the genius, and the breath of England.
Thou Æsculapius of the Christian world!
Methinks the Queen, in all her majesty,
Hemmed with a pomp of rusty swords, and duller brains,
When thou art absent is a naked monarch,
And fills an idle throne till Cecil comes
To head her councils, and inspire her generals.
Thy uncouth self that seems a scourge to nature
For so maliciously deforming thee,
Is by the heavenly powers stamped with a soul
That like the sun breaks through dark mists, when none
Beholds the cloud but wonders at the light.

Burl. O spare that angel's voice till the last day:
Such heavenly praise is lost on such a subject.

C. Nott. Let none presume to say while Burleigh lives
A woman wears the crown; fourth Richard rather,
Heir to the third in magnanimity,
In person, courage, wit, and bravery all,
But to his vices none, nor to his end,
I hope.

Burl. You torture me with this excess—
Were but my flesh cast in a purer mould,
Then you might see me blush, but my hot blood,
Burnt with continual thought, does inward glow;
Thought like the sun still goes its daily round,
And scorches, as in India, to the root.—
But to the wretched cause of your disturbance;
Say, shall I guess? Is Essex not the man?

C. Nott. Oh, name not Essex! Hell and tortures rather,
Poisons, and vultures to the breast of man
Are not so cruel as the name of Essex.—
Speak, good my lord; nay, never speak nor think

24 cabal] secret 26 two nations] England and Ireland 47 person] Like Cecil, Richard III was a 'crook-back'.

Again, unless you can assuage this worse
Than fury in my breast.
Burl. Tell me the cause;
Then cease your rage, and study to revenge.
C. Nott. My rage! It is the wing by which I'll fly
To be revenged—I'll ne'er be patient more.
Lift me, my rage, nay, mount me to the stars,
Where I may hunt this peacock though he lies
Close in the lap to Juno-Elizabeth,
Though the Queen circles him with charms of power,
And hides her minion like another Circe.
Burl. Still well-instructed rage, but pray disclose
The reason of the Earl's misfortune.
C. Nott. You are,
My Friend, the cabinet of all my frailties;
From you, as from just Heaven, I hope for absolution;
Yet pray, though anger makes me red, when I
Discourse the reason of my rage, be kind,
And say it is my sex's modesty.
Know then,
This base imperious man I loved, loved so,
Till lingering with the pain of fierce desire,
And shame that strove to torture me alike,
At last I passed the limits of our sex,
And (O kind Cecil, pity and forgive me)
Sent this opprobrious man my mind a slave;
In a kind letter broke the silence of
My love, which rather should have broke my heart.
Burl. But pray, what answer did you get from him?
C. Nott. Such as has made an earthquake in my soul,
Shook ev'ry vital in these tender limbs,
And raised me to the storm you found me in.
At first he charmed me with a thousand hopes,
Else 'twas my love thought all his actions so.—
Just now from Ireland I received this letter,
Which take and read, but now I think you shall not—
I'll tear it in a thousand pieces first,
Tear it as I would Essex with my will,
To bits, to morsels hack the mangled slave,
Till every atom of his cursed body

68 Peacock] proud, vainglorious creature. The peacock was sacred to Juno (l. 69).

Severed, and flew like dust before the wind.
[Tears the letter in a rage.
Now do I bless the chance, all else may blame
Me for revealing of my foolish passion.—
Did I e'er think these celebrated charms
Which I so often have been blessed and praised for
Should once be destined to so mean a price
As a refusal!—Are there friends above
That protect innocence, and injured love?
Hear me, and curse me straight with wrinkled age,
With leprosy—derision, all your plagues
On earth, and Hell hereafter, if I'm not revenged.

Burl. [*Aside.*] Else say she is no woman, or no widow.—
The sacred guardians of your slighted beauties
Have had more pity on their lovely charge
Than to behold you swallowed in his ruin.
The best and worst that Fortune could propose
To you, in Essex' love, was to have brought
A helpless, short-lived traitor to your arms.

C. Nott. Ha! Traitor, say you! Speak that word again—
Yet do not; 'tis enough if Burleigh says it:
His wit has power to damn the man that thinks it,
And t'extract treason from infected thought.
The nation's safety like a ship he steers,
When tempests blow, raised by designs of false
And ignorant statesmen; by his wit alone
They're all dispersed, and by his breath she sails,
His prosperous counsels all her gentle gales.

Enter a Gentleman.

Gent. My Lord, the Queen expects you straight.
Burl. Madam,
Be pleased to attend her Majesty i'th' presence,
Where you shall hear such misdemeanours offered,
Such articles against the Earl of Essex,
As will both glad the nation, and yourself.

Gent. My Lord, I see the haughty Earl of Southampton
Coming this way.
Burl. Madam, retire.
C. Nott. I go

102 Me for revealing] *Q.* 2–4; Me for; revealing *Q.* 1

With greater expectation of delight
Than a young bridegroom on his marriage night.
[*Exit* Countess of Nottingham.

Burl. Southampton! he's the chief of Essex' faction,
His friend and sworn brother; and I fear
Too much a friend and partner of his revels
To be a stranger to the other's guilt.—
'Tis not yet time to lop this haughty bough,
Till I have shaken first the tree that bears it.

Enter Southampton.

South. My Lord, I hear unwelcome news; 'tis said
Some factious members of the house, headed
By you, have voted an address for leave
T'impeach the Earl of Essex of strange articles,
Of treason.

Burl. Treason, 'tis most true, is laid
To Essex' charge, but that I am the cause
They do me wrong; th' occasion is too public:
For those dread storms in Ireland raised by him
Have blown so rudely on our English coasts,
That they have shipwrecked quite the nation's peace,
And waked its very statues to abhorring.

South. Mere argument; your nice and fine distinctions
To make a good man vicious, or a bad
Man virtuous, even as please the sophisters.—
My Lord, you are engend'ring snakes within you,
I fear you have a subtle stinging heart;
And give me leave to tell you that this treason,
If any, has been hatched in Burleigh's school.
I see ambition in the fair pretence,
Burleigh in all its cunning, dark disguises,
And envious Cecil everywhere.

Burl. My Lord, my Lord, your zeal to this bad Earl
Makes you offend the Queen, and all good men.
Believe it, sir, his crimes have bin so noted,
So plain and open to the State, and her,
That he can now no more deceive the eyes
Of a most gracious mistress, or her council;

148 th' occasion is too public] i.e. the cause of it is only too well known 152 statues] If this is what Banks wrote, it is one of his bolder metaphors. Qy. 'statutes' (?)

Nor can she any longer, if she would,
In pity of his other parts let justice wink,
But rouse herself from cheated slumbering mercy,
And start at his most foul ingratitude.
Nor does it well become the brave Southampton
To plead in his behalf; for fear it pulls
Upon himself suspicion of his crimes.

South. Hold in my fire, and scorch not through my ribs!
Quench, if thou canst, the burning furious pain—
I cannot if I would, but must unload
Some of the torture.—Now, by my wronged self,
And Essex, much more wronged, I swear 'tis false,
False as the rules by which vile statesmen govern,
False as their arts by which the traitors rise,
By cheating nations, and destroying kings,
And false imposing on the common crew.
Essex! By all the hopes of my immortal soul,
There's not one drop of blood of that brave man
But holds more honour, truth and loyalty
Than thy whole mass besides, and all thy brains
Stuffed with cabals, and projects for the nation;
Than thou that seem'st a good St. Christopher
Carrying thy country's genius on thy back,
But art indeed a devil, and takest more hire
Than half the kingdom's wealth can satisfy.
I say again that thou, and all thy race
With Essex' base accusers, ev'ry one
Put in a scale together, weigh not half
The merit that's in one poor hair of his.

Burl. Thank you, my Lord.—See, I can bear the scandal,
And cannot choose but smile to see you rage.

South. It is because thy guilty soul's a coward,
And has not spirit enough to feign a passion.

Burl. It is the token of my innocence.—
But let Southampton have a special care
To keep his close designs from Cecil's way,
Lest he disturb the genius of the nation,

190 St. Christopher] 'Many legends have gathered round his name. One represents him as a powerful giant who earned his living by carrying travellers across a river, and on one occasion numbered among his passengers a small child who caused him to bow beneath his burden, since the child was none other than the Christ and His weight that of the whole world' (*Oxford Dictionary of the Christian Church*).

As you were pleased to call me; and beware
The fate of Essex. [*Exit* Burleigh.
South. Ha! The fate of Essex!
Thou liest, proud statesman, 'tis above thy reach;
As high above thy malice as is heaven
Beyond a Cecil's hopes.—Despair not, Essex,
Nor his brave friends, since a just Queen's his judge;
She that saw once such wonders in thy person,
A scarce fledged youth, as loading thee with honours,
At once made thee Earl-Marshall, Knight o'th' Garter,
Chief Councillor, and Admiral at Sea.—
She comes, she comes, bright goddess of the day,
And Essex's foes she drives like mists away.

Enter the Queen, Burleigh, Lord Chancellor, Countess of Nottingham, Countess of Rutland, *Lords and Attendants*; Queen *on a chair of state, Guards.*

Queen. My Lords, we hear not anything confirms
The new designs were dreaded of the Spaniards:
Our letters lately from our agent there
Say nothing of such fears, nor do I think
They dare.
Burl. To dare, most high illustrious Princess,
Is such a virtue Spaniard never knew;
His courage is as cold as he is hot,
And faith is as adulterate as his blood.
What truth can we expect from such a race
Of mongrels, Jews, Mahometans, Goths, Moors,
And Indians with a few of Old Castilians,
Shuffled in nature's mould together?
That Spain may truly now be called the place
Where Babel first was built. These men
With all false tenets chopped and mashed together,
Sucked from the scum of ev'ry base religion,
Which they have since transformed to Romish mass,
Are now become the Mitre's darling sons,
And Spain is called the Pope's most Catholic King.
Queen. Spoke like true Cecil still, old Protestant.—
But, oh! it joys me with the dear remembrance
Of this romantic huge invasion.

239 romantic] fantastic, extravagant

From the Pope's closet where 'twas first begot,
Bulls, absolutions, pardons, frightful bans
Flew o'er the Continent and narrow seas,
Some to reward, and others to torment;
Nay, worse, the Inquisition was let loose
To teach the very atheists Purgatory.
Then were a thousand holy hands employed,
As cardinals, bishops, abbots, monks, and Jesuits;
Not a poor mendicant or begging friar
But thought he should be damned to leave the work.

South. Whole shoals of benedictions were dispersed;
Nay, the good Pope himself so wearied was
With giving blessings to these holy warriors
That flew to him from ev'ry part, as thick
As hornets to their nest, it gave his arms
The gout.

Burl. O faithless, incourageous hands!
They should have both been burnt for heretics.

Queen. But when this huge and mighty fleet was ready,
Altars were stripped of shining ornaments:
Their images, their pictures, palls, and hangings
By nuns and Persians wrought,
All went to help their great Armado forth;
Relics of all degrees of saints
Were there distributed, and not a ship
Was blessed without one; ev'ry sail amongst 'em
Boasted to carry, as a certain pledge
Of victory, some of the real Cross.

South. Long live that day, and never be forgotten
The gallant hour, when to th' immortal fame
Of England, and the more immortal Drake,
That proud Armado was destroyed; yet was
The fight not half so dreadful as th' event
Was pleasant. When the first broadsides were given,
A tall brave ship, the tallest of the rest,
That seemed the pride of all their big half-moon,
Whether by chance, or by a lucky shot
From us, I know not, but she was blown up,
Bursting like thunder, and almost as high,
And then did shiver in a thousand pieces,

271 th' event] the outcome 274 half-moon] ships in crescent formation

Whilst from her belly crowds of living creatures
Broke like untimely births, and filled the sky:
Then might be seen a Spaniard catch his fellow,
And wrestling in the air fall down together;
A priest for safety riding on a Cross,
Another that had none, crossing himself;
Friars, with long big sleeves like magpie's wings
That bore them up, came gently sailing down:
One with a Don that held him by the arms,
And cried, 'Confess me straight!' but as he just
Had spoke the words, they tumbled down together.

Burl. Just Heaven, that never ceased to have a care
Of your most gracious Majesty and kingdoms,
By valiant soldiers and by faithful leaders
Confounded in one day the vast designs
Of Italy and Spain against our liberties;
So may Tyrone and Irish rebels fall,
And so may all your captains henceforth prove
To be as loyal and as stout commanders.

Queen. Is there no fresher news from Ireland yet?

Burl. None better than the last, that seems too ill
To be repeated in your gracious hearing.

Queen. Why, what was that?

South. [*Aside.*] Now, now the subtle fiend
Begins to conjure up a storm.

Burl. How soon your gracious Majesty forgets
Crimes done by any of your subjects!

Queen. What?
That Essex did defer his journey to
The North, and therefore lost the season quite:
Was not that all?

Burl. And that he met Tyrone
At his request, and treated with him private.
A ford dividing them, they both rode in,
Wading their horses knee-deep on each side;
But that the distance from each other was
So great, and they were forced to parley loud,
Orders were given to keep the soldiers off;
Nay, not an officer in all the army

307 Tyrone] Hugh O'Neill, second Earl of Tyrone (1540?–1616). In April 1599 Essex landed in Ireland to put down Tyrone's rebellion, but met with little success. Early in September he made the truce with Tyrone that aroused Elizabeth's anger.

But was denied to hear what passed between them.—
What followed then the parley was the truce,
So shameful (if I may be bold to call
It so) both to your Majesty and England.

Queen. Enough, enough, good Cecil, you begin
To be inveterate. 'Twas his first fault;
And though that crimes done to the nation's hurt
Admit of no excuse or mitigation
From th' author's many virtues or misfortunes,
Yet you must all confess that he is brave,
Valiant as any, and 'as done as much
For you as e'er Alcides did for Greece.
Yet I'll not hide his faults, but blame him too,
And therefore I have sent him chiding letters,
Forbidding him to leave the kingdom till
He has dispatched the war, and killed Tyrone.

Enter Sir Walter Rawleigh, *attended by some other Members of the House.*

Burl. Most royal Madam, here's the gallant Rawleigh,
With others in commission from the House,
Who 'ttend your Majesty with some few bills
And humblest of addresses, that you would
Be pleased to pass 'em for the nation's safety.

Queen. Welcome, my people, welcome to your Queen,
Who wishes still no longer to be so
Than she can govern well, and serve you all;
Welcome again, dear people (for I'm proud
To call you so), and let it not be boasting
In me to say, I love you with a greater love
Than ever kings before showered down on subjects,
And that I think ne'er did a people more
Deserve than you. Be quick,
And tell me your demands; I long to hear:
For know, I count your wants are all my own.

Raw. Long live the bright Imperial Majesty
Of England, virgin star of Christendom,
Blessing and guide of all your subjects' lives,
Who wish the sun may sooner be extinguished
From the bright orb he rules in than their Queen

326 Alcides] Hercules 333 'ttend] *Q.* 1; attend *Q.* 2

Should e'er descend the throne she now makes happy.
Your parliament, most blessed of sovereigns,
Calling to mind the providence of Heaven
In guarding still your people under you,
And sparing your most precious life,
Do humbly offer to your royal pleasure
Three bills to be made living Acts hereafter,
All for the safety of your crown and life,
More precious than ten thousand of your slaves.

Queen. Let Cecil take, and read what they contain.

Cecil *takes the papers and reads the contents.*

Burl. *An act for settling and establishing*
A strong militia out of ev'ry county,
And likewise for levying a new army
Consisting of six thousand foot at least,
And horse three thousand, quickly to be ready,
As a strong guard for the Queen's sacred person,
And to prevent what clandestine designs
The Spaniards or the Scots may have.

Queen. Thanks to
My dear and loving people. I will pass it.

Burl. This second Act is for the speedy raising
Two hundred thousand pounds to pay the army,
And to be ordered as the Queen shall please;
This to be gathered by a benevolence
And subsidy, in six months time from hence.

Queen. What mean my giving subjects! It shall pass.

Burl. The third has several articles at large,
With an address subscribed, most humbly offered
For the impeaching Robert Earl of Essex
Of several misdemeanours of high treason.

Queen. Ha!
[*Aside.*] This unthought blast has shocked me like an ague:
It has alarumed every sense, and spoiled me
Of all the awful courage of a queen;
But I'll recover.—Say, my Nottingham,
And Rutland, did you ever hear the like!
But are you well assured I am awake?
Bless me, and say it is a horrid vision,

374 benevolence] forced loan

That I am not upon the throne—
Ha! Is't not so?—Yes, traitors, I'll obey you.— [*She rises in a rage.*
Here, sit you in my place; take Burleigh's staff,
The Chancellor's seal, and Essex' valiant head,
And leave me none but such as are yourselves,
Knaves for my council, fools for magistrates,
And cowards for commanders.—[*Aside.*] Oh my heart!

South. O horrid imposition on a throne!
Essex! that has so bravely served the nation,
That I may boldly say Drake did not more;
That has so often beat its foes on land,
Stood like a promontory in its defence,
And sailed with dragon's wings to guard the seas!
Essex! that took as many towns in Spain
As all this island holds, beggared their fleet
That came with loads of half their mines in India,
And took a mighty carrack of such value,
That held more gold in its prodigious deck
Than served the nation's riot in a year.

Queen. Ingrateful people! Take away my life:
'Tis that you'd have; for I have reigned too long.—
You too well know that I'm a woman, else
You durst not use me thus.—Had you but feared
Your Queen as you did once my royal father,
Or had I but the spirit of that monarch,
With one short syllable I should have rammed
Your impudent petitions down your throats,
And made four hundred of your factious crew
Tremble, and grovel on the earth for fear.

Raw. Thus prostrate at your feet we beg for pardon,
And humbly crave your Majesty's forgiveness. [*Petitioners kneel.*

Queen. No more.—Attend me in the House tomorrow.

Burl. Most mighty Queen! Blessed and adored by all,
Torment not so your royal breast with passion:
Not all of us, our lives, estates and country,
Are worth the least disturbance of your mind.

Queen. Are you become a pleader for such traitors!
Ha! I suspect that Cecil too is envious,
And Essex is too great for thee to grow—

393 council] counsell *Q.* 1–4 401 Essex . . . Spain] The one success of Essex was the storming of Cadiz, in 1596. 404 carrack] large merchant ship, galleon 405 its] *Q.* 1; his *Q.* 2–4

A shrub that never shall be looked upon
Whilst Essex, that's a cedar, stands so nigh.—
Tell me, why was not I acquainted with
This close design; for I am sure thou know'st it.

Burl. Madam—

Queen. Be dumb; I will hear no excuses.—
I could turn cynic, and outrage the wind,
Fly from all courts, from business, and mankind,
Leave all like Chaos in confusion hurled;
For 'tis not reason now that rules the world:
There's order in all states but man below,
And all things else do to superiors bow;
Trees, plants and fruits rejoice beneath the sun,
Rivers and seas are guided by the moon;
The lion rules through shades and ev'ry green,
And fishes own the dolphin for their queen;
But man, the verier monster, worships still
No god but lust, no monarch but his will.

[*Exeunt omnes.*

ACT II SCENE I

Countess of Essex.

C. Ess. Is this the joy of a new-married life?
This all the taste of pleasures that are feigned
To flow from sweet and everlasting springs?
By what false optics do we view those sights,
And by our ravenous wishes seem to draw
Delights so far beyond a mortal's reach,
And bring 'em home to our deluded breasts?
'Tis not yet long since that blessed day was past,
A day I wished that should for ever last;
The night once gone, I did the morning chide,
Whose beams betrayed me by my Essex' side,
And whilst my blushes and my eyes he blessed,
I strove to hide 'em in his panting breast,

442 verier] truer, more real 1 new-married] Essex had married in 1590 (some ten years before the events of this play) the widow of Sir Philip Sidney. It is true that this secret marriage had angered the Queen, but she had long since forgiven him.

And my hot cheeks close to his bosom laid,
List'ning to what the guest within it said,
Where fire to fire the noble heart did burn
Close like a phœnix in her spicy urn:
I sighed, and wept for joy, a shower of tears,
And felt a thousand sweet and pleasant fears,
Too rare for sense, too exquisite to say;
Pain we can count, but pleasure steals away.
But business now, and envious glory's charms
Have snatched him from these ever faithful arms;
Ambition, that's the highest way to woe,
Cruel ambition, love's eternal foe.

Enter Southampton.

South. Thou dearest partner of my dearest friend,
The brightest planet of thy shining sex,
Forgive me for the unwelcome news I bring—
Essex is come, the most deplored of men!
C. Ess. Now by the sacred joy that fills my heart,
What fatal meaning can there be in that?
Is my Lord come? say, speak.
South. Too sure he's come.—
But oh, that seas, as wide as waters flow,
Or burning lakes, as broad and deep as Hell,
Had rather parted you for ever,
So Essex had been safe on th' other side!
C. Ess. My Lord, you much amaze me.—
Pray what of ill has happened since this morning
That the Queen guarded him with so much mercy,
And then refused to hear his false impeachers?
South. Too soon, alas, h'as forfeited his honours,
Places and wealth, but more his precious life,
Condemned by the too cruel nation's laws
For leaving his commission and returning,
When the Queen's absolute commands forbid him.
C. Ess. Fond hopes! Must then our meeting prove so fatal?
South. Say, madam, now what help will you propose?
Can the Queen's pity any more protect him?
Never; it is no longer in her power;
She must, though gainst her will, deliver him
A sacrifice to all his greedy foes.

44 leaving his commission] Essex had returned to England at the end of September 1599.

C. Ess. Where is my Lord?
South. Blount left him on the way,
And came disguised in haste to give me notice.
C. Ess. Let him go back, and give my Essex warning,
Conjuring him from us to stir no further,
But straight return to Ireland ere 'tis known
He left the place.
South. Alas, it is no secret;
Besides, he left the town almost as soon
As Blount, and is expected every moment.
C. Ess. How could it be revealed so suddenly?
South. I know not that, unless from Hell it came,
Where Cecil too is privy councillor,
And knows as much as any devil there.
I met the cunning fiend and Rawleigh whispering;
And the fair treacherous Nottingham
I saw bedecked with an ill-natured smile,
That showed malicious beauty to the height.
C. Ess. Hold, hold, my Lord, my fears begin to rack me,
And danger now in all its horrid shapes,
Stalks in my way, and makes my blood run cold,
Worse than a thousand glaring spirits could do.
Assist me straight, thou Damon to my Essex,
Help me, thou more than friend in misery.—
I'll to the Queen, and straight declare our marriage;
She will have mercy on my helpless state,
Pity these tears, and all my humble postures;
If not for me, nor for my Essex' sake,
Yet for the illustrious offspring that I bear.
I'll go, I'll run, I'll hazard all this moment. [*Offers to be gone.*
South. Led by vain hopes, you fly to your destruction;
There wants but that dread secret to be known,
To tumble you for ever to despair,
And leave you both condemned without the hopes
Of the Queen's pity, or remorse hereafter.
C. Ess. Cursed be the stars that flattered at our births!
That shone so bright, with such unusual lustre
As cheated the whole world into belief
Our lives alone were all their chiefest care.

52 Blount] Sir Christopher Blount (1565?–1601), executed for taking part in the Essex rising
72 Damon] a philosopher whose friendship with Pythias became proverbial. When Damon was condemned to death by Dionysius, Pythias volunteered to take his place.

South. Be comforted, rely on Essex' fate,
And the Queen's mercy—
Behold she comes; our good or evil fate
In discontented characters wrote on
Her brow.

Enter the Queen, Burleigh, Countess of Nottingham, Rawleigh, *Attendant Guards.*

Queen. Is Essex then arrived?
Burl. He is.
Queen. [*Aside.*] Then he has lost me all the flattering hopes
I ever had to save him.—Come, say you!
Who else came with him?
Burl. Some few attendants.
Queen. Durst the most vile of traitors serve me thus?—
Double my strength about me, draw out men,
And set a guard before the palace gates,
And bid my valiant friends the citizens
Be ready straight—I shall be murdered else,
And, faithful Cecil, if thou lovest thy Queen,
See all this done; for how can I be safe,
If Essex that I favoured seeks my life?
Burl. Will't please your Majesty to see the Earl?
Queen. No.
Burl. Shall I publish straight your royal order,
That may forbid his coming to the court,
Until your Majesty command him?
Queen. Neither.—
How durst you seem t'interpret what's my pleasure!
No, I will see him if 'a comes, and then
Leave me to act without your saucy aid,
If I have any royal power.
C. Ess. [*Aside.*] Blessed be the Queen, blessed be the pitying God
That has inspired her.
South. Most admired of queens,
Thus low unto the ground I bend my body,
And wish I could sink lower through the earth,
To suit a posture to my humble heart.
I tremble to excuse my gallant friend
In contradiction to your heavenly will,
Who like a god knows all, and 'tis enough
You think him innocent, and he is so;

But yet your Majesty's most royal soul,
That soars so high above the humble malice
Of base and sordid wretches under you,
Perhaps is ignorant the valiant Earl
Has foes—foes that are only so because
Your Majesty has crowned him with your favours,
And lifted him so far above their sights
That 'tis a pain to all their envious eyes
To look so high above him; and of these
Some grow too near your royal person,
As the ill angels did at first in Heaven,
And daily seek to hurt this brave man's virtue.

Queen. Help me, thou infinite Ruler of all things,
That sees at once far as the sun displays,
And searches every soul of humankind,
Quick, and unfelt, as light infuses beams,
Unites, and makes all contradictions centre,
And to the sense of man, which is more strange,
Governs innumerable distant parts
By one entire same providence at once.
Teach me so far thy holy art of rule
As in a mortal reason may distinguish
Betwixt bold subjects, and a monarch's right.

Burl. May't please your Majesty, the Earl is come
And waits your pleasure.

Queen. Let him be admitted.—
[*Aside.*] Now, now support thy royalty,
And hold thy greatness firm; but oh, how heavy
A load is state where the free mind's disturbed!
Now happy a maid is she that always lives
Far from high honour, in a low content,
Where neither hills nor dreadful mountains grow,
But in a vale where springs and pleasures flow;
Where sheep lie round instead of subjects' throngs,
The trees for music, birds instead of songs;
Instead of Essex one poor faithful hind,
He as a servant, she a mistress kind,
Who with garlands for his coming crowns her door,
And all with rushes strews her little floor,
Where at their mean repast no fears attend
Of a false enemy, or falser friend;

138 centre] agree 158 his coming] her coming *Q.* 1-4

No care of sceptres, nor ambitious frights
Disturb the quiet of their sleep at nights.—
He comes, this proud invader of my rest,
'A comes; but I intend so to receive him—

Enter the Earl of Essex, *with attendants.*

Essex *kneels. The* Queen *turns to the* Countess of Nottingham.

Essex. Long live the mightiest, most adored of queens,
The brightest power on earth that Heaven e'er formed;
Awed and amazed the trembling Essex kneels,
Essex that stood the dreadful voice of cannons,
Hid in a darker field of smoke and fire
Than that where Cyclops blow the forge, and sweat
Beneath the mighty hill, whilst bullets round me
Flew like the bolts of heaven when shot with thunder,
And lost their fury on my shield and corslet;
And stood these dangers unconcerned and dauntless.
But you, the most majestic, brightest form
That ever ruled on earth, have caught my soul,
Surprised its virtues all with dread and wonder;
My humble eyes durst scarcely look up to you,
Your dazzling mien and sight so fill the place,
And every part celestial rays adorn.
Queen. [*Aside.*] Ha!
Essex. 'Tis said I have been guilty—
I dare not rise, but crawl thus on the earth,
Till I have leave to kiss your sacred robe,
And clear before the justest, best of queens,
My wronged and wounded innocence.
Queen. [*Aside.*] What saidst thou, Nottingham? what said the Earl?
Essex. What, not a word! a look! not one blessed look!
Turn, turn your cruel brow, and kill me with
A frown; it is a quick and surer way
To rid you of your Essex
Than banishment, than fetters, swords, or axes.—
What, not that neither! Then I plainly see
My fate, the malice of my enemies
Triumphant in their joyful faces; Burleigh,
With a glad coward's smile, that knows h'as got
Advantage o'er his valiant foe, and Rawleigh's proud

194 My] *Om. Q.* 1–4 196 h'as] *Q.* 2–4; 'has *Q.* 1

To see his dreaded Essex kneel so long,
Essex that stood in his great mistress' favour
Like a huge oak, the loftiest of the wood,
Whilst they no higher could attain to be
Than humble suckers nourished by my root,
And like the ivy twined their flatt'ring arms
About my waist, and lived but by my smiles—

Queen. [*Aside.*] I must be gone; for if I stay I shall
Here wrack my conduct, and my fame for ever.
Thus the charmed pilot, list'ning to the Sirens,
Lets his rich vessel split upon a rock,
And loses both his life and wealth together.

Essex. Still am I shunned as if I wore destruction.— [*Rises.*
Here, here my faithful and my valiant friends,
Dearest companions of the fate of Essex,
Behold this bosom studded o'er with scars,
This marble breast that has so often held,
Like a fierce battlement against the foes
Of England's Queen, that made a hundred breaches;
Here, pierce it straight, and through this wild of wounds
Be sure to reach my heart, this loyal heart,
That sits consulting 'midst a thousand spirits
All at command, all faithful to my Queen.

Queen. [*Aside.*] If I had ever courage, haughtiness
Or spirit, help me but now, and I am happy!
He melts; it flows, and drowns my heart with pity;
If I stay longer I shall tell him so.——
What, is this traitor in my sight!
All that have loyalty, and love their queen,
Forsake this horrid wretch, and follow me.

Exeunt Queen *and her attendants, manet* Essex *solus.*

Essex. She's gone, and darted fury as she went—
Cruellest of queens!
Not heard! Not hear your soldier speak one word!
Essex that once was all day listened to;
Essex that like a cherub held thy throne,
Whilst thou didst dress me with thy wealthy favours,
Cheered me with smiles, and decked me round with glories;
Nor was thy crown scarce worshipped on thy head

206 wrack] shipwreck 213 studded] *Q.* 2–4; studdied *Q.* 1

Without me by thy side; but now art deaf
As adders, winds, or the remorseless seas,
Deaf as thy cunning sex's ears to those
That make unwelcome love.—

Enter Southampton.

What news, my friend?
South. Such as I dare not tell; but pardon me,
As an ill bird that perches on the side
Of some tall ship foretells a storm at hand,
I come to give you warning of the danger.—
See Cecil with a message from the Queen.
Essex. Then does my wrack come rolling on a-pace;
That foul Leviathan ne'er yet appeared
Without a horrid tempest from his nostrils.

Enter to them Burleigh *and* Rawleigh.

Burl. Hear, Robert Earl of Essex,
Hear what the Queen, my Lord, by us pronounces;
She now divests you of your offices,
Your dignities of Governor of Ireland,
Earl Marshall, Master of her Horse, General
Of all her forces both by land and sea,
And Lord Lieutenant of the several counties,
Of Essex, Hereford, and Westmorland.
Essex. A vast and goodly sum, all at one cast
By an unlucky hand thrown quite away.
Burl. Also her pleasure is, that in obedience
To her commands you send your staff by us,
Then leave the court, and stir no farther than
Your house, till order from the Queen and Council.
Essex. Thanks my misfortunes, for you fall with weight
Upon me, and Fate shoots her arrows thick;
'Tis hard if they not find one mortal place
About me.—
Burl. My Lord, what shall we tell her Majesty?
What is your answer, for the Queen expects us?
Essex. Wilt thou then promise to be just, and tell her?
Give her a caution of her worst of foes,
Thy greedy self, the lands-infesting giant,

Exacting heads from her best subjects daily;
Worse than the Phrygian monster: he was more
Cheaply compounded with, and but devoured
Seven virgins in a week, and spared the rest.
South. Hold, my brave friend, waste not the noble breath
Of Essex on so base and mean a subject.—
[*To* Burleigh.] Thou traitor to thy sovereign and her kingdoms,
More full of guilt than e'er thou didst devise
To lay on Essex, whom thou fear'st and hatest;
And thou, because thy sordid soul and person
Ne'er fitted thee
For gallant actions, thinkest the world so too:
For he that looks through a foul glass that's stained,
Sees all things stained like the foul perspective he uses!
'Tis crime enough in any to be valiant,
To win a battle or be fortunate,
Whilst thou stand'st by the Queen to intercept,
Or else determine favours from her hands;
'Tis not who is to blame, or who deserves,
Nor whom the Queen would look on with a grace,
But whom proud Cecil pleases to reward,
Or punish, and the valiant never 'scape thee;
Cursed be the brave that fall into such hands;
For cowards still are cruel and malicious.
Burl. This I dare tell, and that Southampton said it.
South. And put her too in mind of thy vain glories,
Such impudence and ostentation in thee,
And so much horrid pride and costliness
As would undo a monarch to supply.
Essex. So thrives the lazy gown, and such as sleep
On woolsacks, and on seats of injured justice,
Or learn to prate at council tables; but
How miserable is fortune to the valiant!
Were but commanders half so well rewarded
For all their winter's camps, and summer's fights,
Then they might eat, and the poor soldiers' widows,
And children too, might all be kept from starving.
Raw. My Lord, in speaking thus you tax the Queen
Of weakness and injustice both, and that
She favours none but worthless persons.

287 determine] decide upon, fix 288 to] *Q.* 1 too

Burl. Must we return this stubborn answer to her?
You'll not obey her Majesty, nor here
Resign your staff of offices to us?
Essex. Tell her whate'er thy malice can invent;
Yet if thou say'st I'll not obey the Queen,
I tell thee, lord,
'Tis false, false as thy most inveterate soul
That looks through the foul prison of thy body,
And curses all she sees at liberty.
I tell thee, creeping thing, the Queen's too good,
More merciful than to condemn a slave,
Much less her Essex, without hearing him.
I will appeal to her—
Burl. You'll not believe us,
Nor that it was by her command we came.
Essex. I do not.
Burl. Fare you well, my Lords.
[*Exeunt* Burleigh *and* Rawleigh.
Essex. Go thou,
My brave Southampton, follow to the Queen,
And quickly ere my cruel foes are heard,
Tell her that thus her faithful Essex says:
This star she decked me with; and all these honours else,
In one blessed hour, when scarce my tender years
Had reached the age of man, she heaped upon me,
As if the sun, that sows the seeds of gems
And golden mines, had showered upon my head,
And dressed me like the bridegroom of her favour.
This thou beheld'st, and nations wondered at;
The world had not a favourite so great,
So loved as I.
South. And I am witness, too,
How many gracious smiles she blessed 'em with,
And parted with a look with every favour
Was doubly worth the gift, whilst the whole court
Was so well pleased, and showed their wondrous joy
In shouting louder than the Roman bands
When Julius and Augustus were made consuls.
Essex. Thou canst remember too (for all she said was signal)
That at the happy time she did invest

328 star] the star worn by Knights of the Garter

Her Essex with this robe of shining glories,
She bade me prize 'em as I would my life,
Defend 'em as I would her crown and person:
Then a rich sword she put into my hand,
And wished me Cæsar's fortune; so she graced me.

South. So young Alcides, when he first wore arms,
Did fly to kill the Erymanthean boar,
And so Achilles, first by Thetis made
Immortal, hasted to the siege of Troy.

Essex. Go thou, Southampton, for thou art my friend,
And such a friend's an angel in distress;
Now the false globe that flattered me is gone,
Thou art to me more wealth, more recompence
Than all the world was then.—Entreat the Queen
To bless me with a moment's sight,
And I will lay her relics humbly down,
As travelling pilgrims do before the shrines
Of saints they went a thousand leagues to visit,
And her bright virgin honours all untainted,
Her sword not spoiled with rust, but wet with blood,
All nations' blood that disobeyed my Queen;
This staff that disciplined her kingdoms once,
And triumphed o'er an hundred victories;
And if she will be pleased to take it, say
My life, the life of once her darling Essex.

South. I fly, my Lord, and let your hopes repose
On the kind zeal Southampton has to serve you.

[*Exit* Southampton.

Essex. Where art thou, Essex! where are now thy glories!
Thy summer's garlands, and thy winter's laurels,
The early songs that ev'ry morning waked thee,
Thy halls and chambers thronged with multitudes
More than the temples of the Persian god,
To worship thy uprising; and when I appeared,
The blushing Empress of the East, Aurora,
Gladded the world not half so much as I.
Yesterday's sun saw his great rival thus,
The spiteful planet saw me thus adored;

351 the Erymanthean boar] the fourth labour of Hercules was to bring back alive a wild boar that ravaged the neighbourhood of Erymanthus. 352 Thetis] the mother of Achilles, who tried to make her son immortal by dipping him in the waters of Styx 356 globe] a troop, a body of persons (*O.E.D.* 8; Latin, *globus*)

And as some tall-built pyramid, whose height
And golden top confronts him in his sky,
He tumbles down with lightning in his rage,
So on a sudden has he snatched my garlands,
And with a cloud impaled my gaudy head,
Struck me with thunder, dashed me from the heavens,
And oh! 'tis doomsday now, and darkness all with me.
Here I'll lie down—Earth will receive her son.
Take pattern all by me, you that hunt glory,
You that do climb the rounds of high ambition;
Yet when y'ave reached, and mounted to the top,
Here you must come by just degrees at last,
If not fall headlong down at once like me—
Here I'll abide close to my loving centre:
For here I'm sure that I can fall no further.

Enter Countess of Rutland ⟨i.e. of Essex⟩.

Ha! what makes thou here? Tell me, fairest creature!
Why art thou so in love with misery,
To come to be infected with my woe,
And disobey the angry Queen for me?

C. Ess. Bless me, my angel, guard me from such sounds;
Is this the language of a welcome husband!
Are these fit words for Essex' bride to hear!
Bride I may truly call myself, for love
Had scarce bestowed the blessing of one night,
But snatched thee from these arms.

Essex. My soul, my love!
Come to my breast, thou purest excellence,
And throw thy lovely arms about my neck,
More soft, more sweet, more loving than the vine.
Oh! I'm o'ercome with joy, and sink beneath [*They embrace.*
Thy breast.

C. Ess. Take me along with thee, my dear—
My Essex, wake my love, I say:
I am grown jealous of each bliss without thee;
There's not a dream, an ecstasy or joy,
But I will double in thy ravished senses.
Come, let's prepare, and mingle souls together,

382 as] *Om. Q.* 1-4 386 impaled] surrounded 395 centre] i.e. the earth

Thou shalt lose nothing, but a gainer be:
Mine is as full of love as thine can be.

Essex. Where have I been! But yet I have thee still
Come, sit thee down upon this humble floor,
It was the first kind throne that love e'er had.
Thus, like the first bright couple, let's embrace,
And fancy all around is Paradise.
It must be so; for all is Paradise
Where thou remains't, thou lovelier far than Eve.

C. Ess. And thou more brave, and nobler person far,
Than the first man, whom Heaven's peculiar care
Made for a pattern for ingenious Nature,
Which ne'er till thee excelled th' original.

Essex. Thus when th' Almighty formed the lovely maid,
And sent her to the bower where Adam lay,
The first of men awaked, and starting from
His mossy flow'ry bed whereon he slept,
Lifted his eyes, and saw the virgin coming,
Saw the bright maid that glittered like a star;
Stars he had seen, but ne'er saw one so fair.
Thus they did meet, and thus they did embrace,
Thus in the infancy of pure desire,
Ere, lust, displeasures, jealousies, and fears
Debauched the world, and plagued the breast of man;
Thus in the dawn of golden time, when love,
And only love, taught lovers what to do.

C. Ess. O thou most dear, most prized of all mankind,
I burn, I faint, I'm ravished with thy love;
The fever is too hot,
It scorches, flames like pure ethereal fire,
And 'tis not flesh and blood but spirits can bear it,
And those the brightest of angelic forms.

Essex. That is thyself, thy only self, thou fairest;
There's not in heaven so bright a cherubin,
No angel there but for thy love would die:
The Thrones are all less happy there than I.

C. Ess. O my best lord! The Queen, the Queen, my love!
Ah, what have we committed to undo us!
The powers are angry, and have sent the Queen,
The jealous Queen of all our innocent joys,

439 jealousies] suspicions 452 Thrones] the third of the nine orders of angels

To drive us from our paradise of love;
And oh, my Lord! she will not, ere't be long,
Allow us this poor plat, this ground to mourn on.

Essex. Weep not, my soul, my love, my infinite all.
Ah, what could I express if there were words
To tell how much, how tenderly, my thoughts
Adore thee!—Ah, these tears are drops of blood,
Thy Essex' blood, my world, my heaven, my bride!—
Ay, there's the start of all my joys beside,
Blest that I am that I can call thee wife,
That loves so well, and is so well beloved.

C. Ess. Ah, hold my Lord! what shall I say of you,
That best deserves a love so well you speak of?

Essex. Again thou weep'st.—By heaven, there's not a tear.
But weighs more than the wealth of England's crown.
O thou bright storer of all virtues, were there.
But so much goodness in thy sex beside,
It were enough to save all womankind,
And keep 'em from damnation.—Still thou weep'st.
Come, let me kiss thy eyes, and catch those pearls;
Hold thy cheeks close to mine that none may fall,
And spare me some of these celestial drops.
Thus as two turtles driven by a storm,
Dropping and weary, sheltered on a bough,
Begin to join their melancholy voices,
Then thus they bill, and thus renew their joys,
With quivering wings, and cooing notes repeat
Their loves, and thus like us bemoan each other.

Enter a Lady.

Lady. Madam, the Queen expects you instantly.

C. Ess. Ah, what would wish to be of human kind!
Man in his life scarce finds a moment's bliss,
But counts a thousand pains for one short pleasure,
And when that comes 'tis snatched away like ours.

Essex. Go, my best hopes, obey the cruel Queen—
I had forgot: thy love, thy beauties charmed me,
Dearer than Albion to the sailor's sight
Whom many years barred from his native country;
Looking on thee, I gazed my soul away,
And quite forgot the dangerous wrecks below.

459 plat] plot

Farewell!—Nay then, thou'lt soften me to fondness—
The Queen may change, and we may meet again.
C. Ess. Farewell!
Essex. So have I seen a tall rich ship of India
Of mighty bulk teeming with golden ore,
With prosperous gales come sailing nigh the shore,
Her train of pendants borne up by the wind;
The gladsome seas, proud of the lovely weight,
Now lift her up above the sky in height,
And then as soon th' officious waves divide,
Hug the gay thing, and clasp her like a bride,
Whilst fishes play, and dolphins gather round,
And Tritons with their coral trumpets sound;
Till on a hidden rock at last she's borne,
Swift as our fate, and thus in pieces torn.

[*Exeunt severally*.

ACT III SCENE I

Countess of Nottingham, Burleigh.

C. Nott. Now, famous Cecil, England owes to thee
More than Rome's state did once to Cicero pay,
That crushed the vast designs of Catiline.
But what did he? Quelled but a petty consul,
And saved a commonwealth; but thou'ast done more,
Pulled down a haughtier far than Catiline,
The nation's sole dictator for twelve years,
And saved a queen and kingdoms by thy wisdom.
Burl. But what the Roman senate then allowed,
Nay, and proud Cicero himself to Fulvia,
Fulvia the lovely saver of her country,
Must all and more be now ascribed to you,
To the sole wit of beauteous Nottingham;

496 fondness] foolish tenderness, weakness 501 pendants] pennants 504 officious] eager to do good offices, kind 10 Cicero] During his consulship Cicero exposed Catiline's conspiracy. Catiline tried to have him assassinated, but thanks to Fulvia (not the Fulvia who married Mark Antony) his life was saved.

But I will cease and let the nation praise thee,
And fix thy statue high as was Minerva's,
The great Palladium that protected Ilium.—
I came t'attend the Queen. Where is she gone?

C. Nott. She went to her closet, where she's now alone.
As she passed by, I saw her lovely eyes
Clouded in sorrow, and before she spied me,
Sad murmurs echoed from her troubled breast,
And straight some tears followed the mournful sound,
Which, when she did perceive me, she'd have hid,
And with a piteous sigh she strove to wipe
The drops away, but with her haste she left
Some sad remains upon her dewy cheeks.

Burl. What should the reason be?

C. Nott. At Essex' answer.

Burl. What said she then? No doubt th' affront had stung her;
But kind Southampton, faithful to his friend
In all things, came and with a cunning tale,
Which she too willingly inclined to hear,
Turned her to mildness, and at his request,
Promised to see the Earl, and hear him speak
To vindicate his crimes, which bold Southampton
Declared to be his enemies' aspersions;
And now is Essex sent for to the court.

C. Nott. Then I am lost, and my designs unravelled.
If once she sees him, all's undone again—

Burl. Behold the closet opens.—See, the Queen!—
'Tis dangerous to interrupt her. Let's retire.

C. Nott. Be you not seen; I'll wait within her call.

Enter the Queen *alone as from her closet. Exit* Burleigh.

Queen. Where am I now? Why wander I alone?
What drags my body forth without a mind,
In all things like a statue but in motion?
There's something I would say, but know not what,
Nor yet to whom.—O wretched state of princes!
That never can enjoy, nor wish to have,
What is but meanly in itself a crime,
But 'tis a plague, and reigns through all the world.
Faults done by us are like licentious laws,

16 Palladium] the great statue of Pallas Athena (Minerva) in Troy (Ilium) 28 What said she then?] wrongly given in *Q.* 1 as part of the reply of the Countess to Burleigh.

Adored by all the rabble, and are easier,
And sooner far obeyed, than what are honest;
And comets are less dreadful than our failings.—
⟨*To Nottingham.*⟩ Where hast thou bin?
I thought, dear Nottingham, I'd been alone.
C. Nott. Pardon this bold intrusion, but my duty
Urges me farther.—On my knees I first
Beg pardon that I am so bold to ask it,
Then, that you would disclose what 'tis afflicts you;
Something hangs heavy on your royal mind,
Or else I fear you are not well.
Queen. Rise, prithee.—
I am in health, and thank thee for thy love,
Only a little troubled at my people.
I have reigned long, and they're grown weary of me:
New crowns are like new garlands, fresh, and lovely;
My royal sun declines towards its west,
They're hot, and tired beneath its autumn beams.—
Tell me, what says the world of Essex' coming?
C. Nott. Much they do blame him for't, but think him brave.
Queen. What, when the traitor served me thus!
C. Nott. Indeed, it was not well.
Queen. Not well; and was that all?
C. Nott. It was a very bold, and heinous fault.
Queen. Ay, was it not? and such a base contempt
As he deserves to die for? Less than that
Has cost a hundred nearer favourites' heads,
Since the first Saxon king that reigned in England;
And lately, in my royal father's time,
Was not brave Buckingham for less condemned,
And lost not Wolsey all his church revenues,
Nay, and his life, too, but that he was a coward
And durst not live to feel the stroke of justice?
Thou know'st it too, and this most vile of men,
That brave Northumberland, and Westmorland,
For lesser crimes than his were both beheaded.

78 Buckingham] Edward Stafford, third Duke of Buckingham (1478–1521), was executed on trumped-up charges in the reign of Henry VIII. His father had suffered the same fate in 1483, during the reign of Richard III. 83 Northumberland . . . Westmorland] In 1569 those two Catholic earls headed a rebellion on behalf of Mary, Queen of Scots. Northumberland was beheaded in 1572: Westmorland escaped to the Continent, and died in 1601.

C. Nott. Most true.—Can Essex then be thought so guilty,
And not deserve to die?
Queen. To die! to wrack;
And as his treasons are the worst of all men's,
So I will have him plagued above the rest,
His limbs cut off, and placed to th' highest view,
Not on low bridges, gates, and walls of towns,
But on vast pinnacles that touch the sky,
Where all that pass may in derision say,
Lo, there is Essex, proud ingrateful Essex,
Essex that braved the justice of his Queen!—
Is not that well? Why dost not speak?
And help thy queen to rail against this man?
C. Nott. Since you will give me leave, I will be plain,
And tell your Majesty what all the world
Says of that proud ingrateful man.
Queen. Do so.
Prithee, what says the world of him, and me?
C. Nott. Of you they speak no worse than of dead saints,
And worship you no less than as their god,
Than peace, than wealth, or their eternal hopes;
Yet do they often wish with kindest tears,
Sprung from the purest love, that you'd be pleased
To heal their grievances on Essex charged,
And not protect the traitor by your power,
But give him up to justice and to shame
For a revenge of all your wrongs, and theirs.
Queen. What! would they then prescribe me rules to govern?
C. Nott. No more but with submission as to Heaven;
But upon Essex they unload reproaches,
And give him this bad character:
They say he is a person (bating his treasons)
That in his noblest, best array of parts,
He scarcely has enough to make him pass
For a brave man, nor yet a hypocrite,
And that he wears his greatness and his honours
Foolish, and proud as lackeys wear gay liveries:
Valiant they will admit he is, but then
Like beasts precipitately rash, and brutish,
Which is no more commendable in him

86 wrack] undergo ruin

Than in a bear, a leopard, or a wolf.
He never yet had courage over fortune,
And which too shows his natural pride the more,
He roars and staggers under small affronts,
And can no more endure the pain than Hell;
Then he's as covetous, and more ambitious,
Than that first fiend that sowed the vice in heaven,
And therefore was dethroned and tumbled thence;
And so they wish that Essex too may fall.

Queen. Enough, th'ast railed thyself quite out of breath;
I'll hear no more.—[*Aside.*] Blisters upon her tongue.—
'Tis baseness, though in thee but to repeat,
What the rude world maliciously has said;
Nor dare the vilest of the rabble think,
Much less profanely speak, such horrid treasons.
Yet 'tis not what they say, but what you'd have 'em.

C. Nott. Did not your Majesty command me speak?

Queen. I did, but then I saw thee on a sudden
Settle thy senses all in eager postures,
Thy lips, thy speech, and hands were all prepared,
A joyful red painted thy envious cheeks,
Malicious flames flashed in a moment from
Thy eyes, like lightning from thy o'ercharged soul,
And fired thy breast, which, like a hard rammed piece,
Discharged unmannerly upon my face.

C. Nott. Pardon, bright Queen, most royal and beloved,
The manner of expressing of my duty;
But you yourself began and taught me first.

Queen. I am his queen, and therefore may have leave:
May not myself have privilege to mould
The thing I made, and use it as I please?
Besides, he has committed monstrous crimes
Against my person, and has urged me far
Beyond the power of mortal suffering.
Me he has wronged, but thee he never wronged.
What has poor Essex done to thee? Thou hast
No crown that he could hope to gain,
No laws to break, no subjects to molest,
Nor throne that he could be ambitious of—
What pleasure couldst thou take to see
A drowning man knocked on the head, and yet
Not wish to save the miserable wretch?

C. Nott. I was too blame.
Queen. No more:
Thou seest thy queen, the world, and destiny
Itself against this one bad man, and him
Thou canst not pity nor excuse.
C. Nott. Madam—
Queen. Begone, I do forgive thee; and bid Rutland
Come to me straight. [*Exit* Nottingham.]—Ha! what have I disclosed?
Why have I chid my woman for a fault
Which I wrung from her, and committed first?
Why stands my jealous and tormented soul
A spy to listen, and divulge the treasons
Spoke against Essex?—O you mighty powers!
Protectors of the fame of England's queen,
Let me not know it for a thousand worlds;
'Tis dangerous.—But yet it will discover,
And I feel something whispering to my reason,
That says it is.—O blotted be the name
Forever from my thoughts! If it be so,
And I am stung with thy almighty dart,
I'll die, but I will tear thee from my heart,
Shake off this hideous vapour from my soul,
This haughty Earl, the prince of my control;
Banish this traitor to his queen's repose,
And blast him with the malice of his foes:
Were there no other way his guilt to prove,
'Tis treason to infect the throne with love.

Enter Countess of Essex.

How now, my Rutland? I did send for you—
I have observed you have been sad of late.
Why wearest thou black so long? and why that cloud,
That mourning cloud about thy lovely eyes?
Come, I will find a noble husband for thee.
C. Ess. Ah, mighty Princess, most adored of queens!
Your royal goodness ought to blush when it
Descends to care for such a wretch as I am.
Queen. Why say'st thou so? I love thee well; indeed
I do, and thou shalt find by this 'tis truth.—
Injurious Nottingham and I had some
Dispute, and 'twas about my Lord of Essex—

165 blame] blameworthy, culpable 178 discover] discover itself, come to light

C. Ess. [*Aside.*] Ha!
Queen. So much that she displeased me strangely,
And I did send her from my sight in anger.
C. Ess. [*Aside.*] O that dear name o'th'sudden how it starts me!
Makes ev'ry vein within me leave its channel,
To run, and to protect my feeble heart;
And now my blood as soon retreats again
To crowd with blushes full my guilty cheeks.—
Alas, I fear.
Queen. Thou blushest at my story!
C. Ess. Not I, my gracious mistress, but my eyes
And cheeks, fired and amazed with joy, turned red
At such a grace that you were pleased to show me.
Queen. I'll tell thee, then, and ask thee thy advice.
There is no doubt, dear Rutland, but thou hear'st
The daily clamours that my people vent
Against the most unhappy Earl of Essex,
The treasons that they would impeach him of;
And which is worse, this day he is arrived
Against my strict commands, and left affairs
In Ireland desp'rate, headless, and undone.
C. Ess. Might I presume to tell my humble mind,
Such clamours very often are designed
More by the people's hate than any crimes
In those they would accuse.
Queen. Thou speak'st my sense;
But oh, dear Rutland, he has been to blame!—
Lend me thy breast to lean upon.—Oh! 'tis
A heavy yoke they would impose on me
Their queen, and I am weary of the load,
And want a friend like thee to lull my sorrows.
C. Ess. Behold these tears, sprung from fierce pain and joy,
To see your wondrous grief, your wondrous pity.
Oh, that kind Heaven would but instruct my thoughts,
And teach my tongue such soft'ning, healing words,
That it might charm your soul, and cure your breast
For ever!
Queen. Thou art my better angel then,
And sent to give me everlasting quiet—
Say, is't not pity that so brave a man,
And one that once was reckoned as a god,
That he should be the author of such treasons!

That he, that was like Cæsar, and so great,
Has had the power to make, and unmake kings,
Should stoop to gain a petty throne from me.

C. Ess. I can't believe 'tis in his soul to think,
Much less to act, a treason against you,
Your Majesty, whom I have heard him so
Commend, that angels' words did never flow
With so much eloquence, so rare, so sweet,
That nothing but the subject could deserve.

Queen. Hast thou then heard him talk of me?

C. Ess. I have,
And as of so much excellence as if
He meant to make a rare encomium on
The world, the stars, or what is brighter, heaven.
'She is', said he, 'the goddess of her sex,
So far beyond all womankind beside,
That what in them is most adored and loved,
Their beauties, parts, and other ornaments,
Are but in her the foils to greater lustre,
And all perfections else, how rare soever,
Are in her person but as lesser gleams,
And infinite beams that usher still the sun,
But scarce are visible amidst her other brightness.
And then she is so good, it might be said
That whilst she lives a goddess reigns in England:
For all her laws are registered in heaven,
And copied thence by her.'—But then he cried,
With a deep sigh fetched from his loyal heart,
'Well may the world bewail that time at last,
When so much goodness shall on earth be mortal,
And wretched England break its stubborn heart.'

Queen. Did he say all this?

C. Ess. All this! nay more,
A thousand times as much. I never saw him
But his discourse was still in praise of you;
Nothing but raptures fell from Essex' tongue:
And all was still the same, and all was you.

Queen. Such words spoke loyalty enough.

C. Ess. Then does
Your Majesty believe that he can be
A traitor?

Queen. No; yet he has broke the laws,

And I for shame no longer can protect him;
Nay, durst not see him.
C. Ess. What, not see him, say you!
By that bright star of mercy in your soul,
And glistening through your eyes, let me entreat:
'Tis good, 'tis god-like, and like England's queen,
Like only her to pity the distressed.—
Will you not grant that he shall see you once?
Queen. What, he
That did defy my absolute commands,
And brings himself audaciously before me!
C. Ess. Impute it not to that, but to his danger,
That hearing what proceedings here had passed
Against his credit and his life, he comes
Loyal, though unadvised, to clear himself.
Queen. Well, I will see him then, and see him straight.—
Indeed my Rutland, I would fain believe
That he is honest still, as he is brave.
C. Ess. Oh, nourish that most kind belief, 'tis sprung
From justice in your royal soul.—Honest!
By your bright majesty, he's faithful still,
The pure and virgin light is less untainted.
The glorious body of the sun breeds gnats
And insects that molest its curious beams;
The moon has spots upon her crystal face,
But in his soul are none.—And for his valour,
The Christian world records its wondrous story.
Baseness can never mingle with such courage.
Remember what a scourge he was to rebels,
And made your Majesty adored in Spain
More than their king, that bribed you with his Indies
And made himself so dreadful to their fears,
His very name put armies to the rout;
It was enough to say 'Here's Essex come!'
And nurses stilled their children with the fright.
Queen. ⟨*Aside.*⟩ Ha! she's concerned, transported!
I'll try her further.—Then he has a person!
C. Ess. Ay, in his person, there you sum up all.
Ah, loveliest Queen, did you e'er see the like?
The limbs of Mars and awful front of Jove,

281 glistening] *Q.* 1–2; listening *Q.* 3–4   316 front] forehead (here, perhaps = face)

With such a harmony of parts as put
To blush the beauties of his daughter Venus;
A pattern for the gods to make a perfect man by,
And Michael Angelo to frame a statue
To be adored through all the wond'ring world.

Queen. ⟨*Aside.*⟩ I can endure no more.—Hold, Rutland!
Thy eyes are moist, thy senses in a hurry,
Thy words come crowding one upon another.
Is it a real passion, or extorted,
Is it for Essex' sake or for thy Queen's,
That makes this furious transport in thy mind?
⟨*Aside.*⟩ She loves him.—Ah, 'tis so.—What have I done?
Conjured another storm to rack my rest?
Thus is my mind with quiet never blessed,
But like a loaded bark finds no repose,
When 'tis becalmed, nor when the weather blows.

Enter Burleigh, Countess of Nottingham, Rawleigh, *Lords*, *Attendants and Guards.*

Burl. May't please your Majesty, the Earl of Essex,
Returned by your command, entreats to kneel
Before you.

Queen. [*Aside.*] Now hold out, my treacherous heart!
Guard well the breach that this proud man has made.—
Rutland, we must defer this subject till
Some other time.—Come hither, Nottingham.

Enter the Earls of Essex *and* Southampton *attended.*

Essex. Behold, your Essex kneels to clear himself
Before his Queen, and now receive his doom.

Queen. ⟨*Aside.*⟩ I must divert my fears: I see he takes the way
To bend the sturdy temper of my heart.—
Well, my Lord, I see you can
Withstand my anger, as you lately boasted
You did your enemies'.—Were they such foes
As bravely did resist, or else the same
You parleyed with? It was a mighty courage.

Essex. Well, well, you cruel fates! well have you found
The way to shock the basis of a temper,
That all your malice else could ne'er invent,
And you, my Queen, to break your soldier's heart.

347 parleyed with] i.e. when Essex made a truce with Tyrone

Thunder and earthquakes, prodigies on land
I've borne, devouring tempests on the seas,
And all the horrid strokes beside
That Nature e'er invented; yet to me
Your scorn is more.—Here take this traitor,
Since you will have me so; throw me to dungeons,
Lash me with iron rods, fast bound in chains,
And like a fiend in darkness let me roar:
It is the nobler justice of the two.

Queen. I see you want no cunning skill to talk,
And daub with words a guilt you would evade.
But yet, my Lord, if you would have us think
Your virtues wronged, wash off the stain you carry,
And clear yourself of parleying with the rebels.—
[*Aside.*] Grant Heaven he does but that, and I am happy.

Essex. My parleying with the enemy?

Queen. Yes,
Your secret treating with Tyrone I mean,
And making articles with England's rebels.

Essex. Is that alleged against me for a fault,
Put in your royal breast by some that are
My false accusers for a crime? Just Heaven!
How easy 'tis to make a great man fall,
'Tis wise, 'tis Turkish policy in courts.
For treating!
Am I not yet your general, and was
I not so there by virtue of this staff?
I thought your Majesty had given me power,
And my commission had been absolute
To treat, to fight, give pardons, or disband:
So much and vast was my authority,
That you were pleased to say as mirth to others,
I was the first of English kings that reigned
In Ireland.

Queen. [*Aside.*] Oh, how soon would I believe!
How willingly approve of such excuses,
His answers which to all the crowd are weak.—
That large commission had in it no power
That gave you leave to treat with rebels
Such as Tyrone, and wanted not authority
To fight 'em on the least advantage.

Essex. The reason why

I led not forth the army to the north,
And fought not with Tyrone, was that my men
Were half consumed with fluxes and diseases,
And those that lived, so weakened and unfit,
That they could scarce defend them from the vultures
That took 'em for the carrion of an army.

Queen. [*Aside.*] Oh, I can hold no longer! He'll not hide his guilt.
I fear he will undo himself and me.—
Name that no more for shame of thee the cause,
Nor hide thy guilt by broaching of a worse;
Fain I would tell, but whisper it in thy ear,
That none besides may hear, nay, not myself:
How vicious thou hast been.—Say, was not Essex
The plague that first infected my poor soldiers,
And killed 'em with diseases? Was't not he
That loitered all the year without one action,
Whilst all the rebels in the north grew bold,
And rallied daily to thy Queen's dishonour?
Meanwhile thou stood'st and saw thy army rot
In fenny and unwholesome camps.—Thou hast
No doubt a just excuse for coming too,
In spite of all the letters that I sent
With my commands to hinder thee.—Be silent!
If thou makest more such impudent excuses,
Thou'lt raise an anger will be fatal to thee.

Essex. Not speak! Must I be tortured on the rack,
And not be suffered to discharge a groan!
Speak! Yes I will were there a thousand deaths
Stood ready to devour me; 'tis too plain
My life's conspired, my glories all betrayed:
That vulture Cecil there with hungry nostrils
Waits for my blood, and Rawleigh for my charge,
Like birds of prey that seek out fighting fields,
And know when battle's near: nay, and my Queen
Has passed her vote, I fear, to my destruction.

Queen. [*Aside.*] Oh I'm undone! How he destroys my pity!
Could I bear this from any other man!
He pulls and tears the fury from my heart,
With greater grief and pain than a forked arrow
Is drawn from forth the bosom where 'twas lodged.
Mild words are all in vain, and lost upon him.—
Proud and ingrateful wretch, how durst thou say it!

Know, monster, that thou hast no friend but me,
And I have no pretence for it but one,
And that's in contradiction to the world,
That curses and abhors thee for thy *crimes.*
Stir me no more with anger, for thy life;
Take heed how thou dost shake my wrongs too much,
Lest they fall thick and heavy on thy head.
Yet thou shalt see what a rash fool thou art.—
Know, then, that I forgive thee from this moment
All that is past, and this unequalled boldness;
Give thee that life thou saidst I did conspire against:
But for your offices—

Essex. I throw 'em at your feet.

[*Lays his general's staff down.*

Now banish him that planted strength about you,
Covered this island with my spreading laurels,
Whilst your safe subjects slept beneath their shade.
Give 'em to courtiers, sycophants and cowards
That sell the land for peace and children's portions,
Whilst I retreat to Afric in some desert,
Sleep in a den and herd with valiant brutes,
And serve the King of Beasts; there's more reward,
More justice there than in all Christian courts:
The lion spared the man that freed him from
The toil, but England's Queen abhors her Essex.

South. My Lord—

C. Ess. [*Aside.*] Ah, what will be th'event of this!

Queen. Audacious traitor!

Essex. Ha!

South. My Lord, my Lord, recall your temper.

Essex. You said that I was bold, but now who blames
My rage? Had I been rough as storms and tempests,
Rash as Cethegus, mad as Ajax was,
Yet this has rammed more powder in my breast,
And blown a magazine of fury up.—
A traitor! Yes, for serving you so well;
For making England like the Roman Empire
In great Augustus' time, renowned in peace
At home and war abroad; enriching you

455 toil] a trap or net for catching animals 461 Cethegus] one of Catiline's associates, who was deputed to murder Cicero

With spoils both of the wealthy sea and land,
More than your Thames does bring you in an age,
And setting up your fame to such a height
That it appears the column of the world;
For tumbling down the proud rebellious earls,
Northumberland and Westmorland, which caused
The cutting both their heads off with an axe
That saved the crown on yours.—This Essex did,
And I'll remove the traitor from your sight. [Essex *offers to go.*

Queen. Stay, sir, take your reward along with you—
[*The* Queen *comes up to him and gives him a box on the ear.*

Essex. Ha! Furies, death and hell! a blow!
Has Essex had a blow!—(*Lays hand on his sword.*) Hold, stop my arm,
Some god!—Who is't has given it me? The Queen!

South. What do you mean, my Lord!

Queen. Unhand the villain.—
Durst the vile slave attempt to murder me!

Essex. No, y'are my Queen; that charms me. But, by all
The subtlety and woman in your sex,
I swear that had you been a man you durst not,
Nay, your bold father Harry durst not this
Have done.—Why say I him? not all the Harrys,
Nor Alexander's self were he alive,
Should boast of such a deed on Essex done
Without revenge.

Queen. Rail on, despair, and curse thy foolish breath,
I'll leave thee like thy hopes at th'hour of death,
Like the First Slayer wandering with a mark,
Shunning the light, and wishing for the dark,
In torments worse than Hell, when thou shalt see
Thou hast by this cursed chance lost heaven and me.
[*Exeunt* Queen, *etc. Manent* Essex *and* Southampton.

South. What have you done, my Lord! Your haughty carriage
Has ruined both yourself and all your friends.
Follow the Queen, and humbly on your knees
Implore her mercy, and confess your fault.

Essex. Ha! And tell her that I'll take a blow!
Thou wouldst not wish thy friend were such a slave.
By heaven! my cheek has set on fire my soul,
And the disgrace sticks closer to my heart,

473 Northumberland and Westmorland] cf. p. 221, l. 83n. At the time of the Northumberland–Westmorland rebellion Essex was three years old.

Than did the son of old Antipater's,
Which cost the life of his proud master.—Stand off,
Beware you lay not hands upon my ruin,
I have a load would sink a legion that
Should offer but to save me.

South. My Lord, let us retire,
And shun this barbarous place.

Ess. Ay, there thou say'st it.—
Abhor all courts if thou art brave and wise,
For then thou never shalt be sure to rise;
Think not by doing well a fame to get,
But be a villain, and thou shalt be great.
Here virtue stands by't self, or not at all,
Fools have foundations, only brave men fall;
But if ill fate and thy own merits bring
Thee once to be a favourite to a king,
It is a curse that follows loyalty:
Cursed in thy merits, more in thy degree,
In all the sport of chance its chiefest aim,
Mankind's the *hunt*, a favourite is the *game*.

[*Exeunt*.

ACT IV SCENE I

Countess of Nottingham, Rawleigh.

C. Nott. Sir, did you ever see so strange a scene
As Essex' boldness? Nay, and which is more
To be admired, the Queen's prodigious patience!

Raw. So strange, that naught but such a miracle
Had saved him from death upon the place.

C. Nott. She's of a nature wondrous in her sex,
Not hasty to admire the beauties, wisdom,
Valour and parts in others though extreme,

505 the son of old Antipater's] Antipater was one of Alexander the Great's generals, suspected of poisoning his 'proud master'. At his death he appointed Polyperchon his successor as Governor of Macedonia, passing over his own son Cassander, who, however, purged his 'disgrace' by making himself master of Macedonia. 3 admired] wondered at

Because there's so much excellence in herself,
And thinks that all mankind should be so too;
But when once entertained, none cherishes,
Exalts or favours virtue more than she,
Slow to be moved, and in her rage discreet.
But then the Earl's like an ungoverned steed,
That yet has all the shapes and other beauties
That are commendable, or sought in one:
His soul with sullen beams shines in itself,
More jealous of men's eyes than is the sun,
That will not suffer to be looked into;
And there's a mine of sulphur in his breast,
Which, when 'tis touched or heated, straight takes fire,
And tears and blows up all his virtues with it.

Raw. Ambitious minds feed daily upon passion,
And ne'er can be at rest within themselves,
Because they never meet with slaves enough
To tread upon, mechanics to adore 'em,
And lords and statesmen to have cringes from;
Like some of those strange seas that I've been on,
Whose tides are always violent and rough,
Where winds are seldom blowing to molest 'em.
Sh'had done a nobler justice, if instead of
That schoolboy's punishment a blow,
Sh'had snatched a halberd from her nearest guard,
And thrust it to his heart; for less than that
Did the bold Macedonian monarch kill
Clytus his friend, and braver soldier far.

C. Nott. But worse had been th'event of such a deed,
For if th'afflicted King was hardly brought
From Clytus' body, she'd have died o'er his.
But how proceed the bold rebellious lords
In Essex' house?

Raw. Still they increase in number.
The Queen has sent four of her chiefest lords,
And since I hear the guards are gone. 'Tis said,
For his excuse, that Blount, that fiend of Hell,
And brand of all his master's wicked counsels,

11 entertained] accepted 18 jealous] apprehensive, suspicious 26 mechanics] manual labourers (often used contemptuously) 26 to adore] *Q*. 4; do adore *Q*. 1–3
35 Macedonian monarch] Alexander, who killed his friend Clytus at a feast in a moment of passion.

Has spread abroad this most abhorred of lies,
That I and the Lord Grey should join to murder him.

C. Nott. Already then he's hunted to the toil,
Where let him roar, and lash himself with fury,
But never, never shall get out with struggling.
Oh, it o'erjoyed th'affront within my soul,
To see the man by all the world adored,
That like a comet shined above, and ruled below,
To see him on a sudden from our eyes
Drop like a star, and vanish in the ground;
To see him how he bit the cursed torture
That durst no further venture than his lips,
When he passed by the guards to hear no noise,
No 'Room for mighty Essex!' was proclaimed;
No caps, no knees, nor welcomes to salute him.
Then how he chafed, and started like a deer
With the fierce dart fast sticking in his side,
And finds his speedy death where'er he runs!

Raw. Behold the Queen and the whole court appear.

Enter the Queen, Burleigh, *Lords, Attendants and Guards.*

Queen. Are the rebellious earls then apprehended?

Burl. They are, thanks to the almighty powers,
And the eternal fortune of your Majesty.

Queen. And how did you proceed with my commands?
And how did the rebels act?

Burl. Most audaciously:
The four lords, chiefest of your Private Council,
Sent thither by your Majesty's commission,
Came to the rebel's house, but found the gates
Guarded, and shut against them; yet at last
Telling they brought a message from the Queen,
They were admitted, all besides but him
That bore the seal before the Chancellor
Denied. Ent'ring, they saw the outward court
Filled with a number of promiscuous persons,
The chief of which bold traitors in the midst
Stood the two earls of Essex and Southampton,
Of whom your faithful messengers with loud

47 Lord Grey] Thomas Grey, fifteenth Baron Grey of Wilton (d. 1614), who had served under Essex in Ireland and quarrelled with him

And loyal voices did demand the cause
Of their unjust assembly, telling them
All real grievances should be redressed;
But straight their words were choked by louder cries,
And by the Earl's command with insolence
The people drove 'em to a strong apartment
Belonging to the house, setting a guard
Of muskets at the door, and threat'ning them
That they should there be kept close prisoners
Till the next morning that the Earl returned
From visiting his friends the citizens.

Queen. O horrid insolence! Attempt my Council!
My nearest friends! [*Aside.*] Well, Essex, well,
I thank thee for the cure of my disease;
Thou goest the readiest way to give me ease.—
The City say'st! What did he in the City?

Burl. There, as I learnt from many that confessed,
He was informed the citizens would rise,
Which to promote, he went disguised like one
Whom evil fortune had bereaved of sense,
And almost seemed as pitiful a wretch
As Harpagus, that fled all o'er dismembered
To fond Astyages, to gain the trust
Of all his Median army to betray it.
His head was bare, the heat and dust had made
His manly face compassionate to behold, which he
So well did use, that sometimes with a voice
That ushered tears both from himself and them,
And sometimes with a popular rage he ran
With fury through the streets. To those that stood
Far off he bended and made taking signs:
To those about him raised his voice aloud,
And humbly did beseech 'em for a guard,
Told 'em he was attempted to be murdered
By some the chief of th' court, then counted all his wounds,
Unstripped his vest, and showed his naked scars,
Telling them what great wonders he had done,
And would do more to serve 'em and their children;

103–4 Harpagus . . . Astyages] Astyages, King of Media, had the son of Harpagus, one of his officers, cut to pieces, and the dismembered body served to Harpagus at supper. Harpagus fled, stirred up the Medes against Astyages, and helped Cyrus, the King's grandson, to depose him. 104 fond] beguile, deceive 112 taking] engaging, alluring

Begging still louder to the stinking rabble,
And sweated too so many eager drops, as if
He had been pleading for Rome's consulship.

Queen. How came he taken?

Burl. After he had used
Such subtle means to gain your subjects' hearts
(Your citizens that ever were most faithful,
And too well grounded in their loyalties
To be seduced from such a Queen), and finding
That none began to arm in his behalf,
Fear and confusion of his horrid guilt
Possessed him, and despairing of success,
Attempted straight to walk through Ludgate home;
But being resisted by some companies
Of the trained bands that stood there in defence,
He soon retreated to the nearest stairs,
And so came back by water at the time
When your most valiant soldiers with their leader
Entered his house, and took Southampton and the rest.
Th'affrighted Earl, defenceless both in mind
And body, without the power to help himself,
And being full of horror in his thoughts,
Was forced to run for shelter in the room
Of a small summer house upon the Thames,
Which, when the soldiers came to search, and found him,
Who then had eyes, and did not melt for pity!
To see the high, the gallant Essex there
Trembling and panting like the frighted quarry
Whom the fierce hawk had in his eager eye.

Queen. ⟨*Aside.*⟩ Ha! By my stars, I think the mournful tale
Has almost made thee weep. Can Essex' miseries
Then force compassion from thy flinty breast!
'A weeps, the crocodile weeps o'er his prey!
How wretched and how low then art thou fallen,
That even thy barbarous hunters can neglect
Their rage, and turn their cruel sport to pity!
What then must be my lot? how many sighs,
How many griefs, repentances and horrors
Must I eternally endure for this!—
Where is the Earl?

Burl. Under sufficient guard
In order to his sending to the Tower.

Queen. Ha, In the Tower! How durst they send him there
Without my order?
Burl. Th' Earls are yet without
In the Lieutenant's custody, who waits
But to receive your Majesty's command
To carry 'em thither.
Queen. [*Aside.*] What shall I do now?
Wake me, thou watchful genius of thy Queen,
Rouse me, and arm now against my foe,
Pity's my enemy, and love's my foe,
And both have equally conspired with Essex.
Ha! Shall I then refuse to punish him!
Condemn the slave that disobeyed my orders,
That braved me to my face, and did attempt
To murder me, then went about to gain
My subjects' hearts, and seize my crown!
Now, by my thousand wrongs, 'a dies, dies quickly,
And I could stab this heart, if I but thought
The traitor in it to corrupt it.—Away!
And send him to the Tower with speed.—Yet hold.
C. Nott. [*Aside.*] The Queen's distracted how to save the Earl:
Her study puts my hatred on the rack.
Queen. [*Aside.*] Who is it thou wouldst kill with so much haste?
Is it not Essex? Him thou didst create,
And crowned his morning with full rays of honours?
Whilst he returned 'em with whole springs of laurels,
Fought for thy fame a hundred times in blood,
And ventured twice as many lives for thee;
And shall I then for one rash act of his,
Of which I was the cruel cause, condemn him?
C. Nott. [*Aside.*] Her rage ebbs out, and pity flows apace.
Queen. [*Aside.*] Do what you will, my stars, do as you please,
Just Heaven, and censure England's Queen for it,
Yet Essex I must see; and then whoe'er thou art
That when I'm dead shall call this tender fault,
This only action of my life in question,
Thou canst at worst but say that it was love,
Love that does never cease to be obeyed,
Love that has all my power and strength betrayed,
Love that sways wholly like the cause of things.
Kings may rule subjects, but love reigns o'er kings,

175 this] *Q.* 1; his *Q.* 2–4 183 springs] sprigs

Sets bounds to Heaven's high wrath when 'tis severe,
And is the greatest bliss and virtue there.—
Carry Southampton to the Tower straight,
But Essex I will see before he goes.—
⟨*Aside.*⟩ Now help me, art, check ev'ry pulse within me,
And let me feign a courage though I've none.

Enter Essex *with Guards.*

[*Aside.*] Behold 'a comes with such a pomp of misery!
Greatness in all he shows, and nothing makes
Him less, but turns to be majestic in him.—
All that are present for a while withdraw,
And leave the prisoner here with me unguarded.
[*Exeunt* ⟨Burleigh, Rawleigh, Countess of Nottingham, etc.⟩.
Manent Queen *and* Essex.

Essex. Thus, though I am condemned and hated by you,
A traitor by your royal will proclaimed; [Essex *kneels.*
Thus do I bless my Queen, and all those powers
That have inspired her with such tender mercy,
As once to hear her dying Essex speak,
And now receive his sentence from your lips,
Which, let it be my life or death, they're both
Alike to me, from you my royal mistress:
And thus I will receive my doom, and wish
My knees might ever till my dying minute
Cleave to the earth, as now they do in token of
The choicest, humblest begging of the blessing.

Queen. Pray rise, my Lord. You see that I dare venture
To leave myself without a guard between us.

Essex. Fairest that e'er was England's queen, you need not.
The time has been that Essex has been thought
A guard, and being near you, has been more
Than crowds of mercenary slaves;
And is he not so now? Oh, think me rather,
Think me a traitor, if I can be so
Without a thought against your precious life,
But wrong me not with that; for by yourself,
By your bright self that rules o'er all my wishes,
I swear I would not touch that life to be
As great as you, the greatest prince on earth;
Lightning should blast me first,

Ere I would touch the person of my Queen
Less gentle than the breeze.

Queen. Oh y'are become a wondrous penitent,
My Lord; the time has been you were not so:
Then you were haughty, and because you urged me,
Urged me beyond the suffering of a saint,
To strike you, which a king would have obeyed,
Then straight your malice led you to the City,
Tempting my loyal subjects to rebel,
Laying a plot how to surprise the court,
Then seize my person with my chiefest Council
To murder them, and I to beg your mercy;
This, this the wondrous faithful Essex did,
Thou whom I raised from the vile dust of man,
And placed thee as a jewel in my crown,
And bought thee dearly for my favour, at the rate
Of all my people's grievances and curses:
Yet thou didst this, ingrateful monster, this
And all, for which as surely thou shalt die,
Die like the foulest and the worst ingrate;
But fetters now have humbled you, I see.

Essex. Oh hear me speak, most injured majesty,
Brightest of queens, goddess of mercy too,
Oh, think not that the fear of death or prisons
Can e'er disturb a heart like mine, or make it
More guilty, or more sensible of guilt!
All that y'are pleased to say, I now confess,
Confess my misery, my crime, my shame;
Yet neither death nor Hell should make me own it,
But true remorse and duty to yourself,
And love—I dare stand candidate with Heaven,
Who loves you most and purest.

Queen. [*Aside*.] Now he awakes me,
And all my faculties begin to listen,
Steal to my eyes, and tread soft paces to
My ears as loth to be discovered, yet
As loth to lose the siren's charming song.
Help me a little now, my cautious angel.
I must confess I formerly believed so,
And I acknowledged it by my rewards.

Essex. You have, but oh, what has my rashness done!
And what has not my guilt condemned me to!

Seated I was in Heaven, where once that angel,
That haughty spirit, reigned that tempted me,
But now thrown down, like him, to worse than Hell.

Queen. Ay, think on that, and like that fiend roar still
In torments, when thou may'st have been most happy!—
[*Aside.*] There I outdid my strength, and feel my rage
Recoil upon me, like a foolish child
Who, firing of a gun as much as he can lift,
Is blasted with the fury of the blow.

Essex. Most blessed of queens! Her doom, her very anger's kind,
And I will suffer it as willingly
As your loud wrongs instruct you to inflict.
I know my death is nigh, my enemies
Stand like a guard of furies ready by you
To intercept each sigh, kind wish, or pity,
Ere it can reach to Heaven in my defence,
And dash it with a cloud of accusations.

Queen. [*Aside.*] Ha! I begin to dread the danger nigh;
Like an unskilful swimmer that has waded
Beyond his depth, I'm caught, and almost drowned,
In pity.—What! And no one near to help me!

Essex. My father once, too truly skilled in fate,
In my first blooming age to rip'ning glory
Bid me beware my six and thirtieth year:
'That year', said he, 'will fatal to thee prove,
Something like death, or worse than death will seize thee'.
Too well I find that cruel time's at hand,
For what can e'er more fatal to me prove
Than my lost fame, and losing of my Queen?

Queen. [*Aside.*] 'Tis so, 'tis true, nor is it in my power
To help him. Ha! Why is it not? What hinders!
Who dares, or thinks to contradict my will!
Is it my subjects or my virtue stays me?
No, virtue's patient and abhors revenge,
Nay, sometimes weeps at justice. 'Tis not love
(Ah, call it any thing but that!); 'tis mercy,
Mercy that pities foes when in distress,
Mercy the heavens delights.——
My Lord, I fear your hot-spur violence
Has brought you to the very brink of fate,
And 'tis not in my power, if I'd the will,

305 fame] reputation

To save you from the sentence of the law.
The lords that are to be your equal judges
The House has chose already, and tomorrow,
So soon your trial is to be. The people
Cry loud for justice; therefore I'll no more
Repeat my wrongs, but think you are the man
That once was loyal.

Essex. Once!—

Queen. Hold! For that reason I will not upbraid you;
To triumph o'er a miserable man
Is base in any, in a queen far worse.
Speak now, my Lord, and think what's in my power
That may not wrong your queen, and I will grant you.—
[*Aside.*] So—I am sure in this I have not erred.

Essex. Blessed be my Queen, in mercy rich as Heaven!——
Now, now my chains are light. Come, welcome death,
Come, all you spirits of immortality,
And waft my soul unto his bright abode
That gives my Queen this goodness. Let me then
Most humbly and devoutly ask two things:
The first is, if I am condemned,
That execution may be done within
The Tower walls, and so I may not suffer
Upon a public scaffold to the world.

Queen. I grant it.—[*Aside.*] Oh, and wish I could do more!

Essex. Eternal blessings crown your royal head!
The next, the extremest bliss my soul can covet
And carry with it to the other world,
As a firm passport to the powers incensed,
Say you have pardoned me, and have forgot
The rage, the guilt, and folly of your Essex.

Queen. [*Aside.*] Ha! What shall I do now!
Look to thyself, and guard thy character.—
Go, cure your fame, and make yourself but what I wish you;
Then you shall find that I am still your Queen.
But that you may not see I'm covetous
Of my forgiveness, take it from my heart;
I freely pardon now whate'er y'ave done
Amiss to me, and hope you will be quitted;
Nay, I not only hope it, but shall pray for it,

319 equal] equitable, impartial   352 covetous] miserly, niggard   355 quitted] acquitted   quitted] quited *Q.* 1

My prayers to Heaven shall be that you may clear
Yourself.

Essex. Oh, most renowned and god-like Mercy!
Oh, let me go! your goodness is too bright
For sinful eyes like mine, or like the Fiend
Of Hell, when dashed from the ethereal light,
I shall shoot downwards with my weight of curses,
Cleave and be chained for ever to the centre.

Queen. [*Aside.*] He is going, ay, but whither? To his trial,
To be condemned perhaps, and then to die;
If so, what mercy hast thou showed in that!
Pity and pardon! Poor amends for life!
If those be well, a crocodile is blameless
That weeps for pity, yet devours his prey.
And dare not I do more for Essex, I
That am a woman, and in womankind
Pity's their nature? Therefore I'm resolved
It shall be in's own power to save his life.
If I shall sin in this, witness, just Heaven,
'Tis mercy like yourselves that draws me to't,
And you'll forgive me, though the world may not.—
My Lord, perhaps we ne'er may meet again,
And you in person may not have the power
T'implore what I too freely grant you; therefore,
That you may see you have not barely forced
An empty pity from me, here's a pledge:
I give it from my finger with this promise,
That whensoever you return this ring, [*Gives him a ring.*
To grant in lieu of it whate'er you ask.

Essex. Thus I receive it with far greater joy [*Receives it on his knees.*
Than the poor remnant of mankind that saw
The rainbow token in the heavens, when straight
The floods abated, and the hills appeared,
And a new smiling world the waves brought forth.

Queen. No more; begone, fly with thy safety hence,
Lest horrid, dread repentance seize my soul,
And I recall this strange misdeed.——

Enter the rest with the Guards.

Here take
Your prisoner; there he is, to be condemned
Or quitted by the law. Away with him!— [*Exeunt Guard with the* Earl.

Now Nottingham, thy Queen is now at rest,
And Essex' fate is now my least of troubles.

Enter Countess of Essex *running and weeping, then kneels before the* Queen *and holds her by her robe.*

C. Ess. Where is my Queen? Where is my royal mistress?—
I throw myself for mercy here.
Queen. What mean'st thou!
C. Ess. Here I will kneel, here with my humble body,
Fast rooted to the earth as I'm to sorrow,
No moisture but my tears to nourish me,
Nor air but sighs, till I shall grow at last
Like a poor shrivelled trunk blasted with age
And grief, and never think to rise again
Till I've obtained the mercy I implore.
Queen. Thou dost amaze me.
C. Ess. Here let me grow the abject'st thing on earth,
A despised plant beneath the mighty cedar;
Yet if you will not pity me I swear
These arms shall never cease, but grasping still
Your royal robe, shall hold you thus for ever.
Queen. Prithee be quick, and tell me what thou'dst have.
C. Ess. I dare not, yet I must.—My silence will
Be death, my punishment can be no more.
Prepare to hear, but learn to pity first,
For 'tis a story that will start your patience.—
Oh, save the Earl of Essex, save his life,
My lord whom you've condemned to prisons straight,
And save my life, who am no longer Rutland,
But Essex' faithful wife.—He is my husband.
Queen. Thy husband!
C. Ess. Yes, too true it is, I fear,
By th'awful darting fury in your eyes,
The threat'ning prologue of our utter ruins.
Married we were in secret ere my lord
Was sent by you t'his fatal government.
In Ireland.
Queen. Then thou art wedded to thy grave.
Dost think by this, in multiplying treasons,
And boldly braving me with them before
My face, to save thy wicked husband's life?

416 start] startle

[*Aside.*] What will my restless fate do with me now!—
Why dost thou hold me so? Take off thy hands.
C. Ess. Alas, I ask not mine; if that will please you
I'll glut you with my torments; act whate'er
Your fury can invent; but 'tis for him,
My lord, my love, the soul of my desires.
My love's not like the common rate of women's,
It is a phoenix, there's not one such more:
How gladly would I burn like that rare bird,
So that the ashes of my heart could purchase
Poor Essex' life and favour of my princess.
Queen. [*Aside.*] Would I were loose 'mong wilds, or anywhere
In any hell but this.—Why say I hell?
Can there be melting lead or sulphur yet
To add more pain to what my breast endures!—
Why dost thou hang on me, and tempt me still?
C. Ess. Oh, throw me not away!—Would you but please
To feel my throbbing breast, you might perceive
At ev'ry name, and very thought of Essex,
How my blood starts, and pulses beat for fear,
And shake and tear my body like an earthquake;
And ah! which cannot choose but stir your heart
The more to pity me, th'unhappy frighted infant,
The tender offspring of our guilty joys,
Pleads for its father in the very womb,
As now its wretched mother does.
Queen. Quickly.
Unloose her hands, and take her from my sight.
C. Ess. Oh, you will not—you'll hear me first, and grant me,
Grant me poor Essex' life.—Shall Essex live?
Say but you'll pardon him before I go?—
Queen. Help me.—Will no one ease me of this burden?
C. Ess. Oh, I'm too weak for these inhuman creatures!
[*The women take off her hold.*
My strength's decayed, my joints and fingers numbed,
And can no longer hold, but fall I must.
Thus like a miserable wretch that thinks
H'as scaped from drowning, holding on a rock
With fear and pain, and his own weight oppressed,
And dashed by ev'ry wave that shrinks his hold,
[*She falls down with faintness.*

445 tempt] make an attempt upon, try to win over

At length lets go, and drops into the sea,
And cries for help, but all in vain like me.
Queen. Begone, and be delivered of thy shame;
Let the vile insect live, and grow to be
A monster baser, hotter, worser far
Than the ingrateful parents that begot it.
C. Ess. Ah, cruel, most remorseless princess, hold!
What has it done to draw such curses from you?
Queen. Go, let her be close prisoner in her chamber.
C. Ess. Since I must go, and from my Essex part,
Despair and death at once come seize my heart;
Shut me from light, from day, ne'er to be seen,
By human kind, nor my more cruel Queen;
Yet bless her, Heaven, and hear my loyal prayer:
May you ne'er love like me, nor ne'er despair,
Ne'er see the man at his departing breath
Whom you so love, and fain would save from death;
Let Heaven be deaf as you are to my cry,
And you run mad, and be as cursed as I.
[*Exit* Countess of Essex, *carried away by women.*
Queen. ⟨*Aside.*⟩ She's gone, but at her parting shot a truth
Into my breast, has pierced my soul.—
Why was I Queen? And why was I not Rutland?
Then had my princess, as myself did now,
Given Essex such a ring, and the reward
Had then been mine as now the torment is.—
O wretched state of monarchs! theirs is still
The business of the world, and all the pains,
Whilst happy subjects sleep beneath their gains;
The meanest hind rules in his humble house,
And nothing but the day sees what he does,
But princes, like the Queen of Night so high,
Their spots are seen by ev'ry vulgar eye;
And as the sun, the planets' glorious king,
Gives life and growth to ev'ry mortal thing,
And by his motion all the world is blessed,
Whilst he himself can never be at rest;
So, if there are such blessings in a throne,
Kings rain 'em down, while they themselves have none.
[*Exeunt omnes.*

505 rain] raign *Q.* 1–4

ACT V SCENE I

Sir Walter Rawleigh *with the Queen's Guards*,
the Lieutenant of the Tower.

Raw. Mr. Lieutenant, here expires my charge;
I received orders from Her Majesty,
And the Lord Steward to return the prisoners
Safe in your custody, and with you I leave 'em,
With charge to have 'em in a readiness,
For execution will be very speedy.
Lieut. I shall, sir.

Enter the Countess of Nottingham.

Raw. Ha! the Lady Nottingham!
What makes her here?
C. Nott. Where is my Lord of Essex?
I am commanded straight to speak with him,
And bring a message from Her Majesty.
Raw. Madam, what news can this strange visit bring?
How fares the Queen? Are her resolves yet steadfast?
C. Nott. No; when she heard that Essex was condemned,
She started and looked pale, then blushing red,
And said that execution should be straight;
Then stopped, and said she'd hear first from the Earl:
So she retired and passed an hour in thought,
None daring t'interrupt her till in haste
She sent for me, commanding me to go
And tell my Lord from her, she could resist
No longer her subjects' loud demands for justice,
And therefore wished, if he had any reasons
That were of weight to stay his execution,
That he would send 'em straight by me; then blushed
Again, and sighed, and pressed my hand,
And prayed me to be secret, and deliver
What Essex should return in answer to her.
Raw. I know not what she means, but doubt th'event:
You can tell best the cause of her disturbance.
I will to Burleigh, and then both of us
Will make attempts to recollect the Queen.
[*Exit* Rawleigh *and Guards*.

31 recollect] bring to a reconsideration

C. Nott. Pray bring me to my lord.
Lieut. Madam, I will acquaint him that y'are here. [*Exit* Lieutenant.
C. Nott. Now dragon's blood distil through all my veins,
And gall instead of milk swell up my breasts,
That nothing of the woman may appear,
But horrid cruelty, and fierce revenge!

Enter Essex.

He comes with such a gallantry and port,
As if his miseries were harbingers,
And death the state to set his person out.—
Wrongs less than mine, though in a tiger's breast,
Might now be reconciled to such an object;
But slighted love my sex can ne'er forget.
Essex. Madam, this is a miracle of favour,
A double goodness in my royal mistress,
T'employ the fair, the injured Nottingham;
And 'tis no less in you to condescend
To see a wretch like me that has deserved
No favour at your hands.
C. Nott. No more, my Lord. The Queen,
The gracious Queen commends her pity to you,
Pity by me that owe a great deal more
You know, and wish that I were once your queen,
To give you what my heart has had so long in store.
Essex. Then has my death more charms than life can promise,
Since my Queen pities me, and you forgive me.
C. Nott. Hold, good my Lord, that is not all; she sends
To know if you can anything propose
To mitigate your doom, and stay your death,
Which else can be no longer than this day.
Next, if y'are satisfied with ev'ry passage
In your late trial; if 'twere fair and legal;
And if y'ave those exceptions that are real,
She'll answer them.
Essex. Still is my death more welcome,
And life would be a burden to my soul,
Since I can ne'er requite such royal goodness.
Tell her then, fair and charitable messenger,
That Essex does acknowledge every crime,

50 commends] kindly conveys 51 owe] own, possess

His guilt unworthy of such wondrous mercy;
Thanks her bright justice, and the lords his judges,
For all was gracious and divine like her;
And I have now no injustice to accuse,
Nor enemy to blame that was the cause,
Nor innocence to save me but the Queen.

C. Nott. [*Aside.*] Ha, is this true! How he undoes my hopes!—
And is that all? Have you not one request
To ask, that you can think the Queen will grant you?

Essex. I have, and humbly 'tis that she would please
To spare my life; not that I fear to die,
But in submission to her heavenly justice.
I own my life a forfeit to her power,
And therefore ought to beg it of her mercy.

C. Nott. [*Aside.*] If this be real, my revenge is lost.—
Is there naught else that you rely upon,
Only submitting to the Queen's mere mercy,
And barely asking her so great a grace?
Have you no other hopes?

Essex. Some hopes I have.

C. Nott. What are they, pray, my Lord? Declare 'em boldly,
For to that only purpose I am sent.

Essex. Then I am happy, happiest of mankind,
Blest in the rarest mercy of my Queen,
And such a friend as you, blessed in you both;
The ecstasy will let me hold no longer.—
Behold this ring, the passport of my life;
At last y'ave pulled the secret from my heart.
This precious token,
Amidst my former triumphs in her favour
She took from off her finger, and bestowed
On me.—Mark, with the promise of a queen,
Of her bright self less failing than an oracle,
That in what exigence or state soe'er
My life was in, that time when I gave back,
Or should return this ring again to her,
She'd then deny me nothing I could ask.

C. Nott. Oh, give it me, my Lord, and quickly let
Me bear it to the Queen, and ask your life.

Essex. Hold, generous madam, I received it on
My knees, and on my knees I will restore it.

[*Kneels, and gives the* Countess of Nottingham *the ring.*

Here take it, but consider what you take:
'Tis the life, blood, and very soul of Essex.
I've heard that by a skilful artist's hand
The bowels of a wretch were taken out,
And yet he lived; you are that gallant artist,
Oh, touch it as you would the seals of life,
And give it to my royal mistress' hand,
As you would pour my blood back in its empty channels,
That gape and thirst like fishes on the ooze
When streams run dry, and their own element
Forsakes 'em. If this should in the least miscarry,
My life's the purchase that the Queen will have for't.

C. Nott. Doubt you my care, my Lord? I hope you do not.

Essex. I will no more suspect my fate, nor you:
Such beauty and such merits must prevail.

Enter a Gentleman.

Gent. Th' Earl of Southampton having leave,
Desires to speak with you, my Lord.

C. Nott. Repose
Your mind, and take no thought but to be happy;
I'll send you tidings of a lasting life.

Essex. A longer and much happier life attend
Both my good Queen and you! [*Exit* Essex.

C. Nott. Farewell, my Lord.—
Yes, a much longer life than thine, I hope,
And if thou chance to dream of such strange things,
Let it be there where lying poets feign
Elysium is, where myrtles lovely spread,
Trees of delicious fruit invite the taste,
And sweet Arabian plants delight the smell,
Where pleasant gardens, dressed with curious care
By lovers' ghosts, shall recreate thy fancy,
And there perhaps thou soon shalt meet again
With amorous Rutland, for she cannot choose
But be romantic now, and follow thee.

Enter a Gentlewoman.

Woman. Madam, the Queen.

C. Nott. Ha! that's unlucky.—She come to the Tower!

113 seals] i.e. covenant, promise 116 ooze] The quarto reads 'Ouse': Banks may be referring to the river of that name.

Yet 'tis no matter; see him I am sure
She will not, or at worst will be persuaded.

Enter the Queen.

Queen. How now, dear Nottingham, hast seen the Earl?
I left Whitehall because I could not rest
For crowds that hollowed for their executions,
And others that petitioned for the traitors.
Quick, tell me, hast thou done as I commanded?
C. Nott. Yes, Madam, I have seen, and spoke with him.
Queen. And what has he said to thee for himself?
C. Nott. At my first converse with him I did find him
Not totally despairing, nor complaining;
But yet a haughty melancholy
Appeared in all his looks, that showed him rather
Like one that had more care
Of future life than this.
Queen. Well, but what said he,
When thou awaked'st him with the hopes of pity?
C. Nott. To my first question put by your command,
Which was to know if he were satisfied
In the proceedings of his lawful trial,
He answered, with a careless tone and gesture,
That it was true, and he must needs confess
His trial looked most fair to all the world;
But yet he too well knew,
The law that made his actions treason
Consulted but with foes and circumstances,
And never took from Heaven, or Essex' thoughts,
A precedent or cause that might condemn him;
For if they had the least been read in either,
They would have quickly found his innocence.
Queen. Ha!
C. Nott. That was but the prologue; mark what follows.
Queen. What, durst he be so bold to brand my justice!
C. Nott. I prayed that he would urge that sense no more,
But, since he was condemned and stood in need
Of mercy, to implore it of your Majesty,
And beg his life which you would not deny;
For to that end I said that you were pleased

157 awaked'st] *Q.* 4; awakest *Q.* 1–3 166 Consulted . . . with] took into consideration

To send me to him, and then told him all,
Nay, more than you commanded me to say.

Queen. What said he then? That altered him, I hope.

C. Nott. No, not at all; but as I've seen a lion
That has been played withal with gentle strokes,
Has at the last been jested into madness,
So on a sudden started into passion,
The furious Earl, his eyes grew fiery red,
His words precipitate, and speech disordered;
'Let the Queen have my blood', said he; ''tis that
She longs for; pour it to my foes to drink,
As hunters, when the quarry is run down,
Throw to the hounds his entrails for reward.
I have enough to spare, but by the heavens
I swear, were all my veins like rivers full,
And if my body held a sea of blood,
I'd lose it all to the last innocent drop
Before I'd like a villain beg my life.'

Queen. Hold, Nottingham, and say th'art not in earnest.—
Can this be true? So impudent a traitor!

C. Nott. That's but the gloss, the colour of his treason,
But after he did paint himself to th'life.
'Would the Queen', said he, 'have me own a treason,
Impose upon myself a crime the law
Has found me guilty of by her command;
And so by asking of my forfeit life,
Clear and proclaim her justice to the world,
And stain myself forever? No, I'll die first.'

Queen. Enough, I'll hear no more; you wrong him; 'tis
Impossible he should be such a devil.

C. Nott. Madam, I've done.

Queen. I prithee pardon me.
But could he say all this?

C. Nott. He did, and more;
But 'tis no matter, 'twill not be believed,
If I should tell the half of what he uttered,
How insolent, and how profane he used you.

Queen. You need not, I had rather
Believe it all than put you to the trouble
To tell it o'er again, and me to hear it.
[*Aside.*] Then I am lost, betrayed by this false man,

My courage, power, my pity, all betrayed;
And like that giant, patriarch of the Jews,
Bereft at once both of his sight and strength
By treacherous foes, I wander in the dark,
By Essex weakened, and by Essex blinded;
But then, as hc prayed that his strength might grow,
At once to be revenged on them and die,
So grant me, Heaven, but so much resolution
To grope my way where I may lay but hold
On whatsoe'er this huge Colossus stands;
I'll pull the scaffold down, though o'er my head,
And lose my life to be revenged on his.—
Well, Nottingham, I have but one word more:
Talked not this wicked creature of no reason,
No obligation that I had to save
His life?

C. Nott. No, but far worse than I have told you.

Queen. Sure thou art most unhappy in ill news!
No promise, nor no token did he speak of?

C. Nott. Not the least word, and if there are such things,
I do suppose he keeps 'em to himself
For reasons that I know not.

Queen. 'Tis most false;
He needs must tell thee all, and thou betray'st him.

C. Nott. Your Majesty does me wrong—

Queen. Hear me—
Oh, I can hold no longer.—Say, sent he
No ring, no token, nor no message by thee?

C. Nott. Not any, on the forfeit of my life.

Queen. Thou liest!—Can Earth produce so vile a creature!—
Hence from my sight, and see my face no more—
Yet tarry, Nottingham.—Come back again.
[*Aside.*] This may be true, and I am still the wretch
To blame and to be pitied.—Prithee, pardon me;
Forget my rage, thy Queen is sorry for't.

C. Nott. I would your Majesty instead of me
Had sent a person that you could confide in,
Or else that you would see the Earl yourself.

Queen. Prithee, no more. Go to him!
No, but I'll send a message for his head.
His head's the token that my wrongs require,

217 courage] inclination, desire (*O.E.D.*, 2) 222 he] i.e. Samson

And his base blood the stream to quench my fury.—
Prithee invent, for thou art wondrous witty
At such inventions; teach my feeble malice
How to torment him with a thousand deaths,
Or what is worse than death.—Speak, my Medea,
And thou wilt then oblige thy Queen forever.

C. Nott. First sign an order for his execution.

Queen. Say it is done, but how to torture him!

C. Nott. Then, as the lords are carrying to the block,
Condoling both their sad misfortunes,
Which to departing souls is some delight,
Order a pardon for Southampton's life;
It will be worse than Hell to Essex' soul,
Where 'tis a going, to see his friend snatched from him,
And make him curse his so much pride and folly
That lost his own life, in exchange for his.

Queen. That was well thought on!

C. Nott. This is but the least.
The next will be a fatal stroke, a blow indeed,
A thousand heads to lose is not so dreadful.
Let Rutland see him at the very moment
Of her expiring husband; she will hang
Worse than his guilt upon him, lure his mind,
And pull it back to earth again; double
All the fierce pangs of thought and death upon him,
And make his loaded spirits sink to Hell.

Queen. O th'art the Machiavile of all thy sex,
Thou bravest, most heroic for invention!
Come, let's dispatch.—

Enter Burleigh, Rawleigh, *Lords*, *Attendants*, *and Guards*.

My Lords, see execution done on Essex;
But for Southampton, I will pardon him:
His crimes he may repent of; they were not
So great, but done in friendship to the other.
Act my commands with speed, that both of us
May straight be out of torment.—My Lord Burleigh,
And you Sir Walter Rawleigh, see't performed;
I'll not return till you have brought the news.
[*Exeunt* Queen *and* Countess of Nottingham.

280 Machiavile] Anglicized name of Niccolò Machiavelli, who became a byword for unscrupulous statecraft. 281 bravest] finest

Raw. I would she were a hundred leagues from hence,
Well, and the crown upon her head; I fear
She'll not continue in this mind a moment.
Burl. Then't shall be done this moment.—Who attends?
Bid the Lieutenant have his prisoners ready.— [*Exit Officer.*
Now we may hope to see fair days again
In England, when this hovering cloud is vanished,
Which hung so long betwixt our royal sun
And us, but soon will visit us with smiles,
And raise her drooping subjects' hearts.—

Enter the two Earls, *the* Lieutenant *and Guards.*

[*To Essex.*] My Lord,
We bring an order for your execution,
And hope you are prepared; for you must die
This very hour.
South. Indeed the time is sudden!
Essex. Is death th'event of all my flattered hopes?
False sex, and Queen more perjured than them all!—
But die I will without the least complaint;
My soul shall vanish silent as the dew
Attracted by the sun from verdant fields,
And leaves of weeping flowers.—Come, my dear friend,
Partner in fate, give me thy body in
These faithful arms; and oh, now let me tell thee,
And you, my Lords, and Heaven's my witness too,
I have no weight, no heaviness on my soul
But that I've lost my dearest friend his life.
South. And I protest by the same powers divine,
And to the world, 'tis all my happiness,
The greatest bliss my mind yet e'er enjoyed,
Since we must die, my Lord, to die together.
Burl. The Queen, my Lord Southampton, has been pleased
To grant particular mercy to your person;
And has by us sent you a reprieve from death,
With pardon of your treasons, and commands
You to depart immediately from hence.
South. O my unguarded soul! Sure never was
A man with mercy wounded so before.
Essex. Then I am loose to steer my wandering voyage,
Like a glad vessel that has long been crossed,

304 th' event] the outcome 327 crossed] met adversely

And bound by adverse winds, at last gets liberty,
And joyfully makes all the sail she can
To reach its wished-for port.—Angels protect
The Queen; for her my chiefest prayers shall be,
That as in time sh'as spared my noble friend,
And owns his crimes worth mercy, may she ne'er
Think so of me too late when I am dead.—
Again, Southampton, let me hold thee fast,
For 'tis my last embrace.

South. Oh, be less kind, my friend, or move less pity,
Or I shall sink beneath the weight of sadness;
Witness the joy I have in life to part
With you; witness these woman's throbs and tears;
I weep that I am doomed to live without you,
And should have smiled to share the death of Essex.

Essex. Oh, spare this tenderness for one that needs it,
For her that I'll commit to all that I
Can claim of my Southampton.—Oh, my wife!
Methinks that very name should stop thy pity,
And make thee covetous of all as lost
That is not meant to her.—Be a kind friend
To her as we have been to one another.
Name not the dying Essex to thy Queen
Lest it should cost a tear, nor ne'er offend her.

South. Oh stay, my Lord, let me have one word more,
One last farewell before the greedy axe
Shall part my friend, my only friend from me,
And Essex from himself.—I know not what
Are called the pangs of death, but sure I am
I feel an agony that's worse than death.—
Farewell!

Essex. Why, that's well said.—Farewell to thee!
Then let us part, just like two travellers
Take distant paths, only this difference is,
Thine is the longest, mine the shortest way.—
Now let me go. If there's a throne in heaven
For the most brave of men, and best of friends,
I will bespeak it for Southampton.

340 throbs] heart-beats 346–8 Methinks . . . to her] The very mention of my wife's name should stop your pity for *me*, and make you wish that all such expressions of pity were for her, since otherwise they would be lost (i.e. thrown away on the wrong subject).

South. And I, while I have life, will hoard thy memory;
When I am dead, we then shall meet again.
Essex. Till then, farewell.
South. Till then, farewell.
Essex. Now on, my Lords, and execute your office. [*Exit* Southampton.

Enter Countess of Essex *and Women.*

My wife! Nay then, my stars will ne'er have done.
Malicious planets reign; I'll bear it all
To your last drop of venom on my head.—
Why, cruel lovely creature, dost thou come
To add to sorrow, if't be possible,
A figure more lamenting? Why this kindness,
This killing kindness now at such a time,
To add more woes to thine and my misfortunes?
C. Ess. The Queen, my Lord, has been so merciful,
Or cruel, name it as you please, to let
Me see my Essex ere he dies.
Essex. Has she!
Then let's improve this very little time
Our niggard fate allows us; for w'are owing
To this short space all the dear love we had
In store for many happy promised years.
C. Ess. What hinders then but that we should be happy?
Whilst others live long years, and sip, and taste
Like niggards of their loves, we'll take whole draughts.
Essex. Then let's embrace in ecstasies and joys,
Drink all our honey up in one short moment,
That should have served us for our winter store,
Be lavish, and profuse like wanton heirs
That waste their whole estates at once;
For the kind Queen takes care and has ordained
That we shall never live to want.
Burl. My Lord,
Prepare; the very utmost time's at hand,
And we must straight perform the Queen's command
In leading you to justice.
C. Ess. Hold, good Lucifer,
Be kind a little, and defer damnation,
Thou canst not think how I will worship thee;
No Indian shall adore thee as I will,
Thou shalt have martyrs, and whole hecatombs

Of slaughtered innocents to suck their blood,
Widows' estates, and orphans without number,
Manors and parks more than thy lust requires,
Till thou shalt die and leave a king's estate
Behind thee.

Essex. Prithee spare thy precious heart,
That fluttering so with passion in thy breast,
Has almost bruised its tenderness to death.

C. Ess. Why ask I him, and think of pity there!
From him on whom kind Heaven has set a mark,
A heap of rubbish at the door to show
No cleanly virtue can inhabit there.—
Malicious toad, and which is worse, foul Cecil,
I tell thee Essex soon shall reign in Heaven,
While thou shalt grovel in the den of Hell,
Roar like the damned, and tremble to behold him.
Go share dominions with the powers of Hell;
For Lucifer himself will ne'er dispute
Thy great desert in wickedness above him,
Nor who's the uglier fiend, thyself or he.

Raw. My Lord, you think not of the Queen's commands,
And can you stand thus unconcerned, and hear
Yourself so much abused.

Burl. Be patient, Rawleigh,
The pain is all her own, and hurts not Cecil;
She will be weary sooner than myself.—
Poor innocent and most unhappy lady,
I pity her.

C. Ess. Why, dost thou pity me!
Nay, then I'm fall'n into a low estate
Indeed; if Hell compassionates my miseries,
They must be greater than the damned endure.—
I prithee pardon me.—Ah, my loved lord,
My heart begins to break; let me go with thee,
And see the fatal blow given to my Essex:
That will be sure to rid me soon of torments;
And 'twill be kindness in thee.—Do, my Lord,
Then we shall both be quit of pain together.

Essex. Ah! why was I condemned to this? What man
But Essex ever felt a weight like this!

426 Why, dost] *Q.* 3–4; Why dost *Q.* 1–2

C. Ess. Oh, we must never part.—Support my head,
My sinking head, and lay it to the pulse,
The throbbing pulse that beats about thy heart.
'Tis music to my senses.—Oh, my love!
I have no tears left in me that should ease
A wretch that longs for pity—I am past
All pity, and my poor tormented heart
And spirits within are quite consumed; and tears,
Which is the balm, the scorpion's blood that cures
The biting pain of sorrow, quite have left me,
And I am now a wretched hopeless creature,
Full of substantial misery without
One drop of remedy.
Essex. Th'art pale; thy breath
Grows chill, and like the morning air on roses,
Leaves a cold dew upon thy redder lips.—
She strives, and holds me like a drowning wretch.—
Oh now, my Lords, if pity ever blessed you,
If you were never nursed by tigers, help me.—
Now, now, you cruel Heavens, I plainly see,
'Tis not your swords, your axes, nor diseases
Which make the death of man so feared and painful,
But 'tis such horrid accidents as these.—
She opens her eyes, which with a waning look,
Like sickly stars give a faint glimmering light.
C. Ess. Where is my love?
Oh, think not to get loose, for I'm resolved
To stick more close to thee than life; and when
That's going, mine shall run the race with thine,
And both together reach the happy goal.
Essex. Now I am shocked, torn up, and rooted all
That's human in me.—What, you merciless Heavens,
What is't that makes poor man distracted, mad,
Profane, to curse the day, himself, the Heavens
That made him, but less miseries than mine?
Why, why, you Powers, do you exact from man
More than your world, and all that live beside!
The sea is never calm when tempests blow,
Tall woods and cedars murmur at the wind,
And when your horrid earthquakes cleave the ground,

467 rooted] uprooted (i.e. all is uprooted . . .)

The centre groans, and Nature takes its part,
As if they did design to break your laws,
And shake your fetters off, nay your own heavens,
When thunders roar, rebel, the sun engages,
And all the warring elements resist;
Heaven, seas, and land are suffered to contend,
But man alone is cursed if he complain.—
Farewell, my everlasting love; 'tis vain,
'Tis all in vain against resistless Fate
That pulls me from thee. [*Gives her a letter.*
Here, give this paper to the Queen, which when
She reads, perhaps she will be kind to thee.

C. Ess. Wilt thou not let me go?
I am prepared to see the deadly stroke,
And at that time the fatal axe falls on thee,
It will be sure to cut the twisted cord
Of both our lives asunder.

Essex. We must part.—
Thou miracle of love and virtues all,
Farewell, and may thy Essex' sad misfortunes
Be doubled all in blessings on thy soul!—
Still, still thou grasp'st me like th'fangs of death.—
Ha! now she faints, and like a wretch
Striving to climb a steep and slippery beach,
With many hard attempts gets up, and still
Slides down again, so she lets go at last
Her eager hold, and sinks beneath her weight.—
Support her, all!

Burl. My Lord, she will recover;
Pray leave her with her women, and make use
Of this so kind an opportunity
To part with her.

Essex. Cruel hard-hearted Burleigh!
Most barbarous Cecil!

Burl. See, my Lord,
She soon will come t'herself, and you must leave her.—
Haste, away!

Lieut. Make way there.

Ess. Look to her, faithful servants; while she lives
She'll be a tender mistress to you all.—

480 engages] becomes involved 497 grasp'st] grasps *Q.* 1–4 th' fangs] *Q.* 1–2; th' pangs *Q.* 3–4 499 beach] *Q.* 1; breach *Q.* 2–4

Come, push me off then; since I must swim o'er,
Why do I stand thus shivering on the shore!
'Tis but a breath, and I no more shall think,
Mix with the sun, or into atoms shrink.—
⟨*To his wife.*⟩ Lift up thy eyes no more in search of mine
Till I am dead, then glad the world with thine.—
This kiss (Oh, that it would for forever last!)
Gives me of immortality a taste.—
Farewell;
May all that's passed, when thou recover'st, seem
Like a glad waking from a fearful dream.

[*Exeunt* Essex *to execution*, Burleigh, Rawleigh, Lieutenant *and Guards. Manent* Countess of Essex *with Women.*

Woman. See, she revives.
C. Ess. Where is my Essex, where?
Woman. Alas, I fear by this time he's no more.
C. Ess. Why did you wake me then from such bright objects?
I saw my Essex mount with angel's wings,
(Whilst I rode on the beauteous cherubin),
And took me on 'em, bore me o'er the world
Through everlasting skies, eternal light.
Woman. Be comforted.
C. Ess. Sure we're the only pair
Can boast of such a pomp of misery,
And none was e'er substantially so cursed
Since the first couple that knew sorrow first;
Yet they were happy, and for Paradise
Found a new world unskilled, unfraught with vice,
No tyrant to molest 'em, nor no sword,
All that had life obedience did afford;
No pride but labour there, and healthful pains,
Nor thief to rob them of their honest gains:
Ambition, now the plague of ev'ry thought,
Then was not known, or else was unbegot.

Enter the Queen, Countess of Nottingham, *Lords and Attendants.*

Queen. Behold where the poor Rutland lies, almost
As dead and low as Essex in his grave
Can be, and I want but a very little
To be more miserable than 'em both.—
Rise, rise, unfortunate and mournful Rutland,
I know not what to call thee now, but wish

I could not call thee by the name of Essex.—
Rise, and behold thy Queen, I say,
That bends to take thee in her arms.

C. Essex. Oh, never think to charm me with such sounds,
Such hopes that are too distant from my soul,
For 'tis but preaching heaven to one that's damned.
Oh, take your pity back, most cruel Queen,
Give it to those that want it for a cure,
My griefs are mortal, remedies are vain,
And thrown away on such a wretch as I.—
Here is a paper from my lord to you;
It was his last request that you would read it.

Queen. Giv't me.—⟨*Aside.*⟩ But oh, how much more welcome had
The ring been in its stead! [*Reads to herself.*

C. Nott. [*Aside.*] Ha! I'm betrayed.

Queen. Haste! See if execution yet be done;
If not, prevent it. Fly with angel's wings!— [*Officer goes out.*
Oh, thou far worse than serpent—worse than woman!
Ah, Rutland! here's the cruel cause of both our woes:
Mark this, and help to curse her for thy husband.

The Queen *reads the letter.*

Madam,

I receive my death with the willingness and submission of a subject, and as it is the will of Heaven and of Your Majesty, with this request that you would be pleased to bestow that royal pity on my poor wife which is denied to me, and my last, flying breath shall bless you. I have but one thing to repent of since my sentence, which is, that I sent the ring by Nottingham, *fearing it should once put my Queen in mind of her broken vow.*

Essex.

Repentance, horrors, plagues, and deadly poisons,
Worse than a thousand deaths, torment thy soul.

C. Nott. Madam—

Queen. Condemn me first to hear the groans of ghosts,
The croaks of ravens, and the damned in torments,
Just Heaven! 'tis music to what thou canst utter;
Begone! Fly to that utmost verge of earth,
Where the globe's bounded with eternity,
And never more be seen of human kind;
Cursed with long life and with a fear to die,
With thy guilt ever in thy memory,
And Essex' ghost be still before thy eye.

C. Nott. I do confess—
Queen. Quick, bear her from my sight, her words are blasting,
Her eyes are basilisks, infection reigns
Where'er she breathes; go shut her in a cave,
Or chain her to some rock whole worlds from hence,
The distance is too near. There let her live
Howling to th'seas to rid her of her pain,
For she and I must never meet again—
Away with her!
C. Nott. I go—but have this comfort in my doom;
I leave you all with greater plagues at home.
[*Exit* Countess of Nottingham.

Enter Burleigh *and* Rawleigh.

Burl. Madam, your orders came too late—
The Earl was dead—
Queen. Then I wish thou wert dead that say'st it,
But I'll be just and curse none but myself.—
What said he when he came so soon to die?
Burl. Indeed, his end, made so by woeful casualties,
Was very sad and full of pity;
But at the block all hero he appeared,
Or else, to give him a more Christian title,
A martyr armed with resolution;
Said little, but did bless your Majesty,
And died full of forgiveness to the world,
As was no doubt his soul that soon expired.
Queen. Come, thou choice relict of lamented Essex,
Call me no more by th' name of Queen, but friend.
When thy dear husband's death revenged shall be,
Pity my fate, but lay no guilt on me,
Since 'tis th'Almighty's pleasure, though severe,
To punish thus his faithful regents here,
To lay on kings his hardest task of rule,
And yet has given 'em but a human soul.
The subtle paths of traitors' hearts to view
Reason's too dark, a hundred eyes too few;
Yet when by subjects we have been betrayed,
The blame is ours, their crimes on us are laid,
And that which makes a monarch's happiness,
Is not in reigning well, but with success.

[*Exeunt omnes.*

EPILOGUE

By Mr. Dryden

We act by fits and starts, like drowning men,
But just peep up, and then dop down again;
Let those who call us wicked change their sense,
For never men lived more on Providence;
Not Lott'ry Cavaliers are half so poor,
Nor broken cits, nor a vacation whore,
Not courts nor courtiers living on the rents,
Of the three last ungiving parliaments.
So wretched that if Pharaoh could divine,
He might have spared his dreams of seven lean kine,
And changed the vision for the Muses nine.
The comet which they say portends a dearth,
Was but a vapour drawn from playhouse earth,
Pent here since our last fire, and Lilly says,
Foreshows our change of state and thin third days.
'Tis not our want of wit that keeps us poor,
For then the printer's press would suffer more:
Their pamphleteers their venom daily spit,
They thrive by treason and we starve by wit.
Confess the truth, which of you has not laid [To the upper gallery.
Four farthings out to buy the Hatfield Maid?
Or what is duller yet, and more to spite us,
Democritus *his wars with* Heraclitus?

2 *dop*] sink suddenly 5 *Lott'ry Cavaliers*] 'poor loyal officers, to whom the right of keeping lotteries was granted by patent in Charles II's reign' (*O.E.D.*) 6 *broken cits*] bankrupt citizens 8 *ungiving parliaments*] of 1679, 1680, 1681. During their short existence none of them had voted money for the King's use. 10 *seven lean kine*] see Genesis 41: 1–4 12 *comet*] One had appeared in the winter of 1680. 14 *fire*] the Theatre Royal in Bridges Street was destroyed by fire in January 1672 *Lilly*] William Lilly (1602–81), a celebrated astrologer. 15 *third days*] the days on which the author of a play received his benefit 21 Hatfield Maid] In 1681 one Elizabeth Freeman of Bishop's-Hatfield, Herts, claimed to have seen, on four separate occasions, the apparition of a woman in white. Dryden alludes to a pamphlet describing the occurrences. 22 *to*] *Q.* 1; does *Q.* 2–4 23 Democritus . . . Heraclitus] *Heraclitus Ridens* was a Tory paper (1681–2); it gave rise to a short-lived Whig paper, *Democritus Ridens*.

These are the authors that have run us down,
And exercise you critics of the Town;
Yet these are pearls to your lampooning rhymes,
Y' abuse yourselves more dully than the times;
Scandal, *the glory of the* English *nation,*
Is worn to rags and scribbled out of fashion;
Such harmless thrusts, as if like fencers wise,
You had agreed your play before the prize.
Faith, you may hang your harps upon the willows,
'Tis just like children when they box with pillows.
Then put an end to civil wars for shame,
Let each knight errant who has wronged a dame,
Throw down his pen, and give her if he can,
The satisfaction of a gentleman.

30 *fencers*] The allusion is to professional swordsmen, who practised 'the noble art of self-defence' for prize money. 32 *willows*] see Psalms 137: 2

PROLOGUE

Intended to be spoken, Written by the Author

'Tis said, when the renowned Augustus *reigned,*
That all the world in peace and wealth remained,
And though the school of action, war, was o'er,
Arms, arts, and letters then increased the more.
All these sprung from our royal virgin's bays,
And flourished better than in Cæsar's days;
And only in her time at once was seen
So brave a soldier, statesman, and a queen.*
Her reign may be compared to that above,
As the best poet, Cæsar's, did to Jove:
For as great Julius built the mightiest throne,
And left Rome's first large empire to his son,
Under whose weight, till her, we all did groan;
So her great father was the first that struck
Rome's triple crown; but she threw off the yoke:
Straight at her birth new light the heavens adorned,
Which more than fifteen hundred years had mourned.—
But hold, I'm bid to let you understand,
That when our poet took this work in hand,
He trembled straight like prophets in a dream;
Her awful genius stood, and threatened him;
Her modest beauties only he has shown,
And has her character so nicely drawn,
That if herself in purest robes of light,
Should come from heaven, and bless us with her sight,
She would not blush to hear what he has writ.
Therefore—
To all the shining sex this play's addressed,
But more the Court, *the planets of the rest;*

* Essex *and* Burleigh.

10 *the best poet*] Virgil 15 *triple crown*] the papal tiara 23 *nicely*] scrupulously

You who on earth are man's best, softest fate,
So that when heaven with some rough piece has met,
It sends him you to mould, and new create.
Strange ways to virtue, some may think to prove,
But yet the best and surest path is love;
Love, like the ermine, is so nice a guest,
It never enters in a vicious breast.—
If you are pleased, we will be bold to say,
This modest poem is the ladies' play.

33 *prove*] attempt 35 *ermine*] The cleanliness of the ermine (stoat) was often remarked.

VENICE PRESERVED

Thomas Otway

1652–1685

Venice Preserved, the sixth and last of Otway's tragedies, was produced at the Duke's Theatre, Dorset Garden, early in February 1682. With this and some earlier plays, notably *Don Carlos* and *The Orphan*, Otway gave Restoration tragedy a new direction. Although the dilemma of Jaffeir may seem to recall the old love-and-honour situation of the heroic drama, Otway's heroes are different in kind from the Almanzors of Dryden: they suffer and agonize rather than act. The emphasis falls on fate and circumstance combining to strike at a character who is noble and well-meaning, but who is unable to cope with the forces ranged against him. The effect is therefore one of pathos, of misfortunes closing in on a doomed hero and heroine, and this change of emphasis is increased by the domestic setting of both *The Orphan* and *Venice Preserved*. The move towards a domestic tragedy becomes more evident a generation later in Nicholas Rowe, who described his tragedy, *The Fair Penitent*, as 'a melancholy tale of private woes', and told his audience that it was a mistake to think of tragedy as being restricted to kings and princes,

> As if misfortune made the throne her seat,
> And none could be unhappy but the great . . .
> No princes here lost royalty bemoan,
> But you shall meet with sorrows like your own.

A new sentimentalism, then, was creeping into the drama, and it is to be found in varying degrees in *The Unhappy Favourite* of Banks and in Southerne's *Oroonoko*.

In its own day *Venice Preserved* had also a topical interest, and this was spelt out in the sub-title, 'A Plot Discovered'. From 1678, when the infamous Titus Oates swore to the existence of a Jesuit plot to murder Charles II and his evidence was seized upon by the Whigs, led by Shaftesbury, to secure a Protestant succession, the country had been in a political ferment. By 1681 the King was beginning to recover control, and it was possible to have Shaftesbury arrested for high treason in the summer of that year. When *Venice Preserved* was produced in 1682 the tide had turned, but political feeling was still running high. Since Otway's play, with its satirical portrayal of Shaftesbury as the lecherous Antonio, had a clear anti-Whig bias, there was no danger of its being banned (as *Lucius Junius Brutus* had been); but one of the unexplained mysteries of the Restoration theatre is how, with playgoers fairly evenly divided between Whig and Tory, a play with such a pronounced political slant was ever given a quiet hearing by that part of the audience that disagreed with it. So far as *Venice Preserved* is concerned, the contemporary audience may well have been in a rather muddled state of mind. The republic of Venice, against which the plot was hatched, was traditionally held up by Whig political writers as the ideal state, and its possible overthrow should not have worried any good Tory. Again, the Venetian senate (which is presumably to be equated with the House of Lords, or the Lords and Commons) is shown as selfish and perjured, and one of the senators, Antonio, is more contemptible and corrupt than any of the conspirators—one of whom, Jaffier, is the hero of the tragedy, and another, Pierre, the only character of complete integrity. This ambivalence extends to some of the *dramatis personae*, notably Jaffier, who is an oddly unheroic hero. At all events the tragedy appears to have delighted the contemporary audience, and it survived as a stock play all through the eighteenth century and into the nineteenth.

Otway's source was a work by César Vischard, Abbé de Saint-Réal, which was translated into English in 1675 with the title, *A Conspiracy of the Spaniards against the State of Venice*. Here he found Jaffier, Pierre, Bedamore (the Marquis of Bedamar) and the other conspirators. Belvidera is his own invention; and Otway uses her, after she has disclosed to her husband the lecherous advances of old Renault, to motivate Jaffier's revulsion from the conspirators and the conspiracy.

Texts collated: *Q.* 1 (1682); *Works* (Collected Works, 1712); Ghosh (*The Works of Thomas Otway*, ed. J. C. Ghosh, Oxford, 1932). See Selected Bibliography, pp. 439–41.

Venice Preserv'd,

OR,

A Plot Discover'd.

A

TRAGEDY.

As it is Acted at the

DUKE'S THEATRE.

Written by *THOMAS OTWAY.*

LONDON,

Printed for *Jos. Hindmarsh* at the Sign of the
Black Bull, over against the Royal
Exchange in *Cornhill.* 1682.

EPISTLE DEDICATORY

To Her GRACE the DUCHESS OF PORTSMOUTH

MADAM,

Were it possible for me to let the world know how entirely your Grace's goodness has devoted a poor man to your service; were there words enough in speech to express the mighty sense I have of your great bounty towards me; surely I should write and talk of it for ever. But your Grace has given me so large a theme, and laid so very vast a foundation, that imagination wants stock to build upon it. I am as one dumb when I would speak of it, and when I strive to write, I want a scale of thought sufficient to comprehend the height of it. Forgive me then, madam, if (as a poor peasant once made a present of an apple to an emperor) I bring this small tribute, the humble growth of my little garden, and lay it at your feet. Believe it is paid you with the utmost gratitude, believe that so long as I have thought to remember how very much I owe your generous nature, I will ever have a heart that shall be grateful for it too. Your Grace, next Heaven, deserves it amply from me; that gave me life, but on a hard condition, till your extended favour taught me to prize the gift, and took the heavy burden it was clogged with from me: I mean hard fortune. When I had enemies that with malicious power kept back and shaded me from those royal beams whose warmth is all I have, or hope to live by, your noble pity and compassion found me where I was far cast backward from my blessing down in the rear of fortune, called me up, placed me in the shine, and I have felt its comfort. You have in that restored me to my native right, for a steady faith, and loyalty to my Prince, was all the inheritance my father left me; and however hardly my ill fortune deal with me, 'tis what I prize so well that I ne'er pawned it yet, and hope I ne'er shall part with it. Nature and fortune were certainly in

Title. Duchess of Portsmouth] Louise Renée de Quéroualle, the French mistress of Charles II
10 apple] A peasant presented an apple of great beauty to Theodosius II, who gave it to his empress, Eudocia. She in turn made a present of it to her favourite Paulinus, who then offered it to the Emperor. The suspicions of Theodosius were aroused, and Paulinus was banished and later killed.

league when you were born, and as the first took care to give you beauty enough to enslave the hearts of all the world, so the other resolved to do its merit justice, that none but a monarch fit to rule that world should e'er possess it, and in it he had an empire. The young prince you have given him, by his blooming virtues early declares the mighty stock he came from; and as you have taken all the pious care of a dear mother and a prudent guardian to give him a noble and generous education, may it succeed according to his merits and your wishes. May he grow up to be a bulwark to his illustrious father, and a patron to his loyal subjects, with wisdom and learning to assist him, whenever called to his councils, to defend his right against the encroachments of republicans in his senates, to cherish such men as shall be able to vindicate the royal cause, that good and fit servants to the Crown may never be lost for want of a protector. May he have courage and conduct, fit to fight his battles abroad, and terrify his rebels at home; and that all these may be yet more sure, may he never, during the spring-time of his years, when those growing virtues ought with care to be cherished, in order to their ripening—may he never meet with vicious natures, or the tongues of faithless, sordid, insipid flatterers to blast 'em. To conclude: may he be as great as the hand of fortune (with his honour) shall be able to make him; and may your Grace, who are so good a mistress, and so noble a patroness, never meet with a less grateful servant, than,

Madam,

Your Grace's entirely

Devoted creature,

Thomas Otway.

29 prince] Charles Lennox, first Duke of Richmond, b. 1672

PROLOGUE

In these distracted times, when each man dreads
The bloody stratagems of busy heads;
When we have feared three years we know not what,
Till witnesses begin to die o' th' rot,
What made our poet meddle with a plot?
Was't that he fancied, for the very sake
And name of Plot, his trifling play might take?
For there's not in't one inch-board evidence,
But 'tis, he says, to reason plain and sense,
And that he thinks a plausible defence.
Were truth by sense and reason to be tried,
Sure all our swearers might be laid aside:
No, of such tools our author has no need,
To make his plot, or make his play succeed;
He of black bills has no prodigious tales,
Or Spanish pilgrims cast ashore in Wales;
Here's not one murdered magistrate at least,
Kept rank like ven'son for a City feast,
Grown four days stiff, the better to prepare
And fit his pliant limbs to ride in chair.

1 *these distracted times*] From 1678 to 1682 the country was in a state of political ferment over the Popish Plot and the question of a Protestant succession. 4 *witnesses*] The first witness was Titus Oates, but he was followed by various other unscrupulous perjurers. 8 *inch-board evidence*] evidence sworn to through thick and thin 15 *black bills*] halberds painted black. (At the trial of Edward Coleman, the Duchess of York's Catholic secretary, Oates had testified that '40,000 black bills . . . were provided to be sent into Ireland' to arm the rebels there.) 16 *Spanish pilgrims*] At the trial of Richard Langhorne, another Catholic victim of the Popish Plot, William Bedloe swore that Langhorne had received a letter from the Irish Jesuits at Salamanca telling him that some Irish cashiered soldiers were to be landed at Milford Haven 'under the colour of pilgrims'. 17 *murdered magistrate*] On 17 October 1678, the body of Sir Edmond Berry Godfrey, justice of the peace for Westminster, was found in a ditch at Primrose Hill, near Hampstead. Early in September Oates had visited him to make his first depositions on oath about the Popish Plot, and it was generally assumed that Godfrey had been murdered by Roman Catholic priests. 20 *ride in chair*] At the subsequent trial of the three men accused of his murder, evidence was given that Godfrey had been strangled at Somerset House, and his body conveyed in a sedan chair to Primrose Hill.

Yet here's an army raised, though under ground,
But no man seen, nor one commission found;
Here is a traitor too, that's very old,
Turbulent, subtle, mischievous and bold,
Bloody, revengeful, and to crown his part,
Loves fumbling with a wench, with all his heart;
Till after having many changes passed,
In spite of age (thanks Heaven) is hanged at last:
Next is a senator that keeps a whore,
In Venice none a higher office bore;
To lewdness every night the lecher ran,
Show me, all London, such another man,
Match him at Mother Cresswold's if you can.
Oh Poland, Poland! had it been thy lot,
T' have heard in time of this Venetian plot,
Thou surely chosen hadst one king from thence,
And honoured them as thou hast England since.

29 *senator*] Antonio, Otway's caricature of the Whig statesman, the Earl of Shaftesbury
33 *Mother Cresswold's*] Mrs. Cresswold (more frequently Cresswell) was a celebrated procuress.
34 *Poland*] One of the favourite jokes of the Tory party was that Shaftesbury aspired to the (elective) throne of Poland; or, alternatively, that he had actually been chosen king by the Diet (cf. l. 37).

DRAMATIS PERSONÆ

DUKE OF VENICE		*Mr. D. Williams*
PRIULI, father to Belvidera, a Senator		*Mr. Bowman*
ANTONIO, a fine speaker in the Senate		*Mr. Leigh*
JAFFEIR		*Mr. Betterton*
PIERRE		*Mr. Smith*
RENAULT	Conspirators	*Mr. Wilshire*
BEDAMORE	Conspirators	*Mr. Gillo*
SPINOSA	Conspirators	*Mr. Percival*
THEODORE	Conspirators	
ELIOT	Conspirators	
REVELLIDO	Conspirators	
DURAND	Conspirators	
MEZZANA	Conspirators	
BRAINVEIL	Conspirators	
TERNON	Conspirators	
BRABE	Conspirators	
⟨RETROSI⟩	Conspirators	
BELVIDERA		*Mrs. Barry*
AQUILINA		*Mrs. Currer*

TWO WOMEN, attendants on Belvidera
TWO WOMEN, servants to Aquilina
THE COUNCIL OF TEN
OFFICER
GUARDS
FRIAR
EXECUTIONER AND RABBLE

Venice Preserved,

OR

A Plot Discovered

ACT I SCENE I

Enter Priuli *and* Jaffeir.

Priu. No more! I'll hear no more; begone and leave.
Jaff. Not hear me! by my sufferings but you shall!
My lord, my lord; I'm not that abject wretch
You think me. Patience! where's the distance throws
Me back so far, but I may boldly speak
In right, though proud oppression will not hear me!
Priu. Have you not wronged me?
Jaff. Could my nature e'er
Have brooked injustice or the doing wrongs,
I need not now thus low have bent myself,
To gain a hearing from a cruel father!
Wronged you?
Priu. Yes! wronged me, in the nicest point:
The honour of my house; you have done me wrong.
You may remember (for I now will speak,
And urge its baseness), when you first came home
From travel, with such hopes as made you looked on
By all men's eyes a youth of expectation;
Pleased with your growing virtue, I received you,
Courted, and sought to raise you to your merits:
My house, my table, nay my fortune too,
My very self, was yours; you might have used me
To your best service. Like an open friend,
I treated, trusted you, and thought you mine;

When, in requital of my best endeavours,
You treacherously practised to undo me,
Seduced the weakness of my age's darling,
My only child, and stole her from my bosom.
Oh, Belvidera!

Jaff. 'Tis to me you owe her;
Childless you had been else, and in the grave,
Your name extinct, nor no more Priuli heard of.
You may remember, scarce five years are past,
Since in your brigantine you sailed to see
The Adriatic wedded by our Duke,
And I was with you. Your unskilful pilot
Dashed us upon a rock; when to your boat
You made for safety, entered first yourself:
The affrighted Belvidera following next,
As she stood trembling on the vessel side,
Was by a wave washed off into the deep,
When instantly I plunged into the sea,
And buffeting the billows to her rescue,
Redeemed her life with half the loss of mine.
Like a rich conquest in one hand I bore her,
And with the other dashed the saucy waves
That thronged and pressed to rob me of my prize.
I brought her, gave her to your despairing arms:
Indeed you thanked me, but a nobler gratitude
Rose in her soul; for from that hour she loved me,
Till for her life she paid me with herself.

Priu. You stole her from me, like a thief you stole her,
At dead of night; that cursed hour you chose
To rifle me of all my heart held dear.
May all your joys in her prove false like mine;
A sterile fortune, and a barren bed,
Attend you both. Continual discord make
Your days and nights bitter and grievous; still
May the hard hand of a vexatious need
Oppress and grind you, till at last you find
The curse of disobedience all your portion.

Jaff. Half of your curse you have bestowed in vain;
Heaven has already crowned our faithful loves
With a young boy, sweet as his mother's beauty.

32 wedded] in the annual ceremony (on Ascension day), when the Doge, in the presence of the senate and nobility, cast a gold ring into the Adriatic

May he live to prove more gentle than his grandsire,
And happier than his father!
Priu. Rather live
To bait thee for his bread, and din your ears
With hungry cries, whilst his unhappy mother
Sits down and weeps in bitterness of want.
Jaff. You talk as if it would please you.
Priu. 'Twould by Heaven!
Once she was dear indeed; the drops that fell
From my sad heart when she forgot her duty,
The fountain of my life was not so precious:
But she is gone, and if I am a man
I will forget her.
Jaff. Would I were in my grave.
Priu. And she too with thee;
For, living here, you're but my cursed remembrancers
I once was happy.
Jaff. You use me thus because you know my soul
Is fond of Belvidera. You perceive
My life feeds on her, therefore thus you treat me.
Oh! could my soul ever have known satiety!
Were I that thief, the doer of such wrongs
As you upbraid me with, what hinders me
But I might send her back to you with contumely,
And court my fortune where she would be kinder!
Priu. You dare not do't.—
Jaff. Indeed, my lord, I dare not.
My heart that awes me is too much my master:
Three years are past since first our vows were plighted,
During which time, the world must bear me witness,
I have treated Belvidera like your daughter,
The daughter of a Senator of Venice;
Distinction, place, attendance and observance,
Due to her birth, she always has commanded.
Out of my little fortune I have done this,
Because (though hopeless e'er to win your nature)
The world might see I loved her for herself,
Not as the heiress of the great Priuli.—
Priu. No more!
Jaff. Yes! all, and then adieu for ever.
There's not a wretch that lives on common charity
But's happier than me: for I have known

The luscious sweets of plenty; every night
Have slept with soft content about my head,
And never waked but to a joyful morning,
Yet now must fall like a full ear of corn,
Whose blossom 'scaped, yet's withered in the ripening.

Priu. Home and be humble, study to retrench;
Discharge the lazy vermin of thy hall,
Those pageants of thy folly;
Reduce the glittering trappings of thy wife
To humble weeds, fit for thy little state;
Then to some suburb cottage both retire;
Drudge to feed loathsome life: get brats, and starve— [*Exit* Priuli.
Home, home, I say—

Jaff. Yes, if my heart would let me,
This proud, this swelling heart. Home I would go,
But that my doors are hateful to my eyes,
Filled and dammed up with gaping creditors,
Watchful as fowlers when their game will spring;
I have now not fifty ducats in the world,
Yet still I am in love, and pleased with ruin.
Oh, Belvidera! oh, she's my wife—
And we will bear our wayward fate together,
But ne'er know comfort more.

Enter Pierre.

Pierre. My friend, good morrow!
How fares the honest partner of my heart?
What, melancholy! not a word to spare me?

Jaff. I'm thinking, Pierre, how that damned starving quality
Called honesty got footing in the world.

Pierre. Why, pow'rful villainy first set it up
For its own ease and safety. Honest men
Are the soft easy cushions on which knaves
Repose and fatten. Were all mankind villains,
They'd starve each other; lawyers would want practice,
Cut-throats rewards; each man would kill his brother
Himself, none would be paid or hanged for murder.
Honesty was a cheat invented first
To bind the hands of bold deserving rogues,
That fools and cowards might sit safe in power,
And lord it uncontrolled above their betters.

Jaff. Then honesty is but a notion.
Pierre. Nothing else;
Like wit, much talked of, not to be defined;
He that pretends to most too, has least share in't;
'Tis a ragged virtue. Honesty! no more on't.
Jaff. Sure thou art honest.
Pierre. So indeed men think me,
But they're mistaken, Jaffeir: I am a rogue
As well as they;
A fine gay bold faced villain, as thou seest me.
'Tis true, I pay my debts when they're contracted;
I steal from no man; would not cut a throat
To gain admission to a great man's purse,
Or a whore's bed; I'd not betray my friend,
To get his place or fortune; I scorn to flatter
A blown-up fool above me, or crush the wretch beneath me:
Yet, Jaffeir, for all this, I am a villain!
Jaff. A villain—
Pierre. Yes, a most notorious villain:
To see the suff'rings of my fellow creatures,
And own myself a man; to see our senators
Cheat the deluded people with a show
Of liberty, which yet they ne'er must taste of.
They say, by them our hands are free from fetters,
Yet whom they please they lay in basest bonds;
Bring whom they please to infamy and sorrow;
Drive us like wracks down the rough tide of power,
Whilst no hold's left to save us from destruction:
All that bear this are villains; and I one,
Not to rouse up at the great call of nature,
And check the growth of these domestic spoilers,
That make us slaves and tell us 'tis our charter.
Jaff. Oh, Aquilina! Friend, to lose such beauty,
The dearest purchase of thy noble labours;
She was thy right by conquest, as by love.
Pierre. Oh, Jaffeir! I'd so fixed my heart upon her;
That wheresoe'er I framed a scheme of life
For time to come, she was my only joy
With which I wished to sweeten future cares.
I fancied pleasures—none but one that loves
And dotes as I did can imagine like 'em:
When in the extremity of all these hopes,

In the most charming hour of expectation,
Then when our eager wishes soar the highest,
Ready to stoop and grasp the lovely game,
A haggard owl, a worthless kite of prey,
With his foul wings sailed in and spoiled my quarry.

Jaff. I know the wretch, and scorn him as thou hat'st him.

Pierre. Curse on the common good that's so protected,
Where every slave that heaps up wealth enough
To do much wrong, becomes a lord of right!
I, who believed no ill could e'er come near me,
Found in the embraces of my Aquilina
A wretched old but itching senator;
A wealthy fool, that had bought out my title,
A rogue, that uses beauty like a lambskin,
Barely to keep him warm: that filthy cuckoo too
Was in my absence crept into my nest,
And spoiling all my brood of noble pleasure.

Jaff. Didst thou not chase him thence?

Pierre. I did, and drove
The rank old bearded Hirco stinking home.
The matter was complained of in the Senate,
I summoned to appear, and censured basely,
For violating something they call *privilege*—
This was the recompense of my service:
Would I'd been rather beaten by a coward!
A soldier's mistress, Jaffeir,'s his religion;
When that's profaned, all other ties are broken;
That even dissolves all former bonds of service,
And from that hour I think myself as free
To be the foe as e'er the friend of Venice—
Nay, dear revenge, whene'er thou call'st I am ready.

Jaff. I think no safety can be here for virtue,
And grieve, my friend, as much as thou to live
In such a wretched state as this of Venice,
Where all agree to spoil the public good,
And villains fatten with the brave man's labours.

Pierre. We have neither safety, unity, nor peace,
For the foundation's lost of common good;
Justice is lame as well as blind amongst us;
The laws (corrupted to their ends that make 'em)

178 haggard] wild, untamed   193 Hirco] goat

Serve but for instruments of some new tyranny,
That every day starts up to enslave us deeper:
Now could this glorious cause but find out friends
To do it right! Oh, Jaffeir! then mightst thou
Not wear these seals of woe upon thy face;
The proud Priuli should be taught humanity,
And learn to value such a son as thou art.
I dare not speak! But my heart bleeds this moment!

Jaff. Cursed be the cause, though I thy friend be part on't!
Let me partake the troubles of thy bosom,
For I am used to misery, and perhaps
May find a way to sweeten't to thy spirit.

Pierre. Too soon it will reach thy knowledge—

Jaff. Then from thee
Let it proceed. There's virtue in thy friendship
Would make the saddest tale of sorrow pleasing,
Strengthen my constancy, and welcome ruin.

Pierre. Then thou art ruined!

Jaff. That I long since knew,
I and ill fortune have been long acquaintance.

Pierre. I passed this very moment by thy doors,
And found them guarded by a troop of villains;
The sons of public rapine were destroying.
They told me, by the sentence of the law
They had commission to seize all thy fortune,
Nay, more; Priuli's cruel hand hath signed it.
Here stood a ruffian with a horrid face
Lording it o'er a pile of massy plate,
Tumbled into a heap for public sale:
There was another making villainous jests
At thy undoing; he had ta'en possession
Of all thy ancient most domestic ornaments,
Rich hangings, intermixed and wrought with gold;
The very bed which on thy wedding night
Received thee to the arms of Belvidera,
The scene of all thy joys, was violated
By the coarse hands of filthy dungeon villains,
And thrown amongst the common lumber.

Jaff. Now thanks Heaven—

Pierre. Thank Heaven! for what?

Jaff. That I am not worth a ducat.

Pierre. Curse thy dull stars, and the worse fate of Venice,

Where brothers, friends, and fathers, all are false;
Where there's no trust, no truth; where innocence
Stoops under vile oppression, and vice lords it.
Hadst thou but seen, as I did, how at last
Thy beauteous Belvidera, like a wretch
That's doomed to banishment, came weeping forth,
Shining through tears, like April suns in showers
That labour to o'ercome the cloud that loads 'em,
Whilst two young virgins, on whose arms she leaned,
Kindly looked up, and at her grief grew sad,
As if they catched the sorrows that fell from her:
Even the lewd rabble that were gathered round
To see the sight stood mute when they beheld her;
Governed their roaring throats and grumbled pity:
I could have hugged the greasy rogues; they pleased me.

Jaff. I thank thee for this story from my soul,
Since now I know the worst that can befall me.
Ah, Pierre! I have a heart that could have borne
The roughest wrong my fortune could have done me;
But when I think what Belvidera feels,
The bitterness her tender spirit tastes of,
I own myself a coward. Bear my weakness,
If throwing thus my arms about thy neck,
I play the boy, and blubber in thy bosom.
Oh! I shall drown thee with my sorrows!

Pierre. Burn!
First burn, and level Venice to thy ruin.
What, starve like beggars' brats in frosty weather,
Under a hedge, and whine ourselves to death!
Thou, or thy cause, shall never want assistance
Whilst I have blood or fortune fit to serve thee;
Command my heart: thou art every way its master.

Jaff. No: there's a secret pride in bravely dying.

Pierre. Rats die in holes and corners, dogs run mad;
Man knows a braver remedy for sorrow:
Revenge! the attribute of gods; they stamped it
With their great image on our natures. Die!
Consider well the cause that calls upon thee;
And if thou art base enough, die then. Remember
Thy Belvidera suffers: Belvidera!
Die—damn first!—What, be decently interred
In a churchyard, and mingle thy brave dust

With stinking rogues that rot in dirty winding sheets,
Surfeit-slain fools, the common dung o'th' soil.
Jaff. Oh!
Pierre. Well said, out with't; swear a little—
Jaff. Swear!
By sea and air! by earth, by Heaven and Hell,
I will revenge my Belvidera's tears!
Hark thee, my friend—Priuli—is—a senator!
Pierre. A dog!
Jaff. Agreed.
Pierre. Shoot him.
Jaff. With all my heart.
No more. Where shall we meet at night?
Pierre. I'll tell thee:
On the Rialto every night at twelve
I take my evening's walk of meditation;
There we two will meet, and talk of precious
Mischief.—
Jaff. Farewell.
Pierre. At twelve.
Jaff. At any hour: my plagues
Will keep me waking. [*Exit* Pierre.
Tell me why, good Heaven,
Thou mad'st me what I am, with all the spirit,
Aspiring thoughts and elegant desires
That fill the happiest man? Ah! rather why
Didst thou not form me sordid as my fate,
Base-minded, dull, and fit to carry burdens?
Why have I sense to know the curse that's on me?
Is this just dealing, nature? Belvidera!
Poor Belvidera!

Enter Belvidera.

Belv. Lead me, lead me, my virgins,
To that kind voice! My lord, my love, my refuge!
Happy my eyes, when they behold thy face:
My heavy heart will leave its doleful beating
At sight of thee, and bound with sprightful joys.
Oh, smile, as when our loves were in their spring,
And cheer my fainting soul.
Jaff. As when our loves
Were in their spring? Has then my fortune changed?

Art thou not Belvidera, still the same,
Kind, good, and tender as my arms first found thee?
If thou art altered, where shall I have harbour?
Where ease my loaded heart? Oh! where complain?
Belv. Does this appear like change, or love decaying?
When thus I throw myself into thy bosom,
With all the resolution of a strong truth,
Beats not my heart as 'twould alarm thine
To a new charge of bliss? I joy more in thee
Than did thy mother when she hugged thee first,
And blessed the gods for all her travail past.
Jaff. Can there in woman be such glorious faith?
Sure all ill stories of thy sex are false.
Oh Woman! lovely Woman! Nature made thee
To temper Man: we had been brutes without you.
Angels are painted fair, to look like you;
There's in you all that we believe of Heaven,
Amazing brightness, purity and truth,
Eternal joy, and everlasting love.
Belv. If love be treasure, we'll be wondrous rich:
I have so much, my heart will surely break with't;
Vows cannot express it; when I would declare
How great's my joy, I am dumb with the big thought,
I swell, and sigh, and labour with my longing.
Oh lead me to some desert wide and wild,
Barren as our misfortunes, where my soul
May have its vent; where I may tell aloud
To the high heavens, and every list'ning planet,
With what a boundless stock my bosom's fraught;
Where I may throw my eager arms about thee,
Give loose to love with kisses, kindling joy,
And let off all the fire that's in my heart.
Jaff. Oh Belvidera! double I am a beggar,
Undone by fortune, and in debt to thee;
Want! worldly want! that hungry meagre fiend
Is at my heels, and chases me in view;
Canst thou bear cold and hunger? Can these limbs,
Framed for the tender offices of love,
Endure the bitter gripes of smarting poverty?
When banished by our miseries abroad
(As suddenly we shall be) to seek out
(In some far climate where our names are strangers)

364 climate] region

For charitable succour; wilt thou then,
When in a bed of straw we shrink together,
And the bleak winds shall whistle round our heads—
Wilt thou then talk thus to me? Wilt thou then
Hush my cares thus, and shelter me with love?

Belv. Oh, I will love thee, even in madness love thee:
Though my distracted senses should forsake me,
I'd find some intervals when my poor heart
Should swage itself and be let loose to thine.
Though the bare earth be all our resting-place,
Its roots our food, some clift our habitation,
I'll make this arm a pillow for thy head;
As thou sighing liest, and swelled with sorrow,
Creep to thy bosom, pour the balm of love
Into thy soul, and kiss thee to thy rest;
Then praise our God, and watch thee till the morning.

Jaff. Hear this, you Heavens, and wonder how you made her!
Reign, reign, ye monarchs that divide the world,
Busy rebellion ne'er will let you know
Tranquillity and happiness like mine.
Like gaudy ships, th' obsequious billows fall
And rise again, to lift you in your pride;
They wait but for a storm and then devour you:
I, in my private bark, already wrecked,
Like a poor merchant driven on unknown land,
That had by chance packed up his choicest treasure
In one dear casket, and saved only that,
Since I must wander further on the shore,
Thus hug my little, but my precious store;
Resolved to scorn, and trust my fate no more. [*Exeunt.*

ACT II [SCENE I]

Enter Pierre *and* Aquilina.

Aquil. By all thy wrongs, thou art dearer to my arms
Than all the wealth of Venice. Prithee stay,
And let us love tonight.

Pierre. No. There's fool,

373 swage] assuage 375 clift] cliff 385 obsequious] obedient

There's fool about thee. When a woman sells
Her flesh to fools, her beauty's lost to me;
They leave a taint, a sully where th'ave passed,
There's such a baneful quality about 'em
Even spoils complexions with their own nauseousness,
They infect all they touch. I cannot think
Of tasting any thing a fool has palled.

Aquil. I loathe and scorn that fool thou mean'st, as much
Or more than thou canst, but the beast has gold
That makes him necessary; power too,
To qualify my character, and poise me
Equal with peevish virtue that beholds
My liberty with envy. In their hearts
Th'are loose as I am; but an ugly power
Sits in their faces, and frights pleasures from 'em.

Pierre. Much good may't do you, madam, with your senator.

Aquil. My senator! Why, canst thou think that wretch
E'er filled thy Aquilina's arms with pleasure?
Think'st thou, because I sometimes give him leave
To foil himself at what he is unfit for—
Because I force myself to endure and suffer him,
Think'st thou I love him? No, by all the joys
Thou ever gav'st me, his presence is my penance;
The worst thing an old man can be's a lover,
A mere *memento mori* to poor woman.
I never lay by his decrepit side
But all that night I pondered on my grave.

Pierre. Would he were well sent thither!

Aquil. That's my wish too:
For then, my Pierre, I might have cause with pleasure
To play the hypocrite. Oh! how I could weep
Over the dying dotard, and kiss him too,
In hopes to smother him quite; then, when the time
Was come to pay my sorrows at his funeral,
(For he has already made me heir to treasures
Would make me out-act a real widow's whining),
How could I frame my face to fit my mourning!
With wringing hands attend him to his grave,
Fall swooning on his hearse; take mad possession,
Even of the dismal vault where he lay buried;

14 qualify] make less reprehensible 17 Th'are] Are *Q.* 1; They're *Works*

There like the Ephesian Matron dwell, till thou,
My lovely soldier, comest to my deliverance;
Then throwing up my veil, with open arms
And laughing eyes run to new dawning joy.

Pierre. No more! I have friends to meet me here to night,
And must be private. As you prize my friendship,
Keep up your coxcomb. Let him not pry nor listen,
Nor fisk about the house as I have seen him,
Like a tame mumping squirrel with a bell on;
Curs will be abroad to bite him if you do.

Aquil. What friends to meet? May I not be of your council?

Pierre. How! a woman ask questions out of bed?
Go to your senator, ask him what passes
Amongst his brethren, he'll hide nothing from you;
But pump not me for politics. No more!
Give order that whoever in my name
Comes here, receive admittance. So, good night.

Aquil. Must we ne'er meet again? Embrace no more?
Is love so soon and utterly forgotten?

Pierre. As you henceforward treat your fool, I'll think on't.

Aquil. Cursed be all fools, and doubly cursed myself,
The worst of fools.—⟨*Aside.*⟩ I die if he forsakes me;
And now to keep him, Heaven or Hell instruct me. [*Exeunt.*

SCENE [II]

The Rialto.

Enter Jaffeir.

Jaff. I am here; and thus, the shades of night around me,
I look as if all Hell were in my heart,
And I in Hell. Nay, surely 'tis so with me;
For every step I tread, methinks some fiend
Knocks at my breast, and bids it not be quiet.
I've heard how desperate wretches, like myself,
Have wandered out at this dead time of night
To meet the foe of mankind in his walk:

43 Ephesian Matron] the widowed lady in the story of Petronius whose passionate mourning for her dead husband yielded to the charms of a handsome living soldier 49 Keep up] i.e. keep [him] shut up, confined 50 fisk] scamper 51 mumping] grimacing

Sure, I am so cursed that, though of Heaven forsaken,
No minister of darkness cares to tempt me.
Hell! Hell! why sleepest thou?

Enter Pierre.

Pierre. Sure I have stayed too long:
The clock has struck, and I may lose my proselyte.
Speak, who goes there?
Jaff. A dog, that comes to howl
At yonder moon. What's he that asks the question?
Pierre. A friend to dogs, for they are honest creatures,
And ne'er betray their masters; never fawn
On any that they love not. Well met, friend:
Jaffeir!
Jaff. The same. Oh Pierre! Thou art come in season,
I was just going to pray.
Pierre. Ah that's mechanic;
Priests make a trade on't, and yet starve by it too:
No praying, it spoils business, and time's precious.
Where's Belvidera?
Jaff. For a day or two
I've lodged her privately, till I see farther
What fortune will do with me. Prithee, friend,
If thou wouldst have me fit to hear good counsel,
Speak not of Belvidera—
Pierre. Speak not of her?
Jaff. Oh no!
Pierre. Nor name her? May be I wish her well.
Jaff. Who well?
Pierre. Thy wife, thy lovely Belvidera.
I hope a man may wish his friend's wife well,
And no harm done!
Jaff. Y' are merry Pierre!
Pierre. I am so:
Thou shalt smile too, and Belvidera smile;
We'll all rejoice. Here's something to buy pins;
Marriage is chargeable.
Jaff. I but half wished
To see the Devil, and he's here already.
Well!

20 mechanic] vulgar, belonging to the 'lower orders'

What must this buy? Rebellion, murder, treason?
Tell me which way I must be damned for this.

Pierre. When last we parted, we had no qualms like these,
But entertained each other's thoughts like men
Whose souls were well acquainted. Is the world
Reformed since our last meeting? What new miracles
Have happened? Has Priuli's heart relented?
Can he be honest?

Jaff. Kind Heaven! let heavy curses
Gall his old age; cramps, aches, rack his bones,
And bitterest disquiet wring his heart;
Oh, let him live till life become his burden!
Let him groan under't long, linger an age
In the worst agonies and pangs of death,
And find its ease but late.

Pierre. Nay, couldst thou not
As well, my friend, have stretched the curse to all
The Senate round, as to one single villain?

Jaff. But curses stick not. Could I kill with cursing,
By Heaven, I know not thirty heads in Venice
Should not be blasted: senators should rot
Like dogs on dunghills; but their wives and daughters
Die of their own diseases. Oh for a curse
To kill with!

Pierre. Daggers, daggers are much better!

Jaff. Ha!

Pierre. Daggers.

Jaff. But where are they?

Pierre. Oh, a thousand
May be disposed in honest hands in Venice.

Jaff. Thou talk'st in clouds.

Pierre. But yet a heart half wronged,
As thine has been, would find the meaning, Jaffeir.

Jaff. A thousand daggers, all in honest hands;
And have not I a friend will stick one here?

Pierre. Yes, if I thought thou wert not to be cherished
To a nobler purpose, I'd be that friend.
But thou hast better friends, friends, whom thy wrongs
Have made thy friends; friends, worthy to be called so.
I'll trust thee with a secret: there are spirits

45 aches] This word was pronounced as a disyllable. 69 spirits] men of spirit

This hour at work. But as thou art a man
Whom I have picked and chosen from the world,
Swear that thou wilt be true to what I utter,
And when I have told thee that which only gods
And men like gods are privy to, then swear
No chance or change shall wrest it from thy bosom.

Jaff. When thou wouldst bind me, is there need of oaths?—
Green-sickness girls lose maidenheads with such counters—
For thou art so near my heart that thou may'st see
Its bottom, sound its strength and firmness to thee:
Is coward, fool, or villain in my face?
If I seem none of these, I dare believe
Thou wouldst not use me in a little cause,
For I am fit for honour's toughest task,
Nor ever yet found fooling was my province;
And for a villainous inglorious enterprise,
I know thy heart so well, I dare lay mine
Before thee, set it to what point thou wilt.

Pierre. Nay, its a cause thou wilt be fond of, Jaffeir,
For it is founded on the noblest basis:
Our liberties, our natural inheritance.
There's no religion, no hypocrisy in't;
We'll do the business, and ne'er fast and pray for't:
Openly act a deed the world shall gaze
With wonder at, and envy when it is done.

Jaff. For liberty!

Pierre. For liberty, my friend!
Thou shalt be freed from base Priuli's tyranny,
And thy sequestered fortunes healed again.
I shall be freed from opprobrious wrongs,
That press me now, and bend my spirit downward;
All Venice free, and every growing merit
Succeed to its just right. Fools shall be pulled
From wisdom's seat—those baleful unclean birds,
Those lazy owls, who (perched near fortune's top)
Sit only watchful with their heavy wings
To cuff down new fledged virtues that would rise
To nobler heights, and make the grove harmonious.

Jaff. What can I do?

Pierre. Canst thou not kill a senator?

Jaff. Were there one wise or honest, I could kill him
For herding with that nest of fools and knaves.

By all my wrongs, thou talk'st as if revenge
Were to be had, and the brave story warms me.

Pierre. Swear then!

Jaff. I do, by all those glittering stars,
And yond great ruling planet of the night!
By all good pow'rs above, and ill below!
By love and friendship, dearer than my life!
No pow'r or death shall make me false to thee.

Pierre. Here we embrace, and I'll unlock my heart.
A council's held hard by, where the destruction
Of this great empire's hatching. There I'll lead thee!
But be a man, for thou art to mix with men
Fit to disturb the peace of all the world,
And rule it when it's wildest—

Jaff. I give thee thanks
For this kind warning. Yes, I will be a man,
And charge thee, Pierre, whene'er thou see'st my fears
Betray me less, to rip this heart of mine
Out of my breast, and show it for a coward's.
Come, let's begone, for from this hour I chase
All little thoughts, all tender human follies
Out of my bosom. Vengeance shall have room:
Revenge!

Pierre. And liberty!

Jaff. Revenge! revenge! [*Exeunt.*

[SCENE III]

The scene changes to Aquilina'*s house, the Greek courtesan.*

Enter Renault.

Ren. Why was my choice ambition, the first ground
A wretch can build on? It's indeed at distance
A good prospect, tempting to the view;
The height delights us, and the mountain top
Looks beautiful because it's nigh to heaven,
But we ne'er think how sandy's the foundation,
What storm will batter, and what tempest shake us!
Who's there?

1 first] *Q.* 1; worst *Works*

Enter Spinosa.

Spino. Renault, good morrow! for by this time
I think the scale of night has turned the balance,
And weighs up morning. Has the clock struck twelve?
Ren. Yes, clocks will go as they are set; but man,
Irregular man's ne'er constant, never certain.
I've spent at least three precious hours of darkness
In waiting dull attendance; 'tis the curse
Of diligent virtue to be mixed like mine
With giddy tempers, souls but half resolved.
Spin. Hell seize that soul amongst us it can frighten!
Ren. What's then the cause that I am here alone?
Why are we not together?

Enter Eliot.

Oh, sir, welcome!
You are an Englishman: when treason's hatching
One might have thought you'd not have been behind-hand.
In what whore's lap have you been lolling?
Give but an Englishman his whore and ease,
Beef and a sea-coal fire, he's yours for ever.
Eliot. Frenchman, you are saucy.
Ren. How!

Enter Bedamore *the ambassador*, Theodore, Brainveil, Durand, Brabe, Revellido, Mezzana, Ternon, Retrosi, *conspirators.*

Bed. At difference? fie!
Is this a time for quarrels? Thieves and rogues
Fall out and brawl. Should men of your high calling,
Men separated by the choice of providence
From the gross heap of mankind, and set here
In this great assembly as in one great jewel,
T'adorn the bravest purpose it e'er smiled on;
Should you like boys wrangle for trifles?
Ren. Boys!
Bed. Renault, thy hand!
Ren. I thought I'd given my heart
Long since to every man that mingles here,
But grieve to find it trusted with such tempers
That can't forgive my froward age its weakness.
Bed. Eliot, thou once had'st virtue; I have seen

Thy stubborn temper bend with god-like goodness,
Not half thus courted: 'tis thy nation's glory,
To hug the foe that offers brave alliance.
Once more embrace, my friends—we'll all embrace—
United thus, we are the mighty engine
Must twist this rooted empire from its basis!
Totters it not already?

Eliot. Would it were tumbling!

Bed. Nay, it shall down: this night we seal its ruin.

Enter Pierre.

Oh Pierre! thou art welcome!
Come to my breast, for by its hopes thou look'st
Lovelily dreadful, and the fate of Venice
Seems on thy sword already. Oh, my Mars!
The poets that first feigned a god of war
Sure prophesied of thee.

Pierre. Friends! was not Brutus,
(I mean that Brutus who in open senate
Stabbed the first Cæsar that usurped the world)
A gallant man?

Ren. Yes, and Catiline too,
Though story wrong his fame; for he conspired
To prop the reeling glory of his country:
His cause was good.

Bed. And ours as much above it,
As Renault thou art superior to Cethegus,
Or Pierre to Cassius.

Pierre. Then to what we aim at.
When do we start? Or must we talk for ever?

Bed. No, Pierre, the deed's near birth: fate seems to have set
The business up, and given it to our care.
I hope there's not a heart nor hand amongst us
But is firm and ready.

All. All! We'll die with Bedamore.

Bed. Oh men,
Matchless, as will your glory be hereafter!
The game is for a matchless prize, if won;
If lost, disgraceful ruin.

Ren. What can lose it?

58 Cethegus] a Roman tribune who took part in Catiline's conspiracy against the senate

The public stock's a beggar; one Venetian
Trusts not another. Look into their stores
Of general safety: empty magazines,
A tattered fleet, a murmuring unpaid army,
Bankrupt nobility, a harassed commonalty,
A factious, giddy, and divided senate
Is all the strength of Venice: let's destroy it!
Let's fill their magazines with arms to awe them,
Man out their fleet, and make their trade maintain it;
Let loose the murmuring army on their masters,
To pay themselves with plunder; lop their nobles
To the base roots, whence most of 'em first sprung;
Enslave the rout, whom smarting will make humble;
Turn out their droning senate, and possess
That seat of empire which our souls were framed for.

Pierre. Ten thousand men are armed at your nod,
Commanded all by leaders fit to guide
A battle for the freedom of the world;
This wretched state has starved them in its service,
And by your bounty quickened, they're resolved
To serve your glory, and revenge their own!
Th' have all their different quarters in this city,
Watch for th' alarm, and grumble 'tis so tardy.

Bed. I doubt not, friend, but thy unwearied diligence
Has still kept waking, and it shall have ease;
After this night it is resolved we meet
No more, till Venice own us for her lords.

Pierre. How lovely the Adriatic whore,
Dressed in her flames, will shine! devouring flames!
Such as shall burn her to the watery bottom
And hiss in her foundation.

Bed. Now if any
Amongst us that owns this glorious cause
Have friends or interest he'd wish to save,
Let it be told. The general doom is sealed;
But I'd forgo the hopes of a world's empire,
Rather than wound the bowels of my friend.

Pierre. I must confess you there have touched my weakness:
I have a friend; hear it, such a friend!
My heart was ne'er shut to him. Nay, I'll tell you,
He knows the very business of this hour;
But he rejoices in the cause, and loves it:

W' have changed a vow to live and die together,
And he's at hand to ratify it here.
Ren. How! all betrayed?
Pierre. No—I've dealt nobly with you;
I've brought my all into the public stock:
I had but one friend, and him I'll share amongst you!
Receive and cherish him. Or if, when seen
And searched, you find him worthless, as my tongue
Has lodged this secret in his faithful breast,
To ease your fears I wear a dagger here
Shall rip it out again, and give you rest.
Come forth, thou only good I e'er could boast of.

Enter Jaffeir *with a dagger.*

Bed. His presence bears the show of manly virtue.
Jaff. I know you'll wonder all, that thus uncalled
I dare approach this place of fatal counsels;
But I am amongst you, and by Heaven it glads me
To see so many virtues thus united,
To restore justice and dethrone oppression!
Command this sword, if you would have it quiet,
Into this breast; but if you think it worthy
To cut the throats of reverend rogues in robes,
Send me into the cursed assembled Senate;
It shrinks not, though I meet a father there.
Would you behold this city flaming? Here's
A hand shall bear a lighted torch at noon
To the arsenal, and set its gates on fire.
Ren. You talk this well, sir.
Jaff. Nay—by Heaven I'll do this!
Come, come, I read distrust in all your faces,
You fear me a villain, and indeed it's odd
To hear a stranger talk thus at first meeting
Of matters that have been so well debated;
But I come ripe with wrongs as you with counsels;
I hate this senate, am a foe to Venice,
A friend to none but men resolved like me
To push on mischief. Oh, did you but know me,
I need not talk thus!
Bed. Pierre! I must embrace him,
My heart beats to this man as if it knew him.

131 father] i.e. father-in-law

Ren. I never loved these huggers.
Jaff. Still I see
The cause delights me not. Your friends survey me
As I were dangerous—but I come armed
Against all doubts, and to your trust will give
A pledge, worth more than all the world can pay for.—
My Belvidera! Ho! my Belvidera!
Bed. What wonder next?
Jaff. Let me entreat you,
As I have henceforth hopes to call ye friends,
That all but the ambassador, this
Grave guide of counsels, with my friend that owns me,
Withdraw a while to spare a woman's blushes.
[*Exeunt all but* Bedamore, Renault, Jaffeir, Pierre.
Bed. Pierre, whither will this ceremony lead us?
Jaff. My Belvidera! Belvidera!

Enter Belvidera.

Belv. Who,
Who calls so loud at this late peaceful hour?
That voice was wont to come in gentler whispers,
And fill my ears with the soft breath of love.
Thou hourly image of my thoughts, where art thou?
Jaff. Indeed, 'tis late.
Belv. Oh! I have slept, and dreamt,
And dreamt again. Where hast thou been thou loiterer?
Though my eyes closed, my arms have still been opened,
Stretched every way betwixt my broken slumbers,
To search if thou wert come to crown my rest;
There's no repose without thee. Oh, the day
Too soon will break, and wake us to our sorrow;
Come, come to bed, and bid thy cares good-night.
Jaff. Oh, Belvidera! we must change the scene
In which the past delights of life were tasted:
The poor sleep little, we must learn to watch
Our labours late, and early every morning,
Midst winter frosts, thin clad and fed with sparing,
Rise to our toils, and drudge away the day.
Belv. Alas! where am I? whither is't you lead me?
Methinks I read distraction in your face!

147 The cause delights me not] This seems to be Jaffier's (unidiomatic) way of saying: 'The conspirators don't like me.' 175 thin clad] *Works*; then clad *Q.* 1

Something less gentle than the fate you tell me:
You shake and tremble too! your blood runs cold!
Heavens guard my love, and bless his heart with patience!

Jaff. That I have patience, let our fate bear witness,
Who has ordained it so, that thou and I
(Thou the divinest good man e'er possessed,
And I the wretched'st of the race of man)
This very hour, without one tear, must part.

Belv. Part! must we part? Oh! am I then forsaken?
Will my love cast me off? Have my misfortunes
Offended him so highly that he'll leave me?
Why drag you from me? whither are you going?
My dear! my life! my love!

Jaff. Oh friends!

Belv. Speak to me.

Jaff. Take her from my heart,
She'll gain such hold else, I shall ne'er get loose.
I charge thee take her, but with tender'st care,
Relieve her troubles and assuage her sorrows.

Ren. Rise, madam! and command amongst your servants!

Jaff. To you, sirs, and your honours, I bequeath her,
And with her this: when I prove unworthy— [*Gives a dagger.*
You know the rest—Then strike it to her heart;
And tell her, he who three whole happy years
Lay in her arms, and each kind night repeated
The passionate vows of still increasing love,
Sent that reward for all her truth and sufferings.

Belv. Nay, take my life, since he has sold it cheaply;
Or send me to some distant clime your slave,
But let it be far off, lest my complainings
Should reach his guilty ears, and shake his peace.

Jaff. No, Belvidera, I've contrived thy honour;
Trust to my faith, and be but fortune kind
To me, as I'll preserve that faith unbroken,
When next we meet, I'll lift thee to a height
Shall gather all the gazing world about thee,
To wonder what strange virtue placed thee there.
But if we ne'er meet more—

Belv. Oh thou unkind one,
Never meet more! have I deserved this from you?
Look on me, tell me, tell me, speak, thou dear deceiver,
Why am I separated from thy love?

If I am false, accuse me; but if true,
Don't, prithee don't in poverty forsake me.
But pity the sad heart that's torn with parting.
Yet hear me! yet recall me—

[*Exeunt* Renault, Bedamore, *and* Belvidera.

Jaff. Oh my eyes!
Look not that way, but turn yourselves awhile
Into my heart, and be weaned all together!
My friend, where art thou?

Pierre. Here, my honour's brother.

Jaff. Is Belvidera gone?

Pierre. Renault has led her
Back to her own apartment: but, by Heaven!
Thou must not see her more till our work's over.

Jaff. No?

Pierre. Not for your life.

Jaff. Oh Pierre, wert thou but she,
How I could pull thee down into my heart,
Gaze on thee till my eye-strings cracked with love,
Till all my sinews with its fire extended,
Fixed me upon the rack of ardent longing;
Then swelling, sighing, raging to be blessed,
Come like a panting turtle to thy breast,
On thy soft bosom hovering, bill and play,
Confess the cause why last I fled away;
Own 'twas a fault, but swear to give it o'er,
And never follow false ambition more. [*Exeunt ambo.*

ACT III [SCENE I]

Enter Aquilina *and her Maid.*

Aquil. Tell him I am gone to bed; tell him I am not at home; tell him I've better company with me, or anything; tell him in short I will not see him, the eternal troublesome vexatious fool. He's worse company than an ignorant physician—I'll not be disturbed at these unseasonable hours.

Maid. But madam! He's here already, just entered the doors.

228 No?] No. *Q.* 1, *Works*

Aquil. Turn him out again, you unnecessary, useless, giddy-brained ass! If he will not begone, set the house afire and burn us both: I had rather meet a toad in my dish than that old hideous animal in my chamber tonight.

Enter Antonio.

Anto. Nacky, Nacky, Nacky—how dost do, Nacky? Hurry durry! I am come, little Nacky; past eleven a clock, a late hour; time in all conscience to go to bed, Nacky—Nacky did I say? Ay, Nacky; Aquilina, lina, lina, quilina, quilina, quilina, Aquilina, Naquilina, Naquilina, Acky, Acky, Nacky, Nacky, Queen Nacky—come, let's to bed—you fubs, you pug you—you little puss—purree tuzzey—I am a senator. 14

Aquil. You are fool, I am sure.

Anto. May be so too, sweetheart. Never the worse senator for all that. Come, Nacky, Nacky, let's have a game at rump, Nacky.

Aquil. You would do well signior to be troublesome here no longer, but leave me to myself; be sober and go home, sir.

Anto. Home, Madonna!

Aquil. Ay, home, sir. Who am I?

Anto. Madonna, as I take it you are my—you are—thou art my little Nicky Nacky—that's all!

Aquil. I find you are resolved to be troublesome, and so to make short of the matter in few words, I hate you, detest you, loathe you, I am weary of you, sick of you—hang you, you are an old, silly, impertinent, impotent, solicitous coxcomb, crazy in your head, and lazy in your body, love to be meddling with everything, and if you had not money, you are good for nothing. 29

Anto. Good for nothing! Hurry durry, I'll try that presently. Sixty-one years old, and good for nothing; that's brave [*To the Maid.*] Come, come, come, Mistress Fiddle-faddle, turn you out for a season; go, turn out, I say, it is our will and pleasure to be private some moments—out, out, when you are bid to—[*Puts her out and locks the door.*] Good for nothing, you say.

Aquil. Why what are you good for?

Anto. In the first place, madam, I am old, and consequently very wise, very wise, Madonna, d'ye mark that? In the second place take notice, if you please, that I am a senator, and when I think fit can make speeches, Madonna. Hurry durry, I can make a speech in the senate-house now and then—would make your hair stand on end, Madonna. 41

13 fubs . . . pug] terms of endearment 14 tuzzey] (tuzzy-muzzy: the female genitals) 15 fool] *Q.* 1; a fool *Works* 17 rump] possibly an alternative spelling of 'romp', but Antonio's meaning is probably more indecent 30–1 Sixty-one years old] Shaftesbury (Antonio) was born in 1621

Aquil. What care I for your speeches in the senate-house? If you would be silent here, I should thank you.

Anto. Why, I can make speeches to thee too, my lovely Madonna; for example— [*Takes out a purse of gold, and at every pause shakes it.*]

My cruel fair one, since it is my fate,
That you should with your servant angry prove;
Though late at night—I hope 'tis not too late
With this to gain reception for my love.

—There's for thee, my little Nicky Nacky—take it, here take it—I say take it, or I'll throw it at your head—how now, rebel!

Aquil. Truly, my illustrious senator, I must confess your honour is at present most profoundly eloquent indeed.

Anto. Very well. Come, now let's sit down and think upon't a little—come sit, I say—sit down by me a little, my Nicky Nacky, hah!—[*Sits down.*] Hurry durry—good for nothing—

Aquil. No, sir, if you please, I can know my distance and stand.

Anto. Stand! How? Nacky up and I down! Nay then, let me exclaim with the poet:

Show me a case more pitiful who can,
A standing woman, and a falling man.

Hurry durry—not sit down?—See this, ye gods—
You won't sit down?

Aquil. No, sir.

Anto. Then look you now, suppose me a bull, a Basan bull, the bull of bulls, or any bull. Thus up I get and with my brows thus bent—I broo, I say I broo, I broo, I broo. You won't sit down will you?—I broo— [*Bellows like a bull, and drives her about.*]

Aquil. Well, sir, I must endure this. [*She sits down.*] Now your honour has been a bull, pray what beast will your worship please to be next?

Anto. Now I'll be a senator again, and thy lover, little Nicky Nacky! [*He sits by her.*] Ah toad, toad, toad, toad! spit in my face a little, Nacky—spit in my face prithee, spit in my face, never so little: spit but a little bit—spit, spit, spit, spit, when you are bid, I say; do, prithee spit—now, now, now, spit: what, you won't spit, will you? Then I'll be a dog.

Aquil. A dog, my lord?

Anto. Ay, a dog—and I'll give thee this t'other purse to let me be a dog—and to use me like a dog a little. Hurry durry—I will—here 'tis.— [*Gives the purse.*]

Aquil. Well, with all my heart. But let me beseech your dogship to play

65 Basan bull] cf. Psalms, 22: 12

your tricks over as fast as you can, that you may come to stinking the sooner, and be turned out of doors as you deserve.

Anto. Ay, ay—no matter for that [*He gets under the table.*]—that shan't move me—Now, bough waugh waugh, bough waugh— [*Barks like a dog.*]

Aquil. Hold, hold, hold, sir, I beseech you: what is't you do? If curs bite, they must be kicked, sir. Do you see, kicked thus.

Anto. Ay, with all my heart: do kick, kick on; now I am under the table, kick again—kick harder—harder yet, bough waugh waugh, waugh, bough—'od, I'll have a snap at thy shins—bough waugh wough, waugh, bough—'od, she kicks bravely.—

Aquil. Nay then, I'll go another way to work with you; and I think here's an instrument fit for the purpose. [*Fetches a whip and bell.*] What, bite your mistress, sirrah! Out, out of doors, you dog, to kennel and be hanged.—Bite your mistress by the legs, you rogue!— [*She whips him.*]

Anto. Nay, prithee, Nacky, now thou art too loving. Hurry durry, 'od, I'll be a dog no longer.

Aquil. Nay, none of your fawning and grinning; but be gone, or here's the discipline. What, bite your mistress by the legs, you mongrel? Out of doors—hout, hout, to kennel, sirrah! Go.

Anto. This is very barbarous usage, Nacky, very barbarous. Look you, I will not go—I will not stir from the door, that I resolve—hurry durry, what, shut me out? [*She whips him out.*]

Aquil. Ay, and if you come here any more tonight I'll have my footmen lug you, you cur. What, bite your poor mistress Nacky, sirrah!

Enter Maid.

Maid. Heavens, madam! What's the matter? [*He howls at the door like a dog.*]

Aquil. Call my footmen hither presently.

Enter two footmen.

Maid. They are here already, madam; the house is all alarmed with a strange noise that nobody knows what to make of.

Aquil. Go all of you, and turn that troublesome beast in the next room out of my house.—If I ever see him within these walls again, without my leave for his admittance, you sneaking rogues—I'll have you poisoned all, poisoned, like rats: every corner of the house shall stink of one of you. Go, and learn hereafter to know my pleasure. So now for my Pierre:

Thus when godlike lover was displeased,
We sacrifice our fool and he's appeased. [*Exeunt.*

SCENE II

Enter Belvidera.

Belv. I'm sacrificed! I am sold! betrayed to shame!
Inevitable ruin has enclosed me!
No sooner was I to my bed repaired,
To weigh, and (weeping) ponder my condition,
But the old hoary wretch, to whose false care
My peace and honour was entrusted, came
(Like Tarquin) ghastly with infernal lust.
Oh, thou Roman Lucrece! thou couldst find friends to vindicate [thy wrong;
I never had but one, and he's proved false;
He that should guard my virtue has betrayed it;
Left me! undone me! Oh, that I could hate him!
Where shall I go? Oh, whither, whither wander?

Enter Jaffeir.

Jaff. Can Belvidera want a resting place
When these poor arms are open to receive her?
Oh, 'tis in vain to struggle with desires
Strong as my love to thee; for every moment
I am from thy sight, the heart within my bosom
Moans like a tender infant in its cradle
Whose nurse had left it. Come, and with the songs
Of gentle love persuade it to its peace.
Belv. I fear the stubborn wanderer will not own me;
'Tis grown a rebel to be ruled no longer,
Scorns the indulgent bosom that first lulled it,
And like a disobedient child disdains
The soft authority of Belvidera.
Jaff. There was a time—
Belv. Yes, yes, there was a time,
When Belvidera's tears, her cries, and sorrows,
Were not despised; when if she chanced to sigh,
Or look but sad—there was indeed a time
When Jaffeir would have ta'en her in his arms,
Eased her declining head upon his breast,
And never left her till he found the cause.
But let her now weep seas,
Cry, till she rend the earth, sigh till she burst

Her heart asunder; still he bears it all;
Deaf as the wind, and as the rocks unshaken.

Jaff. Have I been deaf? am I that rock unmoved,
Against whose root tears beat and sighs are sent?
In vain have I beheld thy sorrows calmly!
Witness against me, Heavens, have I done this?
Then bear me in a whirlwind back again,
And let that angry dear one ne'er forgive me!
Oh thou too rashly censur'st of my love!
Couldst thou but think how I have spent this night,
Dark and alone, no pillow to my head,
Rest in my eyes, nor quiet in my heart,
Thou wouldst not, Belvidera, sure thou wouldst not
Talk to me thus, but like a pitying angel
Spreading thy wings come settle on my breast,
And hatch warm comfort there ere sorrows freeze it.

Belv. Why then, poor mourner, in what baleful corner
Hast thou been talking with that witch the night?
On what cold stone hast thou been stretched along,
Gathering the grumbling winds about thy head,
To mix with theirs the accents of thy woes?
Oh, now I find the cause my love forsakes me!
I am no longer fit to bear a share
In his concernments: my weak female virtue
Must not be trusted; 'tis too frail and tender.

Jaff. Oh Portia! Portia! What a soul was thine!

Belv. That Portia was a woman, and when Brutus
Big with the fate of Rome (Heaven guard thy safety!),
Concealed from her the labours of his mind,
She let him see her blood was great as his,
Flowed from a spring as noble, and a heart
Fit to partake his troubles as his love:
Fetch, fetch that dagger back, the dreadful dower
Thou gav'st last night in parting with me; strike it
Here to my heart; and as the blood flows from it,
Judge if it run not pure as Cato's daughter's.

Jaff. Thou art too good, and I indeed unworthy,
Unworthy so much virtue. Teach me how
I may deserve such matchless love as thine,
And see with what attention I'll obey thee.

43 censur'st] judgest 64 her blood] Portia gashed her thigh to prove to Brutus that she had sufficient fortitude to be allowed to share his secrets and would never betray them.

Belv. Do not despise me: that's the all I ask.
Jaff. Despise thee! Hear me—
Belv. Oh, thy charming tongue
Is but too well acquainted with my weakness;
Knows, let it name but love, my melting heart
Dissolves within my breast; till with closed eyes
I reel into thy arms, and all's forgotten.
Jaff. What shall I do?
Belv. Tell me! be just, and tell me
Why dwells that busy cloud upon thy face?
Why am I made a stranger? why that sigh,
And I not know the cause? Why, when the world
Is wrapped in rest, why chooses then my love
To wander up and down in horrid darkness,
Loathing his bed, and these desiring arms?
Why are these eyes blood-shot, with tedious watching?
Why starts he now, and looks as if he wished
His fate were finished? Tell me, ease my fears,
Lest, when we next time meet, I want the power
To search into the sickness of thy mind,
But talk as wildly then as thou look'st now.
Jaff. Oh Belvidera!
Belv. Why was I last night delivered to a villain?
Jaff. Hah, a villain!
Belv. Yes! to a villain! Why at such an hour
Meets that assembly all made up of wretches
That look as Hell had drawn 'em into league?
Why, I in this hand, and in that a dagger,
Was I delivered with such dreadful ceremonies?
'To you, sirs, and to your honour I bequeath her,
And with her this. Whene'er I prove unworthy,
You know the rest, then strike it to her heart?'
Oh! why's that 'rest' concealed from me? Must I
Be made the hostage of a hellish trust?
For such I know I am; that's all my value!
But by the love and loyalty I owe thee,
I'll free thee from the bondage of these slaves;
Straight to the Senate, tell 'em all I know,
All that I think, all that my fears inform me!
Jaff. Is this the Roman virtue! this the blood
That boasts its purity with Cato's daughter!
Would she have e'er betrayed her Brutus?

Belv. No;
For Brutus trusted her. Wert thou so kind,
What would not Belvidera suffer for thee?
Jaff. I shall undo myself, and tell thee all.
Belv. Look not upon me as I am a woman,
But as a bone, thy wife, thy friend, who long
Has had admission to thy heart, and there
Studied the virtues of thy gallant nature;
Thy constancy, thy courage and thy truth
Have been my daily lesson: I have learnt them,
Am bold as thou, can suffer or despise
The worst of fates for thee; and with thee share them.
Jaff. Oh you divinest powers! look down and hear
My prayers! instruct me to reward this virtue!
Yet think a little, ere thou tempt me further:
Think I have a tale to tell will shake thy nature,
Melt all this boasted constancy thou talk'st of
Into vile tears and despicable sorrows—
Then if thou shouldst betray me!
Belv. Shall I swear?
Jaff. No: do not swear. I would not violate
Thy tender nature with so rude a bond:
But as thou hop'st to see me live my days,
And love thee long, lock this within thy breast;
I've bound myself by all the strictest sacraments,
Divine and human—
Belv. Speak!—
Jaff. To kill thy father—
Belv. My father!
Jaff. Nay, the throats of the whole Senate
Shall bleed, my Belvidera: he amongst us
That spares his father, brother, or his friend,
Is damned. How rich and beauteous will the face
Of ruin look when these wide streets run blood;
I and the glorious partners of my fortune
Shouting, and striding o'er the prostrate dead,
Still to new waste; whilst thou, far off in safety
Smiling, shalt see the wonders of our daring;
And when night comes, with praise and love receive me.
Belv. Oh!
Jaff. Have a care, and shrink not even in thought!
For if thou dost—

Belv. I know it, thou wilt kill me.
Do, strike thy sword into this bosom; lay me
Dead on the earth, and then thou wilt be safe.
Murder my father! Though his cruel nature
Has persecuted me to my undoing,
Driven me to basest wants, can I behold him
With smiles of vengeance, butchered in his age?
The sacred fountain of my life destroyed?
And canst thou shed the blood that gave me being?
Nay, be a traitor too, and sell thy country;
Can thy great heart descend so vilely low,
Mix with hired slaves, bravoes, and common stabbers,
Nose-slitters, alley-lurking villains! join
With such a crew, and take a ruffian's wages,
To cut the throats of wretches as they sleep?
Jaff. Thou wrong'st me, Belvidera! I've engaged
With men of souls, fit to reform the ills
Of all mankind: there's not a heart amongst them,
But's as stout as death, yet honest as the nature
Of man first made, ere fraud and vice were fashions.
Belv. What's he, to whose cursed hands last night thou gav'st me?
Was that well done? Oh! I could tell a story
Would rouse thy lion heart out of its den,
And make it rage with terrifying fury.
Jaff. Speak on, I charge thee!
Belv. Oh my love! if e'er
Thy Belvidera's peace deserved thy care,
Remove me from this place. Last night, last night!
Jaff. Distract me not, but give me all the truth.
Belv. No sooner wert thou gone, and I alone,
Left in the pow'r of that old son of mischief;
No sooner was I lain on my sad bed,
But that vile wretch approached me, loose, unbuttoned,
Ready for violation. Then my heart
Throbbed with its fears: oh, how I wept and sighed,
And shrunk and trembled; wished in vain for him
That should protect me. Thou, alas! wert gone!
Jaff. Patience, sweet Heaven, till I make vengeance sure!
Belv. He drew the hideous dagger forth thou gav'st him,
And with upbraiding smiles he said, 'Behold it;

163 Nose-slitters] After an attack of this kind in 1670 on Sir John Coventry, an act was passed declaring nose-slitting to be an act of felony, without benefit of clergy.

This is the pledge of a false husband's love!'
And in my arms then pressed, and would have clasped me;
But with my cries I scared his coward heart,
Till he withdrew, and muttered vows to Hell.
These are thy friends! with these thy life, thy honour,
Thy love, all's staked, and all will go to ruin.

Jaff. No more: I charge thee keep this secret close;
Clear up thy sorrows, look as if thy wrongs
Were all forgot, and treat him like a friend,
As no complaint were made. No more; retire,
Retire, my life, and doubt not of my honour;
I'll heal its failings, and deserve thy love.

Belv. Oh, should I part with thee, I fear thou wilt
In anger leave me, and return no more.

Jaff. Return no more! I would not live without thee
Another night to purchase the creation.

Belv. When shall we meet again?

Jaff. Anon at twelve!
I'll steal myself to thy expecting arms,
Come like a travelled dove and bring thee peace.

Belv. Indeed!

Jaff. By all our loves!

Belv. 'Tis hard to part:
But sure no falsehood e'er looked so fairly.
Farewell.—Remember twelve. [*Exit* Belvidera.

Jaff. Let Heaven forget me
When I remember not thy truth, thy love,
How cursed is my condition, tossed and justled,
From every corner! Fortune's common fool,
The jest of rogues, an instrumental ass
For villains to lay loads of shame upon,
And drive about just for their ease and scorn!

Enter Pierre.

Pierre. Jaffeir!

Jaff. Who calls?

Pierre. A friend, that could have wished
T' have found thee otherwise employed. What, hunt
A wife on the dull foil! sure a staunch husband
Of all hounds is the dullest? Wilt thou never,
Never be weaned from caudles and confections?

221 foil] track (of a hunted animal) staunch] a term used of sporting dogs that 'may be trusted to find or follow the *scent*, or to mark the game; dependable' (*O.E.D.*, 5)

What feminine tale hast thou been listening to,
Of unaired shirts; catarrhs and toothache got
By thin-soled shoes? Damnation! that a fellow,
Chosen to be a sharer in the destruction
Of a whole people, should sneak thus in corners
To ease his fulsome lusts, and fool his mind.

Jaff. May not a man then trifle out an hour
With a kind woman and not wrong his calling?

Pierre. Not in a cause like ours.

Jaff. Then, friend, our cause
Is in a damned condition; for I'll tell thee,
That canker-worm called lechery has touched it;
'Tis tainted vilely. Wouldst thou think it, Renault
(That mortified old withered winter rogue)
Loves simple fornication like a priest?
I found him out for watering at my wife:
He visited her last night like a kind guardian.
Faith, she has some temptations, that's the truth on't.

Pierre. He durst not wrong his trust!

Jaff. 'Twas something late, though,
To take the freedom of a lady's chamber.

Pierre. Was she in bed?

Jaff. Yes, faith, in virgin sheets
White as her bosom, Pierre; dished neatly up,
Might tempt a weaker appetite to taste.
Oh, how the old fox stunk, I warrant thee,
When the rank fit was on him!

Pierre. Patience guide me!
He used no violence?

Jaff. No, no! out on't, violence!
Played with her neck; brushed her with his grey beard,
Struggled and toused, tickled her till she squeaked a little,
May be, or so—but not a jot of violence—

Pierre. Damn him!

Jaff. Ay, so say I. But hush, no more on't;
All hitherto is well, and I believe
Myself no monster yet, though no man knows
What fate he's born to. Sure 'tis near the hour
We all should meet for our concluding orders.
Will the ambassador be here in person?

238 watering at] i.e. with the mouth watering in anticipation 250 toused] tousled, handled rudely 254 monster] cuckold

Pierre. No; he has sent commission to that villain,
Renault, to give the executing charge;
I'd have thee be a man if possible
And keep thy temper; for a brave revenge
Ne'er comes too late.
Jaff. Fear not, I am cool as patience:
Had he completed my dishonour, rather
Than hazard the success our hopes are ripe for,
I'd bear it all with mortifying virtue.
Pierre. He's yonder coming this way through the hall;
His thoughts seem full.
Jaff. Prithee retire, and leave me
With him alone: I'll put him to some trial,
See how his rotten part will bear the touching.
Pierre. Be careful then.
Jaff. Nay never doubt, but trust me. [*Exit* Pierre.
What, be a devil! take a damning oath
For shedding native blood! Can there be a sin
In merciful repentance. Oh, this villain!

Enter Renault.

Ren. Perverse! and peevish! what a slave is man!
To let his itching flesh thus get the better of him!
Dispatch the tool her husband—that were well.
Who's there?
Jaff. A man.
Ren. My friend, my near ally!
The hostage of your faith, my beauteous charge,
Is very well.
Jaff. Sir, are you sure of that?
Stands she in perfect health? beats her pulse even?
Neither too hot nor cold?
Ren. What means that question?
Jaff. Oh, women have fantastic constitutions,
Inconstant as their wishes, always wavering,
And ne'er fixed. Was it not boldly done
Even at first sight to trust the thing I loved
(A tempting treasure too!) with youth so fierce
And vigorous as thine? But thou art honest.
Ren. Who dares accuse me?
Jaff. Cursed be him that doubts
Thy virtue; I have tried it, and declare,

Were I to choose a guardian of my honour
I'd put it into thy keeping—for I know thee.
Ren. Know me!
Jaff. Ay, know thee: there's no falsehood in thee.
Thou look'st just as thou art. Let us embrace.
Now wouldst thou cut my throat or I cut thine?
Ren. You dare not do't.
Jaff. You lie sir.
Ren. How!
Jaff. No more!
'Tis a base world, and must reform, that's all.

Enter Spinosa, Theodore, Eliot, Revellido, Durand, Brainveil, *and the rest of the conspirators.*

Ren. Spinosa! Theodore!
Spin. The same.
Ren. You are welcome!
Spin. You are trembling, sir.
Ren. 'Tis a cold night indeed, I am aged,
Full of decay and natural infirmities.

Pierre *re-enters.*

We shall be warm, my friend, I hope tomorrow.
Pierre. ⟨*Aside to* Jaffeir.⟩ 'Twas not well done; thou shouldst have stroked [him
And not have galled him.
Jaff. Damn him, let him chew on't.——
⟨*Aside*.⟩ Heaven! where am I? beset with cursed fiends,
That wait to damn me. What a devil's man,
When he forgets his nature!—Hush, my heart!
Ren. My friends, 'tis late. Are we assembled all?
Where's Theodore?
Theo. At hand.
Ren. Spinosa.
Spin. Here.
Ren. Brainveil.
Brain. I am ready.
Ren. Durand and Brabe.
Dur. Command us,
We are both prepared!
Ren. Mezzana, Revellido,
Ternon, Retrosi; oh, you are men, I find

Fit to behold your fate, and meet her summons.
Tomorrow's rising sun must see you all
Decked in your honours! Are the soldiers ready?

Omnes. All, all.

Ren. You, Durand, with your thousand must possess
St. Mark's; you, captain, know your charge already:
'Tis to secure the ducal palace. You,
Brabe, with a hundred more must gain the Secque;
With the like number Brainveil to the Procuralle.
Be all this done with the least tumult possible,
Till in each place you post sufficient guards:
Then sheath your swords in every breast you meet.

Jaff. ⟨*Aside.*⟩ Oh reverend cruelty! Damned bloody villain!

Ren. During this execution, Durand, you
Must in the midst keep your battalia fast,
And Theodore be sure to plant the cannon
That may command the streets; whilst Revellido,
Mezzana, Ternon and Retrosi guard you.
(This done!) we'll give the general alarm,
Apply petards, and force the Ars'nal gates;
Then fire the city round in several places,
Or with our cannon (if it dare resist)
Batter't to ruin. But above all I charge you
Shed blood enough, spare neither sex nor age,
Name nor condition; if there live a senator
After tomorrow, though the dullest rogue
That e'er said nothing, we have lost our ends.
If possible, let's kill the very name
Of senator, and bury it in blood.

Jaff. ⟨*Aside.*⟩ Merciless, horrid slave!—⟨*Aloud.*⟩ Ay, blood enough!
Shed blood enough, old Renault. How thou charm'st me!

Ren. But one thing more, and then farewell till fate
Join us again, or separate us ever:
First, let's embrace. Heaven knows who next shall thus
Wing ye together. But let's all remember
We wear no common cause upon our swords;
Let each man think that on his single virtue
Depends the good and fame of all the rest,
Eternal honour or perpetual infamy.

319 Secque] the Mint 320 Procuralle] the home of the Procurator, the most important magistrate in Venice after the Doge 326 keep your battalia fast] keep the main body of the troops in firm order

Let's remember through what dreadful hazards
Propitious fortune hitherto has led us;
How often on the brink of some discovery
Have we stood tottering, and yet still kept our ground
So well, the busiest searchers ne'er could follow
Those subtle tracks which puzzled all suspicion—
⟨*To Jaffeir.*⟩ You droop, sir.

Jaff. No; with a most profound attention
I've heard it all, and wonder at thy virtue.

Ren. Though there be yet few hours 'twixt them and ruin,
Are not the Senate lulled in full security,
Quiet and satisfied, as fools are always?
Never did so profound repose forerun
Calamity so great. Nay, our good fortune
Has blinded the most piercing of mankind:
Strengthened the fearfull'st, charmed the most suspectful,
Confounded the most subtle; for we live,
We live, my friends, and quickly shall our life
Prove fatal to these tyrants. Let's consider
That we destroy oppression, avarice,
A people nursed up equally with vices
And loathsome lusts which Nature most abhors,
And such as without shame she cannot suffer.

Jaff. ⟨*Aside.*⟩ Oh, Belvidera, take me to thy arms
And show me where's my peace, for I've lost it. [*Exit* Jaffeir.

Ren. Without the least remorse then let's resolve
With fire and sword t'exterminate these tyrants;
And when we shall behold those cursed tribunals,
Stained by the tears and sufferings of the innocent,
Burning with flames rather from Heaven than ours,
The raging, furious and unpitying soldier
Pulling his reeking dagger from the bosoms
Of gasping wretches, death in every quarter,
With all that sad disorder can produce,
To make a spectacle of horror: then,
Then let's call to mind, my dearest friends,
That there's nothing pure upon the earth,
That the most valued things have most allays,
And that in change of all those vile enormities,
Under whose weight this wretched country labours,
The means are only in our hands to crown them.

360 security] over-confidence, carelessness 387 allays] alloys

Pierre. And may those powers above that are propitious
To gallant minds record this cause, and bless it.
Ren. Thus happy, thus secure of all we wish for,
Should there, my friends, be found amongst us one
False to this glorious enterprise, what fate,
What vengeance were enough for such a villain?
Eliot. Death here without repentance, Hell hereafter.
Ren. Let that be my lot, if as here I stand
Listed by fate amongst her darling sons,
Though I had one only brother, dear by all
The strictest ties of nature; though one hour
Had given us birth, one fortune fed our wants,
One only love, and that but of each other,
Still filled our minds—could I have such a friend
Joined in this cause, and had but ground to fear
Meant foul play, may this right hand drop from me,
If I'd not hazard all my future peace,
And stab him to the heart before you. Who
Would do less? Wouldst not thou, Pierre, the same?
Pierre. You have singled me, sir, out for this hard question,
As if 'twere started only for my sake!
Am I the thing you fear? Here, here's my bosom,
Search it with all your swords! am I a traitor?
Ren. No; but I fear your late commended friend
Is little less. Come, sirs, 'tis now no time
To trifle with our safety. Where's this Jaffeir?
Spin. He left the room just now in strange disorder.
Ren. Nay, there is danger in him: I observed him,
During the time I took for explanation,
He was transported from most deep attention
To a confusion which he could not smother.
His looks grew full of sadness and surprise,
All which betrayed a wavering spirit in him,
That laboured with reluctancy and sorrow;
What's requisite for safety must be done
With speedy execution; he remains
Yet in our power: I for my own part wear
A dagger.
Pierre. Well.
Ren. And I could wish it—
Pierre. Where?
Ren. Buried in his heart.

Pierre. Away! w'are yet all friends;
No more of this, 'twill breed ill blood amongst us.
Spin. Let us all draw our swords, and search the house,
Pull him from the dark hole where he sits brooding
O'er his cold fears, and each man kill his share of him.
Pierre. Who talks of killing? who's he'll shed the blood
That's dear to me? Is't you? or you? or you sir?
What, not one speak? How you stand gaping all
On your grave oracle, your wooden god there!
Yet not a word? ⟨*To Renault.*⟩ Then, sir, I'll tell you a secret,
Suspicion's but at best a coward's virtue!
Ren. A coward— [*Handles his sword.*
Pierre. Put, put up thy sword, old man,
Thy hand shakes at it; come, let's heal this breach,
I am too hot: we yet may live friends.
Spin. Till we are safe, our friendship cannot be so.
Pierre. Again: who's that?
Spin. 'Twas I.
Theo. And I.
Rev. And I.
Eliot. And all.
Ren. Who are on my side?
Spin. Every honest sword.
Let's die like men and not be sold like slaves.
Pierre. One such word more, by Heaven I'll to the Senate
And hang ye all, like dogs in clusters.
Why peep your coward swords half out their shells?
Why do you not all brandish them like mine?
You fear to die, and yet dare talk of killing?
Ren. Go to the Senate and betray us, hasten,
Secure thy wretched life; we fear to die
Less than thou dar'st be honest.
Pierre. That's rank falsehood,
Fear'st not thou death? Fie, there's a knavish itch
In that salt blood, an utter foe to smarting.
Had Jaffeir's wife proved kind, he had still been true.
Foh! how that stinks!
Thou die! thou kill my friend! or thou, or thou,
Or thou, with that lean withered wretched face!
Away! disperse all to your several charges,
And meet tomorrow where your honour calls you;
I'll bring that man whose blood you so much thirst for,

And you shall see him venture for you fairly—
Hence, hence, I say. [*Exit* Renault *angrily*.
Spin. I fear we have been too blame,
And done too much.
Theo. 'Twas too far urged against the man you loved.
Rev. Here, take our swords and crush 'em with your feet.
Spin. Forgive us, gallant friend.
Pierre. Nay, now y' have found
The way to melt and cast me as you will.
I'll fetch this friend and give him to your mercy;
Nay, he shall die if you will take him from me,
For your repose I'll quit my heart's jewel,
But would not have him torn away by villains
And spiteful villainy.
Spin. No; may you both
For ever live and fill the world with fame!
Pierre. Now you are too kind. Whence rose all this discord?
Oh, what a dangerous precipice have we 'scaped!
How near a fall was all we had long been building!
What an eternal blot had stained our glories,
If one the bravest and the best of men
Had fallen a sacrifice to rash suspicion!
Butchered by those whose cause he came to cherish!
Oh, could you know him all as I have known him,
How good he is, how just, how true, how brave,
You would not leave this place till you had seen him;
Humbled yourselves before him, kissed his feet,
And gained remission for the worst of follies.
Come but tomorrow, all your doubts shall end,
And to your loves me better recommend,
That I've preserved your fame, and saved my friend.
[*Exeunt omnes*.

466 too blame] too blameworthy too blame *Q*. 1; to blame *Works*

ACT IV [SCENE I]

Enter Jaffeir *and* Belvidera.

Jaff. Where dost thou lead me? Every step I move,
Methinks I tread upon some mangled limb
Of a racked friend. Oh, my dear charming ruin!
Where are we wand'ring?
Belv. To eternal honour;
To do a deed shall chronicle thy name
Among the glorious legends of those few
That have saved sinking nations. Thy renown
Shall be the future song of all the virgins
Who by thy piety have been preserved
From horrid violation; every street
Shall be adorned with statues to thy honour,
And at thy feet this great inscription written:
Remember him that propped the fall of Venice.
Jaff. Rather remember him who, after all
The sacred bonds of oaths and holier friendship,
In fond compassion to a woman's tears
Forgot his manhood, virtue, truth and honour,
To sacrifice the bosom that relieved him.
Why wilt thou damn me?
Belv. Oh, inconstant man!
How will you promise? how will you deceive?
Do, return back, replace me in my bondage,
Tell all thy friends how dangerously thou lov'st me;
And let thy dagger do its bloody office.
Oh, that kind dagger, Jaffeir, how twill look
Stuck through my heart, drenched in my blood to th' hilts!
Whilst these poor dying eyes shall with their tears
No more torment thee, then thou wilt be free:
Or if thou think'st it nobler, let me live
Till I am a victim to the hateful lust
Of that infernal devil, that old fiend
That's damned himself and would undo mankind.
Last night, my love!
Jaff. Name, name it not again.
It shows a beastly image to my fancy
Will wake me into madness. Oh, the villain,

That durst approach such purity as thine
On terms so vile! Destruction, swift destruction
Fall on my coward head, and make my name
The common scorn of fools if I forgive him;
If I forgive him, if I not revenge
With utmost rage and most unstaying fury
Thy sufferings, thou dear darling of my life, love!
Belv. Delay no longer then, but to the Senate;
And tell the dismal'st story e'er was uttered;
Tell 'em what bloodshed, rapines, desolations,
Have been prepared, how near's the fatal hour!
Save thy poor country, save the reverend blood
Of all its nobles, which tomorrow's dawn
Must else see shed. Save the poor tender lives
Of all those little infants which the swords
Of murderers are whetting for this moment.
Think thou already hear'st their dying screams,
Think that thou seest their sad distracted mothers
Kneeling before thy feet, and begging pity
With torn dishevelled hair and streaming eyes,
Their naked mangled breasts besmeared with blood,
And even the milk with which their fondled babes
Softly they hushed, dropping in anguish from 'em.
Think thou seest this, and then consult thy heart.
Jaff. Oh!
Belv. Think too, if thou lose this present minute,
What miseries the next day bring upon thee.
Imagine all the horrors of that night,
Murder and rapine, waste and desolation,
Confusedly ranging. Think what then may prove
My lot! The ravisher may then come safe,
And midst the terror of the public ruin
Do a damned deed; perhaps to lay a train
May catch thy life. Then where will be revenge,
The dear revenge that's due to such a wrong?
Jaff. By all Heaven's powers, prophetic truth dwells in thee,
For every word thou speak'st strikes through my heart
Like a new light, and shows it how 't has wandered.
Just what th' hast made me, take me, Belvidera,
And lead me to the place where I'm to say
This bitter lesson, where I must betray
My truth, my virtue, constancy and friends.

Must I betray my friends? Ah, take me quickly,
Secure me well before that thought's renewed;
If I relapse once more, all's lost for ever.
Belv. Hast thou a friend more dear than Belvidera?
Jaff. No, th' art my soul itself; wealth, friendship, honour,
All present joys, and earnest of all future,
Are summed in thee. Methinks when in thy arms
Thus leaning on thy breast, one minute's more
Than a long thousand years of vulgar hours.
Why was such happiness not given me pure?
Why dashed with cruel wrongs, and bitter wantings?
Come, lead me forward now like a tame lamb
To sacrifice. Thus in his fatal garlands,
Decked fine and pleased, the wanton skips and plays,
Trots by the enticing flattering priestess' side,
And much transported with his little pride,
Forgets his dear companions of the plain
Till by her, bound, he's on the altar lain
Yet then too hardly bleats, such pleasure's in the pain.

Enter Officer *and six Guards.*

Offic. Stand! who goes there?
Belv. Friends.
Jaff. Friends, Belvidera! hide me from my friends.
By Heaven, I'd rather see the face of Hell,
Than meet the man I love.
Offic. But what friends are you?
Belv. Friends to the Senate and the state of Venice.
Offic. My orders are to seize on all I find
At this late hour, and bring 'em to the Council,
Who now are sitting.
Jaff. Sir, you shall be obeyed.
Hold, brutes, stand off, none of your paws upon me!
Now the lot's cast, and fate, do what thou wilt. [*Exeunt guarded.*

SCENE [II]

The Senate House.

Where appear sitting, the Duke of Venice, Priuli, Antonio, *and eight other* Senators.

Duke. Antony, Priuli, Senators of Venice,
Speak; why are we assembled here this night?
What have you to inform us of concerns
The state of Venice' honour, or its safety?
Priu. Could words express the story I have to tell you,
Fathers, these tears were useless, these sad tears
That fall from my old eyes; but there is cause
We all should weep, tear off these purple robes,
And wrap ourselves in sackcloth, sitting down
On the sad earth, and cry aloud to Heaven.
Heaven knows if yet there be an hour to come
Ere Venice be no more!
All Senators. How!
Priu. Nay, we stand
Upon the very brink of gaping ruin,
Within this city's formed a dark conspiracy
To massacre us all, our wives and children,
Kindred and friends; our palaces and temples
To lay in ashes: nay, the hour too fixed,
The swords, for aught I know, drawn even this moment,
And the wild waste begun. From unknown hands
I had this warning: but if we are men
Let's not be tamely butchered, but do something
That may inform the world in after ages,
Our virtue was not ruined though we were.

A noise without.

Room, room, make room for some prisoners!
2 *Senator.* Let's raise the city.

Enter Officer *and Guard.*

Priu. Speak there, what disturbance?
Offic. Two prisoners have the guard seized in the streets,
Who say they come to inform this reverend Senate
About the present danger.

19 waste] destruction

Enter Jaffeir *and* Belvidera *guarded.*

All. Give 'em entrance—
Well, who are you?
Jaff. A villain.
Anto. Short and pithy.
The man speaks well.
Jaff. Would every man that hears me
Would deal so honestly, and own his title!
Duke. 'Tis rumoured that a plot has been contrived
Against this state; that you have a share in't too.
If you are a villain, to redeem your honour,
Unfold the truth and be restored with mercy.
Jaff. Think not that I to save my life come hither,
I know its value better; but in pity
To all those wretches whose unhappy dooms
Are fixed and sealed. You see me here before you,
The sworn and covenanted foe of Venice.
But use me as my dealings may deserve
And I may prove a friend.
Duke. The slave capitulates;
Give him the tortures.
Jaff. That you dare not do;
Your fears won't let you, nor the longing itch
To hear a story which you dread the truth of—
Truth which the fear of smart shall ne'er get from me.
Cowards are scared with threat'nings, boys are whipped
Into confessions; but a steady mind
Acts of itself, ne'er asks the body counsel.
Give him the tortures! Name but such a thing
Again, by Heaven I'll shut these lips for ever;
Not all your racks, your engines or your wheels
Shall force a groan away—that you may guess at.
Anto. A bloody-minded fellow, I'll warrant;
A damned bloody-minded fellow.
Duke. Name your conditions.
Jaff. For myself full pardon,
Besides the lives of two and twenty friends [*Delivers a list.*
Whose names are here enrolled. Nay, let their crimes
Be ne'er so monstrous, I must have the oaths
And sacred promise of this reverend Council,

42 capitulates] makes conditions, bargains

That in a full assembly of the senate
The thing I ask be ratified. Swear this,
And I'll unfold the secrets of your danger.
All. We'll swear.
Duke. Propose the oath.
Jaff. By all the hopes
Ye have of peace and happiness hereafter,
Swear.
All. We all swear.
Jaff. To grant me what I've asked,
Ye swear?
All. We swear.
Jaff. And as ye keep the oath,
May you and your posterity be blessed,
Or cursed for ever.
All. Else be cursed for ever.
Jaff. Then here's the list, and with't the full disclose
[*Delivers another paper.*
Of all that threatens you.—Now, Fate, thou hast caught me.

Anto. Why, what a dreadful catalogue of cut-throats is here! I'll warrant you not one of these fellows but has a face like a lion. I dare not so much as read their names over.

Duke. Give orders that all diligent search be made
To seize these men: their characters are public.
The paper intimates their rendezvous
To be at the house of a famed Grecian courtesan
Called Aquilina; see that place secured.

Anto. What, my Nicky Nacky, hurry durry, Nicky, Nacky in the plot!—
I'll make a speech. Most noble senators,
What headlong apprehension drives you on,
Right noble, wise and truly solid Senators,
To violate the laws and right of nations?
The lady is a lady of renown.
'Tis true, she holds a house of fair reception,
And though I say't myself, as many more
Can say as well as I—
2 *Senator.* My lord, long speeches
Are frivolous here, when dangers are so near us;
We all well know your interest in that lady,
The world talks loud on't.
Anto. Verily I have done,
I say no more.

Duke. But since he has declared
Himself concerned, pray, captain, take great caution
To treat the fair one as becomes her character,
And let her bed-chamber be searched with decency.
You, Jaffeir, must with patience bear till morning
To be our prisoner.
Jaff. Would the chains of death
Had bound me fast ere I had known this minute!
I've done a deed will make my story hereafter
Quoted in competition with all ill ones;
The history of my wickedness shall run
Down through the low traditions of the vulgar,
And boys be taught to tell the tale of Jaffeir.
Duke. Captain, withdraw your prisoner.
Jaff. Sir, if possible,
Lead me where my own thoughts themselves may lose me,
Where I may doze out what I've left of life,
Forget myself and this day's guilt and falsehood.
Cruel remembrance, how shall I appease thee! [*Exit guarded.*
[*Noise without.*] More traitors; room, room, make room there!
Duke. How's this? Guards!
Where are our guards? Shut up the gates, the treason's
Already at our doors.

Enter Officer.

Offic. My lords, more traitors:
Seized in the very act of consultation;
Furnished with arms and instruments of mischief.—
Bring in the prisoners.

Enter Pierre, Renault, Theodore, Eliot, Revillido *and other conspirators, in fetters, guarded.*

Pierre. You, my lords and fathers,
(As you are pleased to call yourselves) of Venice;
If you sit here to guide the course of justice,
Why these disgraceful chains upon the limbs
That have so often laboured in your service?
Are these the wreaths of triumphs ye bestow
On those that bring you conquests home and honours?
Duke. Go on, you shall be heard, sir.
Anto. And be hanged too, I hope.

Pierre. Are these the trophies I've deserved for fighting
Your battles with confederated powers,
When winds and seas conspired to overthrow you,
And brought the fleets of Spain to your own harbours?
When you, great Duke, shrunk trembling in your palace,
And saw your wife, th'Adriatic, ploughed
Like a lewd whore by bolder prows than yours,
Stepped not I forth, and taught your loose Venetians
The task of honour and the way to greatness,
Raised you from your capitulating fears
To stipulate the terms of sued-for peace?
And this my recompense? If I am a traitor,
Produce my charge; or show the wretch that's base enough
And brave enough to tell me I am a traitor.
Duke. Know you one Jaffeir? [*All the conspirators murmur.*
Pierre. Yes, and know his virtue.
His justice, truth, his general worth and sufferings
From a hard father taught me first to love him.

Enter Jaffeir *guarded.*

Duke. See him brought forth.
Pierre. My friend too bound? Nay then,
Our fate has conquered us, and we must fall.
Why droops the man whose welfare's so much mine
They're but one thing? These reverend tyrants, Jaffeir,
Call us all traitors. Art thou one, my brother?
Jaff. To thee I am the falsest, veriest slave
That e'er betrayed a generous trusting friend,
And gave up honour to be sure of ruin.
All our fair hopes which morning was to have crowned
Has this cursed tongue o'erthrown.
Pierre. So, then all's over:
Venice has lost her freedom; I my life.
No more; farewell.
Duke. Say, will you make confession
Of your vile deeds and trust the Senate's mercy?
Pierre. Cursed be your Senate! Cursed your constitution!
The curse of growing factions and division
Still vex your councils, shake your public safety,
And make the robes of government you wear
Hateful to you, as these base chains to me!

129 your wife, th'Adriatic] cf. p. 280, n.

Duke. Pardon or death?
Pierre. Death, honourable death!
Ren. Death's the best thing we ask or you can give.
All Conspirators. No shameful bonds, but honourable death!
Duke. Break up the Council. Captain, guard your prisoners.
Jaffeir, y'are free, but these must wait for judgement.
[*Exeunt all the Senators*.
Pierre. Come, where's my dungeon? Lead me to my straw:
It will not be the first time I've lodged hard
To do your senate service.
Jaff. Hold one moment.
Pierre. Who's he disputes the judgement of the Senate?
Presumptuous rebel—on!— [*Strikes* Jaffeir.
Jaff. By Heaven, you stir not.
I must be heard, I must have leave to speak.
Thou hast disgraced me, Pierre, by a vile blow:
Had not a dagger done thee nobler justice?
But use me as thou wilt, thou canst not wrong me,
For I am fallen beneath the basest injuries;
Yet look upon me with an eye of mercy,
With pity and with charity behold me;
Shut not thy heart against a friend's repentance,
But, as there dwells a god-like nature in thee,
Listen with mildness to my supplications.
Pierre. What whining monk art thou? what holy cheat
That wouldst encroach upon my credulous ears
And cant'st thus vilely? Hence! I know thee not;
Dissemble and be nasty. Leave me, hypocrite!
Jaff. Not know me, Pierre?
Pierre. No, know thee not. What art thou?
Jaff. Jaffeir, thy friend, thy once loved, valued friend,
Though now deservedly scorned, and used most hardly.
Pierre. Thou Jaffeir! Thou my once loved, valued friend?
By Heavens, thou liest! The man so called, my friend,
Was generous, honest, faithful, just and valiant,
Noble in mind, and in his person lovely,
Dear to my eyes and tender to my heart:
But thou a wretched, base, false, worthless coward,
Poor even in soul, and loathsome in thy aspect;
All eyes must shun thee, and all hearts detest thee.
Prithee avoid, nor longer cling thus round me,
Like something baneful that my nature's chilled at.

Jaff. I have not wronged thee, by these tears I have not,
But still am honest, true, and hope, too, valiant;
My mind still full of thee: therefore still noble.
Let not thy eyes then shun me, nor thy heart
Detest me utterly. Oh, look upon me,
Look back and see my sad sincere submission!
How my heart swells, as even 'twould burst my bosom;
Fond of its gaol, and labouring to be at thee!
What shall I do? what say to make thee hear me?

Pierre. Hast thou not wronged me? dar'st thou call thyself
Jaffeir, that once loved, valued friend of mine,
And swear thou hast not wronged me? Whence these chains?
Whence the vile death which I may meet this moment?
Whence this dishonour but from thee, thou false one?

Jaff. —All's true, yet grant one thing, and I've done asking.

Pierre. What's that?

Jaff. To take thy life on such conditions
The Council have proposed. Thou and thy friends
May yet live long, and to be better treated.

Pierre. Life! Ask my life! Confess! record myself
A villain for the privilege to breathe,
And carry up and down this cursed city
A discontented and repining spirit,
Burdensome to itself, a few years longer,
To lose, it may be, at last in a lewd quarrel
For some new friend, treacherous and false as thou art!
No, this vile world and I have long been jangling,
And cannot part on better terms than now,
When only men like thee are fit to live in't.

Jaff. By all that's just—

Pierre. Swear by some other powers,
For thou hast broke that sacred oath too lately.

Jaff. Then by that Hell I merit, I'll not leave thee,
Till to thyself at least thou'rt reconciled,
However thy resentments deal with me.

Pierre. Not leave me!

Jaff. No, thou shalt not force me from thee.
Use me reproachfully, and like a slave,
Tread on me, buffet me, heap wrongs on wrongs
On my poor head; I'll bear it all with patience,
Shall weary out thy most unfriendly cruelty,
Lie at thy feet and kiss 'em though they spurn me,

Till, wounded by my sufferings, thou relent,
And raise me to thy arms with dear forgiveness.
Pierre. Art thou not—
Jaff. What?
Pierre. A traitor?
Jaff. Yes.
Pierre. A villain?
Jaff. Granted.
Pierre. A coward, a most scandalous coward,
Spiritless, void of honour, one who has sold
Thy everlasting fame for shameless life?
Jaff. All, all, and more, much more: my faults are numberless.
Pierre. And wouldst thou have me live on terms like thine?
Base as thou art false—
Jaff. No, 'tis to me that's granted.
The safety of thy life was all I aimed at,
In recompense for faith and trust so broken.
Pierre. I scorn it more because preserved by thee,
And as when first my foolish heart took pity
On thy misfortunes, sought thee in thy miseries,
Relieved thy wants, and raised thee from thy state
Of wretchedness in which thy fate had plunged thee,
To rank thee in my list of noble friends,
All I received in surety for thy truth,
Were unregarded oaths, and this, this dagger,
Given with a worthless pledge thou since hast stol'n—
So I restore it back to thee again,
Swearing by all those powers which thou hast violated,
Never from this cursed hour to hold communion,
Friendship or interest with thee, though our years
Were to exceed those limited the world.
Take it—farewell!—for now I owe thee nothing.
Jaff. Say thou wilt live then.
Pierre. For my life, dispose it
Just as thou wilt, because 'tis what I'm tired with.
Jaff. Oh, Pierre!
Pierre. No more!
Jaff. My eyes won't lose the sight of thee,
But languish after thine, and ache with gazing.
Pierre. Leave me!—Nay, then thus, thus, I throw thee from me,
And curses, great as is thy falsehood, catch thee! [*Exit* Pierre.
Jaff. Amen.

He's gone, my father, friend, preserver,
And here's the portion he has left me. [*Holds the dagger up.*
This dagger, well rememb'red, with this dagger
I gave a solemn vow of dire importance,
Parted with this and Belvidera together—
Have a care, mem'ry, drive that thought no farther.
No, I'll esteem it as a friend's last legacy,
Treasure it up in this wretched bosom,
Where it may grow acquainted with my heart,
That when they meet, they start not from each other.
So; now for thinking: a blow, called traitor, villain,
Coward, dishonourable coward, fogh!
Oh for a long sound sleep, and so forget it!
Down, busy devil—.

Enter Belvidera.

Belv. Whither shall I fly?
Where hide me and my miseries together?
Where's now the Roman constancy I boasted?
Sunk into trembling fears and desperation!
Not daring now to look up to that dear face
Which used to smile even on my faults, but down
Bending these miserable eyes to earth,
Must move in penance, and implore much mercy.
Jaff. Mercy! Kind Heaven has surely endless stores
Hoarded for thee of blessings yet untasted;
Let wretches loaded hard with guilt as I am
Bow with the weight and groan beneath the burden,
Creep with a remnant of that strength th' have left,
Before the footstool of that Heaven th' have injured.
Oh Belvidera! I'm the wretched'st creature
E'er crawled on earth; now if thou hast virtue, help me,
Take me into thy arms, and speak the words of peace
To my divided soul that wars within me,
And raises every sense to my confusion.
By Heaven, I am tottering on the very brink
Of peace, and thou art all the hold I've left.
Belv. Alas! I know thy sorrows are most mighty;
I know th' hast cause to mourn; to mourn, my Jaffeir,
With endless cries, and never ceasing wailings;
Th' hast lost—
Jaff. Oh I have lost what can't be counted.

My friend too, Belvidera, that dear friend,
Who, next to thee, was all my health rejoiced in,
Has used me like a slave, shamefully used me;
'Twould break thy pitying heart to hear the story.
What shall I do? Resentment, indignation,
Love, pity, fear, and mem'ry how I've wronged him,
Distract my quiet with the very thought on't,
And tear my heart to pieces in my bosom.

Belv. What has he done?

Jaff. Thou'dst hate me, should I tell thee.

Belv. Why?

Jaff. Oh, he has used me—yet, by Heaven, I bear it!—
He has used me, Belvidera—but first swear
That when I've told thee, thou'lt not loathe me utterly,
Though vilest blots and stains appear upon me,
But still at least with charitable goodness,
Be near me in the pangs of my affliction,—
Not scorn me, Belvidera, as he has done.

Belv. Have I then e'er been false that now I am doubted?
Speak, what's the cause I am grown into distrust?
Why thought unfit to hear my love's complainings?

Jaff. Oh!

Belv. Tell me.

Jaff. Bear my failings, for they are many.
Oh, my dear angel! in that friend I've lost
All my soul's peace; for every thought of him
Strikes my sense hard, and deads it in my brains.
Wouldst thou believe it?—

Belv. Speak.

Jaff. Before we parted,
Ere yet his guards had led him to his prison,
Full of severest sorrows for his suff'rings,
With eyes o'erflowing and a bleeding heart,
Humbling myself almost beneath my nature,
As at his feet I kneeled, and sued for mercy,
Forgetting all our friendship, all the dearness
In which w' have lived so many years together,
With a reproachful hand he dashed a blow,
He struck me, Belvidera; by Heaven, he struck me!
Buffeted, called me traitor, villain, coward.
Am I a coward? am I a villain? Tell me:

306 health] well-being

Th'art the best judge, and mad'st me, if I am so.
Damnation! Coward!

Belv. Oh! forgive him, Jaffeir.
And if his sufferings wound thy heart already,
What will they do tomorrow?

Jaff. Hah!

Belv. Tomorrow,
When thou shalt see him stretched in all the agonies
Of a tormenting and a shameful death,
His bleeding bowels, and his broken limbs,
Insulted o'er by a vile butchering villain;
What will thy heart do then? Oh, sure 't will stream
Like my eyes now.

Jaff. What means thy dreadful story?
Death, and tomorrow? broken limbs and bowels?
Insulted o'er by a vile butchering villain?
By all my fears I shall start out to madness
With barely guessing, if the truth's hid longer.

Belv. The faithless senators, 'tis they've decreed it.
They say according to our friend's request,
They shall have death, and not ignoble bondage;
Declare their promised mercy all as forfeited,
False to their oaths, and deaf to intercession;
Warrants are passed for public death tomorrow.

Jaff. Death! doomed to die! condemned unheard! unpleaded!

Belv. Nay, cruel'st racks and torments are preparing
To force confessions from their dying pangs;
Oh, do not look so terribly upon me,
How your lips shake, and all your face disordered!
What means my love?

Jaff. Leave me, I charge thee leave me—strong temptations
Wake in my heart.

Belv. For what?

Jaff. No more, but leave me.

Belv. Why?

Jaff. Oh! by Heaven, I love thee with that fondness
I would not have thee stay a moment longer,
Near these cursed hands. Are they not cold upon thee?

Belv. No, everlasting comfort's in thy arms.

[⟨Jaffeir⟩ *pulls the dagger half out of his bosom and puts it back again.*

To lean thus on thy breast is softer ease
Than downy pillows decked with leaves of roses.

Jaff. Alas, thou thinkest not of the thorns 'tis filled with.
Fly ere they gall thee: there's a lurking serpent
Ready to leap and sting thee to thy heart.
Art thou not terrified?
Belv. No.
Jaff. Call to mind
What thou hast done, and whither thou hast brought me.
Belv. Hah!
Jaff. Where's my friend? my friend, thou smiling mischief?
Nay, shrink not; now 'tis too late. Thou shouldst have fled
When thy guilt first had cause, for dire revenge
Is up and raging for my friend. He groans;
Hark, how he groans! his screams are in my ears
Already. See, th'have fixed him on the wheel,
And now they tear him—Murder! perjured senate!
Murder—Oh!—Hark thee, traitress, thou hast done this;
[*Fumbling for his dagger.*
Thanks to thy tears and false persuading love.
How her eyes speak! Oh, thou bewitching creature!
Madness cannot hurt thee. Come, thou little trembler,
Creep, even into my heart, and there lie safe;
'Tis thy own citadel—hah!—yet stand off,
Heaven must have justice, and my broken vows
Will sink me else beneath its reaching mercy;
I'll wink and then 'tis done—.
Belv. What means the lord
Of me, my life and love? What's in thy bosom
Thou grasp'st at so? Nay, why am I thus treated?
[⟨Jaffeir⟩ *draws the dagger, offers to stab her.*
What wilt thou do? Ah, do not kill me, Jaffeir,
Pity these panting breasts, and trembling limbs,
That used to clasp thee when thy looks were milder,
That yet hang heavy on my unpurged soul,
And plunge it not into eternal darkness.
Jaff. No, Belvidera, when we parted last
I gave this dagger with thee as in trust
To be thy portion, if I e'er proved false.
On such condition was my truth believed;
But now 'tis forfeited and must be paid for. [*Offers to stab her again.*
Belv. [*Kneeling.*] Oh, mercy!

375 gall] *Works*; call *Q.* 1

Jaff. Nay, no struggling.
Belv. Now then kill me,
[*Leaps upon his neck and kisses him.*
While thus I cling about thy cruel neck,
Kiss thy revengeful lips and die in joys
Greater than any I can guess hereafter.
Jaff. I am, I am a coward; witness't, Heaven,
Witness it, earth, and every being witness!
'Tis but one blow; yet, by immortal love,
I cannot longer bear a thought to harm thee,
[*He throws away the dagger and embraces her.*
The seal of providence is sure upon thee,
And thou wert born for yet unheard of wonders:
Oh, thou wert either born to save or damn me!
By all the power that's given thee o'er my soul,
By thy resistless tears and conquering smiles,
By the victorious love that still waits on thee,
Fly to thy cruel father; save my friend,
Or all our future quiet's lost for ever:
Fall at his feet, cling round his reverend knees,
Speak to him with thy eyes, and with thy tears
Melt the hard heart, and wake dead nature in him,
Crush him in th'arms, and torture him with thy softness;
Nor, till thy prayers are granted, set him free, 428
But conquer him, as thou hast vanquished me. [*Exeunt ambo.*

ACT V [SCENE I]

Enter Priuli *solus.*

Priu. Why, cruel Heaven, have my unhappy days
Been lengthened to this sad one? Oh! dishonour
And deathless infamy is fall'n upon me.
Was it my fault? Am I a traitor? No.
But then, my only child, my daughter, wedded;
There my best blood runs foul, and a disease
Incurable has seized upon my memory,

414 one blow; yet,] one blow yet: *Q.* 1 426 the] Ghosh; thy *Q.* 1; his *Works*

To make it rot and stink to after ages.
Cursed be the fatal minute when I got her;
Or would that I'd been anything but man,
And raised an issue which would ne'er have wronged me.
The miserablest creatures (man excepted)
Are not the less esteemed though their posterity
Degenerate from the virtues of their fathers;
The vilest beasts are happy in their offsprings,
While only man gets traitors, whores and villains.
Cursed be the names, and some swift blow from fate
Lay his head deep, where mine may be forgotten!

Enter Belvidera *in a long mourning veil.*

Belv. He's there, my father, my inhuman father,
That, for three years, has left an only child
Exposed to all the outrages of fate,
And cruel ruin—oh!—
Priu. What child of sorrow
Art thou that com'st thus wrapped in weeds of sadness,
And mov'st as if thy steps were towards a grave?
Belv. A wretch who from the very top of happiness
Am fallen into the lowest depths of misery,
And want your pitying hand to raise me up again.
Priu. Indeed, thou talk'st as thou hadst tasted sorrows;
Would I could help thee.
Belv. 'Tis greatly in your power.
The world, too, speaks you charitable, and I,
Who ne'er asked alms before, in that dear hope
Am come a-begging to you, sir.
Priu. For what?
Belv. Oh, well regard me; is this voice a strange one?
Consider too, when beggars once pretend
A case like mine, no little will content 'em.
Priu. What wouldst thou beg for?
Belv. Pity and forgiveness.
[*Throws up her veil.*
By the kind tender names of child and father,
Hear my complaints and take me to your love.
Priu. My daughter?
Belv. Yes, your daughter, by a mother
Virtuous and noble, faithful to your honour,
Obedient to your will, kind to your wishes,

Dear to your arms. By all the joys she gave you,
When in her blooming years she was your treasure,
Look kindly on me; in my face behold
The lineaments of hers y'have kissed so often,
Pleading the cause of your poor cast-off child.

Priu. Thou art my daughter.

Belv. Yes—and y'have oft told me
With smiles of love and chaste paternal kisses,
I'd much resemblance of my mother.

Priu. Oh!
Hadst thou inherited her matchless virtues
I'd been too blessed.

Belv. Nay, do not call to memory
My disobedience, but let pity enter
Into your heart, and quite deface the impression;
For could you think how mine's perplexed, what sadness
Fears and despairs distract the peace within me,
Oh, you would take me in your dear, dear arms,
Hover with strong compassion o'er your young one,
To shelter me with a protecting wing
From the black gathered storm that's just, just breaking.

Priu. Don't talk thus.

Belv. Yes, I must, and you must hear too.
I have a husband.

Priu. Damn him.

Belv. Oh, do not curse him!
He would not speak so hard a word towards you
On any terms, howe'er he deal with me—

Priu. Hah! what means my child?

Belv. Oh, there's but this short moment
'Twixt me and fate, yet send me not with curses
Down to my grave, afford me one kind blessing
Before we part; just take me in your arms
And recommend me with a prayer to Heaven,
That I may die in peace, and when I'm dead—

Priu. How my soul's catched!

Belv. Lay me, I beg you, lay me
By the dear ashes of my tender mother.
She would have pitied me, had fate yet spared her.

Priu. By Heaven, my aching heart forebodes much mischief,
Tell me thy story, for I'm still thy father.

63 howe'er] *Works*; oh! e'r *Q*. 1

Belv. No, I'm contented.
Priu. Speak.
Belv. No matter.
Priu. Tell me.
By you, blessed Heaven, my heart runs o'er with fondness.
Belv. Oh!
Priu. Utter't.
Belv. Oh, my husband, my dear husband
Carries a dagger in his once kind bosom
To pierce the heart of your poor Belvidera.
Priu. Kill thee?
Belv. Yes, kill me. When he passed his faith
And covenant against your state and senate,
He gave me up as hostage for his truth,
With me a dagger and a dire commission,
Whene'er he failed, to plunge it through this bosom.
I learnt the danger, chose the hour of love
T'attempt his heart, and bring it back to honour;
Great love prevailed and blessed me with success:
He came, confessed, betrayed his dearest friends
For promised mercy; now they're doomed to suffer.
Galled with remembrance of what then was sworn,
If they are lost, he vows t'appease the gods
With this poor life, and make my blood th' atonement.
Priu. Heavens!
Belv. Think you saw what passed at our last parting;
Think you beheld him like a raging lion,
Pacing the earth and tearing up his steps,
Fate in his eyes, and roaring with the pain
Of burning fury; think you saw his one hand
Fixed on my throat, while the extended other
Grasped a keen threat'ning dagger! Oh 'twas thus,
We last embraced, when, trembling with revenge,
He dragged me to the ground, and at my bosom
Presented horrid death, cried out, 'My friends,
Where are my friends?'—swore, wept, raged, threatened, loved,
For he yet loved, and that dear love preserved me
To this last trial of a father's pity.
I fear not death, but cannot bear a thought
That that dear hand should do th' unfriendly office.
If I was ever then your care, now hear me;
Fly to the senate, save the promised lives
Of his dear friends, ere mine be made the sacrifice.

Priu. Oh, my heart's comfort!
Belv. Will you not, my father?
Weep not, but answer me.
Priu. By Heaven, I will.
Not one of 'em but what shall be immortal.
Canst thou forgive me all my follies past,
I'll henceforth be indeed a father; never,
Never more thus expose, but cherish thee,
Dear as the vital warmth that feeds my life,
Dear as these eyes that weep in fondness o'er thee.
Peace to thy heart. Farewell.
Belv. Go, and remember.
'Tis Belvidera's life her father pleads for. [*Exeunt severally.*

[SCENE II]

Enter Antonio.

Hum, hum, hah,
Signior Priuli, my lord Priuli, my lord, my lord, my lord! Now, we lords love to call one another by our titles. My lord, my lord, my lord—Pox on him, I am a lord as well as he, and so let him fiddle. I'll warrant him he's gone to the Senate House, and I'll be there too, soon enough for somebody. 'Od—here's a tickling speech about the plot. I'll prove there's a plot with a vengeance—would I had it without book. Let me see—

Most reverend Senators,

That there is a plot, surely by this time no man that hath eyes or understanding in his head will presume to doubt, 'tis as plain as the light in the cucumber—no—hold there—cucumber does not come in yet—'tis as plain as the light in the sun, or as the man in the moon, even at noon day. It is indeed a pumpkin-plot, which, just as it was mellow, we have gathered; and now we have gathered it, prepared and dressed it, shall we throw it like a pickled cucumber out at the window? No: that it is not only a bloody, horrid, execrable, damnable and audacious plot, but it is, as I may so say, a saucy plot; and we all know, most reverend Fathers, that what is sauce for a goose is sauce for a gander. Therefore, I say, as those bloodthirsty ganders of the conspiracy would have destroyed us geese of the Senate, let us make haste to destroy them; so I humbly move for hanging—hah, hurry durry—I think this will do, though I was something out, at first, about the sun and the cucumber.

114 Canst thou . . . past,] modern editions substitute a mark of interrogation for the comma. But 'Canst thou' is presumably conditional.

Enter Aquilina.

Aquil. Good morrow, Senator.

Anto. Nacky, my dear Nacky, 'morrow, Nacky! 'Od, I am very brisk, very merry, very pert, very jovial—haaaaa—kiss me, Nacky; how dost thou do, my little tory rory strumpet? Kiss me, I say, hussy, kiss me.

Aquil. Kiss me, Nacky! Hang you, sir, coxcomb, hang you, sir!

Anto. Hayty tayty, is it so indeed? With all my heart, faith—'Hey then up go we', faith—'hey then up go we'. Dum dum derum dump. [*Sings.*

Aquil. Signior.

Anto. Madonna.

Aquil. Do you intend to die in your bed?

Anto. About threescore years hence, much may be done, my dear.

Aquil. You'll be hanged, Signior.

Anto. Hanged, sweet heart! prithee be quiet; hanged quoth-a! that's a merry conceit, with all my heart, why, thou jok'st, Nacky, thou art given to joking, I'll swear. Well, I protest, Nacky; nay, I must protest, and will protest that I love joking dearly, man. And I love thee for joking, and I'll kiss thee for joking, and touse thee for joking, and 'od, I have a devilish mind to take thee aside about that business for joking too, 'od I have, and 'Hey then up go we', dum dum derum dump. [*Sings.*

Aquil. See you this, sir? [*Draws a dagger.*

Anto. Oh Laud, a dagger! Oh Laud! it is naturally my aversion, I cannot endure the sight on't; hide it, for Heaven's sake, I cannot look that way till it be gone—hide it, hide it, oh, oh, hide it!

Aquil. Yes, in your heart, I'll hide it.

Anto. My heart! what, hide a dagger in my heart's blood?

Aquil. Yes, in thy heart, thy throat, thou pampered devil;
Thou hast helped to spoil my peace, and I'll have vengeance
On thy cursed life, for all the bloody senate,
The perjured faithless senate. Where's my lord,
My happiness, my love, my god, my hero,
Doomed by thy accursed tongue, amongst the rest,
T' a shameful rack? By all the rage that's in me
I'll be whole years in murdering thee.

Anto. Why, Nacky,
Wherefore so passionate? What have I done? what's the matter, my dear Nacky? Am not I thy love, thy happiness, thy lord, thy hero, thy senator, and everything in the world, Nacky?

Aquil. Thou! Thinkst thou, thou art fit to meet my joys,

146 tory rory] boisterous

To bear the eager clasps of my embraces?
Give me my Pierre, or—

Anto. Why, he's to be hanged, little Nacky, trussed up for treason, and so forth, child.

Aquil. Thou liest! Stop down thy throat that hellish sentence,
Or 'tis thy last: swear that my love shall live,
Or thou art dead.

Anto. Ahhhh!

Aquil. Swear to recall his doom,
Swear at my feet, and tremble at my fury.

Anto. I do. Now if she would but kick a little bit, one kick now. Ahhhh!

Aquil. Swear, or—

Anto. I do, by these dear fragrant foots
And little toes, sweet as, e-e-e-e, my Nacky Nacky Nacky.

Aquil. How!

Anto. Nothing but untie thy shoe-string a little, faith and troth; that's all, that's all, as I hope to live, Nacky, that's all.

Aquil. Nay, then—

Anto. Hold, hold; thy love, thy lord, thy hero
Shall be preserved and safe.

Aquil. Or may this poniard
Rust in thy heart.

Anto. With all my soul.

Aquil. Farewell. [*Exit* Aquilina.

Anto. Adieu! Why, what a bloody-minded, inveterate, termagant strumpet have I been plagued with! Ohhh, yet more! Nay then, I die, I die— I am dead already. [*Stretches himself out.*

[SCENE III]

Enter Jaffeir.

Jaff. Final destruction seize on all the world!
Bend down, ye heavens, and shutting round this earth,
Crush the vile globe into its first confusion;
Scorch it with elemental flames to one curst cinder
And all us little creepers in't, called men,
Burn, burn to nothing. But let Venice burn
Hotter than all the rest: here kindle Hell
Ne'er to extinguish, and let souls hereafter
Groan here, in all those pains which mine feels now!

Enter Belvidera.

Belv. My life— [*Meeting him.*
Jaff. My plague— [*Turning from her.*
Belv. Nay then, I see my ruin.
If I must die!—
Jaff. No, death's this day too busy.
Thy father's ill-timed mercy came too late.
I thank thee for thy labours though, and him too,
But all my poor betrayed unhappy friends
Have summons to prepare for fate's black hour;
And yet I live.
Belv. Then be the next my doom.
I see thou hast passed my sentence in thy heart,
And I'll no longer weep or plead against it,
But with the humblest, most obedient patience
Meet thy dear hands, and kiss 'em when they wound me;
Indeed I am willing, but I beg thee do it
With some remorse, and where thou giv'st the blow,
View me with eyes of a relenting love,
And show me pity, for 'twill sweeten justice.
Jaff. Show pity to thee?
Belv. Yes, and when thy hands,
Charged with my fate, come trembling to the deed,
As thou hast done a thousand thousand dear times,
To this poor breast, when kinder rage has brought thee,
When our stinged hearts have leaped to meet each other,
And melting kisses sealed our lips together,
When joys have left me gasping in thy arms,
So let my death come now, and I'll not shrink from't.
Jaff. Nay, Belvidera, do not fear my cruelty,
Nor let the thoughts of death perplex thy fancy,
But answer me to what I shall demand
With a firm temper and unshaken spirit.
Belv. I will when I've done weeping—
Jaff. Fie, no more on't—
How long is't since the miserable day
We wedded first—
Belv. Ohhh!
Jaff. Nay, keep in thy tears,
Lest they unman me too.
Belv. Heaven knows I cannot;

The words you utter sound so very sadly
These streams will follow—
Jaff. Come, I'll kiss 'em dry then.
Belv. But, was't a miserable day?
Jaff. A cursed one.
Belv. I thought it otherwise, and you've oft sworn
In the transporting hours of warmest love
When sure you spoke the truth, you've sworn you blessed it.
Jaff. 'Twas a rash oath.
Belv. Then why am I not cursed too?
Jaff. No, Belvidera; by th' eternal truth,
I doat with too much fondness.
Belv. Still so kind?
Still then do you love me?
Jaff. Nature, in her workings,
Inclines not with more ardour to creation,
Than I do now towards thee; man ne'er was blessed,
Since the first pair first met, as I have been.
Belv. Then sure you will not curse me.
Jaff. No, I'll bless thee.
I came on purpose, Belvidera, to bless thee.
'Tis now, I think, three years w'have lived together.
Belv. And may no fatal minute ever part us,
Till, reverend grown for age and love, we go
Down to one grave, as our last bed, together,
There sleep in peace till an eternal morning.
Jaff. When will that be? [*Sighing.*
Belv. I hope long ages hence.
Jaff. Have I not hitherto (I beg thee tell me
Thy very fears) used thee with tender'st love?
Did e'er my soul rise up in wrath against thee?
Did I e'er frown when Belvidera smiled,
Or, by the least unfriendly word, betray
A bating passion? have I ever wronged thee?
Belv. No.
Jaff. Has my heart, or have my eyes e'er wandered
To any other woman?
Belv. Never, never—
I were the worst of false ones should I accuse thee.
I own I've been too happy, blessed above
My sex's charter.
Jaff. Did I not say I came to bless thee?
Belv. Yes.

Jaff. Then hear me, bounteous Heaven;
Pour down your blessings on this beauteous head,
Where everlasting sweets are always springing.
With a continual giving hand, let peace,
Honour and safety always hover round her;
Feed her with plenty, let her eyes ne'er see
A sight of sorrow, nor her heart know mourning,
Crown all her days with joy, her nights with rest,
Harmless as her own thoughts, and prop her virtue,
To bear the loss of one that too much loved,
And comfort her with patience in our parting.
Belv. How, parting, parting!
Jaff. Yes, for ever parting,
I have sworn, Belvidera. By yon Heaven,
That best can tell how much I lose to leave thee,
We part this hour for ever.
Belv. Oh, call back
Your cruel blessings, stay with me and curse me!
Jaff. No, 'tis resolved.
Belv. Then hear me too, just Heaven:
Pour down your curses on this wretched head
With never-ceasing vengeance, let despair,
Danger or infamy, nay all, surround me;
Starve me with wantings, let my eyes ne'er see
A sight of comfort, nor my heart know peace,
But dash my days with sorrow, nights with horrors
Wild as my own thoughts now, and let loose fury
To make me mad enough for what I lose,
If I must lose him!—If I must! I will not.—
Oh, turn and hear me!
Jaff. Now hold, heart, or never.
Belv. By all the tender days we have lived together,
By all our charming nights, and joys that crowned 'em,
Pity my sad condition; speak, but speak.
Jaff. Ohhh!
Belv. By these arms that now cling round thy neck,
By this dear kiss and by ten thousand more,
By these poor streaming eyes—
Jaff. Murder! Unhold me!
By th'immortal destiny that doomed me [*Draws his dagger.*
To this cursed minute, I'll not live one longer,
Resolve to let me go or see me fall—

Belv. Hold, sir, be patient.
Jaff. Hark, the dismal bell [*Passing-bell tolls.*
Tolls out for death! I must attend its call too,
For my poor friend, my dying Pierre expects me;
He sent a message to require I'd see him
Before he died, and take his last forgiveness.
Farewell for ever.
Belv. Leave thy dagger with me.
Bequeath me something.—Not one kiss at parting?
Oh, my poor heart, when wilt thou break?
[*Going out* ⟨Jaffeir⟩ *looks back at her.*
Jaff. Yet stay,
We have a child, as yet a tender infant:
Be a kind mother to him when I am gone,
Breed him in virtue and the paths of honour,
But let him never know his father's story;
I charge thee guard him from the wrongs my fate
May do his future fortune or his name.
Now—nearer yet— [*Approaching each other.*
Oh, that my arms were riveted
Thus round thee ever! But my friends, my oath!
This and no more. [*Kisses her.*
Belv. Another, sure another,
For that poor little one you've ta'en care of,
I'll giv't him truly.
Jaff. So, now farewell.
Belv. For ever?
Jaff. Heaven knows for ever. All good angels guard thee! ⟨*Exit.*⟩
Belv. All ill ones sure had charge of me this moment.
Cursed be my days, and doubly cursed my nights,
Which I must now mourn out in widowed tears;
Blasted be every herb and fruit and tree,
Cursed be the rain that falls upon the earth,
And may the general curse reach man and beast!
Oh, give me daggers, fire or water;
How I could bleed, how burn, how drown the waves
Huzzing and booming round my sinking head,
Till I descended to the peaceful bottom!
Oh, there's all quiet, here all rage and fury,
The air's too thin, and pierces my weak brain,

140 Huzzing] buzzing

I long for thick substantial sleep. Hell, Hell!
Burst from the centre, rage and roar aloud,
If thou art half so hot, so mad as I am!

Enter Priuli *and* servants.

Who's there?
Priu. Run, seize and bring her safely home, [*They seize her*.
Guard her as you would life. Alas, poor creature!
Belv. What? To my husband then conduct me quickly.
Are all things ready? shall we die most gloriously?
Say not a word of this to my old father:
Murmuring streams, soft shades, and springing flowers,
Lutes, laurels, seas of milk, and ships of amber. [*Exeunt*.

[SCENE IV]

Scene opening discovers a scaffold and a wheel prepared for the executing of Pierre. *Then enter officers*, Pierre *and guards, a Friar, Executioner and a great rabble*.

Offic. Room, room there!—Stand all by, make room for the prisoner.
Pierre. My friend not come yet?
Father. Why are you so obstinate?
Pierre. Why you so troublesome, that a poor wretch
Cannot die in peace,
But you, like ravens, will be croaking round him?
Father. Yet, Heaven—
Pierre. I tell thee Heaven and I are friends.
I ne'er broke peace with't yet by cruel murders,
Rapine, or perjury, or vile deceiving,
But lived in moral justice towards all men;
Nor am a foe to the most strong believers,
Howe'er my own short-sighted faith confine me.
Father. But an all-seeing judge—
Pierre. You say my conscience
Must be mine accuser: I have searched that conscience,
And find no records there of crimes that scare me.
Father. 'Tis strange you should want faith.
Pierre. You want to lead

My reason blindfold, like a hampered lion,
Checked of its nobler vigour; then, when baited,
Down to obedient tameness, make it couch,
And show strange tricks which you call signs of faith.
So silly souls are gulled and you get money.
Away, no more! Captain, I would hereafter
This fellow write no lies of my conversion,
Because he has crept upon my troubled hours.

Enter Jaffeir.

Jaff. Hold. Eyes, be dry; heart, strengthen me to bear
This hideous sight, and humble me to take
The last forgiveness of a dying friend,
Betrayed by my vile falsehood to his ruin.
Oh, Pierre!
Pierre. Yet nearer.
Jaff. Crawling on my knees,
And prostrate on the earth, let me approach thee.
How shall I look up to thy injured face,
That always used to smile with friendship on me?
It darts an air of so much manly virtue,
That I, methinks, look little in thy sight,
And stripes are fitter for me than embraces.
Pierre. Dear to my arms, though thou hast undone my fame,
I cannot forget to love thee. Prithee, Jaffeir,
Forgive that filthy blow my passion dealt thee;
I am now preparing for the land of peace,
And fain would have the charitable wishes
Of all good men, like thee, to bless my journey.
Jaff. Good! I am the vilest creature, worse than e'er
Suffered the shameful fate thou art going to taste of.
Why was I sent for to be used thus kindly?
Call, call me villain, as I am; describe
The foul complexion of my hateful deeds;
Lead me to the rack, and stretch me in thy stead,
I've crimes enough to give it its full load,
And do it credit. Thou wilt but spoil the use on't,
And honest men hereafter bear its figure
About 'em, as a charm from treacherous friendship.
Offic. The time grows short, your friends are dead already.
Jaff. Dead!

25 me to take] Ghosh; me, take *Q.* 1; me: Take *Works*

Pierre. Yes, dead, Jaffeir, they've all died like men too,
Worthy their character.
Jaff. And what must I do?
Pierre. Oh, Jaffeir!
Jaff. Speak aloud thy burdened soul,
And tell thy troubles to thy tortured friend.
Pierre. Friend! Couldst thou yet be a friend, a generous friend,
I might hope comfort from thy noble sorrows.
Heaven knows I want a friend.
Jaff. And I a kind one,
That would not thus scorn my repenting virtue,
Or think, when he is to die, my thoughts are idle.
Pierre. No! live, I charge thee, Jaffeir.
Jaff. Yes, I will live,
But it shall be to see thy fall revenged
At such a rate as Venice long shall groan for.
Pierre. Wilt thou?
Jaff. I will, by Heaven.
Pierre. Then still thou'rt noble,
And I forgive thee. Oh—yet—shall I trust thee?
Jaff. No; I've been false already.
Pierre. Dost thou love me?
Jaff. Rip up my heart, and satisfy thy doubtings.
Pierre. Curse on this weakness! [*He weeps.*
Jaff. Tears! Amazement! Tears!
I never saw thee melted thus before;
And know there's something lab'ring in thy bosom
That must have vent. Though I'm a villain, tell me.
Pierre. Seest thou that engine? [*Pointing to the wheel.*
Jaff. Why?
Pierre. Is't fit a soldier, who has lived with honour,
Fought nations' quarrels, and been crowned with conquest,
Be exposed a common carcass on a wheel?
Jaff. Hah!
Pierre. Speak! Is't fitting?
Jaff. Fitting?
Pierre. Yes. Is't fitting?
Jaff. What's to be done?
Pierre. I'd have thee undertake
Something that's noble, to preserve my memory
From the disgrace that's ready to attaint it.

80 attaint] taint, sully

Offic. The day grows late, sir.
Pierre. I'll make haste! Oh, Jaffeir,
Though thou'st betrayed me, do me some way justice.
Jaff. No more of that: thy wishes shall be satisfied.
I have a wife, and she shall bleed; my child too
Yield up his little throat, and all t'appease thee—
[*Going away* Pierre *holds him.*
Pierre. No—this—no more! [*He whispers* Jaffeir.
Jaff. Hah! is't then so?
Pierre. Most certainly.
Jaff. I'll do't.
Pierre. Remember.
Offic. Sir.
Pierre. Come, now I'm ready.—
[*He and* Jaffeir *ascend the scaffold.*
Captain, you should be a gentleman of honour,
Keep off the rabble, that I may have room
To entertain my fate, and die with decency.
Come! [*Takes off his gown.* Executioner *prepares to bind him.*
Father. Son!
Pierre. Hence, tempter.
Offic. Stand off, priest.
Pierre. I thank you, sir.—
[*To* Jaffeir.] You'll think on't.
Jaff. 'Twon't grow stale before tomorrow.
Pierre. Now, Jaffeir! now I am going. Now—
[Executioner *having bound him.*
Jaff. Have at thee,
Thou honest heart, then—here— [*Stabs him.*
And this is well too. [*Then stabs himself.*
Father. Damnable deed!
Pierre. Now thou hast indeed been faithful.
This was done nobly.—We have deceived the Senate.
Jaff. Bravely.
Pierre. Ha, ha, ha!—Oh, oh! [*Dies.*
Jaff. Now, ye cursed rulers,
Thus of the blood y'have shed I make libation,
And sprinkled mingling. May it rest upon you,
And all your race! Be henceforth peace a stranger
Within your walls! Let plagues and famine waste
Your generations!—Oh, poor Belvidera!
Sir, I have a wife; bear this in safety to her,

A token that with my dying breath I blessed her,
And the dear little infant left behind me.
I am sick—I'm quiet— [Jaffeir *dies.*
Offic. Bear this news to the Senate,
And guard their bodies till there's farther order:
Heaven grant I die so well! [*Scene shuts upon them.*

[SCENE V]

Soft music. Enter Belvidera *distracted, led by two of her women*; Priuli *and servants.*

Priu. Strengthen her heart with patience, pitying Heaven!
Belv. Come, come, come, come, come! Nay, come to bed;
Prithee, my love! The winds! Hark how they whistle!
And the rain beats: oh, how the weather shrinks me!
You are angry now; who cares? pish, no indeed!
Choose then; I say you shall not go, you shall not;
Whip your ill-nature; get you gone then!—Oh! [Jaffeir'*s ghost rises.*
Are you returned? See, father, here he's come again;
Am I to blame to love him! Oh, thou dear one! [*Ghost sinks.*
Why do you fly me? are you angry still then?
Jaffeir! where art thou? Father, why do you do thus?
Stand off, don't hide him from me. He's here somewhere.
Stand off, I say! What, gone? Remember't, tyrant!
I may revenge myself for this trick one day.

Enter Officer *and others.*

I'll do't—I'll do't. Renault's a nasty fellow.
Hang him, hang him, hang him!
Priu. News, what news?
[Officer *whispers* Priuli.
Offic. Most sad, sir.
Jaffeir upon the scaffold, to prevent
A shameful death, stabbed Pierre, and next himself:
Both fell together.
Priu. Daughter!
[*The ghosts of* Jaffeir *and* Pierrc *rise together, both bloody.*
Belv. Hah, look there!
My husband bloody, and his friend too! Murder!
Who has done this? Speak to me, thou sad vision, [*Ghosts sink.*

On these poor trembling knees I beg it. Vanished!—
Here they went down. Oh, I'll dig, dig the den up.
You shan't delude me thus. Hoa, Jaffeir, Jaffeir!
Peep up and give me but a look. I have him!
I've got him, father: oh, now how I'll smuggle him!
My love! my dear! my blessing! help me, help me!
They have hold on me, and drag me to the bottom.
Nay—now they pull so hard—farewell! [*She dies.*

Maid. She's dead.
Breathless and dead.

Priu. Then guard me from the sight on't.
Lead me into some place that's fit for mourning,
Where the free air, light and the cheerful sun
May never enter. Hang it round with black;
Set up one taper that may last a day
As long as I've to live, and there all leave me—
Sparing no tears when you this tale relate,
But bid all cruel fathers dread my fate.

[*Exeunt omnes. Curtain falls.*

FINIS

26 smuggle] cuddle, caress

EPILOGUE

The text is done, and now for application,
And when that's ended pass your approbation.
Though the conspiracy's prevented here,
Methinks I see another hatching there;
And there's a certain faction fain would sway,
If they had strength enough and damn this play,
But this the author bade me boldly say:
If any take his plainness in ill part,
He's glad on't from the bottom of his heart;
Poets in honour of the truth should write,
With the same spirit brave men for it fight;
And though against him causeless hatreds rise,
And daily where he goes of late, he spies
The scowls of sullen and revengeful eyes;
'Tis what he knows with much contempt to bear,
And serves a cause too good to let him fear.
He fears no poison from an incensed drab,
No ruffian's five-foot sword, nor rascal's stab;
Nor any other snares of mischief laid,
Not a Rose-Alley cudgel-ambuscade
From any private cause where malice reigns,
Or general pique all blockheads have to brains:
Nothing shall daunt his pen when Truth does call,
No, not the picture-mangler at Guildhall.

4 *there*] i.e. in the audience (more especially in the 'critic's corner' in the pit) 20 *Rose-Alley*] On 18 December 1679, in Rose Alley near Covent Garden, Dryden was badly beaten up by ruffians, possibly hired by someone who had been offended by his satire. 24 *picture-mangler*] 'The rascal that cut the Duke of York's picture' [Otway]. In January 1682 the Duke's portrait in the Guildhall was 'cut and mangled' by one of 'the rebel tribe', i.e. a Whig. As the Roman Catholic successor to the throne, Charles II's brother was highly unpopular in the years following the Popish Plot.

The rebel tribe, of which that vermin's one,
Have now set forward and their course begun;
And while that Prince's figure they deface,
As they before had massacred his name,
Durst their base fears but look him in the face,
They'd use his person as they've used his fame;
A face, in which such lineaments they read
Of that great martyr's whose rich blood they shed,
That their rebellious hate they still retain,
And in his son would murder him again.
With indignation then, let each brave heart,
Rouse and unite to take his injured part;
Till royal love and goodness call him home,
And songs of triumph meet him as he come;
Till Heaven his honour and our peace restore,
And villains never wrong his virtue more.

32 *martyr's*] i.e. Charles I 37 *call him home*] In October 1679, during the public excitement over the Popish Plot, Charles prudently sent his brother to Scotland as High Commissioner. He returned to London in April 1682, and the first play he saw was *Venice Preserved*, with a loyal prologue written for the occasion by Dryden.

OROONOKO

Thomas Southerne

1660–1746

The story of Oroonoko first appeared in a short novel by Mrs. Aphra Behn, *Oroonoko: Or, The Royal Slave* (1688), and was adapted by Southerne for the stage and performed at Drury Lane around December 1695. The modern reader must inevitably feel that Southerne's tragedy is remote in time and place, but the contemporary playgoer would have seen things differently. In her novel Mrs. Behn, who had actually visited Surinam, claimed that she was an eye-witness of some of the events in Oroonoko's story, and had an account of other events 'from the mouth of the chief actor in this history, the hero himself'. So the action of Southerne's play was not set in the remote, but in the recent, past; and, if Mrs. Behn was to be believed, the hero had really lived in Surinam and suffered at the hands of the English planters there. Again, for the modern reader, the circumstance of slavery and the slave trade is apt to set up a psychological barrier that would not have existed for Southerne's contemporaries, when the slave trade was still a thriving part of the economy and regarded as vital to the new colonial possessions in the West. At no point does Southerne suggest that there is anything wrong with slavery as such; but, like Mrs. Behn before him and Defoe a little after him, he is all in favour of humane treatment for slaves and opposed to brutal exploitation. Like Mrs. Behn, too, he takes several opportunities of contrasting the conduct of so-called Christians with that of the morally good black man whom they thought of as a heathen and an inferior. In some respects Oroonoko is a prototype of 'the noble savage', but, as a prince, he is a man of considerable culture and not just an innocent child of nature.

A good part of Southerne's tragedy is taken up by a comic plot. He had already mixed tragedy and comedy in his previous play, *The Fatal Marriage*, and on that occasion he said why: 'I have given you a little taste of comedy with it, not from my own opinion, but the present humour of the Town: I never contend that, because I think every reasonable man will, and ought, to govern the pleasures he pays for.' Congreve also alludes in the epilogue to the contemporary taste for a mixture of 'mirth and grief', but adds, fairly enough, that they are 'like rain and sunshine mixed, in April weather'. They were so mixed in Shakespeare; and although Southerne is far from being a Shakespeare he has something of his ability to write good earthy comedy based, not on wit and *doubles entendres*, but on the common human animal being abundantly itself—the lusty widow, the nincompoop son—which is all very far removed from tragedy, but does not clash with it.

Texts collated: *Q.* 1 (1696); *Q.* 2 (1699, Printed for H. Playford . . . and B. Tooke); *Q.* 3 (1699, Printed for H. Playford . . . B. Tooke . . . and A. Bettesworth); *Works* (Collected Works, 1713). See Selected Bibliography, pp. 439–41.

Oroonoko:

A

TRAGEDY

As it is Acted at the

Theatre-Royal,

By His MAJESTY's SERVANTS.

Written by *THO. SOUTHERNE.*

----*Quo fata trahunt, virtus secura sequetur.* Lucan.

Virtus recludens immeritis mori
Cœlum, negatâ tentat iter viâ.
Hor. Od. 2. lib. 3.

LONDON:
Printed for *H. Playford* in the *Temple-Change. B. Tooke* at the *Middle-Temple-Gate.* And *S. Buckley* at the *Dolphin* against St. *Dunstan's* Church in *Fleetstreet.*
M DC XC VI.

To His GRACE

WILLIAM

Duke of Devonshire, &c.

Lord Steward of His Majesty's Household, Knight of the Most Noble Order of the Garter, and One of His Majesty's Most Honourable Privy Council.

My Lord,

The best part of the fortune of my last play (*The Innocent Adultery*) was, that it gave me an opportunity of making myself known to Your Grace. You were pleased to countenance the advances which I had been a great while directing and aiming at you, and have since encouraged me into an industry which, I hope, will allow me in this play to own (which is the only way I can) the great obligations I have to you.

I stand engaged to Mrs. Behn for the occasion of a most passionate distress in my last play; and in a conscience that I had not made her a sufficient acknowledgement, I have run further into her debt for *Oroonoko*, with a design to oblige me to be honest, and that every one may find me out for ingratitude when I don't say all that's fit for me upon that subject. She had a great command of the stage; and I have often wondered that she would bury her favourite hero in a novel, when she might have revived him in the scene. She thought either that no actor could represent him; or she could not bear him represented, and I believe the last, when I remember what I have heard from a friend of hers, that she always told his story more feelingly than she writ it. Whatever happened to him at Surinam, he has mended his condition in England. He was born here under Your Grace's influence; and that has carried his fortune farther into the world, than all the poetical stars that I could have solicited for his success. It was your opinion, My Lord, that directed me to Mr. Verbruggen; and it was his

2 *The Innocent Adultery*] *The Fatal Marriage; Or, The Innocent Adultery*, 1694. Southerne 'took the hint of the tragical part of the play' from Mrs. Behn's novel, *The History of the Nun; or, The Fair Vow-Breaker*. 9 conscience] consciousness 14 novel] Mrs. Behn's novel, *Oroonoko; or, The Royal Slave*. 22 Verbruggen] John Verbruggen (fl. 1688–1707?), a natural actor who excelled both in tragedy and comedy.

care to maintain your opinion that directed the Town to me, the better part of it, the people of quality; whose favours as I am proud of, I shall always be industrious to preserve.

My Lord, I know the respect and reverence which in this address I ought to appear in before you, who are so intimate with the ancients, so general a knower of the several species of poetry, and so just a judge in the trials of this kind. You have an absolute power to arraign and convict, but a prevailing inclination to pardon and save; and from the humanity of your temper, and the true knowledge of the difficulties of succeeding this way, never aggravate or insist upon faults

—Quas aut incuria fudit,
Aut humana parum cavit Natura.—

Hor. *Ars Poet.*

to our condemnation, where they are venial, and not against the principles of the art we pretend to. Horace, who found it so, says,

—Gratia Regum
Pieriis tentata modis.

The favour of great men is the poet's inheritance, and all ages have allowed 'em to put in their claim; I only wish that I had merit enough to prefer me to Your Grace, that I might deserve in some measure that patronage which you are pleased to bestow on me; that I were a Horace for such a Mecœnas; that I could describe what I admire, and tell the world what I really think: that as you possess those infinite advantages of nature and fortune in so eminent a degree; that as you so far excel in the perfections of body and mind, you were designed and fashioned a prince, to be the honour of the nation, and the grace and ornament of the Court. Sir, in the fullness of happiness and blessings which you enjoy, I can only bring in my wishes for the continuance of 'em; they shall constantly be devoted to you, with all the services of,

MY LORD,

Your Grace's most obliged, most
thankful, and most Humble Servant,

THO. SOUTHERNE.

33–4 *Quas . . . Natura*] which a careless hand has let drop, or human frailty has failed to avert (*Ars Poetica*, ll. 352–3) 38–9 *Gratia . . . modis*] The favour of kings was sought in Pierian strains (ibid., ll. 404–5) 43 Mecœnas] a famous patron of authors (including Virgil, Horace, and Seneca)

PROLOGUE

Sent by an unknown hand. And spoken by Mr. Powell.

As when in hostile times two neighbouring states
Strive by themselves, and their confederates;
The war at first is made with awkward skill,
And soldiers clumsily each other kill:
Till time at length their untaught fury tames,
And into rules their heedless rage reclaims:
Then every science by degrees is made
Subservient to the man-destroying trade:
Wit, wisdom, reading, observation, art;
A well-turned head to guide a generous heart.
So it may prove with our contending stages,
If you will kindly but supply their wages:
Which you with ease may furnish, by retrenching
Your superfluities of wine and wenching.
Who'd grudge to spare from riot and hard drinking,
To lay it out on means to mend his thinking?
To follow such advice you should have leisure,
Since what refines your sense, refines your pleasure:
Women grown tame by use each fool can get,
But cuckolds all are made by men of wit.
To virgin favours fools have no pretence:
For maidenheads were made for men of sense.
'Tis not enough to have a horse well bred,
To show his mettle, he must be well fed:
Nor is it all in provender and breed,
He must be tried and strained, to mend his speed:
A favoured poet, like a pampered horse,
Will strain his eye-balls out to win the course.

7 *science*] branch of learning or knowledge 11 *contending stages*] The theatres were contending for audiences; but they were also torn by strife and involved in lawsuits. In 1695, Thomas Betterton, the leading actor at Drury Lane, exasperated by Christopher Rich's mercenary management of the playhouse, withdrew from the company, taking with him its two best actresses, Elizabeth Barry and Anne Bracegirdle, and opened at Lincoln's Inn Fields.
26 *strained*] bridled, controlled

Do you but in your wisdoms vote it fit
To yield due succours to this war of wit,
The buskin with more grace shall tread the stage,
Love sigh in softer strains, heroes less rage:
Satire shall show a triple row of teeth,
And comedy shall laugh your fops to death:
Wit shall refine, and Pegasus shall foam,
And soar in search of ancient Greece and Rome.
And since the nation's in the conquering fit,
As you by arms, we'll vanquish France in wit:
The work were over, could our poets write
With half the spirit that our soldiers fight.

37 *conquering fit*] In August 1695 the English and their allies, under the command of King William, had captured Namur after fierce fighting.

DRAMATIS PERSONAE

Men

	BY
OROONOKO	*Mr. Verbruggen*
ABOAN	*Mr. Powell*
LIEUTENANT-GOVERNOR OF SURINAM	*Mr. Williams*
BLANFORD	*Mr. Harland*
STANMORE	*Mr. Horden*
JACK STANMORE	*Mr. Mills*
CAPTAIN DRIVER	*Mr. Ben. Johnson*
DANIEL, son to Widow Lackitt	*Mr. Mich. Lee*
HOTTMAN	*Mr. Sympson*

PLANTERS, INDIANS, NEGROES, MEN, WOMEN, AND CHILDREN

Women

	BY
IMOINDA	*Mrs. Rogers*
WIDOW LACKITT	*Mrs. Knight*
CHARLOTT WELLDON, in man's clothes	*Mrs. Verbruggen*
LUCY WELLDON, her sister	*Mrs. Lucas*

The scene: Surinam, a colony in the West-Indies; at the time of the action of this tragedy in the possession of the English.

Oroonoko

ACT I SCENE I

Enter Welldon ⟨i.e. Charlott⟩ *following* Lucia.

Luc. What will this come to? What can it end in? You have persuaded me to leave dear England, and dearer London, the place of the world most worth living in, to follow you a husband-hunting into America: I thought husbands grew in these plantations.

Well. Why, so they do, as thick as oranges, ripening one under another. Week after week they drop into some woman's mouth. 'Tis but a little patience, spreading your apron in expectation, and one of 'em will fall into your lap at last.

Luc. Ay, so you say indeed.

Well. But you have left dear London, you say: pray, what have you left in London that was very dear to you, that had not left you before?

Luc. Speak for yourself, sister.

Well. Nay, I'll keep you in countenance. The young fellows, you know, the dearest part of the Town, and without whom London had been a wilderness to you and me, had forsaken us a great while.

Luc. Forsaken us! I don't know that they ever had us.

Well. Forsaken us the worst way, child; that is, did not think us worth having; they neglected us, no longer designed upon us, they were tired of us. Women in London are like the rich silks, they are out of fashion a great while before they wear out.—

Luc. The Devil take the fashion, I say.

Well. You may tumble 'em over and over at their first coming up, and never disparage their price; but they fall upon wearing immediately, lower and lower in their value, till they come to the broker at last.

Luc. Ay, ay, that's the merchant they deal with. The men would have us at their own scandalous rates: their plenty makes 'em wanton; and in a little time, I suppose, they won't know what they would have of the women themselves.

23 disparage] lower the value of

Well. Oh, yes, they know what they would have. They would have a woman give the Town a pattern of her person and beauty, and not stay in it so long to have the whole piece worn out. They would have the good face only discovered, and not the folly that commonly goes along with it. They say there is a vast stock of beauty in the nation, but a great part of it lies in unprofitable hands; therefore for the good of the public, they would have a draught made once a quarter, send the decaying beauties for breeders into the country, to make room for new faces to appear, to countenance the pleasures of the Town.

Luc. 'Tis very hard the men must be young as long as they live, and poor women be thought decaying and unfit for the Town at one or two and twenty. I'm sure we were not seven years in London.

Well. Not half the time taken notice of, sister. The two or three last years we could make nothing of it, even in a vizard mask; not in a vizard-mask that has cheated many a man into an old acquaintance. Our faces began to be as familiar to the men of intrigue as their duns, and as much avoided. We durst not appear in public places, and were almost grudged a gallery in the churches. Even there they had their jests upon us, and cried, 'She's in the right on't, good gentlewoman; since no man considers her body, she does very well indeed to take care of her soul'.

Luc. Such unmannerly fellows there will always be.

Well. Then, you may remember, we were reduced to the last necessity, the necessity of making silly visits to our civil acquaintance, to bring us into tolerable company. Nay, the young Inns-of-Court beaus, of but one term's standing in the fashion, who knew nobody but as they were shown 'em by the orange-women, had nicknames for us. How often have they laughed out, 'There goes my landlady; is not she come to let lodgings yet?'

Luc. Young coxcombs that knew no better.

Well. And that we must have come to. For your part, what trade could you set up in? You would never arrive at the trust and credit of a guinea-bawd: you would have too much business of your own ever to mind other people's.

Luc. That is true indeed.

Well. Then, as a certain sign that there was nothing more to be hoped for, the maids at the chocolate-houses found us out, and laughed at us: our *billet doux* lay there neglected for waste paper. We were cried down so low we could not pass upon the City; and became so notorious in our galloping way, from one end of the Town to t'other, that at last we could hardly compass a competent change of petticoats to disguise us to the hackney-coachmen. And then it was near walking a-foot indeed.

35 draught] draft; a detachment or selection of persons for some purpose (e.g. military)
42 vizard-mask] a mask worn (often by prostitutes) to conceal the face

Luc. Nay, that I began to be afraid of.

Well. To prevent which, with what youth and beauty was left, some experience, and the small remainder of fifteen hundred pounds apiece, which amounted to bare two hundred between us both, I persuaded you to bring your person for a venture to the Indies. Everything has succeeded in our voyage. I pass for your brother. One of the richest planters here happening to die just as we landed, I have claimed kindred with him; so, without making his will, he has left us the credit of his relation to trade upon: we pass for his cousins, coming here to Surinam chiefly upon his invitation. We live in reputation; have the best acquaintance of the place; and we shall see our account in't, I warrant you.

Luc. I must rely upon you—

Enter Widow Lackitt.

Wid. Mr. Welldon, your servant. Your servant, Mrs. Lucy. I am an ill visitor, but 'tis not too late, I hope, to bid you welcome to this side of the world. [*Salutes* Lucy.

Well. Gad so, I beg your pardon, widow, I should have done the civilities of my house before; but, as you say, 'tis not too late, I hope—

[*Going to kiss her.*

Wid. What! You think now this was a civil way of begging a kiss; and by my troth, if it were, I see no harm in't; 'tis a pitiful favour indeed that is not worth asking for, though I have known a woman speak plainer before now, and not understood neither.

Well. Not under my roof. Have at you, widow.—

Wid. Why, that's well said, spoke like a younger brother, that deserves to have a widow.— [*He kisses her.*
You're a younger brother, I know, by your kissing.

Well. How so, pray?

Wid. Why, you kiss as if you expected to be paid for't. You have birdlime upon your lips. You stick so close, there's no getting rid of you.

Well. I am akin to a younger brother.

Wid. So much the better: we widows are commonly the better for younger brothers.

Luc. [*Aside.*] Better, or worse, most of you. But you won't be much better for him, I can tell you.—

Well. I was a younger brother; but an uncle of my mother's has maliciously left me an estate, and, I'm afraid, spoiled my fortune.

Wid. No, no; an estate will never spoil your fortune. I have a good estate myself, thank heaven, and a kind husband that left it behind him.

Well. Thank heaven, that took him away from it, widow, and left you behind him.

Wid. Nay, heaven's will must be done; he's in a better place.

Well. A better place for you, no doubt on't. Now you may look about you; choose for yourself, Mrs. Lackitt, that's your business; for I know you design to marry again.

Wid. Oh dear! Not I, I protest and swear; I don't design it. But I won't swear neither; one does not know what may happen to tempt one.

Well. Why, a lusty young fellow may happen to tempt you.

Wid. Nay, I'll do nothing rashly: I'll resolve against nothing. The Devil, they say, is very busy upon these occasions; especially with the widows. But if I am to be tempted, it must be with a young man, I promise you.—Mrs. Lucy, your brother is a very pleasant gentleman: I came about business to him, but he turns everything into merriment.

Well. Business, Mrs. Lackitt. Then, I know, you would have me to yourself. Pray leave us together, sister. [*Exit* Lucy.
[*Aside.*] What am I drawing upon myself here?

Wid. You have taken a very pretty house here; everything so neat about you already. I hear you are laying out for a plantation.

Well. Why, yes truly, I like the country, and would buy a plantation, if I could reasonably.

Wid. Oh! by all means, reasonably.

Well. If I could have one to my mind, I would think of settling among you.

Wid. Oh! you can't do better. Indeed, we can't pretend to have so good company for you as you had in England; but we shall make very much of you. For my own part, I assure you, I shall think myself very happy to be more particularly known to you.

Well. Dear Mrs. Lackitt, you do me too much honour.

Wid. Then as to a plantation, Mr. Welldon, you know I have several to dispose of. Mr. Lackitt, I thank him, has left me, though I say it, the richest widow upon the place; therefore I may afford to use you better than other people can. You shall have one upon any reasonable terms.

Well. That's a fair offer indeed.

Wid. You shall find me as easy as anybody you can have to do with, I assure you. Pray try me, I would have you try me, Mr. Welldon. Well, I like that name of yours exceedingly, Mr. Welldon.

Well. My name!

Wid. Oh, exceedingly! If anything could persuade me to alter my own name, I verily believe nothing in the world would do it so soon as to be called Mrs. Welldon.

Well. Why, indeed Welldon does sound something better than Lackitt.

Wid. Oh! a great deal better. Not that there is so much in a name neither.

But I don't know, there is something: I should like mightily to be called Mrs. Welldon.

Well. I'm glad you like my name.

Wid. Of all things. But then there's the misfortune; one can't change one's name without changing one's condition.

Well. You'll hardly think it worth that, I believe.

Wid. Think it worth what, sir? Changing my condition? Indeed, sir, I think it worth everything. But, alas! Mr. Welldon, I have been a widow but six months; 'tis too soon to think of changing one's condition yet, indeed it is; pray don't desire it of me. Not but that you may persuade me to anything sooner than any person in the world.—

Well. Who, I, Mrs. Lackitt?

Wid. Indeed you may, Mr. Welldon, sooner than any man living. Lord, there's a great deal in saving a decency: I never minded it before. Well, I'm glad you spoke first to excuse my modesty. But what, modesty means nothing, and is the virtue of a girl that does not know what she would be at: a widow should be wiser. Now I will own to you (but I won't confess neither) I have had a great respect for you a great while: I beg your pardon, sir, and I must declare to you, indeed I must, if you desire to dispose of all I have in the world, in an honourable way, which I don't pretend to be any way deserving your consideration, my fortune and person, if you won't understand me without telling you so, are both at your service. Gad so! another time—

Stanmore *enters to them.*

Stan. So, Mrs. Lackitt, your widowhood is waning apace. I see which way 'tis going. Welldon, you're a happy man. The women and their favours come home to you.

Wid. A fiddle of favour, Mr. Stanmore: I am a lone woman, you know it, left in a great deal of business; and business must be followed or lost. I have several stocks and plantations upon my hands, and other things to dispose of, which Mr. Welldon may have occasion for.

Well. We were just upon the brink of a bargain as you came in.

Stan. Let me drive it on for you.

Well. So you must, I believe, you or somebody for me.

Stan. I'll stand by you: I understand more of this business than you can pretend to.

Well. I don't pretend to't; 'tis quite out of my way indeed.

Stan. If the widow gets you to herself, she will certainly be too hard for

164 excuse] save

you. I know her of old: she has no conscience in a corner; a very Jew in a bargain, and would circumcise you to get more of you.

Well. Is this true, widow?

Wid. Speak as you find, Mr. Welldon: I have offered you very fair. Think upon't, and let me hear of you: the sooner the better, Mr. Welldon. [*Exit.*

Stan. I assure you, my friend, she'll cheat you if she can.

Well. I don't know that; but I can cheat her, if I will.

Stan. Cheat her? How?

Well. I can marry her; and then I'm sure I have it in my power to cheat her.

Stan. Can you marry her?

Well. Yes, faith, so she says: her pretty person and fortune (which, one with the other, you know, are not contemptible) are both at my service.

Stan. Contemptible! very considerable, i'gad; very desirable. Why, she's worth ten thousand pounds, man; a clear estate; no charge upon't but a boobily son. He indeed was to have half; but his father begot him, and she breeds him up, not to know or have more than she has a mind to. And she has a mind to something else, it seems.

Well. [*Musing.*] There's a great deal to be made of this.—

Stan. A handsome fortune may be made on't; and I advise you to't, by all means.

Well. To marry her! an old, wanton witch! I hate her.

Stan. No matter for that: let her go to the Devil for you. She'll cheat her son of a good estate for you: that's a perquisite of a widow's portion always.

Well. I have a design, and will follow her at least, till I have a pen'worth of the plantation.

Stan. I speak as a friend when I advise you to marry her. For 'tis directly against the interest of my own family. My cousin Jack has belaboured her a good while that way.

Well. What! Honest Jack! I'll not hinder him. I'll give over the thoughts of her.

Stan. He'll make nothing on't; she does not care for him. I'm glad you have her in your power.

Well. I may be able to serve him.

Stan. Here's a ship come into the river; I was in hopes it had been from England.

Well. From England!

Stan. No, I was disappointed; I long to see this handsome cousin of yours: the picture you gave me of her has charmed me.

192 cheat] chear *Q.* 1 202 boobily] boobyish

Well. You'll see whether it has flattered her or no, in a little time. If she recovered of that illness that was the reason of her staying behind us, I know she will come with the first opportunity. We shall see her, or hear of her death.

Stan. We'll hope the best. The ships from England are expected every day.

Well. What ship is this?

Stan. A rover, a buccaneer, a trader in slaves: that's the commodity we deal in, you know. If you have a curiosity to see our manner of marketing, I'll wait upon you.

Well. We'll take my sister with us. [*Exeunt.*

SCENE II

An open place

Enter Lieutenant-Governor *and* Blanford.

Lt.-Gov. There's no resisting your fortune, Blanford; you draw all the prizes.

Blan. I draw for our Lord Governor, you know; his fortune favours me.

Lt.-Gov. I grudge him nothing this time; but if fortune had favoured me in the last sale, the fair slave had been mine; Clemene had been mine.

Blan. Are you still in love with her?

Lt.-Gov. Every day more in love with her.

Enter Captain Driver, *teased and pulled about by* Widow Lackitt *and several Planters. Enter at another door* Welldon, Lucia, Stanmore, Jack Stanmore.

Wid. Here have I six slaves in my lot, and not a man among 'em, all women and children; what can I do with 'em, Captain? Pray consider, I am a woman myself, and can't get my own slaves, as some of my neighbours do.

1 *Plan.* I have all men in mine. Pray, Captain, let the men and women be mingled together, for procreation's sake, and the good of the plantation.

2 *Plan.* Ay, ay, a man and a woman, Captain, for the good of the plantation.

Capt. Let 'em mingle together and be damned, what care I? Would you have me pimp for the good of the plantation?

1 *Plan.* I am a constant customer, Captain.

Wid. I am always ready money to you, Captain.

1 *Plan.* For that matter, mistress, my money is as ready as yours.

Wid. Pray hear me, Captain.

Capt. Look you, I have done my part by you; I have brought the number of slaves you bargained for; if your lots have not pleased you, you must draw again among yourselves.

3 *Plan.* I am contented with my lot.

4 *Plan.* I am very well satisfied.

3 *Plan.* We'll have no drawing again.

Capt. Do you hear, mistress? You may hold your tongue: for my part, I expect my money.

Wid. Captain, nobody questions or scruples the payment. But I won't hold my tongue; 'tis too much to pray and pay too. One may speak for one's own, I hope.

Capt. Well, what would you say?

Wid. I say no more than I can make out.

Capt. Out with it, then.

Wid. I say, things have not been so fair carried as they might have been. How do I know how you have juggled together in my absence? You drew the lots before I came, I'm sure.

Capt. That's your own fault, mistress; you might have come sooner.

Wid. Then here's a prince, as they say, among the slaves, and you set him down to go as a common man.

Capt. Have you a mind to try what a man he is? You'll find him no more than a common man at your business.

Wid. Sir, you're a scurvy fellow to talk at this rate to me. If my husband were alive, gadsbodykins, you would not use me so.

Capt. Right, mistress, I would not use you at all.

Wid. Not use me! Your betters every inch of you, I would have you to know, would be glad to use me, sirrah. Marry come up here, who are you, I trow? You begin to think yourself a captain, forsooth, because we call you so. You forget yourself as fast as you can; but I remember you; I know you for a pitiful paltry fellow, as you are, an upstart to prosperity, one that is but just come acquainted with cleanliness, and that never saw five shillings of your own without deserving to be hanged for 'em.

Lt.-Gov. She has given you a broadside, Captain; you'll stand up to her.

Capt. Hang her, stink-pot, I'll come no near.

Wid. By this good light, it would make a woman do a thing she never designed: marry again, though she were sure to repent it, to be revenged of such a—

J. Stan. What's the matter, Mrs. Lackitt? Can I serve you?

Wid. No, no, you can't serve me: you are for serving yourself, I'm sure.

30 pray and pay] a proverbial expression: 'It is a pain both to pay and pray.' 54 near] nearer near *Q.* 1, 3; nearer *Q.* 2, *Works*

Pray go about your business, I have none for you: you know I have told you so. Lord! how can you be so troublesome? nay, so unconscionable, to think that every rich widow must throw herself away upon a young fellow that has nothing?

Stan. Jack, you are answered, I suppose.

J. Stan. I'll have another pluck at her.

Wid. Mr. Welldon, I am a little out of order; but pray bring your sister to dine with me. Gad's my life, I'm out of all patience with that pitiful fellow. My flesh rises at him: I can't stay in the place where he is.— [*Exit.*

Blan. Captain, you have used the widow very familiarly.

Capt. This is my way; I have no design, and therefore am not over civil. If she had ever a handsome daughter to wheedle her out of; or if I could make anything of her booby son—

Well. [*Aside.*] I may improve that hint, and make something of him.

Lt.-Gov. She's very rich.

Capt. I'm rich myself. She has nothing that I want. I have no leaks to stop. Old women are fortune-menders. I have made a good voyage, and would reap the fruits of my labour. We plough the deep, my masters, but our harvest is on shore. I'm for a young woman.

Stan. Look about, Captain, there's one ripe, and ready for the sickle.

Capt. A woman indeed! I will be acquainted with her. Who is she?

Well. My sister, sir.

Capt. Would I were akin to her. If she were my sister, she should never go out of the family. What say you, mistress? You expect I should marry you, I suppose.

Luc. I shan't be disappointed, if you don't. [*Turning away.*

Well. She won't break her heart, sir.

Capt. But I mean— [*Following her.*

Well. And I mean—[*Going between him and* Lucia.] that you must not think of her without marrying.

Capt. I mean so too.

Well. Why then, your meaning's out.

Capt. You're very short.

Well. I will grow, and be taller for you.

Capt. I shall grow angry, and swear.

Well. You'll catch no fish then.

Capt. I don't well know whether he designs to affront me, or no.

Stan. No, no, he's a little familiar; 'tis his way.

Capt. Say you so? Nay, I can be as familiar as he, if that be it. Well, sir, look upon me full. What say you? How do you like me for a brother-in-law?

91 out] astray, mistaken 95 You'll catch no fish then] A proverbial expression: 'If you swear, you'll catch no fish'

Well. Why yes, faith, you'll do my business, if we can agree about my sister's. [*Turning him about.*

Capt. I don't know whether your sister will like me, or not: I can't say much to her. But I have money enough; and if you are her brother, as you seem to be akin to her, I know that will recommend me to you.

Well. This is your market for slaves; my sister is a free woman, and must not be disposed of in public. You shall be welcome to my house, if you please; and, upon better acquaintance, if my sister likes you, and I like your offers—

Capt. Very well, sir, I'll come and see her.

Lt.-Gov. Where are the slaves, Captain? They are long a-coming.

Blan. And who is this prince that's fallen to my lot for the Lord Governor? Let me know something of him, that I may treat him accordingly. Who is he?

Capt. He's the devil of a fellow, I can tell you; a prince every inch of him. You have paid dear enough for him, for all the good he'll do you: I was forced to clap him in irons, and did not think the ship safe neither. You are in hostility with the Indians, they say; they threaten you daily: you had best have an eye upon him.

Blan. But who is he?

Lt.-Gov. And how do you know him to be a prince?

Capt. He is son and heir to the great King of Angola, a mischievous monarch in those parts, who, by his good will, would never let any of his neighbours be in quiet. This son was his general, a plaguey fighting fellow: I have formerly had dealings with him for slaves which he took prisoners, and have got pretty roundly by him. But the wars being at an end, and nothing more to be got by the trade of that country, I made bold to bring the prince along with me.

Lt.-Gov. How could you do that?

Blan. What! steal a prince out of his own country? Impossible!

Capt. 'Twas hard indeed; but I did it. You must know, this Oroonoko—

Blan. Is that his name?

Capt. Ay, Oroonoko.

Lt.-Gov. Oroonoko.

Capt. Is naturally inquisitive about the men and manners of the white nations. Because I could give him some account of the other parts of the world, I grew very much into his favour. In return of so great an honour, you know I could do no less upon my coming away than invite him on board me. Never having been in a ship, he appointed his time, and I prepared my entertainment. He came the next evening as privately as he could, with about some twenty along with him. The punch went round; and as many of his attendants as would be dangerous I sent dead drunk on shore; the rest we secured. And so you have the Prince Oroonoko.

1 *Plan.* Gad-a-mercy, Captain, there you were with him, i'faith.

2 *Plan.* Such men as you are fit to be employed in public affairs: the Plantation will thrive by you.

3 *Plan.* Industry should be encouraged.

Capt. There's nothing done without it, boys. I have made my fortune this way.

Blan. Unheard-of villainy!

Stan. Barbarous treachery!

Blan. They applaud him for't.

Lt.-Gov. But, Captain, methinks you have taken a great deal of pains for this Prince Oroonoko; why did you part with him at the common rate of slaves?

Capt. Why, Lieutenant-Governor, I'll tell you; I did design to carry him to England, to have showed him there; but I found him troublesome upon my hands, and I'm glad I'm rid of him.—Oh, ho, here they come.

Black Slaves, Men, women, and children, pass across the stage by two and two; Aboan, *and others of* Oroonoko*'s attendants, two and two*; Oroonoko *last of all in chains.*

Luc. Are all these wretches slaves?

Stan. All sold, they and their posterity all slaves.

Luc. O miserable fortune!

Blan. Most of 'em know no better; they were born so, and only change their masters. But a prince, born only to command, betrayed and sold! My heart drops blood for him.

Capt. Now, Governor, here he comes; pray observe him.

Oro. So, sir, you have kept your word with me.

Capt. I am a better Christian, I thank you, than to keep it with a heathen.

Oro. You are a Christian, be a Christian still:
If you have any god that teaches you
To break your word, I need not curse you more:
Let him cheat you, as you are false to me.
You faithful followers of my better fortune!
We have been fellow-soldiers in the field; [*Embracing his friends.*
Now we are fellow-slaves. This last farewell.
Be sure of one thing that will comfort us,
Whatever world we next are thrown upon,
Cannot be worse than this. [*All slaves go off, but* Oroonoko.

Capt. You see what a bloody pagan he is, Governor; but I took care that

142 you were with him] you were even with him (*O.E.D.*, 22d) 157 wretches] *Q.* 1, 3, *Works*; wretched *Q.* 2

none of his followers should be in the same lot with him, for fear they should undertake some desperate action, to the danger of the colony.

Oro. Live still in fear; it is the villain's curse,
And will revenge my chains: fear even me,
Who have no power to hurt thee. Nature abhors,
And drives thee out from the society
And commerce of mankind, for breach of faith.
Men live and prosper but in mutual trust,
A confidence of one another's truth:
That thou hast violated. I have done.
I know my fortune, and submit to it.

Lt.-Gov. Sir, I am sorry for your fortune, and would help it, if I could.

Blan. Take off his chains. You know your condition; but you are fallen into honourable hands: you are the Lord Governor's slave, who will use you nobly. In his absence it shall be my care to serve you.

[Blanford *applying to him.*

Oro. I hear you, but I can believe no more.

Lt.-Gov. Captain, I'm afraid the world won't speak so honourably of this action of yours as you would have 'em.

Capt. I have the money. Let the world speak and be damned, I care not.

Oro. I would forget myself. (*To* Blanford.) Be satisfied,
I am above the rank of common slaves.
Let that content you. The Christian there that knows me,
For his own sake will not discover more.

Capt. I have other matters to mind. You have him, and much good may do you with your prince. [*Exit.*

The Planters pulling and staring at Oroonoko.

Blan. What would you have there? You stare as if you never saw a man before. Stand further off. [*Turns them away.*

Oro. Let 'em stare on. I am unfortunate, but not ashamed
Of being so. No, let the guilty blush,
The white man that betrayed me: honest black
Disdains to change its colour. I am ready:
Where must I go? Dispose me as you please.
I am not well acquainted with my fortune,
But must learn to know it better: so I know, you say:
Degrees make all things easy.

Blan. All things shall be easy.

210 you say:] *Q.* 1, 3: you say, *Q.* 2, *Works*

Oro. Tear off this pomp, and let me know myself:
The slavish habit best becomes me now.
Hard fare, and whips, and chains may overpower
The frailer flesh, and bow my body down.
But there's another, nobler part of me
Out of your reach, which you can never tame.

Blan. You shall find nothing of this wretchedness
You apprehend. We are not monsters all.
You seem unwilling to disclose yourself:
Therefore for fear the mentioning your name
Should give you new disquiets, I presume
To call you Cæsar.

Oro. I am myself; but call me what you please.

Stan. A very good name, Cæsar.

Lt.-Gov. And very fit for his great character.

Oro. Was Cæsar then a slave?

Lt.-Gov. I think he was; to pirates too: he was a great conqueror, but unfortunate in his friends.—

Oro. His friends were Christians?

Blan. No.

Oro. No! that's strange.

Lt.-Gov. And murdered by 'em.

Oro. I would be Cæsar there. Yet I will live.

Blan. Live to be happier.

Oro. Do what you will with me.

Blan. I'll wait upon you, attend, and serve you. [*Exit with* Oroonoko.

Luc. Well, if the Captain had brought this prince's country along with him, and would make me queen of it, I would not have him, after doing so base a thing.

Well. He's a man to thrive in the world, sister: he'll make you the better jointure.

Luc. Hang him, nothing can prosper with him.

Stan. Enquire into the great estates, and you will find most of 'em depend upon the same title of honesty: the men who raise 'em first are much of the Captain's principles.

Well. Ay, ay, as you say, let him be damned for the good of his family. Come, sister, we are invited to dinner.

Lt.-Gov. Stanmore, you dine with me. [*Exeunt omnes.*

ACT II SCENE I

Widow Lackitt's *house*.

Widow Lackitt, Welldon.

Well. This is so great a favour, I don't know how to receive it.

Wid. Oh dear sir! you know how to receive and how to return a favour as well as anybody, I don't doubt it. 'Tis not the first you have had from our sex, I suppose.

Well. But this is so unexpected.

Wid. Lord, how can you say so, Mr. Welldon? I won't believe you. Don't I know you handsome gentlemen expect everything that a woman can do for you? And by my troth you're in the right on't: I think one can't do too much for a handsome gentleman; and so you shall find it.

Well. I shall never have such an offer again, that's certain. What shall I do? I am mightily divided.— [*Pretending a concern.*

Wid. Divided! Oh dear, I hope not so, sir. If I marry, truly I expect to have you to myself.

Well. There's no danger of that, Mrs. Lackitt. I am divided in my thoughts. My father upon his death-bed obliged me to see my sister disposed of before I married myself. 'Tis that sticks upon me. They say indeed promises are to be broken or kept, and I know 'tis a foolish thing to be tied to a promise; but I can't help it: I don't know how to get rid of it.

Wid. Is that all?

Well. All in all to me. The commands of a dying father, you know, ought to be obeyed.

Wid. And so they may.

Well. Impossible, to do me any good.

Wid. They shan't be your hindrance. You would have a husband for your sister, you say. He must be very well to pass too in the world, I suppose?

Well. I would not throw her away.

Wid. Then marry her out of hand to the sea-captain you were speaking of.

Well. I was thinking of him, but 'tis to no purpose: she hates him.

Wid. Does she hate him? Nay, 'tis no matter; an impudent rascal as he is, I would not advise her to marry him.

Well. Can you think of nobody else?

Wid. Let me see.

Well. Ay, pray do: I should be loth to part with my good fortune in you for so small a matter as a sister. But you find how it is with me.

25 well to pass] well to do, well off

Wid. Well remembered, i'faith. Well, if I thought you would like of it, I have a husband for her: what do you think of my son?

Well. You don't think of it yourself.

Wid. I protest but I do: I am in earnest, if you are. He shall marry her within this half hour, if you'll give your consent to it.

Well. I give my consent! I'll answer for my sister, she shall have him: you may be sure I shall be glad to get over the difficulty.

Wid. No more to be said then, that difficulty is over. But I vow and swear you frightened me, Mr. Welldon. If I had not had a son now for your sister, what must I have done, do you think? Were not you an ill natured thing to boggle at a promise? I could break twenty for you.

Well. I am the more obliged to you. But this son will save all.

Wid. He's in the house; I'll go and bring him myself. (*Going.*) You would do well to break the business to your sister. She's within; I'll send her to you.— [*Going again, comes back.*

Well. Pray do.

Wid. But d'you hear? Perhaps she may stand upon her maidenly behaviour, and blush, and play the fool, and delay. But don't be answered so. What! she is not a girl at these years. Show your authority, and tell her roundly she must be married immediately. I'll manage my son, I warrant you.— [*Goes out in haste.*

Well. The widow's in haste, I see: I thought I had laid a rub in the road about my sister, but she has stepped over that. She's making way for herself as fast as she can, but little thinks where she is going: I could tell her she is going to play the fool, but people don't love to hear of their faults. Besides, that is not my business at present.

Enter Lucia.

So, sister, I have a husband for you.—

Luc. With all my heart: I don't know what confinement marriage may be to the men, but I'm sure the women have no liberty without it. I am for anything that will deliver me from the care of a reputation, which I begin to find impossible to preserve.

Well. I'll ease you of that care: you must be married immediately.

Luc. The sooner the better; for I am quite tired of setting up for a husband. The widow's foolish son is the man, I suppose.

Well. I considered your constitution, sister; and finding you would have occasion for a fool, I have provided accordingly.

Luc. I don't know what occasion I may have for a fool when I'm married; but I find none but fools have occasion to marry.

56 rub] obstacle

Well. Since he is to be a fool, then, I thought it better for you to have one of his mother's making than your own; 'twill save you the trouble.

Luc. I thank you; you take a great deal of pains for me. But, pray tell me, what are you doing for yourself all this while?

Well. You were never true to your own secrets, and therefore I won't trust you with mine. Only remember this, I am your elder sister, and consequently, laying my breeches aside, have as much occasion for a husband as you can have. I have a man in my eye, be satisfied.

Enter Widow Lackitt, *with her son* Daniel.

Wid. Come, Daniel, hold up thy head, child; look like a man. You must not take it as you have done. Gad's my life! there's nothing to be done with twirling your hat, man.

Dan. Why, mother, what's to be done then?

Wid. Why, look me in the face, and mind what I say to you.

Dan. Marry, who's the fool then? What shall I get by minding what you say to me?

Wid. Mrs. Lucy, the boy is bashful; don't discourage him. Pray come a little forward, and let him salute you. [*Going between* Lucia *and* Daniel.

Luc. [*To* Welldon.] A fine husband I am to have, truly.

Wid. Come, Daniel, you must be acquainted with this gentlewoman.

Dan. Nay, I'm not proud, that is not my fault: I am presently acquainted when I know the company; but this gentlewoman is a stranger to me.

Wid. She is your mistress; I have spoke a good word for you. Make her a bow, and go and kiss her.

Dan. Kiss her! Have a care what you say; I warrant she scorns your words. Such fine folk are not used to be slopped and kissed. Do you think I don't know that, mother?

Wid. Try her, try her, man. [Daniel *bows; she thrusts him forward.* Why, that's well done; go nearer her.

Dan. Is the Devil in the woman? [*To his mother.*] Why, so I can go nearer her, if you would let a body alone. [*To* Lucia.] Cry you mercy, forsooth; my mother is always shaming one before company: she would have me as unmannerly as herself, and offer to kiss you.

Well. Why, won't you kiss her?

Dan. Why, pray, may I?

Well. Kiss her, kiss her, man.

Dan. Marry, and I will. (*Kisses her.*) Gadsooks! she kisses rarely! An' please you, mistress, and seeing my mother will have it so, I don't much care if I kiss you again, forsooth. [*Kisses her again.*

89 salute] greet (also, kiss) 92 presently] at once

Luc. Well, how do you like me now?

Dan. Like you! marry, I don't know. You have bewitched me, I think: I was never so in my born days before.

Wid. You must marry this fine woman, Daniel.

Dan. Hey day! marry her! I was never married in all my life. What must I do with her then, mother?

Wid. You must live with her, eat and drink with her, go to bed with her, and sleep with her.

Dan. Nay, marry, if I must go to bed with her, I shall never sleep, that's certain: she'll break me of my rest, quite and clean, I tell you before-hand. As for eating and drinking with her, why, I have a good stomach, and can play my part in any company. But how do you think I can go to bed to a woman I don't know?

Well. You shall know her better.

Dan. Say you so, sir?

Well. Kiss her again. [Daniel *kisses* Lucy.

Dan. Nay, kissing I find will make us presently acquainted. We'll steal into a corner to practise a little, and then I shall be able to do anything.

Well. The young man mends apace.

Wid. Pray, don't baulk him.

Dan. Mother, mother, if you'll stay in the room by me, and promise not to leave me, I don't care for once if I venture to go to bed with her.

Wid. There's a good child. Go in and put on thy best clothes, pluck up a spirit; I'll stay in the room by thee. She won't hurt thee, I warrant thee.

Dan. Nay, as to that matter, I'm not afraid of her, I'll give her as good as she brings: I have a Rowland for her Oliver, and so you may tell her. [*Exit.*

Wid. Mrs. Lucy, we shan't stay for you—you are in a readiness, I suppose?

Well. She's always ready to do what I would have her, I must say that for my sister.

Wid. 'Twill be her own another day. Mr. Welldon, we'll marry 'em out of hand, and then—

Well. And then, Mrs. Lackitt, look to yourself.— [*Exeunt.*

SCENE II

Oroonoko *and* Blanford.

Oro. You grant I have good reason to suspect
All the professions you can make to me.
Blan. Indeed you have.

137 we shan't stay for you?] you won't keep us waiting?

Oro. The dog that sold me did profess as much
As you can do.—But yet I know not why—
Whether it is because I'm fall'n so low,
And have no more to fear.—That is not it:
I am a slave no longer than I please.
'Tis something nobler.—Being just myself,
I am inclining to think others so:
'Tis that prevails upon me to believe you.
Blan. You may believe me.
Oro. I do believe you.
From what I know of you, you are no fool:
Fools only are the knaves, and live by tricks:
Wise men may thrive without 'em, and be honest.
Blan. [*Aside.*] They won't all take your counsel.
Oro. You know my story, and you say you are
A friend to my misfortunes. That's a name
Will teach you what you owe yourself and me.
Blan. I'll study to deserve to be your friend.
When once our noble Governor arrives.
With him you will not need my interest:
He is too generous not to feel your wrongs.
But be assured I will employ my power,
And find the means to send you home again.
Oro. I thank you, sir.—My honest, wretched friends!
Their chains are heavy. [*Sighing.*] They have hardly found
So kind a master. May I ask you, sir,
What is become of 'em? Perhaps I should not.
You will forgive a stranger.
Blan. I'll enquire,
And use my best endeavours, where they are,
To have 'em gently used.
Oro. Once more I thank you.
You offer every cordial that can keep
My hopes alive, to wait a better day.
What friendly care can do, you have applied.
But, oh! I have a grief admits no cure.
Blan. You do not know, sir,—
Oro. Can you raise the dead?
Pursue and overtake the wings of time?
And bring about again the hours, the days,
The years that made me happy?
Blan. That is not to be done.

Oro. No, there is nothing to be done for me.
[*Kneeling and kissing the earth.*
Thou god adored! thou ever-glorious sun!
If she be yet on earth, send me a beam
Of thy all-seeing power to light me to her.
Or if thy sister goddess has preferred
Her beauty to the skies to be a star,
Oh, tell me where she shines, that I may stand
Whole nights, and gaze upon her.
Blan. I am rude,
And interrupt you.
Oro. I am troublesome;
But pray give me your pardon. My swoll'n heart
Bursts out its passage, and I must complain.
Oh! can you think of nothing dearer to me,
Dearer than liberty, my country, friends,
Much dearer than my life, that I have lost?
The tend'rest, best beloved, and loving wife.
Blan. Alas! I pity you.
Oro. Do, pity me:
Pity's akin to love; and every thought
Of that soft kind is welcome to my soul.
I would be pitied here.
Blan. I dare not ask
More than you please to tell me; but if you
Think it convenient to let me know
Your story, I dare promise you to bear
A part in your distress, if not assist you.
Oro. Thou honest-hearted man! I wanted such,
Just such a friend as thou art, that would sit
Still as the night, and let me talk whole days
Of my Imoinda. Oh! I'll tell thee all
From first to last; and pray observe me well.
Blan. I will most heedfully.
Oro. There was a stranger in my father's court,
Valued and honoured much: he was a white,
The first I ever saw of your complexion.
He changed his gods for ours, and so grew great;
Of many virtues, and so famed in arms,
He still commanded all my father's wars.
I was bred under him. One fatal day,
The armies joining, he before me stepped,

Receiving in his breast a poisoned dart
Levelled at me; he died within my arms.
I've tired you already.

Blan. Pray go on.

Oro. He left an only daughter, whom he brought
An infant to Angola. When I came
Back to the court, a happy conqueror,
Humanity obliged me to condole
With this sad virgin for a father's loss,
Lost for my safety. I presented her
With all the slaves of battle to atone
Her father's ghost. But when I saw her face,
And heard her speak, I offered up myself
To be the sacrifice. She bowed and blushed;
I wondered and adored. The sacred power
That had subdued me, then inspired my tongue,
Inclined her heart; and all our talk was love.

Blan. Then you were happy.

Oro. Oh! I was too happy.
I married her; and though my country's custom
Indulged the privilege of many wives,
I swore myself never to know but her.
She grew with child, and I grew happier still.
O my Imoinda! but it could not last.
Her fatal beauty reached my father's ears:
He sent for her to court, where, cursèd court!
No woman comes but for his amorous use.
He raging to possess her, she was forced
To own herself my wife. The furious king
Started at incest; but grown desperate,
Not daring to enjoy what he desired,
In mad revenge, which I could never learn,
He poisoned her, or sent her far, far off,
Far from my hopes ever to see her more.

Blan. Most barbarous of fathers! The sad tale
Has struck me dumb with wonder.

Oro. I have done.
I'll trouble you no farther: now and then
A sigh will have its way; that shall be all.

Enter Stanmore.

Stan. Blanford, the Lieutenant-Governor is gone to your plantation. He desires you would bring the royal slave with you. The sight of his fair mistress, he says, is an entertainment for a prince; he would have his opinion of her.

Oro. Is he a lover?

Blan. So he says himself: he flatters a beautiful slave that I have, and calls her mistress.

Oro. Must he then flatter her to call her mistress?
I pity the proud man who thinks himself
Above being in love. What, though she be a slave,
She may deserve him.

Blan. You shall judge of that when you see her, sir.

Oro. I go with you. [*Exeunt.*

SCENE III

A plantation.

Lieutenant-Governor *following* Imoinda.

Lt.-Gov. I have disturbed you, I confess my fault,
My fair Clemene, but begin again,
And I will listen to your mournful song,
Sweet as the soft complaining nightingales.
While every note calls out my trembling soul,
And leaves me silent as the midnight groves,
Only to shelter you, sing, sing again,
And let me wonder at the many ways
You have to ravish me.

Imo. Oh! I can weep
Enough for you, and me, if that will please you.

Lt.-Gov. You must not weep: I come to dry your tears,
And raise you from your sorrow. Look upon me:
Look with the eyes of kind indulging love,
That I may have full cause for what I say.
I come to offer you your liberty,
And be myself the slave. You turn away. [*Following her.*
But everything becomes you. I may take
This pretty hand: I know your modesty
Would draw it back, but you would take it ill
If I should let it go, I know you would.

You shall be gently forced to please yourself;
That you will thank me for.
[*She struggles, and gets her hand from him; then he offers to kiss her.*
Nay, if you struggle with me, I must take—

Imo. You may, my life, that I can part with freely. [*Exit.*

Enter Blanford, Stanmore, Oroonoko *to him.*

Blan. So, Governor, we don't disturb you, I hope: your mistress has left you. You were making love; she's thankful for the honour, I suppose.

Lt.-Gov. Quite insensible to all I say, and do:
When I speak to her, she sighs, or weeps,
But never answers me as I would have her.

Stan. There's something nearer than her slavery that touches her.

Blan. What do her fellow slaves say of her? Can't they find the cause?

Lt.-Gov. Some of 'em, who pretend to be wiser than the rest, and hate her, I suppose, for being used better than they are, will needs have it that she's with child.

Blan. Poor wretch! if it be so, I pity her:
She has lost a husband, that perhaps was dear
To her, and then you cannot blame her.

Oro. If it be so, indeed you cannot blame her. [*Sighing.*

Lt.-Gov. No, no, it is not so: if it be so,
I still must love her; and desiring still,
I must enjoy her.

Blan. Try what you can do with fair means, and welcome.

Lt.-Gov. I'll give you ten slaves for her.

Blan. You know she is our Lord Governor's. But if I could dispose of her, I would not now, especially to you.

Lt.-Gov. Why not to me?

Blan. I mean against her will. You are in love with her.
And we all know what your desires would have:
Love stops at nothing but possession.
Were she within your power, you do not know
How soon you would be tempted to forget
The nature of the deed, and, maybe, act
A violence you after would repent.

Oro. 'Tis god-like in you to protect the weak.

Lt.-Gov. Fie, fie, I would not force her. Though she be
A slave, her mind is free, and should consent.

Oro. Such honour will engage her to consent:
And then, if you're in love, she's worth the having.
Shall we not see this wonder?

Lt.-Gov. Have a care;
You have a heart, and she has conquering eyes.
Oro. I have a heart; but if it could be false
To my first vows, ever to love again,
These honest hands should tear it from my breast,
And throw the traitor from me. Oh! Imoinda!
Living or dead, I can be only thine.
Blan. [*To* Lieutenant-Governor *and* Stanmore.] Imoinda was his wife: she's either dead,
Or living, dead to him: forced from his arms
By an inhuman father. Another time
I'll tell you all.
Stan. Hark! the slaves have done their work;
And now begins their evening merriment.
Blan. The men are all in love with fair Clemene
As much as you are; and the women hate her
From an instinct of natural jealousy.
They sing, and dance, and try their little tricks
To entertain her, and divert her sadness.
Maybe she is among 'em: shall we see? [*Exeunt.*

The scene drawn shows the slaves, men, women, and children, upon the ground; some rise and dance, others sing the following songs.

A SONG. [By an unknown hand.]

Set by Mr. Courtevill, and sung by the Boy to Miss Cross.

I

A Lass there lives upon the green,
Could I her picture draw;
A brighter nymph was never seen,
That looks and reigns a little queen,
And keeps the swains in awe.

Title: By an unknown hand] In the edition of Southerne's *Works*, 1713, the song is attributed to 'Sir Harry Sheers', i.e. Sir Henry Sheres (d. 1710), military engineer. Courtevill] Ralph Courteville (d. 1735?), organist to the church of St. James's, Westminster. Miss Cross (who is not in the *dramatis personae*) was presumably one of the black children (she was at this time about twelve years old). She had very recently gained notoriety by singing some bawdy songs in D'Urfey's *Comical History of Don Quixote*.

II

Her eyes are Cupid's darts and wings,
Her eyebrows are his bow;
Her silken hair the silver strings,
Which sure and swift destruction brings
To all the vale below.

III

If Pastorella's dawning light
Can warm, and wound us so,
Her noon will shine so piercing bright,
Each glancing beam will kill outright,
And every swain subdue.

A SONG, by Mr. Cheek.

Set by Mr. Courtevill, and sung by Mr. Leveridge.

I

Bright Cynthia's power divinely great,
What heart is not obeying?
A thousand Cupids on her wait,
And in her eyes are playing.

II

She seems the Queen of Love to reign,
For she alone dispenses
Such sweets as best can entertain
The gust of all the senses.

III

Her face a charming prospect brings;
Her breath gives balmy blisses:
I hear an angel, when she sings,
And taste of heaven in kisses.

Title: Cheek] Thomas Cheek: he contributed another song to Southerne's *The Wives Excuse*. Leveridge] Richard Leveridge (1670?–1758), vocalist and composer.

IV

Four senses thus she feasts with joy,
From Nature's richest treasure:
Let me the other sense employ,
And I shall die with pleasure.

During the entertainment, the Lieutenant-Governor, Blanford, Stanmore, Oroonoko *enter as spectators; that ended,* Captain Driver, Jack Stanmore, *and several Planters enter with their swords drawn. A bell rings.*

Capt. Where are you, Governor? Make what haste you can to save yourself, and the whole colony. I bid 'em ring the bell.

Lt.-Gov. What's the matter?

J. Stan. The Indians are come down upon us: they have plundered some of the plantations already, and are marching this way as fast as they can.

Lt.-Gov. What can we do against 'em?

Blan. We shall be able to make a stand till more planters come in to us.

J. Stan. There are a great many more without, if you would show yourself, and put us in order.

Lt.-Gov. There's no danger of the white slaves, they'll not stir. Blanford and Stanmore, come you along with me: some of you stay here to look after the black slaves.

All go out but the Captain, *and six Planters, who all at once seize* Oroonoko.

1 *Plan.* Ay, ay, let us alone.

Capt. In the first place we secure you, sir, as an enemy to the government.

Oro. Are you there, sir? You are my constant friend.

1 *Plan.* You will be able to do a great deal of mischief.

Capt. But we shall prevent you: bring the irons hither. He has the malice of a slave in him, and would be glad to be cutting his masters' throats, I know him. Chain his hands and feet, that he may not run over to 'em: if they have him, they shall carry him on their backs, that I can tell 'em.

As they are chaining him, Blanford *enters, runs to them.*

Blan. What are you doing there?

Capt. Securing the main chance: this is a bosom enemy.

Blan. Away, you brutes! I'll answer with my life for his behaviour; so tell the Governor.

118 white slaves] presumably transported English felons

Capt.
Plan. } Well, sir, so we will. [*Exeunt Captain and Planters.*

Oro. Give me a sword and I'll deserve your trust.

A party of Indians enter, hurrying Imoinda *among the slaves; another party of Indians sustains them retreating, followed at a distance by the* Lieutenant-Governor *with the Planters:* Blanford, Oroonoko *join them.*

Blan. Hell, and the Devil! they drive away our slaves before our faces. Governor, can you stand tamely by and suffer this? Clemene, sir, your mistress, is among 'em.

Lt.-Gov. We throw ourselves away, in the attempt to rescue 'em.

Oro. A lover cannot fall more glorious
Than in the cause of love. He that deserves
His mistress's favour wonnot stay behind:
I'll lead you on, be bold, and follow me.

Oroonoko, *at the head of the Planters, falls upon the Indians with a great shout, beats them off.*

Imoinda *enters.*

Imo. I'm tossed about by my tempestuous fate,
And nowhere must have rest—Indians, or English!
Whoever has me, I am still a slave.
No matter whose I am, since I am no more,
My royal master's, since I'm his no more.
Oh, I was happy! nay, I will be happy,
In the dear thought that I am still his wife,
Though far divided from him. [*Draws off to a corner of the stage.*

After a shout, enter the Lieutenant-Governor *with* Oroonoko, Blanford, Stanmore, *and the Planters.*

Lt.-Gov. Thou glorious man! thou something greater sure
Than Cæsar ever was! that single arm
Has saved us all: accept our general thanks.
All bow to Oroonoko.
And what we can do more to recompense
Such noble services, you shall command.
Clemene too shall thank you,—she is safe—
Look up, and bless your brave deliverer.
[*Brings* Clemene *forward, looking down on the ground.*

Oro. Bless me indeed!

Blan. You start!

Oro. O all you gods,
Who govern this great world, and bring about
Things strange and unexpected, can it be?
Lt.-Gov. What is't you stare at so?
Oro. Answer me, some of you, you who have power,
And have your senses free: or are you all
Struck through with wonder too? [*Looking still fixed on her.*
Blan. What would you know?
Oro. My soul steals from my body through my eyes:
All that is left of life I'll gaze away,
And die upon the pleasure.
Lt.-Gov. This is strange!
Oro. If you but mock me with her image here:
If she be not Imoinda—
[*She looks upon him, and falls into a swoon; he runs to her.*
Ha! she faints!
Nay, then it must be she; it is Imoinda:
My heart confesses her, and leaps for joy
To welcome her to her own empire here.
I feel her all, in every part of me.
Oh! let me press her in my eager arms,
Wake her to life, and with this kindling kiss
Give back that soul she only sent to me. [*Kisses her.*
Lt.-Gov. I am amazed!
Blan. I am as much as you.
Oro. Imoinda! Oh! thy Oroonoko calls. [Imoinda *coming to life.*
Imo. My Oroonoko! Oh! I can't believe
What any man can say. But if I am
To be deceived, there's something in that name,
That voice, that face—[*Staring on him.*] Oh! if I know myself,
I cannot be mistaken. [*Runs, and embraces* Oroonoko.
Oro. Never here;
You cannot be mistaken: I am yours,
Your Oroonoko, all that you would have,
Your tender loving husband.
Imo. All indeed
That I would have: my husband! Then I am
Alive, and waking to the joys I feel:
They were so great, I could not think 'em true.
But I believe all that you say to me:
For truth itself, and everlasting love
Grows in this breast, and pleasure in these arms.

Oro. Take, take me all: enquire into my heart,
(You know the way to every secret there)
My heart, the sacred treasury of love;
And if, in absence, I have misemployed
A mite from the rich store, if I have spent
A wish, a sigh, but what I sent to you,
May I be cursed to wish and sigh in vain,
And you not pity me.

Imo. Oh! I believe,
And know you by myself. If these sad eyes,
Since last we parted, have beheld the face
Of any comfort; or once wished to see
The light of any other heaven but you:
May I be struck this moment blind, and lose
Your blessed sight, never to find you more.

Oro. Imoinda! Oh! this separation
Has made you dearer, if it can be so,
Than you were ever to me. You appear
Like a kind star to my benighted steps,
To guide me on my way to happiness:
I cannot miss it now. Governor, friend,
You think me mad; but let me bless you all
Who, any way, have been the instruments
Of finding her again. Imoinda's found!
And everything that I would have in her.

[*Embracing her in the most passionate fondness.*

Stan. Where's your mistress now, Governor?

Lt.-Gov. Why, where most men's mistresses are forced to be sometimes; with her husband, it seems. [*Aside.*] But I won't lose her so.

Stan. He has fought lustily for her, and deserves her, I'll say that for him.

Blan. Sir we congratulate your happiness: I do most heartily.

Lt.-Gov. And all of us: but how it comes to pass—

Oro. That will require
More precious time than I can spare you now.
I have a thousand things to ask of her,
And she as many more to know of me.
But you have made me happier, I confess,
Acknowledge it, much happier, than I
Have words, or power to tell you. Captain, you,
Ev'n you, who most have wronged me, I forgive.
I won't say you have betrayed me now:

I'll think you but the minister of fate,
To bring me to my loved Imoinda here.
Imo. How, how shall I receive you? how be worthy
Of such endearments, all this tenderness?
These are the transports of prosperity,
When Fortune smiles upon us.—
Oro. Let the fools
Who follow Fortune live upon her smiles.
All our prosperity is placed in love.
We have enough of that to make us happy.
This little spot of earth you stand upon
Is more to me than the extended plains
Of my great father's kingdom. Here I reign
In full delights, in joys to power unknown;
Your love my empire, and your heart my throne. [*Exeunt*.

ACT III SCENE I

Aboan *with several Slaves*, Hottman.

Hott. What! to be slaves to cowards! slaves to rogues!
Who can't defend themselves!
Abo. [*Aside to his own gang*.] Who is this fellow? He talks as if he were acquainted with our design: is he one of us?
Slav. Not yet: but he will be glad to make one, I believe.
Abo. He makes a mighty noise.
Hott. Go, sneak in corners; whisper out your griefs,
For fear your masters hear you; cringe and crouch
Under the bloody whip, like beaten curs
That lick their wounds, and know no other cure.
All, wretches all! you feel their cruelty,
As much as I can feel, but dare not groan.
For my part, while I have a life and tongue,
I'll curse the authors of my slavery.
Abo. Have you been long a slave?
Hott. Yes, many years.
Abo. And do you only curse?
Hott. Curse? only curse? I cannot conjure,

To raise the spirits of other men:
I am but one. Oh! for a soul of fire,
To warm and animate our common cause,
And make a body of us: then I would
Do something more than curse.

Abo. That body set on foot, you would be one,
A limb, to lend it motion.

Hott. I would be
The heart of it: the head, the hand, and heart.
Would I could see the day!

Abo. You will do all yourself.

Hott. I would do more than I shall speak; but I may find a time.

Abo. The time may come to you; be ready for't. ⟨*Exit* Hottman.⟩
Methinks he talks too much: I'll know him more,
Before I trust him farther.

Slav. If he dares half what he says, he'll be of use to us.

Enter Blanford *to them.*

Blan. If there be any one among you here,
That did belong to Oroonoko, speak,
I come to him.

Abo. I did belong to him: Aboan, my name.

Blan. You are the man I want; pray, come with me. [*Exeunt.*

SCENE II

Oroonoko *and* Imoinda.

Oro. I do not blame my father for his love
(Though that had been enough to ruin me):
'Twas Nature's fault, that made you like the sun,
The reasonable worship of mankind.
He could not help his adoration:
Age had not locked his senses up so close
But he had eyes that opened to his soul,
And took your beauties in; he felt your power,
And therefore I forgive his loving you.
But when I think on his barbarity,
That could expose you to so many wrongs;
Driving you out to wretched slavery,
Only for being mine; then I confess,

18 of] *Q.* 1–3; up of *Works*

I wish I could forget the name of son,
That I might curse the tyrant.
Imo. I will bless him,
For I have found you here. Heaven only knows
What is reserved for us: but if we guess
The future by the past, our fortune must
Be wonderful, above the common size
Of good or ill; it must be in extremes:
Extremely happy, or extremely wretched.
Oro. 'Tis in our power to make it happy now.
Imo. But not to keep it so.

Enter Blanford *and* Aboan.

Blan. My royal lord!
I have a present for you.
Oro. Aboan!
Abo. Your lowest slave.
Oro. My tried and valued friend.
This worthy man always prevents my wants:
I only wished, and he has brought thee to me.
Thou art surprised: carry thy duty there,
[Aboan *goes to* Imoinda *and falls at her feet.*
While I acknowledge mine. ⟨*To* Blanford.⟩ How shall I thank you?
Blan. Believe me honest to your interest,
And I am more than paid. I have secured
That all your followers shall be gently used.
This gentleman, your chiefest favourite,
Shall wait upon your person, while you stay
Among us.
Oro. I owe everything to you.
Blan. You must not think you are in slavery.
Oro. I do not find I am.
Blan. Kind Heaven has miraculously sent
Those comforts, that may teach you to expect
Its farther care, in your deliverance.
Oro. I sometimes think myself Heaven is concerned
For my deliverance.
Blan. It will be soon:
You may expect it. Pray, in the meantime,
Appear as cheerful as you can among us.

26 prevents] anticipates

You have some enemies that represent
You dangerous, and would be glad to find
A reason, in your discontent, to fear:
They watch your looks. But there are honest men
Who are your friends: you are secure in them.

Oro. I thank you for your caution.

Blan. I will leave you;
And be assured, I wish your liberty. [*Exit.*

Abo. He speaks you very fair.

Oro. He means me fair.

Abo. If he should not, my lord.

Oro. If he should not!
I'll not suspect his truth: but if I did,
What shall I get by doubting?

Abo. You secure
Not to be disappointed. But besides,
There's this advantage in suspecting him:
When you put off the hopes of other men,
You will rely upon your god-like self:
And then you may be sure of liberty.

Oro. Be sure of liberty! What dost thou mean,
Advising to rely upon myself?
I think I may be sure on't. We must wait:
'Tis worth a little patience. [*Turning to* Imoinda.

Abo. Oh, my lord!

Oro. What dost thou drive at?

Abo. Sir, another time
You would have found it sooner; but I see
Love has your heart, and takes up all your thoughts.

Oro. And canst thou blame me?

Abo. Sir, I must not blame you.
But as our fortune stands there is a passion
(Your pardon, royal mistress, I must speak)
That would become you better than your love:
A brave resentment which, inspired by you,
Might kindle and diffuse a generous rage
Among the slaves, to rouse and shake our chains,
And struggle to be free.

Oro. How can we help ourselves?

Abo. I knew you when you would have found a way,
How help ourselves! The very Indians teach us:
We need but to attempt our liberty,

And we may carry it. We have hands sufficient,
Double the number of our master's force,
Ready to be employed. What hinders us
To set 'em then at work? We want but you
To head our enterprise, and bid us strike.

Oro. What would you do?

Abo. Cut our oppressors' throats.

Oro. And you would have me join in your design
Of murder?

Abo. It deserves a better name:
But be it what it will, 'tis justified
By self-defence, and natural liberty.

Oro. I'll hear no more on't.

Abo. I am sorry for't.

Oro. Nor shall you think of it.

Abo. Not think of it!

Oro. No, I command you not.

Abo. Remember, sir,
You are a slave yourself, and to command,
Is now another's right. Not think of it!
Since the first moment they put on my chains,
I've thought of nothing but the weight of 'em,
And how to throw 'em off: can yours sit easy?

Oro. I have a sense of my condition
As painful, and as quick, as yours can be.
I feel for my Imoinda and myself;
Imoinda much the tenderest part of me.
But though I languish for my liberty,
I would not buy it at the Christian price
Of black ingratitude: they shannot say
That we deserved our fortune by our crimes.
Murder the innocent!

Abo. The innocent!

Oro. These men are so whom you would rise against.
If we are slaves, they did not make us slaves,
But bought us in an honest way of trade:
As we have done before 'em, bought and sold
Many a wretch, and never thought it wrong.
They paid our price for us, and we are now
Their property, a part of their estate,
To manage as they please. Mistake me not,
I do not tamely say that we should bear

All they could lay upon us; but we find
The load so light, so little to be felt,
(Considering they have us in their power,
And may inflict what grievances they please)
We ought not to complain.
Abo. My royal lord!
You do not know the heavy grievances,
The toils, the labours, weary drudgeries,
Which they impose; burdens, more fit for beasts,
For senseless beasts to bear than thinking men.
Then if you saw the bloody cruelties
They execute on every slight offence;
Nay, sometimes in their proud, insulting sport,
How worse than dogs they lash their fellow creatures,
Your heart would bleed for 'em. Oh, could you know
How many wretches lift their hands and eyes
To you, for their relief!
Oro. I pity 'em,
And wish I could with honesty do more.
Abo. You must do more, and may, with honesty.
O royal sir, remember who you are,
A prince, born for the good of other men,
Whose god-like office is to draw the sword
Against oppression, and set free mankind:
And this, I'm sure, you think oppression now.
What though you have not felt these miseries,
Never believe you are obliged to them:
They have their selfish reasons, may be, now,
For using of you well; but there will come
A time, when you must have your share of 'em.
Oro. You see how little cause I have to think so:
Favoured in my own person, in my friends;
Indulged in all that can concern my care,
In my Imoinda's soft society. [*Embracing her.*
Abo. And therefore would you lie contented down
In the forgetfulness and arms of love,
To get young princes for 'em?
Oro. Say'st thou! ha!
Abo. Princes, the heirs of empire, and the last
Of your illustrious lineage, to be born
To pamper up their pride, and be their slaves?
Oro. Imoinda! save me, save me from that thought.

Imo. There is no safety from it: I have long
Suffered it with a mother's labouring pains,
And can no longer. Kill me, kill me now,
While I am blessed, and happy in your love,
Rather than let me live to see you hate me,
As you must hate me; me, the only cause,
The fountain of these flowing miseries.
Dry up this spring of life, this pois'nous spring,
That swells so fast, to overwhelm us all.

Oro. Shall the dear babe, the eldest of my hopes,
Whom I begot a prince, be born a slave?
The treasure of this temple was designed
T'enrich a kingdom's fortune: shall it here
Be seized upon by vile unhallowed hands,
To be employed in uses most profane?

Abo. In most unworthy uses: think of that;
And while you may, prevent it. Oh, my lord!
Rely on nothing that they say to you.
They speak you fair, I know, and bid you wait.
But think what 'tis to wait on promises,
And promises of men who know no tie
Upon their words, against their interest:
And where's their interest in freeing you?

Imo. Oh! where indeed, to lose so many slaves?

Abo. Nay, grant this man you think so much your friend
Be honest, and intends all that he says:
He is but one; and in a government
Where, he confesses, you have enemies
That watch your looks, what looks can you put on
To please these men who are before resolved
To read 'em their own way? Alas! my lord!
If they incline to think you dangerous,
They have their knavish arts to make you so.
And then who knows how far their cruelty
May carry their revenge?

Imo. To everything
That does belong to you; your friends, and me;
I shall be torn from you, forced away,
Helpless, and miserable. Shall I live
To see that day again?

Oro. That day shall never come.

Abo. I know you are persuaded to believe

The Governor's arrival will prevent
These mischiefs, and bestow your liberty:
But who is sure of that? I rather fear
More mischiefs from his coming: he is young,
Luxurious, passionate, and amorous.
Such a complexion, and made bold by power,
To countenance all he is prone to do,
Will know no bounds, no law against his lusts.
If, in a fit of his intemperance,
With a strong hand he should resolve to seize,
And force my royal mistress from your arms,
How can you help yourself?

Oro. Ha! thou hast roused
The lion in his den, he stalks abroad,
And the wide forest trembles at his roar.
I find the danger now: my spirits start
At the alarm, and from all quarters come
To man my heart, the citadel of love.
Is there a power on earth to force you from me?
And shall I not resist it? not strike first
To keep, to save you? to prevent that curse?
This is your cause, and shall it not prevail?
Oh! you were born all ways to conquer me.
Now I am fashioned to thy purpose: speak,
What combination, what conspiracy,
Wouldst thou engage me in? I'll undertake
All thou wouldst have me now for liberty,
For the great cause of love and liberty.

Abo. Now, my great master, you appear yourself.
And since we have you joined in our design,
It cannot fail us. I have mustered up
The choicest slaves, men who are sensible
Of their condition, and seem most resolved:
They have their several parties.

Oro. Summon 'em,
Assemble 'em: I will come forth, and show
Myself among 'em. If they are resolved,
I'll lead their foremost resolutions.

Abo. I have provided those will follow you.

Oro. With this reserve in our proceeding still,

199 complexion] disposition, temperament 229 I'll lead their foremost resolutions] i.e. I'll lead them however far they intend to go.

The means that lead us to our liberty,
Must not be bloody.

Abo. You command in all.
We shall expect you, sir.

Oro. You shannot long.

[*Exeunt* Oroonoko *and* Imoinda *at one door*, Aboan *at another*.

SCENE III

Welldon *coming in before* Widow Lackitt.

Wid. These unmannerly Indians were something unseasonable, to disturb us just in the nick, Mr. Weldon; but I have the parson within call still, to do us the good turn.

Well. We had best stay a little, I think, to see things settled again, had not we? Marriage is a serious thing, you know.

Wid. What do you talk of a serious thing, Mr. Welldon? I think you have found me sufficiently serious: I have married my son to your sister to pleasure you; and now I come to claim your promise to me you tell me marriage is a serious thing.

Well. Why, is it not?

Wid. Fiddle faddle, I know what it is: 'tis not the first time I have been married, I hope. But I shall begin to think you don't design to do fairly by me, so I shall.

Well. Why indeed, Mrs. Lackitt, I am afraid I can't do as fairly as I would by you. 'Tis what you must know, first or last; and I should be the worst man in the world to conceal it any longer. Therefore I must own to you, that I am married already.

Wid. Married! you don't say so, I hope! How have you the conscience to tell me such a thing to my face! have you abused me then, fooled and cheated me? What do you take me for, Mr. Welldon? do you think I am to be served at this rate? But you shan't find me the silly creature, you think me: I would have you to know I understand better things than to ruin my son without a valuable consideration. If I can't have you, I can keep my money. Your sister shan't have the catch of him she expected: I won't part with a shilling to 'em.

Well. You made the match yourself, you know, you can't blame me.

Wid. Yes, yes, I can, and do blame you: you might have told me before you were married.

Well. I would not have told you now, but you followed me so close I was forced to't. Indeed I am married in England; but 'tis as if I were not, for

234 expect] wait for

I have been parted from my wife a great while; and to do reason on both sides, we hate one another heartily. Now I did design and will marry you still, if you'll have a little patience.

Wid. A likely business, truly.

Well. I have a friend in England that I will write to, to poison my wife, and then I can marry you with a good conscience if you love me, as you say you do; you'll consent to that, I'm sure.

Wid. And will he do it, do you think?

Well. At the first word, or he is not the man I take him to be.

Wid. Well, you are a dear devil, Mr. Welldon: and would you poison your wife for me?

Well. I would do anything for you.

Wid. Well, I am mightily obliged to you. But 'twill be a great while before you can have an answer of your letter.

Well. 'Twill be a great while indeed.

Wid. In the mean time, Mr. Welldon—

Well. Why, in the mean time—Here's company: we'll settle that within. I'll follow you. [*Exit* Widow.

Enter Stanmore.

Stan. So, sir, you carry your business swimmingly: you have stolen a wedding, I hear.

Well. Ay, my sister is married; and I am very near being run away with myself.

Stan. The widow will have you then.

Well. You come very seasonably to my rescue. Jack Stanmore is to be had, I hope.

Stan. At half an hour's warning.

Well. I must advise with you. [*Exeunt.*

SCENE IV

Oroonoko *with* Aboan, Hottman, *Slaves.*

Oro. Impossible! nothing's impossible:
We know our strength only by being tried.
If you object the mountains, rivers, woods
Unpassable, that lie before our march—
Woods we can set on fire; we swim by nature:
What can oppose us then but we may tame?
All things submit to virtuous industry:
That we can carry with us, that is ours.

Slave. Great sir, we have attended all you said,
With silent joy and admiration:
And, were we only men, would follow such,
So great a leader through the untried world.
But, oh! consider we have other names,
Husbands and fathers, and have things more dear
To us than life, our children and our wives,
Unfit for such an expedition:
What must become of them?
Oro. We wonnot wrong
The virtue of our women, to believe
There is a wife among 'em would refuse
To share her husband's fortune. What is hard,
We must make easy to 'em in our love.
While we live,
And have our limbs, we can take care for them;
Therefore I still propose to lead our march
Down to the sea, and plant a colony:
Where, in our native innocence, we shall live
Free, and be able to defend ourselves;
Till stress of weather, or some accident
Provide a ship for us.
Abo. An accident!
The luckiest accident presents itself:
The very ship that brought and made us slaves
Swims in the river still; I see no cause
But we may seize on that.
Oro. It shall be so:
There is a justice in it pleases me.
[*To the slaves*.] Do you agree to it?
Omnes. We follow you.
Oro. [*To* Hottman.] You do not relish it?
Hott. I am afraid
You'll find it difficult, and dangerous.
Abo. Are you the man to find the danger first?
You should have given example. Dangerous!
I thought you had not understood the word:
You, who would be the head, the hand, and heart.
Sir, I remember you, you can talk well;
I wonnot doubt but you'll maintain your word.
Oro. [*To* Aboan.] This fellow is not right, I'll try him further.
The danger will be certain to us all,

And death most certain in miscarrying.
We must expect no mercy if we fail.
Therefore our way must be not to expect:
We'll put it out of expectation,
By death upon the place, or liberty.
There is no mean but death or liberty.
There's no man here, I hope, but comes prepared
For all that can befall him.

Abo. Death is all:
In most conditions of humanity
To be desired, but to be shunned in none:
The remedy of many; wish of some;
And certain end of all.
If there be one among us who can fear
The face of death appearing like a friend,
As in this cause of honour death must be,
How will he tremble, when he sees him dressed
In the wild fury of our enemies,
In all the terrors of their cruelty?
For now if we should fall into their hands,
Could they invent a thousand murd'ring ways,
By racking torments, we should feel 'em all.

Hott. What will become of us?

Oro. [*To* Aboan *concerning* Hottman.] Observe him now.—
I could die altogether like a man,
As you, and you, and all of us may do;
But who can promise for his bravery
Upon the rack? where fainting, weary life,
Hunted through every limb, is forced to feel
An agonizing death of all its parts?
Who can bear this? resolve to be impaled?
His skin flead off, and roasted yet alive?
The quivering flesh torn from his broken bones
By burning pincers? Who can bear these pains?

Hott. They are not to be born. [*Discovering all the confusion of fear.*

Oro. You see him now, this man of mighty words!

Abo. How his eyes roll!

Oro. He cannot hide his fear:
I tried him this way, and have found him out.

53–66 Death . . . 'em all] *Q.* 1 gives this speech to Oroonoko. 75 flead] flayed

Abo. I could not have believed it. Such a blaze,
And not a spark of fire!
Oro. His violence,
Made me suspect him first: now I'm convinced.
Abo. What shall we do with him?
Oro. He is not fit—
Abo. Fit! hang him, he is only fit to be
Just what he is, to live and die a slave:
The base companion of his servile fears.
Oro. We are not safe with him.
Abo. Do you think so?
Oro. He'll certainly betray us.
Abo. That he shan't:
I can take care of that: I have a way
To take him off his evidence.
Oro. What way?
Abo. I'll stop his mouth before you, stab him here,
And then let him inform.
[*Going to stab* Hottman, Oroonoko *holds him*.
Oro. Thou art not mad?
Abo. I would secure ourselves.
Oro. It shannot be this way; nay, cannot be:
His murder would alarm all the rest,
Make 'em suspect us of barbarity,
And, may be, fall away from our design.
We'll not set out in blood: we have, my friends,
This night to furnish what we can provide
For our security and just defence.
If there be one among us we suspect
Of baseness or vile fear, it will become
Our common care to have our eyes on him:
I wonnot name the man.
Abo. [*To* Hottman.] You guess at him.
Oro. Tomorrow, early as the breaking day,
We rendezvous behind the citron grove.
That ship secured, we may transport ourselves
To our respective homes. My father's kingdom
Shall open her wide arms to take you in,
And nurse you for her own, adopt you all,
All, who will follow me.
Omn. All, all follow you.
Oro. There I can give you all your liberty;

Bestow its blessings, and secure 'em yours.
There you shall live with honour, as becomes
My fellow-sufferers and worthy friends:
This, if we do succeed. But if we fall
In our attempt, 'tis nobler still to die,
Than drag the galling yoke of slavery.

[*Exeunt omnes.*

ACT IV SCENE I

Welldon *and* Jack Stanmore.

Well. You see, honest Jack, I have been industrious for you: you must take some pains now to serve yourself.

J. Stan. Gad, Mr. Welldon, I have taken a great deal of pains; and if the Widow speaks honestly, faith and troth, she'll tell you what a pains-taker I am.

Well. Fie, fie, not me! I am her husband you know: she won't tell me what pains you have taken with her. Besides, she takes you for me.

J. Stan. That's true: I forgot you had married her. But if you knew all—

Well. 'Tis no matter for my knowing all, if she does—

J. Stan. Ay, ay, she does know, and more than ever she knew since she was a woman, for the time, I will be bold to say; for I have done—

Well. The Devil take you, you'll never have done.

J. Stan. As old as she is, she has a wrinkle behind more than she had, I believe—for I have taught her what she never knew in her life before.

Well. What care I what wrinkles she has? or what you have taught her? If you'll let me advise you, you may; if not, you may prate on, and ruin the whole design.

J. Stan. Well, well, I have done.

Well. Nobody but your cousin, and you, and I, know anything of this matter. I have married Mrs. Lackitt, and put you to bed to her, which she knows nothing of, to serve you. In two or three days I'll bring it about so, to resign up my claim, with her consent, quietly to you.

J. Stan. But how will you do it?

Well. That must be my business. In the mean time, if you should make any noise, 'twill come to her ears, and be impossible to reconcile her.

24–5 make any noise] talk about it at all (cf. 'noise it abroad')

J. Stan. Nay, as for that, I know the way to reconcile her, I warrant you.

Well. But how will you get her money? I am married to her.

J. Stan. That I don't know indeed.

Well. You must leave it to me, you find; all the pains I shall put you to will be to be silent. You can hold your tongue for two or three days?

J. Stan. Truly, not well, in a matter of this nature: I should be very unwilling to lose the reputation of this night's work, and the pleasure of telling.

Well. You must mortify that vanity a little: you will have time enough to brag, and lie of your manhood, when you have her in a bare-faced condition to disprove you.

J. Stan. Well, I'll try what I can do: the hopes of her money must do it.

Well. You'll come at night again? 'Tis your own business.

J. Stan. But you have the credit on't.

Well. 'Twill be your own another day, as the widow says. Send your cousin to me: I want his advice.

J. Stan. I want to be recruited, I'm sure; a good breakfast, and to bed: she has rocked my cradle sufficiently. [*Exit.*

Well. She would have a husband; and if all be as he says, she has no reason to complain. But there's no relying on what the men say upon these occasions: they have the benefit of their bragging by recommending their abilities to other women; theirs is a trading estate that lives upon credit, and increases by removing it out of one bank into another. Now, poor women have not these opportunities: we must keep our stocks dead by us, at home, to be ready for a purchase when it comes—a husband, let him be never so dear, and be glad of him; or venture our fortunes abroad on such rotten security that the principal and interest, nay, very often our persons, are in danger. If the women would agree (which they never will) to call home their effects, how many proper gentlemen would sneak into another way of living, for want of being responsible in this? Then husbands would be cheaper. Here comes the Widow, she'll tell truth: she'll not bear false witness against her own interest, I know.

Enter Widow Lackitt.

Well. Now, Mrs. Lackitt.

Wid. Well, well, Lackitt or what you will now; now I am married to you. I am very well pleased with what I have done, I assure you.

Well. And with what I have done too, I hope.

42 recruited] replenished (with *double entendre*) 53–4 If the women . . . effects] In Southerne's elaborate trading metaphor this appears to mean 'If the women would stop having casual and unprofitable affairs with men'. 55 responsible] of good credit, trustworthy

Wid. Ah! Mr. Welldon! I say nothing, but you're a dear man, and I did not think it had been in you.

Well. I have more in me than you imagine.

Wid. No, no, you can't have more than I imagine; 'tis impossible to have more: you have enough for any woman, in an honest way, that I will say for you.

Well. Then I find you are satisfied.

Wid. Satisfied! No indeed; I'm not to be satisfied, with you or without you: to be satisfied is to have enough of you. Now, 'tis a folly to lie: I shall never think I can have enough of you. I shall be very fond of you. Would you have me fond of you? What do you do to me, to make me love you so well?

Well. Can't you tell what?

Wid. Go; there's no speaking to you: you bring all the blood of one's body into one's face, so you do. Why do you talk so?

Well. Why, how do I talk?

Wid. You know how; but a little colour becomes me, I believe. How do I look to day?

Well. Oh! most lovingly, most amiably.

Wid. Nay, this can't be long a secret, I find, I shall discover it by my countenance.

Well. The women will find you out, you look so cheerfully.

Wid. But do I, do I really look so cheerfully, so amiably? There's no such paint in the world as the natural glowing of a complexion. Let 'em find me out, if they please, poor creatures, I pity 'em; they envy me, I'm sure, and would be glad to mend their looks upon the same occasion. The young gill-flirting girls, forsooth, believe nobody must have a husband but themselves; but I would have 'em to know there are other things to be taken care of besides their green sickness.

Well. Ay, sure, or the physicians would have but little practice.

Wid. Mr. Welldon, what must I call you? I must have some pretty fond name or other for you. What shall I call you?

Well. I thought you liked my own name.

Wid. Yes, yes, I like it, but I must have a nickname for you: most women have nicknames for their husbands—

Well. Cuckold.

Wid. No, no, but 'tis very pretty before company; it looks negligent, and is the fashion, you know.

Well. To be negligent of their husbands, it is indeed.

Wid. Nay then, I won't be in the fashion; for I can never be negligent of

88 gill-flirting] wanton, giddy

dear Mr. Welldon; and to convince you, here's something to encourage you not to be negligent of me. [*Gives him a purse and a little casket.* Five hundred pounds in gold in this; and jewels to the value of five hundred pounds more in this. [Welldon *opens the casket.*

Well. Ay, marry, this will encourage me indeed.

Wid. There are comforts in marrying an elderly woman, Mr. Welldon. Now a young woman would have fancied she had paid you with her person, or had done you the favour.

Well. What do you talk of young women? You are as young as any of 'em, in everything but their folly and ignorance.

Wid. And do you think me so? But I have no reason to suspect you. Was not I seen at your house this morning, do you think?

Well. You may venture again: you'll come at night, I suppose.

Wid. Oh dear! at night? so soon?

Well. Nay, if you think it so soon—

Wid. Oh! no, it is not for that Mr. Welldon, but—

Well. You won't come then?

Wid. Won't! I don't say I won't: that is not a word for a wife. If you command me—

Well. To please yourself.

Wid. I will come to please you.

Well. To please yourself, own it.

Wid. Well, well, to please myself, then; you're the strangest man in the world, nothing can 'scape you: you'll to the bottom of everything.

Enter Daniel, Lucia *following.*

Dan. What would you have? what do you follow me for?

Luc. Why, mayn't I follow you? I must follow you now all the world over.

Dan. Hold you, hold you there: not so far by a mile or two; I have enough of your company already, by'r lady! and something to spare. You may go home to your brother, an you will, I have no farther to do with you.

Wid. Why, Daniel, child, thou art not out of thy wits sure, art thou?

Dan. Nay, marry, I don't know; but I am very near it, I believe. I am altered for the worse mightily since you saw me; and she has been the cause of it there.

Wid. How so, child?

Dan. I told you before what would come on't, of putting me to bed to a strange woman; but you would not be said nay.

Wid. She is your wife now, child; you must love her.

Dan. Why, so I did, at first.

Wid. But you must love her always.

Dan. Always! I loved her as long as I could, mother, and as long as loving was good, I believe, for I find now I don't care a fig for her.

Luc. Why, you lubberly, slovenly, misbegotten blockhead.

Wid. Nay, Mistress Lucy, say anything else, and spare not; but as to his begetting, that touches me; he is as honestly begotten, though I say it, that he is the worse again.

Luc. I see all good nature is thrown away upon you—

Wid. It was so with his father before him: he takes after him.

Luc. And therefore I will use you as you deserve, you tony.

Wid. Indeed, he deserves bad enough, but don't call him out of his name; his name is Daniel, you know.

Dan. She may call me hermophrodite, if she will, for I hardly know whether I'm a boy or a girl.

Well. A boy, I warrant thee, as long as thou liv'st.

Dan. Let her call me what she pleases, mother; 'tis not her tongue that I am afraid of.

Luc. I will make such a beast of thee, such a cuckold!

Wid. Oh, pray, no, I hope; do nothing rashly, Mrs. Lucy.

Luc. Such a cuckold will I make of thee!

Dan. I had rather be a cuckold than what you would make of me in a week, I'm sure: I have no more manhood left in me already than there is, saving the mark, in one of my mother's old under-petticoats here.

Wid. Sirrah, sirrah, meddle with your wife's petticoats, and let your mother's alone, you ungracious bird, you. [*Beats him.*

Dan. Why, is the Devil in the woman? what have I said now? Do you know, if you were asked, I trow? But you are all of a bundle; even hang together; he that unties you makes a rod for his own tail; and so he will find it that has anything to do with you.

Wid. Ay, rogue enough, you shall find it: I have a rod for your tail still.

Dan. No wife, and I care not. 171

Wid. I'll swinge you into better manners, you booby.

[*Beats him off. Exeunt* ⟨Daniel *and* Widow Lackitt⟩.

Well. You have consummated our project upon him.

Luc. Nay, if I have a limb of the fortune, I care not who has the whole body of the fool.

Well. That you shall, and a large one, I promise you.

Luc. Have you heard the news? They talk of an English ship in the river.

Well. I have heard on't; and am preparing to receive it, as fast as I can.

150 tony] simpleton 153 hermophrodite] *O.E.D.* cites this spelling as 'erroneous': no doubt it represents the way Daniel pronounces the word 165 bird] child, youngster 170 tail] backside, bottom 171 No wife] *Q.* 2–3, *Works*; No, wife *Q.* 1

Luc. There's something the matter too with the slaves, some disturbance or other; I don't know what 'tis.

Well. So much the better still. We fish in troubled waters: we shall have fewer eyes upon us. Pray, go you home, and be ready to assist me in your part of the design.

Luc. I can't fail in mine. [*Exit.*

Well. The Widow has furnished me, I thank her, to carry it on. Now I have got a wife, 'tis high time to think of getting a husband. I carry my fortune about me; a thousand pounds in gold and jewels. Let me see— 'Twill be a considerable trust: and I think I shall lay it out to advantage.

Enter Stanmore.

Stan. So, Welldon, Jack has told me his success; and his hopes of marrying the Widow by your means.

Well. I have strained a point, Stanmore, upon your account, to be serviceable to your family.

Stan. I take it upon my account; and am very much obliged to you. But here we are all in an uproar.

Well. So they say; what's the matter?

Stan. A mutiny among the slaves: Oroonoko is at the head of 'em; our Governor is gone out with his rascally militia against 'em. What it may come to nobody knows.

Well. For my part, I shall do as well as the rest; but I'm concerned for my sister, and cousin, whom I expect in the ship from England.

Stan. There's no danger of 'em.

Well. I have a thousand pounds here, in gold and jewels, for my cousin's use, that I would more particularly take care of. 'Tis too great a sum to venture at home; and I would not have her wronged of it. Therefore, to secure it, I think my best way will be to put it into your keeping.

Stan. You have a very good opinion of my honesty.

[*Takes the purse and casket.*

Well. I have, indeed. If anything should happen to me in this bustle, as nobody is secure of accidents, I know you will take my cousin into your protection and care.

Stan. You may be sure on't.

Well. If you hear she is dead, as she may be, then I desire you to accept of the thousand pound as a legacy and token of my friendship; my sister is provided for.

Stan. Why, you amaze me; but you are never the nearer dying, I hope, for making your will?

Well. Not a jot; but I love to be beforehand with fortune. If she comes safe, this is not a place for a single woman, you know. Pray see her married as soon as you can.

Stan. If she be as handsome as her picture, I can promise her a husband.

Well. If you like her when you see her, I wish nothing so much as to have you marry her yourself.

Stan. From what I have heard of her, and my engagements to you, it must be her fault, if I don't. I hope to have her from your own hand.

Well. And I hope to give her to you, for all this.

Stan. Ay, ay, hang these melancholy reflections! Your generosity has engaged all my services.

Well. I always thought you worth making a friend.

Stan. You shan't find your good opinion thrown away upon me: I am in your debt, and shall think so as long as I live. [*Exeunt.*

SCENE II

Enter on one side of the stage Oroonoko, Aboan, *with the Slaves,* Imoinda *with a bow and quiver, the women, some leading, others carrying their children upon their backs.*

Oro. The women, with their children, fall behind.
Imoinda, you must not expose yourself:
Retire, my love: I almost fear for you.
Imo. I fear no danger: life, or death, I will
Enjoy with you.
Oro. My person is your guard.

Abo. Now, sir, blame yourself: if you had not prevented my cutting his throat, that coward there had not discovered us. He comes now to upbraid you.

Enter on the other side Lieutenant-Governor, *talking to* Hottman, *with his rabble.*

Lt.-Gov. This is the very thing I would have wished.
[*To* Hottman.] Your honest service to the government
Shall be rewarded with your liberty.
Abo. His honest service! Call it what it is,
His villainy, the service of his fear.
If he pretends to honest services,
Let him stand out, and meet me, like a man. [*Advancing.*

7 discovered] betrayed

Oro. Hold, you! And you who come against us, hold!
I charge you in a general good to all,
And wish I could command you, to prevent
The bloody havoc of the murdering sword.
I would not urge destruction uncompelled;
But if you follow fate, you find it here.
The bounds are set, the limits of our lives:
Between us lies the gaping gulf of death,
To swallow all. Who first advances—

Enter the Captain *with his crew.*

Capt. Here, here, here they are, Governor! What! seize upon my ship!—
Come, boys, fall on— [*Advancing first,* Oroonoko *kills him.*
Oro. Thou art fallen indeed. Thy own blood be upon thee.
Lt.-Gov. Rest it there.
He did deserve his death. Take him away. [*The body removed.*
You see, sir, you and those mistaken men
Must be our witnesses, we do not come
As enemies, and thirsting for your blood.
If we desired your ruin, the revenge
Of our companion's death had pushed it on.
But that we overlook, in a regard
To common safety and the public good.
Oro. Regard that public good: draw off your men,
And leave us to our fortune. We're resolved.
Lt.-Gov. Resolved, on what? Your resolutions
Are broken, overturned, prevented, lost:
What fortune now can you raise out of 'em?
Nay, grant we should draw off, what can you do?
Where can you move? What more can you resolve?
Unless it be to throw yourselves away.
Famine must eat you up if you go on.
You see our numbers could with ease compel
What we request. And what do we request?
Only to save yourselves.
[*The women with their children gathering about the men.*
Oro. I'll hear no more.
Women. Hear him, hear him. He takes no care of us.
Lt.-Gov. To those poor wretches who have been seduced
And led away, to all, and every one,
We offer a full pardon—
Oro. Then fall on. [*Preparing to engage.*

Lt.-Gov. Lay hold upon't, before it be too late,
Pardon and mercy.

[*The women clinging about the men, they leave* Oroonoko, *and fall upon their faces crying out for pardon.*

Slaves. Pardon, mercy, pardon!

Oro. Let 'em go all. Now, Governor, I see,
I own the folly of my enterprise,
The rashness of this action, and must blush
Quite through this veil of night, a whitely shame,
To think I could design to make those free
Who were by nature slaves; wretches designed
To be their masters' dogs, and lick their feet.
Whip, whip 'em to the knowledge of your gods,
Your Christian gods, who suffer you to be
Unjust, dishonest, cowardly, and base,
And give 'em your excuse for being so!
I would not live on the same earth with creatures
That only have the faces of their kind:
Why should they look like men, who are not so?
When they put off their noble natures for
The grovelling qualities of downcast beasts,
I wish they had their tails.

Abo. Then we should know 'em.

Oro. [*To* Imoinda, Aboan.] We were too few before for victory:
We're still enow to die.

Blanford *enters*

Lt.-Gov. Live, royal sir;
Live, and be happy long on your own terms:
Only consent to yield, and you shall have
What terms you can propose, for you, and yours.

Oro. Consent to yield! Shall I betray myself?

Lt.-Gov. Alas! we cannot fear that your small force,
The force of two, with a weak woman's arm,
Should conquer us. I speak in the regard
And honour of your worth, in my desire
And forwardness to serve so great a man.
I would not have it lie upon my thoughts,
That I was the occasion of the fall
Of such a prince, whose courage, carried on

58 whitely] pale (contrasted with Oroonoko's complexion, 'this veil of night')

In a more noble cause, would well deserve
The empire of the world.

Oro. You can speak fair.

Lt.-Gov. Your undertaking, though it would have brought
So great a loss to us, we must all say
Was generous and noble; and shall be
Regarded only as the fire of youth
That will break out sometimes in gallant souls.
We'll think it but the natural impulse,
A rash impatience of liberty:
No otherwise.

Oro. Think it what you will.
I was not born to render an account
Of what I do, to any but myself.

Blanford *comes forward.*

Blan. [*To the* Lieutenant-Governor] I'm glad you have proceeded by fair [means.
I came to be a mediator.

Lt.-Gov. Try.
What you can work upon him.

Oro. Are you come
Against me too?

Blan. Is this to come against you?
[*Offering his sword to* Oroonoko.
Unarmed to put myself into your hands?
I come, I hope, to serve you.

Oro. You have served me;
I thank you for't. And I am pleased to think
You were my friend while I had need of one;
But now 'tis past. This farewell; and be gone. [*Embraces him.*

Blan. It is not past, and I must serve you still.
I would make up these breaches, which the sword
Will widen more; and close us all in love.

Oro. I know what I have done, and I should be
A child to think they ever can forgive.
Forgive! Were there but that, I would not live
To be forgiven. Is there a power on earth
That I can ever need forgiveness from?

Blan. You sha' not need it.

Oro. No, I wonnot need it.

92 gallant souls] *Q.* 2, *Works*; gallant so *Q.* 1; gallant; so *Q.* 3.

Blan. You see he offers you your own conditions,
For you, and yours.
Oro. I must capitulate?
Precariously compound, on stinted terms,
To save my life?
Blan. Sir, he imposes none.
You make 'em for your own security.
If your great heart cannot descend to treat,
In adverse fortune, with an enemy,
Yet sure your honour's safe: you may accept
Offers of peace, and safety from a friend.
Lt.-Gov. [*To* Blanford.] He will rely on what you say to him:
Offer him what you can; I will confirm,
And make all good. Be you my pledge of trust.
Blan. I'll answer with my life for all he says.
Lt.-Gov. [*Aside.*] Ay, do, and pay the forfeit if you please.
Blan. Consider, sir, can you consent to throw
That blessing from you, you so hardly found, [*Of* Imoinda.
And so much valued once?
Oro. Imoinda! Oh!
'Tis she that holds me on this argument
Of tedius life: I could resolve it soon,
Were this curst being only in debate.
But my Imoinda struggles in my soul:
She makes a coward of me. I confess
I am afraid to part with her in death,
And more afraid of life to lose her here.
Blan. This way you must lose her; think upon
The weakness of her sex, made yet more weak
With her condition, requiring rest,
And soft indulging ease, to nurse your hopes,
And make you a glad father.
Oro. There I feel
A father's fondness, and a husband's love.
They seize upon my heart, strain all its strings,
To pull me to 'em from my stern resolve.
Husband, and father! All the melting art
Of eloquence lives in those soft'ning names.
Methinks I see the babe, with infant hands,
Pleading for life, and begging to be born.
Shall I forbid his birth? Deny him light?
The heavenly comforts of all-cheering light?

And make the womb the dungeon of his death?
His bleeding mother his sad monument?
These are the calls of nature that call loud,
They will be heard, and conquer in their cause:
He must not be a man, who can resist 'em.
No, my Imoinda! I will venture all
To save thee, and that little innocent:
The world may be a better friend to him
Than I have found it. Now I yield myself: [*Gives up his sword.*
The conflict's past, and we are in your hands.

Several men get about Oroonoko *and* Aboan, *and seize them.*

Lt.-Gov. So you shall find you are. Dispose of them
As I commanded you.
Blan. Good Heaven, forbid! You cannot mean—
Lt.-Gov. [*To* Blanford *who goes to* Oroonoko.] This is not your concern.
[*To* Imoinda.] I must take care of you.
Imo. I'm at the end
Of all my care. Here I will die with him. [*Holding* Oroonoko.
Oro. You shall not force her from me. [*He holds her.*
Lt.-Gov. Then I must
[*They force her from him.*
Try other means, and conquer force by force:
Break, cut off his hold, bring her away.
Imo. I do not ask to live; kill me but here.
Oro. O bloody dogs! inhuman murderers!
[Imoinda *forced out of one door by the Lieutenant-Governor and others.*
Oroonoko *and* Aboan *hurried out of another.*
[*Exeunt omnes.*

ACT V SCENE I

Enter Stanmore, Lucia, Charlott.

Stan. 'Tis strange we cannot hear of him. Can nobody give an account of him?

Luc. Nay, I begin to despair: I give him for gone.

Stan. Not so, I hope.

Luc. There are so many disturbances in this devilish country! Would we had never seen it.

Stan. This is but a cold welcome for you, madam, after so troublesome a voyage.

Char. A cold welcome indeed, sir, without my cousin Welldon. He was the best friend I had in the world.

Stan. He was a very good friend of yours indeed, madam.

Luc. They have made him away, murdered him for his money, I believe; he took a considerable sum out with him, I know: that has been his ruin.

Stan. That has done him no injury, to my knowledge; for this morning he put into my custody what you speak of, I suppose a thousand pounds, for the use of this lady.

Char. I was always obliged to him; and he has shown his care of me in placing my little affairs in such honourable hands.

Stan. He gave me a particular charge of you, madam, very particular, so particular that you will be surprised when I tell you.

Char. What, pray sir?

Stan. I am engaged to get you a husband; I promised that before I saw you; and now I have seen you, you must give me leave to offer you myself.

Luc. Nay, cousin, never be coy upon the matter; to my knowledge my brother always designed you for this gentleman.

Stan. You hear, madam, he has given me his interest, and 'tis the favour I would have begged of him. Lord! you are so like him—

Char. That you are obliged to say you like me for his sake.

Stan. I should be glad to love you for your own.

Char. If I should consent to the fine things you can say to me, how would you look at last, to find 'em thrown away upon an old acquaintance? 31

Stan. An old acquaintance!

Char. Lord, how easily are you men to be imposed upon! I am no cousin newly arrived from England, not I; but the very Welldon you wot of.

Stan. Welldon!

Char. Not murdered, nor made away, as my sister would have you believe, but am in very good health, your old friend in breeches that was, and now your humble servant in petticoats.

Stan. I'm glad we have you again. But what service can you do me in petticoats, pray?

Char. Can't you tell what?

Stan. Not I, by my troth: I have found my friend, and lost my mistress, it seems, which I did not expect from your petticoats.

Char. Come, come, you have had a friend of your mistress long enough; 'tis high time now to have a mistress of your friend.

Stan. What do you say?

13 I know: that] I know, that *Q*. 1–3, *Works*

Char. I am a woman, sir.

Stan. A woman!

Char. As arrant a woman as you would have had me but now, I assure you.

Stan. And at my service?

Char. If you have any for me in petticoats.

Stan. Yes, yes, I shall find you employment.

Char. You wonder at my proceeding, I believe.

Stan. 'Tis a little extraordinary, indeed.

Char. I have taken some pains to come into your favour.

Stan. You might have had it cheaper a great deal.

Char. I might have married you in the person of my English cousin, but could not consent to cheat you, even in the thing I had a mind to.

Stan. 'Twas done as you do everything.

Char. I need not tell you I made that little plot, and carried it on only for this opportunity. I was resolved to see whether you liked me as a woman, or not: if I had found you indifferent, I would have endeavoured to have been so too. But you say you like me, and therefore I have ventured to discover the truth.

Stan. Like you! I like you so well that I'm afraid you won't think marriage a proof on't: shall I give you any other?

Char. No, no, I'm inclined to believe you, and that shall convince me. At more leisure I'll satisfy you how I came to be in man's clothes, for no ill I assure you, though I have happened to play the rogue in 'em: they have assisted me in marrying my sister, and have gone a great way in befriending your cousin Jack with the Widow. Can you forgive me for pimping for your family?

Enter Jack Stanmore.

Stan. So, Jack, what news with you?

J. Stan. I am the forepart of the Widow, you know; she's coming after with the body of the family, the young squire in her hand, my son-in-law that is to be, with the help of Mr. Welldon.

Char. Say you so, sir? [*Clapping* Jack *upon the back*.

Enter Widow Lackitt *with her son* Daniel.

Wid. So, Mrs. Lucy, I have brought him about again; I have chastised him, I have made him as supple as a glove for your wearing, to pull on, or throw off, at your pleasure. Will you ever rebel again? Will you, sirrah? But come, come, down on your marrow bones, and ask her forgiveness. [Daniel *kneels*.

Say after me, 'Pray, forsooth, wife'.

49 me but now] *Works*; me. But now *Q*. 1–3 75 forepart] advance party

Dan. 'Pray, forsooth, wife.'

Luc. Well, well, this is a day of good nature, and so I take you into favour. But first take the oath of allegiance. [*He kisses her hand, and rises.* If ever you do so again—

Dan. Nay, marry, if I do, I shall have the worst on't.

Luc. Here's a stranger, forsooth, would be glad to be known to you, a sister of mine; pray salute her.

Wid. [*Starts at* Charlott.] Your sister! Mrs. Lucy! What do you mean? This is your brother, Mr. Welldon. Do you think I do not know Mr. Welldon?

Luc. Have a care what you say. This gentleman's about marrying her: you may spoil all.

Wid. Fiddle faddle, what! You would put a trick upon me.

Char. No, faith, Widow, the trick is over, it has taken sufficiently; and now I will teach you the trick to prevent your being cheated another time.

Wid. How! Cheated, Mr. Welldon!

Char. Why, ay, you will always take things by the wrong handle; I see you will have me Mr. Welldon. I grant you I was Mr. Welldon a little while to please you, or so; but Mr. Stanmore here has persuaded me into a woman again.

Wid. A woman! Pray let me speak with you. [*Drawing her aside*.] You are not in earnest, I hope? A woman!

Char. Really a woman.

Wid. Gads my life! I could not be cheated in everything: I know a man from a woman at these years, or the Devil's in 't. Pray, did not you marry me?

Char. You would have it so.

Wid. And did not I give you a thousand pounds this morning?

Char. Yes indeed, 'twas more than I deserved. But you had your pennyworth for your penny, I suppose: you seemed to be pleased with your bargain.

Wid. A rare bargain I have made on't, truly. I have laid out my money to fine purpose upon a woman.

Char. You would have a husband, and I provided for you as well as I could.

Wid. Yes, yes, you have provided for me.

Char. And you have paid me very well for't, I thank you.

Wid. 'Tis very well; I may be with child too, for aught I know, and may go look for the father.

Char. Nay, if you think so, 'tis time to look about you indeed. Even make up the matter as well as you can, I advise you as a friend, and let us live neighbourly and lovingly together.

Wid. I have nothing else for it, that I know now.

Char. For my part, Mrs. Lackitt, your thousand pounds will engage me not to laugh at you. Then my sister is married to your son; he is to have half your estate, I know. And indeed they may live upon it, very comfortably to themselves, and very creditably to you.

Wid. Nay, I can blame nobody but myself.

Char. You have enough for a husband still, and that you may bestow upon honest Jack Stanmore.

Wid. Is he the man then?

Char. He is the man you are obliged to.

J. Stan. Yes, faith, Widow, I am the man: I have done fairly by you, you find; you know what you have to trust to beforehand.

Wid. Well, well, I see you will have me: even marry me, and make an end of the business.

Stan. Why, that's well said. Now we are all agreed, and all provided for.

A Servant enters to Stanmore.

Serv. Sir, Mr. Blanford desires you to come to him, and bring as many of your friends as you can with you.

Stan. I come to him. You'll all go along with me.

Come, young gentleman, marriage is the fashion, you see; you must like it now.

Dan. If I don't, how shall I help myself?

Luc. Nay, you may hang yourself in the noose, if you please, but you'll never get out on't with struggling.

Dan. Come then, let's even jog on in the old road.
Cuckold, or worse, I must be now contented:
I'm not the first has married, and repented. [*Exeunt.*

SCENE II

Enter Lieutenant-Governor *with* Blanford, *and Planters.*

Blan. Have you no reverence of future fame?
No awe upon your actions from the tongues,
The censuring tongues of men that will be free?
If you confess humanity, believe
There is a God, or Devil, to reward
Our doings here; do not provoke your fate.
The hand of Heaven is armed against these crimes,
With hotter thunder-bolts, prepared to shoot,
And nail you to the earth a sad example,
A monument of faithless infamy.

Enter Stanmore, Jack Stanmore, Charlott, Lucy, Widow, *and* Daniel.

So, Stanmore, you, I know, the women too,
Will join with me. [*To the women.*] 'Tis Oroonoko's cause,
A lover's cause, a wretched woman's cause,
That will become your intercession.

1. *Plan.* Never mind 'em, Governor; he ought to be made an example for the good of the Plantation.

2. *Plan.* Ay, ay, 'twill frighten the negroes from attempting the like again.

1. *Plan.* What, rise against their lords and masters! At this rate no man is safe from his own slaves.

2. *Plan.* No, no more he is. Therefore, one and all, Governor, we declare for hanging.

Om. Plan. Ay, ay, hang him, hang him!

Wid. What! Hang him! Oh! forbid it, Governor.

Char., *Lucy.* We all petition for him.

J. Stan. They are for a holiday. Guilty or not
Is not the business; hanging is their sport.

Blan. We are not sure so wretched to have these,
The rabble, judge for us; the changing crowd;
The arbitrary guard of fortune's power,
Who wait to catch the sentence of her frowns,
And hurry all to ruin she condemns.

Stan. So far from farther wrong that 'tis a shame
He should be where he is. Good Governor,
Order his liberty: he yielded up
Himself, his all, at your discretion.

Blan. Discretion! no, he yielded on your word;
And I am made the cautionary pledge,
The gage, and hostage of your keeping it.
Remember, sir, he yielded on your word;
Your word! which honest men will think should be
The last resort of truth and trust on earth:
There's no appeal beyond it but to Heaven:
An oath is a recognisance to Heaven,
Binding us over in the courts above
To plead to the indictment of our crimes,
That those who 'scape this world should suffer there,
But in the common intercourse of men,

39 gage] pawn, security

(Where the dread majesty is not invoked,
His honour not immediately concerned,
Not made a party in our interests,)
Our word is all to be relied upon.

Wid. Come, come, you'll be as good as your word, we know.

Stan. He's out of all power of doing any harm now, if he were disposed to it.

Char. But he is not disposed to it.

Blan. To keep him where he is will make him soon
Find out some desperate way to liberty:
He'll hang himself, or dash out his mad brains.

Char. Pray try him
By gentle means. We'll all be sureties for him.

Om. All, all.

Luc. We will all answer for him now.

Lt.-Gov. Well, you will have it so; do what you please,
Just what you will with him, I give you leave. [*Exit.*

Blan. We thank you, sir; this way, pray come with me. [*Exeunt.*

The scene drawn shows Oroonoko *upon his back, his legs and arms stretched out, and chained to the ground.*

Enter Blanford, Stanmore, *etc.*

Blan. O miserable sight! Help, everyone;
Assist me all to free him from his chains.
[*They help him up, and bring him forward, looking down.*
Most injured Prince! how shall we clear ourselves?
We cannot hope you will vouchsafe to hear,
Or credit what we say in the defence
And cause of our suspected innocence.

Stan. We are not guilty of your injuries,
No way consenting to 'em, but abhor,
Abominate, and loathe this cruelty.

Blan. It is our curse, but make it not our crime:
A heavy curse upon us, that we must
Share anything in common, even the light,
The elements, and seasons, with such men,
Whose principles, like the famed dragon's teeth,
Scattered, and sown, would shoot a harvest up
Of fighting mischiefs, to confound themselves
And ruin all about 'em.

Stan. Profligates!

Whose bold Titanian impiety
Would once again pollute their mother earth,
Force her to teem with her old monstrous brood
Of giants, and forget the race of men.
Blan. We are not so: believe us innocent.
We come prepared with all our services,
To offer a redress of your base wrongs.
Which way shall we employ 'em?
Stan. Tell us, sir,
If there is anything that can atone
(But nothing can) that may be some amends—
Oro. If you would have me think you are not all
Confederates, all accessory to
The base injustice of your Governor;
If you would have me live, as you appear
Concerned for me, if you would have me live
To thank, and bless you, there is yet a way
To tie me ever to your honest love:
Bring my Imoinda to me; give me her,
To charm my sorrows, and, if possible,
I'll sit down with my wrongs, never to rise
Against my fate, or think of vengeance more.
Blan. Be satisfied you may depend upon us;
We'll bring her safe to you, and suddenly.
Char. We wonnot leave you in so good a work.
Wid. No, no, we'll go with you.
Blan. In the meantime
Endeavour to forget, sir, and forgive;
And hope a better fortune. [*Exeunt.*

Oroonoko *alone*

Oro. Forget! forgive! I must indeed forget,
When I forgive; but while I am a man,
In flesh that bears the living mark of shame,
The print of his dishonourable chains,
My memory still rousing up my wrongs,
I never can forgive this Governor;
This villain, the disgrace of trust, and place,
And just contempt of delegated power.
What shall I do? If I declare myself,
I know him, he will sneak behind his guard
Of followers, and brave me in his fears.

Else, lion-like, with my devouring rage,
I would rush on him, fasten on his throat,
Tear wide a passage to his treacherous heart,
And that way lay him open to the world. [*Pausing.*
If I should turn his Christian arts on him,
Promise him, speak him fair, flatter, and creep,
With fawning steps, to get within his faith,
I could betray him then, as he has me.
But am I sure by that to right myself?
Lying's a certain mark of cowardice;
And when the tongue forgets its honesty.
The heart and hand may drop their functions too,
And nothing worthy be resolved or done.
The man must go together, bad, or good:
In one part frail, he soon grows weak in all.
Honour should be concerned in honour's cause,
That is not to be cured by contraries,
As bodies are, whose health is often drawn
From rankest poisons. Let me but find out
An honest remedy, I have the hand,
A minist'ring hand that will apply it home. [*Exit.*

SCENE III

The Lieutenant-Governor's house.

Enter Lieutenant-Governor.

Lt.-Gov. I would not have her tell me she consents:
In favour of the sex's modesty,
That still should be presumed, because there is
A greater impudence in owning it
Than in allowing all that we can do.
This truth I know, and yet against myself,
(So unaccountable are lovers' ways)
I talk, and lose the opportunities
Which love and she expects I should employ:
Even she expects; for when a man has said
All that is fit, to save the decency,
The women know the rest is to be done.
I wonnot disappoint her. [*Going.*

Enter to him Blanford, *the* Stanmores, Daniel, Mrs. Lackitt, Charlott, *and* Lucy.

Wid. Oh, Governor! I'm glad we have lit upon you.

Lt.-Gov. Why! what's the matter?

Char. Nay, nothing extraordinary. But one good action draws on another. You have given the Prince his freedom: now we come a-begging for his wife. You won't refuse us?

Lt.-Gov. Refuse you? No, no, what have I to do to refuse you?

Wid. You won't refuse to send her to him, she means.

Lt.-Gov. I send her to him!

Wid. We have promised him to bring her.

Lt.-Gov. You do very well; 'tis kindly done of you: ev'n carry her to him, with all my heart.

Luc. You must tell us where she is.

Lt.-Gov. I tell you! why, don't you know?

Blan. Your servants say she's in the house.

Lt.-Gov. No, no, I brought her home at first, indeed; but I thought it would not look well to keep her here: I removed her in the hurry, only to take care of her. What! she belongs to you: I have nothing to do with her.

Char. But where is she now, sir?

Lt.-Gov. Why, faith, I can't say certainly. You'll hear of her at Parham House, I suppose: there, or thereabouts. I think I sent her there.

Blan. [*Aside.*] I'll have an eye on him.

[*Exeunt all but the Lt.-Governor.*

Lt.-Gov. I have lied myself into a little time,
And must employ it. They'll be here again;
But I must be before 'em.

[*Going out, he meets* Imoinda, *and seizes her.*

Are you come!
I'll court no longer for a happiness
That is in mine own keeping: you may still
Refuse to grant, so I have power to take.
The man that asks deserves to be denied.

[*She disengages one hand, and draws his sword from his side upon him;* Lieutenant-Governor *starts and retires;* Blanford *enters behind him.*

Imo. He does, indeed, that asks unworthily.

Blan. You hear her, sir, 'that asks unworthily'.

Lt.-Gov. You are no judge.

32-3 Parham House] presumably the Governor's house. Surinam was colonized by Francis Willoughby, fifth Baron Willoughby of Parham, some years before the Restoration.

Blan. I am of my own slave.
Lt.-Gov. Begone, and leave us.
Blan. When you let her go.
Lt.-Gov. To fasten upon you.
Blan. I must defend myself.
Imo. Help, murder, help!

[Imoinda *retreats towards the door, favoured by* Blanford; *when they are closed, she throws down the sword, and runs out.* Lieutenant-Governor *takes up the sword; they fight, close, and fall,* Blanford *upon him. Servants enter, and part them.*

Lt.-Gov. She shannot 'scape me so. I've gone too far,
Not to go farther. Curse on my delay!
But yet she is, and shall be in my power.
Blan. Nay, then it is the war of honesty:
I know you, and will save you from yourself.
Lt.-Gov. All come along with me. [*Exeunt.*

SCENE IV

Oroonoko *enters.*

Oro. To honour bound! and yet a slave to love!
I am distracted by their rival powers,
And both will be obeyed. O great revenge!
Thou raiser and restorer of fall'n fame!
Let me not be unworthy of thy aid,
For stopping in thy course: I still am thine,
But can't forget I am Imoinda's too.
She calls me from my wrongs to rescue her.
No man condemn me who has never felt
A woman's power, or tried the force of love.
All tempers yield, and soften in those fires;
Our honours, interests resolving down,
Run in the gentle current of our joys,
But not to sink, and drown our memory:
We mount again to action, like the sun,
That rises from the bosom of the sea
To run his glorious race of light anew,
And carry on the world. Love, love will be
My first ambition, and my fame the next.

s.d. *favoured*] aided, supported   s.d. *closed*] at close quarters

Aboan *enters bloody.*

My eyes are turned against me, and combine
With my sworn enemies to represent
This spectacle of honour.—Aboan!
My ever-faithful friend!
Abo. I have no name
That can distinguish me from the vile earth
To which I'm going: a poor, abject worm,
That crawled awhile upon a bustling world,
And now am trampled to my dust again.
Oro. I see thee gashed and mangled.
Abo. Spare my shame
To tell how they have used me; but believe
The hangman's hand would have been merciful.
Do not you scorn me, sir, to think I can
Intend to live under this infamy.
I do not come for pity, to complain.
I've spent an honourable life with you;
The earliest servant of your rising fame,
And would attend it with my latest care:
My life was yours, and so shall be my death.
You must not live.
Bending and sinking, I have dragged my steps
Thus far, to tell you that you cannot live:
To warn you of those ignominious wrongs,
Whips, rods, and all the instruments of death,
Which I have felt, and are prepared for you.
This was the duty that I had to pay.
'Tis done, and now I beg to be discharged.
Oro. What shall I do for thee?
Abo. My body tires,
And wonnot bear me off to liberty:
I shall again be taken, made a slave.
A sword, a dagger yet would rescue me.
I have not strength to go to find out death:
You must direct him to me.
Oro. Here he is. [*Gives him a dagger.*
The only present I can make thee now:
And next the honourable means of life,
I would bestow the honest means of death.
Abo. I cannot stay to thank you. If there is

A being after this, I shall be yours
In the next world, your faithful slave again.
This is to try. [*Stabs himself.*] I had a living sense
Of all your royal favours, but this last
Strikes through my heart. I wonnot say farewell,
For you must follow me. [*Dies.*

Oro. In life, and death,
The guardian of my honour! Follow thee!
I should have gone before thee: then perhaps
Thy fate had been prevented. All his care
Was to preserve me from the barbarous rage
That wronged him, only for being mine.
Why, why, you gods! Why am I so accursed,
That it must be a reason of your wrath,
A guilt, a crime sufficient to the fate
Of anyone, but to belong to me?
My friend has found it, and my wife will soon.
My wife! the very fear's too much for life:
I can't support it. Where? Imoinda! Oh!

Going out, she meets him, running into his arms.

Thou bosom softness! Down of all my cares!
I could recline my thoughts upon this breast
To a forgetfulness of all my griefs,
And yet be happy; but it wonnot be.
Thou art disordered, pale, and out of breath!
If fate pursues thee, find a shelter here.
What is it thou wouldst tell me?

Imo. 'Tis in vain
To call him villain.

Oro. Call him Governor.
Is it not so?

Imo. There's not another, sure.

Oro. Villain's the common name of mankind here,
But his most properly. What! what of him?
I fear to be resolved, and must enquire.
He had thee in his power.

Imo. I blush to think it.

Oro. Blush! to think what?

Imo. That I was in his power.

66 wronged] wrong'd *Q.* 1–3; worry'd *Works*

Oro. He could not use it?
Imo. What can't such men do?
Oro. But did he? durst he?
Imo. What he could, he dared.
Oro. His own gods damn him then; for ours have none,
No punishment for such unheard-of crimes.
Imo. This monster, cunning in his flatteries,
When he had wearied all his useless arts,
Leapt out, fierce as a beast of prey, to seize me.
I trembled, feared.
Oro. I fear, and tremble now.
What could preserve thee; what deliver thee?
Imo. That worthy man you used to call your friend—
Oro. Blanford.
Imo. Came in, and saved me from his rage.
Oro. He was a friend indeed to rescue thee!
And for his sake, I'll think it possible
A Christian may be yet an honest man.
Imo. Oh! did you know what I have struggled through
To save me yours, sure you would promise me
Never to see me forced from you again.
Oro. To promise thee! Oh! do I need to promise?
But there is now no farther use of words.
Death is security for all our fears. [*Shows* Aboan's *body on the floor*.
And yet I cannot trust him.
Imo. Aboan!
Oro. Mangled, and torn, resolved to give me time
To fit myself for what I must expect,
Groaned out a warning to me, and expired.
Imo. For what you must expect?
Oro. Would that were all.
Imo. What! to be butchered thus—
Oro. Just as thou seest.
Imo. By barbarous hands, to fall at last their prey!
Oro. I have run the race with honour. Shall I now
Lag, and be overtaken at the goal?
Imo. No.
Oro. [*Tenderly*.] I must look back to thee.
Imo. You shannot need.
I'm always present to your purpose; say,
Which way would you dispose me?
Oro. Have a care,

Thou'rt on a precipice, and dost not see
Whither that question leads thee. Oh! too soon
Thou dost enquire what the assembled gods
Have not determined, and will latest doom.
Yet this I know of fate, this is most certain,
I cannot, as I would, dispose of thee:
And, as I ought, I dare not. Oh, Imoinda!

Imo. Alas! that sigh! why do you tremble so?
Nay, then 'tis bad indeed, if you can weep.

Oro. My heart runs over; if my gushing eyes
Betray a weakness which they never knew,
Believe, thou, only thou couldst cause these tears.
The gods themselves conspire with faithless men
To our destruction.

Imo. Heaven and earth our foes!

Oro. It is not always granted to the great
To be most happy. If the angry pow'rs
Repent their favours, let 'em take 'em back:
The hopes of empire, which they gave my youth,
By making me a prince, I here resign.
Let 'em quench in me all those glorious fires
Which kindled at their beams. That lust of fame,
That fever of ambition, restless still,
And burning with the sacred thirst of sway,
Which they inspired, to qualify my fate,
And make me fit to govern under them,
Let 'em extinguish. I submit myself
To their high pleasure, and devoted bow
Yet lower, to continue still a slave,
Hopeless of liberty; and if I could
Live after it, would give up honour too,
To satisfy their vengeance, to avert
This only curse, the curse of losing thee.

Imo. If Heaven could be appeased, these cruel men
Are not to be entreated, or believed:
Oh! think on that, and be no more deceived.

Oro. What can we do?

Imo. Can I do anything?

Oro. But we were born to suffer.

Imo. Suffer both,
Both die, and so prevent 'em.

143 qualify] give a certain quality to

Oro. By thy death!
Oh! let me hunt my travelled thoughts again;
Range the wide waste of desolate despair;
Start any hope. Alas! I lose myself,
'Tis pathless, dark, and barren all to me.
Thou art my only guide, my light of life,
And thou art leaving me. Send out thy beams
Upon the wing; let 'em fly all around,
Discover every way. Is there a dawn,
A glimmering of comfort? The great god
That rises on the world must shine on us.
Imo. And see us set before him.
Oro. Thou bespeak'st,
And goest before me.
Imo. So I would, in love:
In the dear unsuspected part of life,
In death for love. Alas! what hopes for me?
I was preserved but to acquit myself,
To beg to die with you.
Oro. And canst thou ask it?
I never durst enquire into myself
About thy fate, and thou resolv'st it all.
Imo. Alas! my lord! my fate's resolved in yours.
Oro. Oh! keep thee there! Let not thy virtue shrink
From my support, and I will gather strength
Fast as I can, to tell thee—
Imo. I must die.
I know 'tis fit, and I can die with you.
Oro. Oh! thou hast banished hence a thousand fears,
Which sickened at my heart, and quite unmanned me.
Imo. Your fear's for me, I know you feared my strength,
And could not overcome your tenderness,
To pass this sentence on me; and indeed
There you were kind, as I have always found you,
As you have ever been: for though I am
Resigned, and ready to obey my doom,
Methinks it should not be pronounced by you.
Oro. Oh! that was all the labour of my grief.
My heart and tongue forsook me in the strife:
I never could pronounce it.

158 travelled] wearied, troubled (travailed) (*O.E.D.*, 7c) 168 Thou bespeak'st] you prognosticate 169 goest] *Works*; goes *Q.* 1–3

Imo. I have for you,
For both of us.
Oro. Alas! for me! my death
I could regard as the last scene of life,
And act it through with joy to have it done.
But then to part with thee—
Imo. 'Tis hard to part.
But parting thus, as the most happy must,
Parting in death, makes it the easier.
You might have thrown me off, forsaken me,
And my misfortunes: that had been a death
Indeed of terror, to have trembled at.
Oro. Forsaken! thrown thee off!
Imo. But 'tis a pleasure more than life can give,
That with unconquered passion to the last
You struggle still, and fain would hold me to you.
Oro. Ever, ever, and let those stars which are my enemies
Witness against me in the other world,
If I would leave this mansion of my bliss,
To be the brightest ruler of their skies.
Oh! that we could incorporate, be one, [*Embracing her.*
One body, as we have been long one mind,
That blended so, we might together mix,
And losing thus our beings to the world,
Be only found to one another's joys.
Imo. Is this the way to part?
Oro. Which is the way?
Imo. The God of Love is blind, and cannot find it.
But quick, make haste, our enemies have eyes
To find us out, and show us the worst way
Of parting; think on them.
Oro. Why dost thou wake me?
Imo. Oh! no more of love.
For if I listen to you, I shall quite
Forget my dangers, and desire to live.
I can't live yours. [*Takes up the dagger.*
Oro. There all the stings of death
Are shot into my heart—what shall I do?
Imo. This dagger will instruct you. [*Gives it him.*
Oro. Ha! this dagger!
Like fate, it points me to the horrid deed.
Imo. Strike, strike it home, and bravely save us both.
There is no other safety.

Oro. It must be—
But first a dying kiss—[*Kisses her.*] This last embrace—[*Embracing her.*]
And now—
Imo. I'm ready.
Oro. Oh! where shall I strike?
Is there a smallest grain of that loved body
That is not dearer to me than my eyes,
My bosomed heart, and all the live blood there?
Bid me cut off these limbs, hew off these hands.
Dig out these eyes, though I would keep them last
To gaze upon thee. But to murder thee!
The joy and charm of every ravished sense,
My wife! Forbid it, Nature.
Imo. Tis your wife,
Who on her knees conjures you. Oh! in time
Prevent those mischiefs that are falling on us.
You may be hurried to a shameful death,
And I too dragged to the vile Governor.
Then I may cry aloud: when you are gone,
Where shall I find a friend again to save me?
Oro. It will be so. Thou unexampled virtue!
Thy resolution has recovered mine:
And now prepare thee.
Imo. Thus with open arms,
I welcome you, and death.
[*He drops his dagger as he looks on her, and throws himself on the ground.*
Oro. I cannot bear it.
Oh! let me dash against this rock of fate.
Dig up this earth, tear, tear her bowels out,
To make a grave, deep as the centre down,
To swallow wide, and bury us together.
It wonnot be. Oh! then some pitying god
(If there be one a friend to innocence)
Find yet a way to lay her beauties down
Gently in death, and save me from her blood.
Imo. Oh, rise, 'tis more than death to see you thus.
I'll ease your love, and do the deed myself—
[*She takes up the dagger; he rises in haste to take it from her.*
Oro. Oh! hold, I charge thee, hold.
Imo. Though I must own
It would be nobler for us both from you.

Oro. Oh! for a whirlwind's wing to hurry us
To yonder cliff which frowns upon the flood:
That in embraces locked we might plunge in,
And perish thus in one another's arms.
Imo. Alas! what shout is that?
Oro. I see 'em coming.
They shannot overtake us. This last kiss.
And now, farewell!
Imo. Farewell, farewell for ever!
Oro. I'll turn my face away, and do it so.
Now, are you ready?
Imo. Now. But do not grudge me
The pleasure in my death of a last look,
Pray look upon me.—Now I'm satisfied.
Oro. So fate must be by this—
[*Going to stab her, he stops short; she lays her hands on his, in order to give the blow.*
Imo. Nay then I must assist you.
And since it is the common cause of both,
'Tis just that both should be employed in it.
Thus, thus 'tis finished, [*Stabs herself.*] and I bless my fate,
That where I lived I die, in these loved arms. [*Dies.*
Oro. She's gone. And now all's at an end with me.
Soft, lay her down. Oh, we will part no more.
[*Throws himself by her.*
But let me pay the tribute of my grief,
A few sad tears to thy loved memory,
And then I follow— [*Weeps over her.*
But I stay too long. [*A noise again.*
The noise comes nearer. Hold, before I go,
There's something would be done. It shall be so.
And then, Imoinda, I'll come all to thee. [*Rises.*

Blanford *and his party enter before the* Lieutenant-Governor *and his party. Swords drawn on both sides.*

Lt.-Gov. You strive in vain to save him. He shall die.
Blan. Not while we can defend him with our lives.
Lt.-Gov. Where is he?
Oro. Here's the wretch whom you would have.
Put up your swords, and let not civil broils

262 flood] sea 290 let not] *Q*. 2–3, *Works*; let *Q*. 1

Engage you in the cursed cause of one
Who cannot live, and now entreats to die.
This object will convince you.
Blan. 'Tis his wife!
[*They gather about the body.*
Alas! there was no other remedy.
Lt.-Gov. Who did the bloody deed?
Oro. The deed was mine.
Bloody I know it is, and I expect
Your laws should tell me so. Thus self-condemned,
I do resign myself into your hands,
The hands of justice.—But I hold the sword
For you—and for myself.
[*Stabs the* Lieutenant-Governor *and himself, then throws himself by* Imoinda'*s body.*
Stan. He has killed the Governor, and stabbed himself.
Oro. 'Tis as it should be now. I have sent his ghost
To be a witness of that happiness
In the next world which he denied us here. [*Dies.*
Blan. I hope there is a place of happiness
In the next world for such exalted virtue.
Pagan or unbeliever, yet he lived
To all he knew; and if he went astray,
There's mercy still above to set him right.
But Christians guided by the heavenly ray,
Have no excuse if we mistake our way.

FINIS

EPILOGUE

Written by Mr. Congreve, and Spoken by Mrs. Verbruggen.

You see, we try all shapes, and shifts, and arts,
To tempt your favours, and regain your hearts.
We weep, and laugh, join mirth and grief together,
Like rain and sunshine mixed in April weather.
Your different tastes divide our poet's cares:
One foot the sock, t'other the buskin wears;
Thus, while he strives to please, he's forced to do't,
Like Volscius, hip-hop, in a single boot.
Critics, he knows, for this may damn his books;
But he makes feasts for friends, and not for cooks.
Though errant-knights of late no favour find,
Sure you will be to ladies-errant kind.
To follow fame, knights-errant make profession:
We damsels fly, to save our reputation;
So they, their valour show, we, our discretion.
To lands of monsters and fierce beasts they go:
We, to those islands where rich husbands grow;
Though they're no monsters, we may make 'em so.
If they're of English growth, they'll bear't with patience,
But save us from a spouse of Oroonoko's nations!
Then bless your stars, you happy London wives,
Who love at large, each day, yet keep your lives;
Nor envy poor Imoinda's doting blindness,
Who thought her husband killed her out of kindness.
Death with a husband ne'er had shown such charms,
Had she once died within a lover's arms.
Her error was from ignorance proceeding:
Poor soul! she wanted some of our town breeding.

6 *buskin*] *Q*. 2; buskins *Q*. 1, 3, *Works* 8 *Volscius*] In *The Rehearsal*, Act III, Buckingham ridicules the love-and-honour debates of the heroic drama by showing Volscius trying to decide whether to put both his boots on or leave them off. The stage direction indicates the result: 'Exit with one boot on, the other off'. 11 *Though errant-knights . . . no favour find*] A sneer at D'Urfey's *The Comical History of Don Quixote* (Part III), which had failed to repeat the success of the two first parts 18 *make 'em so*] make them monsters, i.e. cuckolds 26 *died*] This has the usual sexual connotation

Forgive this Indian's fondness of her spouse;
Their law no Christian liberty allows:
Alas! they make a conscience of their vows!
If virtue in a heathen be a fault,
Then damn the heathen school where she was taught.
She might have learned to cuckold, jilt, and sham,
Had Covent-Garden been in Surinam.

Selected Bibliography

Background and general studies

Henry Hitch Adams and Baxter Hathaway, *Dramatic Essays of the Neoclassic Age* (Columbia, 1950)

Maurice Ashley, *England in the Seventeenth Century* (London, 1952)

E. L. Avery, 'The Restoration Audience' (*Philological Quarterly*, xlv, 1946)

Max Beloff, *Public Order and Popular Disturbances, 1660–1714* (London, 1938)

Sir Arthur Bryant, *The England of Charles II* (London, 1934)

Colley Cibber, *An Apology for his Life* (1740: Everyman edn., London, 1938. Much information on contemporary acting.)

Sir G. N. Clark, *The Later Stuarts 1660–1714* (Oxford, 1956)

K. H. D. Haley, *The First Earl of Shaftesbury* (Oxford, 1968)

Christopher Hill, *The Century of Revolution* (London, 1961)

Leslie Hotson, *The Commonwealth and Restoration Stage* (Cambridge, Mass., 1928)

John Loftis, *The Politics of Drama in Augustan England* (Oxford, 1963)

David Ogg, *England in the Reign of Charles II* (2 vols., Oxford, 1934; repr. 1963)

—— *England in the Reigns of James II and William III* (Oxford, 1955)

Sir John Pollock, *The Popish Plot* (London, 1903; repr. 1944)

W. van Lennep, *The London Stage 1660–1700* (Carbondale, 1965)

G. W. Whiting, 'Political satire in London stage plays, 1680–83' (*Modern Philology*, xxviii, 1930)

Criticism

John Russell Brown and Bernard Harris, eds., *Restoration Theatre* (London, 1964)

K. M. P. Burton, *Restoration Literature* (London, 1958)

Bonamy Dobrée, *Restoration Tragedy* (Oxford, 1929)

J. W. Dodd, *Thomas Southerne, Dramatist* (New Haven, 1933)

Roswell G. Ham, *Otway and Lee* (New Haven, 1931)

Robert D. Hume, *The Development of English Drama in the Late Seventeenth Century* (Oxford, 1976)

Bruce King, *Dryden's Major Plays* (Edinburgh, 1966)

G. Wilson Knight, *The Golden Labyrinth* (London, 1962)

Clifford Leech, 'Restoration tragedy: a reconsideration' (*Durham University Journal*, xlii, 1950)

John Loftis, ed., *Restoration Drama: Modern Essays in Criticism* (New York, 1966)

Earl Miner, ed., *Restoration Dramatists: a Collection of Critical Essays* (Englewood Cliffs, N.J., 1966)

Allardyce Nicoll, *A History of Restoration Drama, 1660–1700* (Cambridge, 1923; rev. edn., 1952)

—— 'Political plays of the Restoration' (*Modern Language Review*, xvi, 1921)

Moody E. Prior, *The Language of Tragedy* (New York, 1947; chapter on 'Tragedy and the heroic play')

E. Rothstein, *Restoration Tragedy: Form and the Process of Change* (Madison, 1961)

—— 'English tragic theory in the late seventeenth century' (*Journal of English Literary History*, xxix, 1962)

Bernard N. Schilling, *Dryden: a Collection of Critical Essays* (Englewood Cliffs, N.J., 1963)

Sarup Singh, *The Theory of Drama in the Restoration Periods* (Calcutta, 1963)

James Sutherland, *English Literature of the late Seventeenth Century* (Oxford, 1969; chapter 2)

Aline M. Taylor, *Next to Shakespeare: Otway's 'Venice Preserved' and 'The Orphan' and their History on the London Stage* (Durham, N.C., 1950)

J. H. Wilson, *A Preface to Restoration Drama* (Boston, 1965)

For *All for Love*: D. W. Hughes, 'The significance of *All for Love*' (*Journal of English Literary History*, xxxvii, 1970); F. R. Leavis, '*Antony and Cleopatra* and *All for Love*: a critical exercise' (*Scrutiny*, v, 1936); Kenneth Muir, 'The imagery of *All for Love*' (*Proceedings of the Leeds Philosophical and Literary Society*, v, 1940); D. T. Starnes, 'Imitation of Shakespeare in Dryden's *All for Love* (*Texas Studies in Literature and Language*, vi, 1964); N. Suckling, 'Dryden in Egypt: reflexions on *All for Love* (*Durham University Journal*, xlv, 1942); H. D. Weinbrot, 'Alexas in *All for Love*: his genealogy and function' (*Studies in Philology*, lxiv, 1967)

For *Venice Preserved*: R. Berman, 'Nature in *Venice Preserved* (*Journal of English Literary History*, xxxvi, 1969); D. R. Hauser, 'Otway preserved: theme and form in *Venice Preserved*' (*Studies in Philology*, lv, 1958); D. W. Hughes, 'A new look at *Venice Preserved*' (*Studies in English Literature*, xi, 1971); John Robert Moore, 'Contemporary satire in Otway's *Venice Preserved*' (*PMLA*, xliii, 1928); T. B. Stroup, 'Otway's bitter pessimism' (*Essays in English Literature . . . presented to Dougald MacMillan*, Chapel Hill, N.C., 1967)

Editions of plays

Bonamy Dobrée, ed., *Five Heroic Plays* (Oxford, 1960)

J. C. Ghosh, ed., *The Works of Thomas Otway* (2 vols., Oxford, 1932; repr. 1968; cited as 'Ghosh')

M. Kelsall, ed., *Thomas Otway: 'Venice Preserved'* (Lincoln, Nebraska, and London, 1969)

John Loftis, ed., *Nathaniel Lee: 'Lucius Junius Brutus'* (Lincoln, Nebraska, and London, 1967; cited as 'Loftis')

T. B. Stroup and A. L. Cooke, eds., *The Works of Nathaniel Lee* (2 vols., New Brunswick, 1954–5; cited as 'Stroup–Cooke')

D. M. Vieth, ed., *John Dryden: 'All for Love'* (Lincoln, Nebraska, and London, 1972)

J. H. Wilson, ed., *Six Restoration Plays* (Boston, 1959)

Louis B. Wright and Virginia A. Lamar, *Four Great Restoration Plays* (New York, 1964)